The RISE *of* *the* MILITARY WELFARE STATE

The RISE *of* *the* MILITARY WELFARE STATE

Jennifer Mittelstadt

Harvard University Press

CAMBRIDGE, MASSACHUSETTS

LONDON, ENGLAND

2015

Second printing

Library of Congress Cataloging-in-Publication Data

Mittelstadt, Jennifer, 1970–
The rise of the military welfare state / Jennifer Mittelstadt.—First edition.
pages cm
Includes bibliographical references and index.
ISBN 978-0-674-28613-9 (hardcover : alk. paper)
1. Military social work—United States. 2. Soldiers—United States—Social conditions—20th century. 3. Families of military personnel—United States—Social conditions—20th century. 4. Families of military personnel—Services for—United States—History—20th century. 5. Military spouses—United States—History—20th century. 6. United States. Army—Social services—Contracting out. 7. United States. Army—Military life—History—20th century. 8. Sociology, Military—United States. 9. Welfare state—United States—History—20th century. I. Title.
UH755.M58 2015
355.1'2—dc23
2015005609

For Aaron

Contents

The RISE *of* *the* MILITARY WELFARE STATE

INTRODUCTION

The Army Takes Care of Its Own

THREADING MY WAY down a busy Brooklyn street ten years ago, I eavesdropped on a cell phone conversation. A tall young man ahead of me moved quickly, speaking loudly to his counterpart. As we made our way down several blocks, a few paces apart, I was drawn into his conversation and began to gather the gist. He was trying to convince a woman to join the U.S. Army. "You'll get good health care," he promised. "They'll get you out of credit card debt and teach you to handle your money." "You can get day care for your kid."

This was not the enticement I expected. As a teenager in the 1980s, I registered the ubiquitous "Be All You Can Be" campaign that promised excitement and personal achievement for soldiers. In my late twenties I watched the "Army of One" campaign that assured a steeled warrior identity for anyone who volunteered. But this recruiter's pledges sounded much less stirring and not at all martial. They sounded more like the opposite—practical, friendly, even nurturing. I couldn't help but wonder, why was a war-fighting institution selling its recruits what sounded like social welfare programs?

I found it difficult to answer the question, as I knew little about the military. As a scholar of domestic politics and social policy, I recognized the significance of the military in American life, especially in the twentieth century, where worldwide conflagrations resulted in dramatic mobilizations that transformed the nation. But though I understood the vital role of the military in these conflicts, and the effects of the conflicts on the American past, I never truly incorporated the armed forces into the stories I told—stories of how and why the United States built social policy and programs. The military operated as an important but distinct, sometimes distant, institution whose history occasionally intersected with the issues about which I cared most.

My inattention to the military arose partly from my unfamiliarity with it. Military history, once a principal historical subfield, occupied a less central space when I trained as a historian two decades ago. Then there was the fact that I had very little personal contact with the institution, like many Americans in the era of the volunteer military. As the wars in Afghanistan and Iraq commenced, I paid closer attention to the military. But as service members have repeatedly reminded Americans in recent years, only one half of 1 percent of citizens currently serve in the armed forces. My uncles joined the navy in the 1950s, but they and our extended family severed direct ties with the institution after their enlistments were up. Neither my professional training nor my personal life augured any special consciousness of the military.

The conversation on the Brooklyn streets changed that. I ran into a bank and copied the recruiter's words onto the back of a deposit slip. What would it mean to bring into to focus the role of the military as a social safety net?

AS IT TURNED out, I was hardly the first to register connections between the military and the welfare state, the broad term describing how nations provide social and economic support to citizens. Military historians of the United States have depicted how the army offered food, shelter, and clothing during the Revolutionary War, essential lures that for many soldiers served more than the purpose of military readiness. Scholars of subsequent wars have linked military service to the history of social welfare by telling the stories of veterans' entitlements—among them pensions after the Civil War, health care after World War I, and education, training, and housing subsidies after World War II.[1] Historians of Europe also have produced voluminous scholarship detailing how war begets welfare states.[2] They have followed in the steps of social theorists from Charles Tilly to Tristram Coffin, who linked war to the state, citizenship rights, and social welfare entitlements.[3]

While these scholars looked to the more distant past of military social provision, a diverse range of military observers have more recently acknowledged what I realized listening to the recruiter—that the volunteer military of the late twentieth and early twenty-first centuries encompassed significant social welfare functions. For the more than 10 million Americans who volunteered for active duty after 1973—and their tens of millions of family members—the military provided an elaborate social and economic safety net: medical and dental programs; housing assistance; subsistence payments; commissary and post exchange privileges; tax advantages; education and training; dozens of family welfare programs; child care; and social services ranging from financial counseling to legal aid (see Appendix).[4] These were multibillion-dollar-per-year programs that at times accounted for nearly 50 percent of the Department of Defense (DoD) budget. Their real costs were hard to find, spreading over several divisions of the defense budget and creating a system of support so vast that in 2009 the department acknowledged that it could not accurately reckon its total expense.[5] In the 1970s, eminent University of Chicago military sociologist Morris Janowitz described these programs as "more of a welfare state than civilian society."[6] And since then, military journalists, active duty officers, and military analysts have dubbed the programs "the Great Society in Camouflage," or "the camouflaged safety net." The military, in the words of one officer, was "deeply and solidly rooted in the paternalistic and socialistic ideas of Franklin Delano Roosevelt's New Deal."[7] Such observations drew on the truism embodied in the old joke among many service members—especially ironic during the days of the Cold War battle against Communism: the United States fought Soviet socialism using the most socialistic organization in the United States—the military.[8]

Whether or not the military's social programs constituted socialism was debatable, but it became clear through my research that social welfare was vital to the military, and likewise that the military was vital to any full history of social welfare in the United States. Political scientists, sociologists and historians of the welfare state have expanded our understanding of the diverse ways in which the United States, as opposed to supposedly "traditional" European welfare states, has organized social and economic support, and the military fits within these frameworks. The American state evolved a complex web of public and private social welfare programs. It included traditionally acknowledged government social welfare such as social insurance and means-tested public assistance programs. But this safety net also arose from less-visible structures, such as the income tax system's incentives and write-offs, and subsidized home mortgages. American social provision included even less recognized ways that government encouraged social welfare—a diverse, government-subsidized system of individual employee benefits.[9] Amidst this complicated patchwork of social provision in the

United States, the military's support for soldiers and their families played a significant role. The question was not whether the history of the military and the history of social welfare connected, but how.

VIEWING THE MILITARY of recent decades as a social welfare institution revealed a unique nexus between the military and welfare, where Americans debated fundamental questions of citizenship, military service, entitlement, and social welfare. The Brooklyn recruiter did not operate within the context of the vast conscript militaries of the Civil War, World War I, or World War II eras but in an altogether different military—the modern All-Volunteer Force (AVF) created in 1973 in the wake of massive opposition to the Vietnam-era draft. As a result, the many benefits he enumerated bore a different relationship to questions of service, entitlement, and citizenship than had earlier programs linking the military to social welfare.

The conscript militaries of the Civil War, World War I, and World War II, which demanded male citizens perform military service, pioneered many social welfare programs in the United States. These were crafted for veterans as rewards for faithful service or compensation for loss. Their political success depended on differentiating the veteran from the civilian and elevating him as worthy of entitlement. Yet because of the broad nature of conscription and the massive mobilizations of these wars, many of these military welfare programs also catalyzed broader social welfare programs for civilians. Civil War pensions pioneered federal retirement and disability payments, planting the seed for civilian retirement pensions decades later.[10] Veterans' health care after World War I created the first model of government health provision, and mobilized veterans demanded expanded pensions and payments as part of the New Deal.[11] And the World War II–era GI Bill vaulted millions of former draftees and their families into the middle class. Even as its programs only reached veterans, they also legitimized government provision of education and housing subsidies for civilian Americans.[12]

Correlations between military service, citizenship, and entitlements to social welfare played out differently in the volunteer era at the end of the twentieth century. Without conscription or mass armies, the benefits the Brooklyn recruiter enumerated did not serve as rewards for the services of citizen soldiers, but rather as programs that lured active duty soldiers into a career force, supported them while on duty, and convinced them to reenlist. In this era the divide between military personnel and civilians grew, perhaps wider than ever before in American history.[13] As a smaller number and narrower cross-section of Americans volunteered for military service, soldiers', sailors', and airmen's links to civilians withered. The same divide emerged in the relationship between military and civilian social welfare programs. The growth of social welfare programs for active duty military personnel and their families did not stimulate civilian social welfare. Instead, in the 1970s and 1980s the military's social and economic supports grew while civilian social welfare contracted. Beginning in the 1970s and extending through the end of the century, a critique of the putative excesses and failures of the Great Society prompted retrenchment of civilian social welfare programs, especially, though not exclusively, for the poor. At the same time, attacks on public sector unions and government facilitated cuts to civilian public employee benefits and to the overall size of the government workforce. Even private sector employment benefits declined as a result of antiunion attacks, the movement of plants to the South and abroad, and the massive outsourcing and merger movements of the 1980s and 1990s. Yet amidst government spending cuts and salvos against welfare clients and public workers, as well as the decline of private employment security, the military expanded its welfare functions.

Connections among military service, citizenship, and entitlement were also unique in the United States compared to its modern industrialized military allies. As the architects of the army's social welfare programs noted, the modern militaries of most North Atlantic Treaty Organization partners did not provide the compendium of support offered by the American military. From Britain to the Netherlands to France, both during the eras of conscription and volunteer forces, soldiers, like other citizens, gained most of their social welfare benefits via universal entitlements granted by the state. Yes, militaries still garrisoned soldiers on posts and provided special social services there. But most social provisions—health care, child allowances, schooling, social services, and other programs—were provided by the state and accessed both by civilians and soldiers alike. In the United States, with its less universal and more hodgepodge system of social welfare, the volunteer army has provided a generous and exceptional safety net.[14]

THIS BOOK EXAMINES how military service intertwined with citizenship and entitlement through the history of welfare provision in the late twentieth-century U.S. Army. While all branches of the U.S. military expanded their benefits and social programs for soldiers and families, the army operated as the vanguard as well as the largest and costliest element of military social welfare.[15] Its frontrunner status was fated by its rocky transition to the volunteer era. Unlike the other branches of the services, which rarely relied on the draft in the long postwar period or even during the Vietnam War, the army used conscription to fill about half of its ranks, with many of the remaining "volunteers" purely motivated to enlist by the draft.[16] As the armed forces abandoned the draft, the army wrestled with how to attract and retain soldiers with greater urgency than the other services. Recruitment proved all the more difficult because of the army's declining prestige as an institution. After the Vietnam War, no branch of the services faced the same degree of ignominy as the army, whose soldiers had fought the bulk of the ground war in Vietnam. Yet the army remained the largest branch of the services, with the most spaces to fill. With so many pressures arrayed against it, the army moved quickly, almost desperately, to determine how to survive.

The story of the army's survival as a modern volunteer force has been told by numerous historians whose scholarship has revealed army leaders' resourceful embrace of a variety of new tools to improve recruitment and retention.[17] No longer able to compel people to join and remain, it had to convince them. The leadership drew on and reflected American consumer society, using the latest advertising technologies and potent themes from popular politics and culture.[18] Higher pay, too, lured soldiers to an institution that offered greater economic stability. Coupled with a newly professionalized image of the military honed by the officer corps, the army drew and retained volunteers.[19]

But a crucial aspect of the volunteer army's survival was its social welfare programs for soldiers and their families. Army leadership determined that expanding its distinct traditional system of economic and social supports could be one of the most potent tools for recruitment and, especially, retention. To ease the conversion from the draft to the volunteer era, the army maintained and broadened its support beyond the limited benefits offered largely to career personnel and officers. At the time, provision of official army support for soldiers and their families, such as family housing, use of the Post Exchange (PX) and commissary, access to medical care and special recreational venues like golf courses and tennis courts, were not extended fully to the first-term or even second-term enlistee or his family. A new soldier could not have his family sponsored for a tour in Germany or qualify for housing there. Even if a new soldier's wife followed him to his post at her own expense, she could not obtain privileges such as use of the commissary and PX. In all areas of army benefits, the most fulsome support represented the privilege of rank. But the army's chiefs of staff and their personnel deputies of the 1970s redefined that privilege, and extended these benefits and supports to the entire army. They undertook a sort of full "officerization" of the force that brought soldiers of every rank, and their families, into a universal system of support.[20]

Army leaders modeled this system on a paternal "Army Family" that, in the words of a revived army motto, "Took Care of Its Own." A string of deputy chiefs of staff for personnel successfully petitioned Congress in the 1970s for the funds to provide a collective soldier and family support system. The programs would not only lure and retain soldiers, they argued, but also foster the morale, cohesion, and commitment necessary for an effective volunteer fighting force. Even amidst the austerity of the post-1973 recession, the army's generals and its personnel argued successfully before Congress that the army could not survive without building an "Army Family" to care for all soldiers.

THE ARMY'S EXPANSION of social welfare did not proceed as smoothly as it hoped, as it confronted resistance from both outside and within. The increasingly antigovernment, free market politics of the late twentieth century shaped one critique of growing social welfare in the military. Free market economists and business leaders first set their sights on transforming the military in the 1960s. Led by scholars at the University of Chicago, the University of Virginia, and the Hoover Institution, they sought to remake the army in their own image. Heading up the President's Commission on the All-Volunteer Force (commonly referred to as the Gates Commission), the 1969 Richard Nixon group that sketched the blueprint for the postdraft era, they advocated not only the end to the draft, but also a broader vision of the military as an ideal free market institution. In their dreams, cash payments and bonuses would drive enlistment and the military's traditional benefits—no better than any other government social program—would be abolished. If abolition proved too difficult, the remaining services and benefits should be contracted out to the private sector. Milton Friedman clashed with General William Westmoreland, the army chief of staff who commenced the transition to the volunteer force, challenging him and his successors to break decisively from their paternalistic adherence to a traditional army and its benefits.

The army's construction of a larger support system was also blocked by opposition within its own ranks and among its staunchest supporters, who worried that the army's combat readiness and public image were threatened by social welfare programs. The influential Beard Report of 1978, commissioned by Representative Robin Beard (R-TN), a member of the Marine Corps Reserves, predicted a disastrous transformation of the army "into a social welfare institution." Joined by the likes of retired naval officer James Webb—later secretary of the navy and a U.S. senator (D-VA)—Beard feared the army becoming a haven for society's misfits, a last resort for those who could not make it in the civilian world and depended on the army as low-income civilians used public assistance programs. They predicted an enervated army, with commanders solving social problems rather than training for battle. They forecast the degradation of the army into a feminized social welfare provider, anathema to the masculine, martial purpose of the institution.

Their concerns were amplified by the changing demographics of the volunteer army in the late 1970s, changes that prompted a many-sided debate that elided into discussions of social welfare. The volunteer era brought fewer white men, less-educated enlistees, more low-income, and more female recruits into the army. Many commanders and army observers worried that the less educated recruits endangered military readiness. But they also fretted about wider implications for the army. They worried that the army was recruiting only "the dregs," low-income Americans without purportedly mainstream values. Others in Congress and the media agonized that the new soldiers were disproportionately African American. Still others in the military community worried that the army admitted too many women who, by dint of their unique reproductive biology, needed and demanded more social provision than male soldiers. Fears of a feminized and overly African American army, one degraded by a culture of poverty, fed anxieties that the army was transforming from a war-fighting institution into a social welfare institution.

The crisis of the army's image as a welfare institution molded a larger campaign by army leadership to distance its soldiers from everyday civilians and the social welfare programs that served them. During the 1970s and 1980s, the army's senior officers and its civilian leaders drew sharp lines differentiating military social and economic supports from civilian ones. Their efforts proved crucial to the growth of the military welfare state.

One campaign to differentiate soldiers' benefits from civilians' concerned the question of whether soldiering constituted a "job," and whether military benefits occupied the same category as employment benefits. The free market economists of the Gates Commission certainly viewed soldiers as employees in a labor market. So, too, did one of the sworn enemies of free market economists—union leaders. In late 1975, the American Federation of Government Employees (AFGE), a public sector union, began a two-year bid to organize the new volunteer soldiers. At the time, recession-era congressional cuts endangered federal employee benefits, both civilian and military, and the threat provided AFGE an opportunity to hitch soldiers' fate to civilians': they could both unite in one union to defend their benefits. Soldiers expressed ambivalence. On the one hand some believed the union had the power to protect their benefits. But on the other hand, many worried about conflating soldiering within "9 to 5" civilian employment. The union debate raised questions fundamental to the volunteer army and its nascent welfare state. Was military service just another type of job? If so, what special benefits and rewards could it command? Was there a unique relationship between military service and entitlements? The discussion spurred new arguments from army leadership and soldiers rejecting comparisons between soldiering and employment and elevating military service as worthier. More importantly, they separated military benefits from civilian ones, and argued for their exclusive protection and growth. Their contention convinced Congress to shore up military social welfare programs, even as those for civilians declined.

President Ronald Reagan built on the army's case, and arguably did more than anyone to advance the belief that military service constituted a special and elevated category. Military social welfare programs progressed in unprecedented fashion in the 1980s thanks to a resurgence of militarization in a nation that had long operated "in the shadow of war."[21] Reagan revived militarization by deploying the military as the symbol of his politics: the military represented the United States and soldiers its ideal citizens.[22] Military spending under Reagan accelerated markedly, facilitating huge corporate mergers of defense contractors seeking higher profits. Americans registered their growing regard for the military in polls, where the military ranked ahead of most all American institutions except the Church.[23] Films featuring the military crowded American cineplexes in the 1980s. The pervasive militarization of the decade fostered significant growth in the army's social welfare programs. And it built sturdier boundaries between the military and civilians.

One way the Reagan administration and the army differentiated between civilians and military personnel was through the revival and reinvention of the GI Bill. Though previously used as an education program to reward veterans for service, the new GI Bill served as a tool to improve the image of the army and justify its special rewards. The army championed a new GI Bill as part of an effort to recast its image from an institution of last resort to an institution offering young Americans socio-economic opportunity. For its part, the Reagan administration used the revival of the GI Bill both to restore the image of the soldier and the army and also to slash civilian social welfare programs, specifically civilian grants and loans for higher education. Reagan officials cut federal loans and grants for civilians as they signed on to the new GI Bill. They praised the sacrifice of young soldiers and implied the shiftlessness of civilian college students. In this way, the military's social welfare programs grew as civilian ones contracted.

Reagan allies among the Christian right helped demarcate the privileged status of military benefits and social services. Evangelical Christians like Dr. James Dobson of Focus on Family saw in the army a chance to advance their political agenda favoring "traditional family values." They cultivated relationships with army leaders and helped guide new army family programs that blossomed in the 1980s. A growing faction of born-again Christian officers and civilian defense leaders welcomed Dobson and other conservative Christians to the army, developing prayer groups and parachurches, and sending missionaries to the Chaplains Corps. Through these mutually reinforcing relationships, civilian and army evangelicals injected conservative Christian ideas into the programs serving soldiers and families. They also used the opportunity to place army families in a special category deserving of generous government support at the same time that the Christian right opposed the extension of government support to civilians who did not meet Christian ideals. Conservative Christian actions distanced army social welfare programs from civilian ones, and this differentiation fed the growth of military benefits and supports.

The expansion of the army's social welfare apparatus in the 1980s also resulted from successful grassroots organizing among army wives, a group occupying a contested position within the emerging army welfare programs. In 1980, a group of officers' wives created a worldwide movement that successfully pressured army leaders to adopt new programs to serve spouses and children. On a separate track from the conservatism that animated the high politics of military social welfare, their efforts resulted from the changing behaviors and expectations of army wives in the 1980s, ones characteristic of the wider population of American women. More army wives pursued education, joined the workforce, and now chafed at the traditional ways in which the army treated them. Long considered by the army as loyal female adjuncts to soldiers and the army's missions, army wives challenged the army to enter with them into a partnership in which the army also served wives. In an institution grappling with the influx of female soldiers, new social welfare programs like day care, and attendant fears of feminization, army wives' demands posed a profound challenge. But in the context of budgetary largesse and the growing prestige and protection afforded the army in the 1980s, army leaders accepted the requests of army wives. They expanded social welfare functions to include a wide range of support services to soldiers' wives and families, from child care and spousal employment assistance to marital counseling and family support services. By the end of the 1980s, the army's social welfare system represented a vast, comprehensive, and effective safety net unique in American life.

IF THE 1980s marked the apogee of the army's social welfare functions, the end of the Cold War and the first Gulf War sparked a transformation that undermined the original foundations of the volunteer army's welfare provisions. Concerns about the feminizing and degrading effects of social welfare on the army erupted again. And the army struggled to cope with the dramatic cuts to its budget during what was referred to as the military "drawdown." The two concurrent phenomena pulled the army to the center of larger developments in the civilian political economy and civilian social welfare in the last decade of the twentieth century. The military's special status eroded amidst debates over the roles of government and the private sector and the scope of the welfare state.

In the wake of the large deployments of the first war in the Persian Gulf in 1991, army leaders expressed renewed concern about whether social welfare programs threatened the military readiness and martial masculinity of the army. During the war, family support leaders observed what some termed excessive "dependency" of army wives upon the newly created support structures of the army, and these worries catalyzed a total reevaluation of the army's family supports. Though it drew on long-term fears of feminizing the army, the ensuing discussion also echoed three decades of attacks on public welfare that culminated in the efforts of President Bill Clinton and the Republican Congress to "end welfare as we know it"—the 1996 Personal Responsibility and Work Opportunity Act (PRWOA). Just as civilian policy makers pressed low-income civilians into the workforce through mandatory employment—achieving what policy makers called "independence" from welfare—so did the army of the 1990s begin to worry about the "dependency" its own support programs produced among soldiers and their wives. Cued by family sociologists and psychologists hired by the army—professionals who also studied civilian welfare clients—the army fixated on fighting dependency on social welfare. Army leadership pursued new policies that promoted "self-support" and "self-reliance" among soldiers and families. Fearful of having its support apparatus labeled as "welfare" and of "encouraging dependency," the army pulled back from its philosophy to "take care of its own" and enjoined soldiers to "take care of themselves." Though army leaders insisted they remained committed to ensuring a high "quality of life" for soldiers, they retrenched their commitment to social and economic support at the same time, and in much the same way, as civilian policy makers. These changes reflected the continued ambivalence with which the military welfare state evolved.

As the army pushed soldiers and families to take care of themselves, it simultaneously transferred its support services to the private sector, contracting out major social welfare functions to corporations. Army generals had succeeded in rebuffing the free market outsourcing agenda in the 1970s and 1980s. Over the previous two decades, free market advocates and business leaders had watched in horror as the military welfare state grew. To them it represented a huge expense added to the federal budget and a model of pure socialism at the heart of the otherwise pro–free enterprise Reagan administration. However, in the late 1980s and 1990s, amidst the post–Cold War drawdown and President Clinton's "Reinvention of Government," the free market agenda succeeded. Clinton's administration imported corporate practices of outsourcing and privatization in government agencies, including both public social welfare programs and the military. Commanders of the army's support structures adopted corporate budget and management strategies, outsourced and privatized elements of soldier and family support programs, and in the process transformed the government-provided social welfare system that it had built over the previous quarter century into a delegated provision of services handled in large part by the private sector.[24]

BY THE TURN of the twenty-first century, when I overheard the army recruiter on the streets of Brooklyn, the army's welfare system was an outsourced entity that had retracted its earlier full-throated commitments to soldiers and families. Outsourcing, privatization, and the demand for "self-reliance" among recipients transformed army support from a public safety net that "took care of its own" to a collection of public funding and private firms and contractors that together encouraged "independence" in the military community. A system that had already detached itself from civilian social welfare now distanced itself from its own soldiers, too.

The legitimacy of the army's social welfare apparatus was, it turned out, never assured. General agreement on the importance of a broad program of social and economic supports for soldiers and families could not quiet concern about what it meant for the army itself to provide social welfare. Fears persisted about the degradation of the army mission, the feminization of the institution, and the taint of poverty, dependency, and welfare. The army struggled to reconcile its need and desire to support the new soldiers of the volunteer era with continual concerns about doing so. The army simultaneously built and denied its welfare state, defended and masked it. Military social welfare constituted a contested arena repeatedly entangled in both the internal politics of the army and the wider political transformations of the era.

The rise and transformation of the army's social welfare programs reflected the constraints on the development of all social welfare programs, both civilian and military, in the "age of fracture" at the end of the twentieth century.[25] Architects and supporters of army social welfare navigated skillfully through the attacks on public welfare programs and public employment benefits in the 1970s and 1980s. But they did not fully outrun them. In an era otherwise marked by extensive militarization, the transformation of the army's social welfare programs in ways similar to civilian ones suggested limits to the power of the military and the privileges for soldiers and military families. Military social welfare in the late twentieth century did not benefit civilians, but nor did it ultimately benefit soldiers in the same manner and to the same degree as originally promised when the army pledged to "take care of its own." The story of its rise and decline revealed the wider shared threats to social welfare for both citizens and soldiers.

THIS BOOK IS structured around the origin, growth, and regression of the army's support programs for soldiers and their families, and their relationships to broader civilian social welfare. The first three chapters describe the army's struggles to define, demarcate, and defend its benefits during the rocky, nascent period of the volunteer army's welfare state. Chapters 4 through 6 chronicle the story of advance and vitalization in army social welfare programs in the 1980s, detailing the contributions of the Reagan administration's military and civilian welfare policies, army wives, and the conservative Christian right. Chapters 7 and 8 recount the end of the flush years and the transformation of the army's social programs by anti-"dependency" ideology and the outsourcing and privatizing of many army support programs in the 1990s. An epilogue links the transformations of the 1990s to present-day crises in the army's welfare state, dilemmas exacerbated by over thirteen years of war in Iraq and Afghanistan.

The stories in these chapters draw on a wide range of sources in the U.S. Army and beyond. The volunteer army's archives constitute a patchwork, and those related to soldier and family support are few and far between. The National Archives has processed only miniscule portions of the papers of the post-Vietnam-era DoD and army. I therefore gratefully turned to Bernard Rostker of RAND, who has gathered some of the otherwise unavailable sources in his own collection of documents on the volunteer force.[26] I found a trove of essential documents in the U.S. Army's Military History Institute at Carlisle Barracks and its Center of Military History at Fort McNair, where various collections allowed me access to the papers of the army's chiefs of staff; personnel and logistics experts; its directors of morale, welfare, and recreation; its studies of soldiers, their spouses, and their families; the newsletters of post commanders; the testimony of its leaders and personnel before Congress; and other vital documents.[27] There and elsewhere I also retrieved oral histories of leaders; after action reports; the minutes of meetings of army spouses; thousands of issues of *Army Times;* and academic studies of military readiness and budgets. The stories I found in the army's various archives also sent me further afield: to the papers of the civilian architects and policy makers of military manpower who oversaw the volunteer force; the collections of labor unions who tried to unionize the military; the writings of free market economists, conservative Christians, sociologists, and psychologists who measured and prescribed solutions for soldiers and their families; and the professional and industrial journals of large military-related corporations.

The sources reveal the history of the army and social welfare from the top down and the bottom up. Many of the chapters that follow emphasize the generals, defense secretaries, members of Congress, and business leaders whose decisions shaped new programs. Other chapters highlight the power of soldiers, their spouses, and civilians in generating new programs, or shaping the politics surrounding benefits. Because the army was (and remains) such a masculinized institution dominated both in membership and symbolism by white men, the stories of relationships between men and women, masculinity and femininity, whiteness and blackness shade the pages of many of the chapters. And because the army's demographics in the volunteer era reflected a more working-class America than during the draft era, many chapters explore recurring class tensions in the army. In these issues and others, ideology mattered, and the chapters take ideas seriously as guides to actions and policies. But they also highlight implementation and practice, and explore what ideas look like—or don't look like—in real, lived experiences. The chapters are also mindful of the complexity of the army's stories. For though the army is often represented as a monolithic institution that speaks and acts with one voice, it is in fact, like so many large institutions, remarkably decentralized in its decision making. As a result, the army juggles enormous, often self-created, contradictions at both the ideological and practical levels, doing what it aims to do and also its opposite, at the same time.[28] This book seeks to do justice to some of the many stories of the army and its benefits in late twentieth-century America.

The book that follows does not comprehensively document every program and benefit that the army has offered soldiers and families in the volunteer era. Instead, it follows the people, programs, issues, and ideas that the evidence suggested were most important in shaping the army's construction and conception of its social welfare apparatus, and those that reverberated within civilian politics and social welfare. Many chapters highlight a particular program or benefit, but all chapters maintain focus on the overall compendium of army support and its relationship to broader national questions. The approach sometimes raises more questions than it answers. But the trade-off is worth it, I hope, in order to train our attention on the vital relationship between the military and social welfare—and the power and limits of both—in the late twentieth century.

1

Army Benefits in a Free Market Era

AT A 1966 meeting at the University of Chicago, Milton Friedman and fellow free market economists met with sympathetic opponents of the draft at the height of the Vietnam War to discuss the possibilities for ending the unpopular system of military conscription. Their meeting hinted at the breadth of the growing antidraft movement, which accommodated both newly elected congressional representative Donald Rumsfeld (R-IL) and Stokely Carmichael in the same camp. Indeed, by 1968, most Americans had come to oppose conscription. But while activists ranging from civil rights leaders to peace groups, from the New Left to religious organizations, all agreed to end the draft, few envisioned the future of the military. For free market economists at the University of Chicago, however, ending the draft was part of a full-blown model of how a new volunteer force would function. This model incorporated the military into their larger worldview of small government and free market principles. Their blueprint called for the army to use solely cash inducements to attract enlistees. It would also forego in-kind and institutional benefits and services like housing, health care, and recreational facilities. Instead free marketers proposed that the army provide cash to allow soldiers to purchase whatever private sector "support," if any, they chose.

In many ways, free market economists succeeded in changing the military. At the most fundamental level, there was no question that the new volunteer army had to enter a labor market for young men, and, to a lesser degree, women, in a way that conscription never fully required. Luring and retaining soldiers, especially into hard-to-fill positions in medical fields and combat arms, necessitated some of the methods of economists. The army also relied more heavily on tools of consumer markets such as advertising. More than ever before, the army in fact did enter the market.[1]

Yet senior army leadership and many soldiers also resisted the redefinition of the army as a market institution, and in no area more than the social welfare function of the army—its benefits and support programs. From the highest leadership—Chief of Staff of the Army (CSA) General William Westmoreland and his deputies as well as secretaries of the army—to its enlisted soldiers, members of the army refused to accept that the army was an institution in which rational choice and utilitarian behavior described by neoclassical economists bore much relevance. In their minds, the army represented an institution steeped in tradition, molded primarily by nonpecuniary and nonquantifiable values. Rather than using market mechanisms, army leadership of the 1970s proposed expanding the paternalist mechanisms of the army's social welfare apparatus in order to lure and retain soldiers in the volunteer force. If there was a model appropriate to the army, it was not a firm in a marketplace. It was more akin to a family—both paternalistic and patriarchal. For the next two decades, the army's view proved more persuasive than the free market economists'.

IN THE SEVERAL decades before Friedman and his cohort trained their vision on the military, the armed forces filled its ranks through combining recruitment of a relatively small cadre who would make the military their career and conscription of a larger group of one-to-two termers through the Selective Service system. Conscription, largely absent from American military history except during times of war, persisted after World War II, when the onset of the Cold War convinced President Harry Truman and much of Congress that the United States had to maintain a large standing army to counter the threat of the Soviet Union.[2] Though the Cold War military technically was composed of two categories—volunteer and conscript—the divisions were never neat. Enlistment formed a continuum. Some volunteers constituted what the military called "true volunteers," men who had dreamt of becoming soldiers, sailors, or airmen, men who had family traditions, or men with a patriotic desire to serve. After their initial enlistment, many planned to make the military a career. However, estimates suggested that no more than 10 percent of army enlisted personnel in their first term and no more than 15 percent of army officers in their first term would have constituted "true volunteers."[3] Many "volunteers" were better labeled "draft-motivated" volunteers. They were men who knew they might be drafted and decided to volunteer in the hopes of exerting some influence over their enlistment. Outside of the Korean conflict and the buildup of the Vietnam War, probably one-third of "volunteers" enlisted to avoid actually being drafted.[4] After both types of volunteers took their places, the rest of military manpower derived from conscripts, a number that varied depending on the timing of conflicts in Korea and Vietnam.[5] Overall, while a small minority of volunteers stayed on to make careers, far fewer conscripts made the same choice.

General military enlistment statistics masked the unique composition of the army. As the largest, least technological, and most likely branch of the armed forces to engage in direct ground combat, the army relied far more heavily on conscripts than the other services.[6] The air force—perceived as modern and technology-driven—never relied on the draft, for example, and the navy and the marines only exceedingly rarely. As a result, almost all draftees of the postwar era ended up in the army, where they filled approximately half of its manpower. The conflict in Vietnam intensified this phenomenon. In 1969, the army had conscripted over half of all its new enlistments, and of the remaining volunteers, half were draft-motivated, having enlisted to avoid being drafted into a system beyond their control. The army endured almost complete "dependency on the draft."[7]

The army, like the other services of the Cold War era, retained its small career cadre by offering a system of economic and institutional supports. Benefits constituted an in-kind exchange that evaded market logic. They depended on the perceived commitment soldiers made to the army. As one senior enlisted man's wife explained to junior wives in a letter to *Army Times*, "The military has decided that when a man has committed himself to a military career and has demonstrated his commitment by serving a required number of years—or has accepted the added responsibilities and duties that go with increased rank—the military command will support him in return." The support was "not a 'right' all dependents can demand," but "a 'privilege.'"[8] As part of earning the honor of rank, senior enlisted men and officers were provided with housing or a housing allowance for them and their families, subsistence allowances, health care, and the use of special facilities like officers' clubs and tennis courts. The army used the promise of these supports to convert first- and second-termers into career personnel, and to keep career personnel through their full minimum twenty-year career.

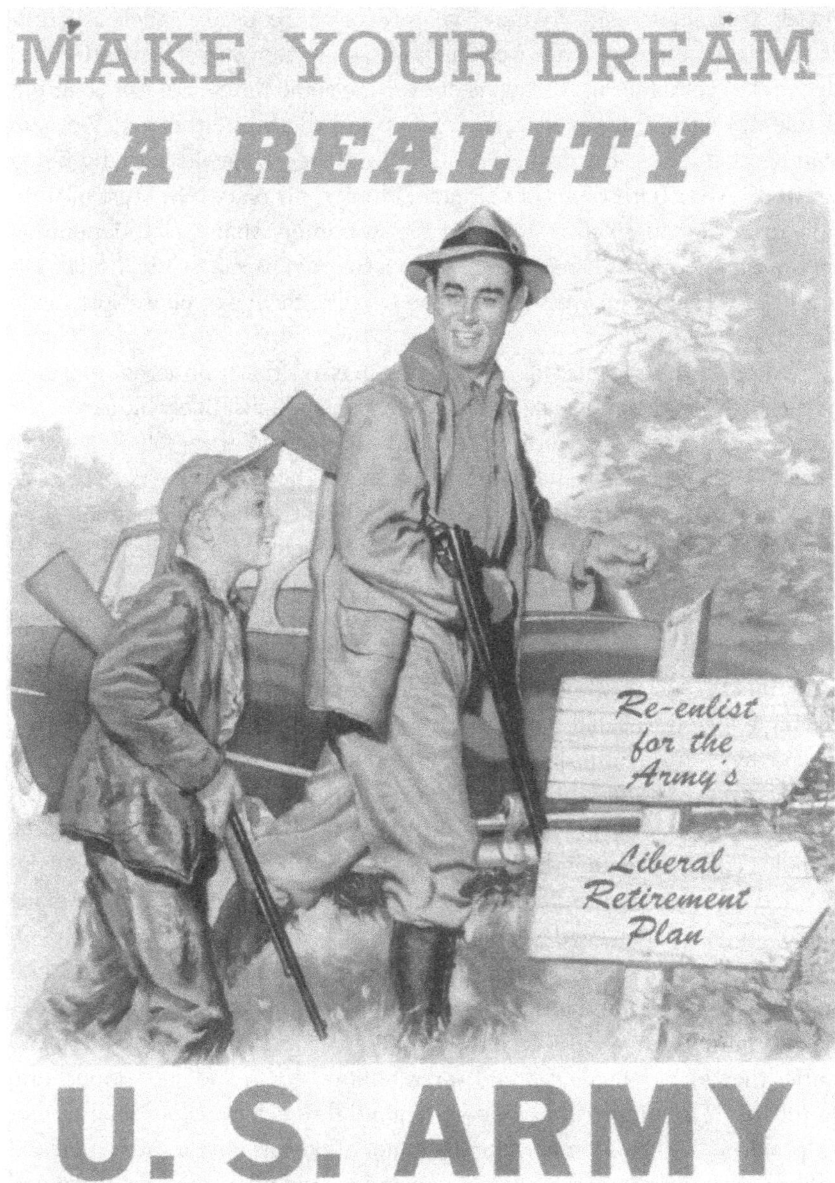

The army advertised its retirement package, for which career personnel were eligible after twenty years, to retain soldiers. Ca. 1950s, courtesy of U.S. Army Recruiting Poster collection, CECOM Historical Office archive, Aberdeen Proving Ground, MD.

Draftees and first-term enlisted volunteers received little of the military's largesse. In the mid-1960s, first-term enlistees received about $2,000 per year in direct pay, plus another $200 or so in additional compensation calculated through subsistence and other allowances.[9] By 1970, with pay raises, the same first-term personnel earned $2,776 per year in direct pay, plus about $475 in other allowances, a total that one government measure judged to be about 53.4 percent of what civilian men of comparable age earned.[10] The enlisted man did not qualify for special housing but lived in the barracks and ate in the mess hall. He did not earn the privilege of the military sponsoring permanent change of station moves by his family, if he had one, nor access to many of the recreation facilities and special programs of career soldiers. Even second-term soldiers—anyone below the enlisted rank E-5 (sergeant)—failed to gain the privileges of support offered to those who made long-term commitments to the military.

In 1971, the lowly pay and conditions of servicemen prompted Senator Barry Goldwater (R-AZ) to lament, "we don't pay the man who carries an M-16 rifle with his head stuck out in front of the enemy as much as we pay the lowest paid domestic in the country."[11] For Goldwater and others, it was unacceptable to compensate manly sacrifice in lesser fashion than banal feminized labor. Perhaps worse, some junior enlisted men relied on civilian social welfare programs to make up for what the army denied them. Beginning in the late 1960s, the media reported that junior enlisted men were using public assistance programs to support their families. The Associated Press investigated the incidence of soldiers and their families using welfare in fall 1969. "From New Jersey to California," it reported, "public welfare agencies are supplementing allotment checks from Vietnam, paying the rent of married draftees or buying groceries for families whose breadwinners are overseas."[12] Several years later, with the transition to the volunteer force under way, the *New York Times* again noted the welfare reliance of junior enlisted families. "These families—now numbering in the tens of thousands—who must depend on food stamps and other forms of welfare to make ends meet" needed far more support.[13] "That a man with or without a child has to be on welfare while serving his country," Senator Mark Hatfield (R-OR) exclaimed, "certainly should put the Senate to shame."[14]

Despite the privation facing the low-ranking soldier, the military's manpower system staffed the armed forces fully and without difficulty from World War II until the mid-1960s. With the escalation of the conflict in Vietnam, however, the system faced a crisis. Many young men did not want to fight a war they opposed. Others objected to the inequities of a manpower system that provided deferments to many middle- and upper-class white men while lower-income and working-class Americans and disproportionate numbers of nonwhites shouldered the burdens of conscription. By 1968, the draft had become so unpopular that every candidate for the presidency from the right to the left announced his opposition to it. In the tense final weeks of the 1968 presidential election, Republican Richard Nixon addressed Americans in a CBS Radio speech. "We have lived with the draft so long," he said, "that too many of us accept it as normal and necessary. . . . I say we take a new look." And with that, Nixon pledged to "bury" the draft.[15] That a hard-line, anticommunist hawk like Nixon felt compelled to make such a promise spoke to the general disgrace into which the system of conscription had fallen. When Nixon won the election, one of his earliest actions was to order the "Defense Department to devise a 'detailed plan' for replacing the military draft with an all-volunteer army," thereby abandoning the conscription system used since World War II.[16]

Though popular support for ending the draft ran high, serious opposition to the volunteer force remained. Staunch military and war supporters in Congress, such as the two heads of the House and Senate Armed Services Committees, Representative F. Edward Hébert (D-LA) and Senator John C. Stennis (D-MS) were skeptical about a volunteer force. They feared declining military readiness with the inevitable waxing and waning of manpower supply that a volunteer system would suffer.[17] President Lyndon Johnson's presidential commission on the draft in 1967 had also rejected a volunteer force as costly and dangerous, creating a gap between the military and civilians in American society.[18] The *New York Times* opined that "in the present chaotic state of the world, it seems rash to try to abandon the draft altogether."[19]

Army leaders despaired. So heavily reliant on the draft to fill their ranks, they expressed open doubts about a volunteer military. In the midst of the protracted and disastrous war in Vietnam, the army was "utterly dependent" on the draft and gloomily faced the prospect of struggling to attract sufficient numbers of soldiers.[20] The prospect for a successful volunteer force was particularly dim given the serious personnel problems the army faced at the time. Crime, alcohol, and drug abuse, overt racism, and resistance to authority plagued the army of the late 1960s and early 1970s. Events like the massacre at My Lai—and its cover-up—and the killing of superior officers by their own soldiers (known as "fragging"), as well as commonplace binge drinking and marijuana smoking, undermined the professionalism and effectiveness of the army. Army leaders "became increasingly convinced that the professional fabric of the institution was unraveling."[21] Persuading hundreds of thousands of soldiers to join a frayed institution during an unpopular war presented a seemingly impossible task.

BEYOND ALREADY enormous challenges in reengineering the army from a conscript to a voluntary force, the army's leaders found that they were not free to define the contours of the new institution. Its generals and civilian staff faced competition in creating a model for a volunteer force from the free market economists increasingly interested in military affairs. At the time that Nixon announced the end of the draft, conservative free market advocates were already setting the agenda for what would be called the All-Volunteer Force (AVF).[22]

Milton Friedman's venture onto military terrain constituted one element of a larger movement of neoclassically trained economists into new areas of American life, where their sojourns revived the power of the private sector in American governance.[23] Though American governance historically had combined, to varying degrees at various moments, public and private provision of services, in the early and mid-twentieth century, as the progressive-era, New Deal, and World War II state grew, the private component of public-private governance waned.[24] Yet as early as the 1950s, the pendulum began to swing back, as opponents of the large federal government, the federal workforce, and government provision of services began an effort to shrink government and replace its functions with the private sector. Free market economists provided the ideological underpinning for this effort from their perches in universities like the University of Chicago, new think tanks and societies like Mont Pelerin and the Foundation for Economic Education, and the widespread adoption of their ideas in the institutions and media of the nascent New Right like the *National Review*.[25] By the mid-1960s, free market perspectives had gained ground and played a significant role in American politics and public policy. In education, for instance, neoclassical economists proposed a radical end to public schools and the creation of cash-value educational vouchers. In public welfare, they advocated an end to social welfare programs providing direct services to the needy and instead invented the notion of a "negative income tax."[26] The military constituted one arena among many in which free market advocates sought to gain influence over American governance.

In 1966, as Friedman helped convene the conference on the draft at the University of Chicago, he and his colleagues drew on the work of a growing number of neoclassical free market economists who had begun to study the military. One of the most prominent was economist Walter Oi of the University of Washington (later the University of Rochester). In the early 1960s, Oi had undertaken research on the economic case for a volunteer armed force, and was becoming what his young followers considered "the godfather of research on the economics of the draft and the all volunteer force."[27] Oi's graduate students joined with others from the University of Virginia to produce a vibrant new body of work making the economic case for the end of the draft and the creation of a volunteer force.[28]

They equated the draft with "involuntary servitude."[29] The "slavery," as they also called it, derived from free marketers' economic framing of the draft: it imposed a "hidden tax" on young men. Conscription forced men not only to provide labor and perhaps their lives, but also compelled them to forgo whatever earnings they might have made in the civilian labor market—opportunity costs, in economists' terms.[30] This economic burden could only be eliminated through a volunteer force in which soldiers chose to enlist and no longer faced compulsion.

Joining this theoretical argument were practical arguments about the economics of the draft—its purported economic inefficiency and costliness due to the vast selective service bureaucracy and the high turnover of drafted military personnel. In articles appearing in some of the most influential journals in the field, including the *American Economic Review* and the *Quarterly Journal of Economics*, economists developed a model of the "enlistment decision" of individuals, plotted supply and demand factors of military volunteers, and developed plans for market-based recruitment and retention of special categories like officers and medical personnel.[31] Friedman drew on these arguments and used them to proselytize to politicians and draft supporters at the conference. He later hailed his conference as the single most "dramatic" success of his career: though the four-day event had begun with two-thirds of participants (mostly the noneconomists) opposed to a volunteer force, it ended with two-thirds supporting it.[32]

Friedman's case convinced economist Martin Anderson, who read the work of both Friedman and Oi coming out of the Chicago conference.

A scholar at the Hoover Institution in Palo Alto, California, Anderson became the most influential policy advocate for the volunteer force. In 1967, he penned his own paper supporting the transition to the volunteer force, basing it largely on the arguments of Friedman and Oi.[33] Anderson circulated his paper among policy makers in Washington, where it received warm reviews among those close to Nixon. Nixon's team set up a meeting with Anderson in which Anderson enumerated not only the free market argument for the volunteer force but also the political advantages of advocating the end of the draft. Nixon was impressed, and Anderson joined Nixon's campaign and penned Nixon's statements officially opposing the draft and advocating its end.[34] After Nixon's victory, Anderson joined the White House staff, where he put together the presidential commission charged with creating the blueprint for the volunteer force—the President's Commission on an All-Volunteer Armed Force. Anderson became so closely associated with the volunteer force that over a decade later when he joined the Reagan administration as chief domestic policy advisor, General Robert Schweitzer of Reagan's National Security Council referred to the volunteer force as "Martin Anderson's volunteer army."[35]

Anderson drew on the community of free market scholars when putting together the membership and research staffs for the presidential commission. He tapped Friedman and like-minded economist Alan Greenspan as the intellectual leaders of the commission.[36] Greenspan and Friedman came with a coterie of young economists, many of whom had been present at the 1966 University of Chicago conference or who had published their own research on neoclassical economics and the draft. Chief among them were Walter Oi, Stewart Altman, Harry Gilman, and David Kassing, each of whom led one of the commission's four research groups. They were joined by staff economists Robert Barro, Larry Sjastaad, Alan Fechter, Ronald Hansen and J. Huston McCullough, many of whom had already penned articles in favor of the volunteer force.[37] After their work transitioning the armed forces from the draft to the volunteer force, many of these economists continued to guide military manpower policy in the years to come at the Brookings Institution and the RAND Corporation, as well as the Department of Defense (DoD).

The free marketers of the presidential commission, commonly referred to as the Gates Commission after its commission chair, former Secretary of Defense Thomas S. Gates, envisioned the military as subject to the laws of the market, and applied neoclassical economic models to recruitment and manning. In earlier eras, defense manpower experts had debated troop levels, training and assignments, and the correct balance between civilian defense workers and uniformed defense employees. But these were not economic questions. They did not venture far into the broader question of a "market" for defense work. The market, however, was the natural language of the new defense experts. They identified their task as an economic inquiry into the dynamics of defense manpower. What economic laws pertained to defense manpower? How could they be represented through a "production function," a mathematical representation of those laws? And how could that production function afford more efficient, less costly manpower policy? The free market economists of the Gates Commission effectively charted the beginning of a new field—market-based defense manpower analysis.

The final report of the Gates Commission advocated free market solutions to the problem of recruiting and retaining an all-volunteer force. Soldiers would be induced to join not mainly with appeals to patriotism or service or tradition, but with money—income incentives. The presumed potential volunteers operated as rational individual actors in a marketplace—a labor market. The military, like any other employer, thus had to gauge the supply of young men, the demand of employers, and adjust its compensation in order to lure the correct number of military personnel at the correct times in order to fill the ranks. During economic slumps, salaries for military personnel need not rise, since unemployment in the civilian sector would render military service more secure. In economic booms and periods of low unemployment, salaries would have to increase to lure potential soldiers. In this way, the military operated as simply one economic actor among many, its fate depending on pay, opportunity costs, and other matters of individual utility.[38] Senator Mark Hatfield (R-OR), a congressional ally of the free market advocates, was certain that "salary increases *alone,* totaling about $4-billion, would supply all the incentive needed to maintain the all-volunteer force." Senator Goldwater, Hatfield's cosponsor of volunteer force bills in both 1969 and 1971, wrote that the secret to the success of the AVF "lies in one word—'incentive'. We must make military services attractive and profitable enough to attract volunteers."[39] For the economists and policy makers favoring the market-based military, there was no need to labor over what was fair, or what kind of special demands military life might place on people. The only question was what wage would deliver men and women to the military's doorstep.

Members of the Gates Commission were particularly skeptical about using what they referred to as "compensation in-kind"—the system of benefits and services that career members of the armed services and officers enjoyed—to recruit and retain soldiers. In-kind compensation consisted of the housing, health care, subsistence and other allowances, clubs, commissaries and the Post Exchange (PX), and more that retained career soldiers. For the career man or the officer with a family, this raft of benefits helped make military lifestyles attractive. Though the full slate of benefits did not reach lower-level enlisted men, in theory they could be liberalized so as to reach them all.

But free market advocates opposed expansions of traditional military benefits as anathema to libertarian, free market principles. In their view, these programs unacceptably extended government power over individuals and the economy. They inhibited the individual's ability to pursue his interests according to his own rational choices. Rather than offering soldiers housing or medical care, the Gates Commission maintained, the army should be providing more cash income and letting soldiers choose individually what "support" they wanted to "buy." The rationale mimicked the argument for education vouchers or a negative taxation program: "Cash," the commission reported, "has an inherent advantage" over benefits in that "it allows each individual to decide how he or she will use whatever he earns."[40] The commission therefore refused "proposals involving increased benefits such as improved housing, dental care for families, or improved in-service or post-service educational programs."[41] Ultimately it "decided against recommending general increases in such benefits or in income-in-kind items of any kind."[42]

Free market economists viewed the commissary, the PX, housing and medical care for families as confounding efficient market mechanisms, distorting otherwise clear incentives, and wasting resources.[43] If soldiers were forced to accept benefits and services they did not want as part of their pay package, the commission explained, neither they nor the government would accrue the full value of the benefits: the soldier would neither use nor feel grateful for them while the government nevertheless would have paid them. Worse, the report explained, the army's insistence on maintaining and advertising the benefits would "encourage . . . [the soldier] to consume more of particular goods or services than he otherwise would." In the view of the commission, military benefits were "of little value to young men and women." Young people, they reasoned, would prefer cash to spend on cars, televisions, or other consumer items.[44] Highly visible, market-based cash salaries, the commission concluded, would obviate the need to use benefits as lures for recruitment or reenlistment.[45] Overall, free market advocates portrayed military benefits and programs for soldiers either as economic drags on the military budget, creating an economic "muddle," and needlessly "overcompensating" the service member, or as quaint traditions—"antiquated" and "paternalistic"—ill-suited to "modern" personnel planning.[46]

Political-economic ideology, as much as efficiency and the market, propelled free marketers' dislike of military benefits. Critics on the right chafed at the growth of military benefits and social services, just as they opposed other government programs such as public education, public assistance, social services, Medicare, or Social Security. The most orthodox among them refused to differentiate between government programs for the military and those for civilians. They categorized both as symptoms of dangerous and inefficient government overreach. A writer for the *National Review* predicted that the army would become the "most socialistic organization in America." The "bennies" of the army, he argued—in a fashion long reserved for attacks on civilian welfare programs—"lull the soldiers into a feeling of security at the expense of his own responsibility." Cutting these programs would free "the overburdened taxpayer" from paying "for one of the most wasteful welfare states in the world."[47]

From the Gates Commission onward through succeeding defense reviews on manpower and compensation, free marketers opposed the expansion of benefits to soldiers in favor of a "competitive salary system" or a "flexible salary structure." These expressed the economists' preference for a free market military and their contempt for military benefits and services.[48] Free market advocates attempted to purge the military of its "socialist" trappings and re-create it as a more market-based institution of their own design.

This purge also would eventually include eliminating the military's performance of "non-essential" support services, also called "commercial services" or "commercial activities" and contracting them out to the private sector. The military of the 1970s already relied on private contractors. Unlike many European nations, the United States had never built massive public arsenals for weapons or materiel. It had always relied heavily on contracts with private firms to build its weapons and stock its depots. In addition, every time the military went to war, as it had most recently in Vietnam, it also relied on private local contractors for logistical and base support. Despite these relationships with private firms, the military nevertheless performed a huge number of its own commercial activities and services. In 1953, the pro–private sector commission of former president Herbert Hoover listed just a few examples: "Air transport, Military Sea Transport Services, Panama Steamship Line, Naval shipyards, Military reserve industrial facilities, Scrap metal Processing, Commissary Stores, Post exchanges, Food services to the Armed Forces, Clothing manufacture, Laundries, Dry Cleaning plants, Medical and dental manufacturing and repair."[49]

Since the 1930s and the days of the Depression-era Liberty League, free market advocates had derided the military's many "commercial activities"—defining them as "a good or service that could be obtained from the private sector and that is not inherently governmental."[50] They considered them part and parcel of the "creeping socialism" of the New Deal and the war years. Beginning in the decade following World War II, free market advocates had begun targeting government-performed "commercial services." Herbert Hoover's postwar commissions had revealed the extent of commercial activities performed not only by the military but also by the government in general. After that, small-government, pro–free enterprise conservatives had taken aim at them by advocating that they be contracted out to the for-profit private sector. In the 1950s, President Dwight D. Eisenhower's Bureau of the Budget began encouraging the military—and government in general—to contract out more of its commercial services. Though President John F. Kennedy stalled contracting in the early 1960s, President Johnson renewed the process in 1965, by then dubbed the A-76 process, according to the name and number of the budget rule.

The Gates Commission economists advocated contracting, but briefly and only in passing. The report recommended private contracting for medical services, explaining that "expanded use of civilians to provide medical care" to soldiers and families would save the Pentagon the difficulties of competing in the labor market for highly paid medical professionals.[51] Within ten years, however, the free marketers of the Gates Commission had pulled private contracting into sharp focus. In 1977, Richard Cooper, a RAND Corporation economist who worked with Walter Oi and Gates Commission veteran Stephen Herbits on a 400-page treatise on the economics of defense manpower, argued that contracting to the private sector would save the DoD precious dollars. "Whereas the average costs for military and direct-hire civilian personnel are within a few hundred dollars of one another," he argued, "contract hires may be several thousand dollars less expensive than either one of these sources of labor input—even if the contractor earns a 10 percent profit on the contract services. . . . The substitution of 250,000 contract hires for 250,000 direct hires could save about $1 billion per year."[52]

At the Brookings Institution, manpower analyst Martin Binkin also advocated contracting out military support services, citing the high costs of manpower and the need to find new places for defense savings. Activities currently performed by government personnel, he argued, could be performed with less expense by the private sector. Surveying the small existing literature on the costs of "in-house" (government) versus contracted (private sector) work, Binkin noted that most studies found significant savings.[53] Private sector firms paid employees less and offered few if any benefits. "Where appropriate," he concluded, "it would be cost-effective for the Pentagon to expand its association with private enterprise." In the end he estimated, "for each 10,000 man-years (the amount of work performed by 10,0000 employees in one year) of activities contracted out. . . . At least $30 million could be saved annually." He cited studies showing cost-saving conversions of government jobs to contracts: laundry and dry cleaning (3 conversions at average savings of 39 percent); custodial services (25 conversions at average savings of 39 percent); refuse collection and disposal (4 conversions at average savings of 47 percent); food services (5 conversions at average savings of 22 percent).[54]

Manpower economists increasingly turned to private-sector contracting in the 1970s to try to minimize the extraordinary defense manpower costs of that decade. By 1972, manpower accounted for over 50 percent of the entire DoD budget—more than construction, procurement, operations and maintenance, and research and development combined. Pumped up by the rising inflation of the 1970s and the salary and benefit increases necessary to convert to an all-recruited career force, defense manpower costs attracted unprecedented attention. The new defense manpower economists offered contracting as the solution to these high costs. "The use of contractors to perform certain activities previously conducted by military personnel (or, for that matter, by direct-hire civilian employees)," promised to cut the defense workforce and get the same work done for less money.[55] Assurances of cost savings rested on the cheaper private sector labor force, and on the assumption that firms would face competition and rules to forestall windfall profits and price gouging.

In the ten years after 1968, as the economy slowed and federal budget pressures rose, free marketers spread the gospel of contracting out. The size of government assumed a primary place in the conservative free market critique of government. Private contracting would transfer federal spending to the private sector and reduce the size and direct function of the federal government. Long-time opponents of the large, active, liberal Democratic state viewed contracting as an unambiguous boon.

Free market advocates cooperated with corporate leaders to increase private contracting in the administrations of presidents Richard Nixon and Gerald Ford. Nixon's "tilt in favor of private industry," as one observer described it, included a Hoover-esque commission charged with improving the efficiency of the federal government, the President's Advisory Council on Executive Re-organization (PACEO).[56] Nixon appointed Roy Ash to head the committee. Ash had built Litton Industries, a huge conglomerate known mostly for its technology divisions and "one of the largest private organizations doing contract business with Uncle Sam"; it conducted over half of its business with the federal government.[57] Under Ash's leadership, the commission recommended the establishment of a new executive agency, the Office of Management and Budget (OMB), that would, under Ash's own leadership, promote vastly expanded contracting out of federal activities and jobs.[58] When in 1974 President Ford took over from Nixon, he altered two of OMB's rules to further encourage contracting.[59] At the same time, the OMB forced federal agencies to meet a quota by creating lists of activities that could be considered for outside contract bids. Agencies were to examine and classify "at least five functions presently performed in-house" that could qualify for "transfer to the private sector."[60]

Though free market opponents of the New Deal order initiated the gospel of contracting, traditional New Deal supporters soon also accepted it. As the federal budget crises deepened in the 1970s and manpower costs continued to rise, politicians from both political parties took aim at the costs of the federal workforce. Democrats proposed widespread transfers to the private sector. When Democrat Jimmy Carter won the presidency in 1976, he continued the policies of the Nixon and Ford years. Carter issued new rules that "favored the contracting options" and gave "private industry an advantage in bidding for new jobs."[61]

Defense manpower economists further pressed the military into the mold of a free market-based institution. From 1973 to 1980, the army was pushed to contract out more services and supports to private firms. Over the first several years, the army contracted out dining facilities at several posts, including Fort Myer in Virginia and Fort Benjamin Harrison in Indiana.[62] Other nonessential supports went too. About half of all mortuary or memorial affairs, preserving and burying the remains of soldiers, were put out to contracts starting in the mid-1970s.[63] In 1975, more than half of the 2,699 deceased soldiers "were prepared by commercial firms under contract with the Army."[64] Starting in 1977, the army began converting its laundry and dry cleaning services—a hefty bill considering soldiers' uniform requirements—to contractors. The army had owned and operated over sixty facilities, all of which were scheduled to go to contractors by 1983.[65] The army contracted the services of medical specialists starting in 1978, as the Gates Commission had recommended ten years before.[66] And in 1979, the army identified nearly 1,000 military police functions that could be considered either for elimination or for contracting out, including "vehicle registration, . . . animal control, money escort service, static security posts, gate guards, information booths, vehicle impoundment operations, and the monitoring of intrusion detection systems."[67] As the army scoured its activities to determine more elements for contracting, even many of those very studies were contracted out to private firms. In 1977, the army's Office of the Deputy Chief of Staff for Personnel (ODCSPER) spent $402,000 on manpower contract studies telling it to contract out its commercial and support services.[68] In these cases, the private sector advocated for the private sector to play an increased role in the volunteer force.

Ten years after the publication of the Gates Commission report, free market economists and their allies had crafted a vision of an American military akin to their political and economic beliefs. The military would be subject to the laws of the market and benefit from its discipline and efficiencies. The military's conversion to market principles would serve the added purpose of bringing the government's role into line with free market principles—circumscribing the military's activities by turning them over to the private sector. Manpower efficiency would increase and government waste and interferences would decrease. The military, they hoped, would emerge as a model of an institution transformed by the power of the free market.

THE ARMY BLOCKED the full realization of this hope. When President Nixon appointed the Gates Commission to draw a blueprint for a volunteer force, the army under General Westmoreland's command countered with its own internal study of a volunteer force: Project Volunteer in Defense of the Nation (PROVIDE). Led by the research of Lieutenant Colonel Jack Butler, a psychologist in the army's Personnel Studies and Research Directorate in ODCSPER, PROVIDE crafted a plan to counter the overly "econometric" perspective of the Gates Commission and dislodge the central assumptions that soldiers were simply "rational economic actors" and the army a market institution.[69] Army leaders blanched at coupling words like "incentive" and "profit" to soldiering. They did not believe that the military was a market institution or even that it could benefit from widely applied market principles. To be sure, many in the army supported budget efficiencies and fiscal discipline per se—indeed General Westmoreland had a business degree from Harvard University. But they opposed the general proposition that the market could or should play a central role in the military. Through PROVIDE, ODCSPER, and in Congress, the army often argued the opposite—leaders denounced a market-based military as detrimental to the goals they envisioned for the new volunteer army.

Army leaders worried that the volunteer force would usher in the age of the mercenary—the bought soldier. General Westmoreland invoked fears—long held in the United States—of the corrupting influence of money on soldiers. In a face-to-face meeting, he blasted Friedman for seeking to transform the forces into "an Army of mercenaries."[70] Army stalwart Senator Stennis, chair of the Senate Armed Services Committee, also voiced concern "about the kinds of men who would come into the army under such a system."[71] Would they be hard-working? Would they be disciplined? Would they be honorable? Stennis warned, "we are abandoning the essential spirit of the modern services when we say we are going out to do whatever is necessary to induce a man solely based on the money."[72]

Westmoreland, Stennis, and their allies probably did not fear actual mercenaries as much as they feared the mercenary image that a free market army projected. Dangling pay in front of young people and comparing the army to "just another job" was not, in their view, likely to produce higher morale or better performance. Recruits motivated only by money might not take army rules and discipline seriously. Secretary of the Army Stanley Resor worried that reliance on income incentives alone would "attract the man on the economic margin," someone not fully committed or able to perform military duties.[73] The army worried that "a political draft would be replaced by an economic draft of the poorest Americans."[74]

ODCSPER argued that free marketers misunderstood the basic reasons why soldiers joined the army and remained part of the institution. In 1974 and 1975, an ODCSPER staff led by Colonel John Johns critiqued the "pure econometric view" of the Gates Commission, "heavily influenced by the University of Chicago's economic viewpoint (Milton Friedman)." They indicted the "limitations of economic theory" for the army and its failure to account for numerous unique aspects of military service. Economic theory could not explain "performance in combat," "motivations for military enlistment," and "the unlimited liability nature of the social commitment" made when soldiers joined the army. Johns and his colleagues charged free market economists with naively imagining a "homogenous mass" of "a youth labor market . . . to be manipulated for service by the Armed Forces." That simplistic view, the ODCSPER staff insisted, did not account for the realities of the way soldiers made their decisions to join, the reasons they remained in the army, or the means by which the military operated.[75]

"The Army," DCSPER General Harold Moore insisted, "is a service—not a job—it cannot buy soldiers. . . . They do not stay in the Army to acquire wealth or luxury." Soldiers' joined and remained in the army for far more encompassing and complex reasons. "The Army is . . . a way of life," he explained. "Dedication and commitment are necessary."[76] Such values were not abstractions, but generated from the lived relationship between soldiers and the army—how soldiers fit into the army and how the army treated soldiers. "A large measure of our success," in recruiting and retaining soldiers, and in training them to fight, Moore explained, "depends on how each soldier views himself in relation to the Army." Such determinations were neither made through a market calculus, nor subject to the laws of supply and demand. Soldiers and army leaders alike viewed their relationship as a web of interdependence, sentiment, and values, not a collection of rational acts. If soldiers joined because of a sense of loyalty and commitment, and if they stayed because of their sense of being accepted, welcomed, and supported, then most of the key policy proposals proffered by free market policy makers were irrelevant, perhaps even counterproductive: exchanges solely of pay and income incentives would not demonstrate the kind of institutional support and commitment that soldiers wanted from the army. Nor would it weave soldiers into a web of army organizations. In sum, the army opposed nearly all of the market innovations of the Gates Commission and supported those that the free marketers loathed. The ODCSPER pressed their case in the mid-1970s, as the details of the volunteer force were hammered out in Congress, the DoD, and in the individual services.

Though free marketers abhorred the large social welfare apparatus of the army, army leaders argued that the benefits and programs—housing, health care, childcare, schools, shopping, and more—all demonstrated precisely the institutional support and commitment that soldiers wanted. The army's "cohesiveness," General Moore insisted in his 1976 annual report to *Army Magazine*, "is based on our ability to provide benefits and services that offset the conditions, unexpected demands and hazards of service."[77] Rather than merely paying the soldier the army proposed to emphasize the cohesion and commitment in the soldier–army relationship and "take care" of the soldier—and his family. This would simultaneously raise soldiers' standards of living and foster institutional loyalty, cohesion, and efficiency. The army recalled and revived a traditional army maxim. Secretary of the Army Martin Hoffman testified to Congress, "The old Army leadership adage 'Take care of your people and they will take care of you' was never more true." Hoffman continued: "The assurance that when . . . in a combat environment or separated from family that the Army will provide for medical care, commissary and exchange privileges, assistance with personal problems and survivors benefits, is probably more important to the individual member than the actual compensation."[78] In the army's view, security for the nation and the success of the volunteer army depended on a broad sense of social security among soldiers and their families—a security the army would provide. Diminishing, or worse eliminating, those benefits would destroy the sense of mutual responsibility between soldiers and army.

Many army leaders doubted the wisdom of free market injunctions to contract out army support activities to the private sector. If the soldier and the army were to enact a relationship of mutual commitment and responsibility, contracting would only confuse the matter of who was responsible to and for whom. The army wanted to demonstrate conspicuously that it—and it alone—provided for the soldiers in order to maintain their loyalty, commitment, and dedication. As a result, the army often dragged its feet as the administrations of Nixon and Ford pushed it to review its "commercial activities" for transfer to the private sector. Its internal evaluations consistently questioned the wisdom of defense manpower economists who equated private contracting with greater cost savings and efficiency. The army, for example, judged contracting "medical specialties," as the Gates Commission had demanded, to be "costly and inefficient."[79] In addition, in an inflationary economy, locked-in contracts became more expensive by the year, leaving the army to request more additional funds from Congress than expected, $431 million more in 1979, for example, just to "offset inflation" in its contracts.[80]

The only activities the army willingly contracted out were those leaders felt directly increased soldier morale. During the fall of 1970, as the army began concerted planning for the inevitable transition to the AVF, General Westmoreland created an office of the Special Assistant for the Modern Volunteer Army (SAMVA) to ease the transition. Its surveys of soldiers revealed that kitchen duty ranked as one of the most hated assignments. It nettled them as unsoldierly, even unmanly, and many felt it was meted out as punishment. Soldiers also abhorred other labor details that post commanders used to help meet service and maintenance requirements—the cleaning of the barracks and other buildings on post, and lawn mowing and other landscape and outdoor cleanup duties. Commanders did not like assigning soldiers to these duties either, since cleaning and mowing stole time from training soldiers to do the job for which the army had recruited them: fighting and winning wars.[81] So the army decided to place kitchen duty out as a contract to the private sector.[82] Yet even these contracts that the army willingly sent out to the private sector did not, according to the army, perform the way that free market economists promised. In 1972, the army undertook a "three-year test" and evaluation of the take-over of dining facilities by commercial contractors, concluding that while "the contract operation was satisfactory, . . . there was no particular advantage in using contract services."[83] Whether it was contracting, cutting army benefits, or relying solely on cash for recruitment and retention, the army resisted free market proposals that diminished its ability to demonstrate to soldiers its commitment to care for them.

To rebut the free market model of the volunteer force, the army preferred a model of masculine familialism, which its leaders believed applied to military service far better than the market. "We in DCSPER . . . argued the notion of a fraternal organization model that would better account for combat motivation," as well as the basic impulses to join and stay in the military.[84] In another report, ODCSPER outlined the familial model less as the imagined brotherhood of the combat unit and more as the paternalism of the benevolent patriarch. The army mounted a defense against free market models of the volunteer force by diminishing the role that money and markets could play in accounting for the sacrifices and loyalty necessary for military service. Its manpower leaders proffered a nonpecuniary paternalist institution in its stead.

The army formalized a colloquial army phrase to breathe life into its paternalist model of the new volunteer army—the "Army Family." The army "took care of its own" because of an "Army Family" ethos. DCSPER Harold Moore used the term officially in his 1976 *Army Magazine* report. "As we moved through the second year of the volunteer force we . . . took a hard look at where we need to go to improve personnel management for members of the Army family."[85] Moore spelled out the Army Family's broad constituency, making the case for "adequate pay and benefits for *all* elements of the military 'family.'"[86] In Moore's terms, terms that became commonplace, soldiers joined the volunteer army because the army was a "family," and it, in turn, took care of the soldier's family. The Army Family thus served as a model and metaphor for the institution as a whole but especially for the many support programs that directly cared for soldiers. The term "Army Family" became the colloquial expression of the economic and social support relationship between the army, soldiers, and their families.

Soldiers themselves seemed to desire the army's model of family "taking care of their own" more than a market model. SAMVA's chief, General George Forsythe, undertook a series of inquiries, pilot projects, and policies that spoke to these wants. Forsythe was an innovator, committed to shaking up the army and listening to soldiers, and one of his most important long-term contributions was his attentiveness to the desire of soldiers for a secure, supportive environment for themselves and their families. Forsythe's research confirmed the faith of leaders in the army that a successful volunteer force required creating a social compact with soldiers and their families in which the army promised to care for them.

Soldiers consistently named benefits and supports such as housing, health care, and the PX as among the most important factors in their decisions about recruitment, and, even more important, about reenlistment. Soldiers' families' well-being profoundly affected their attitudes toward the army. They reported that "frequent moves, family separation, and lack of housing" made their lives difficult.[87] One survey indicated that that this general "dissatisfaction over living conditions was one of the main objections to Army life."[88] Follow-up surveys at specific posts delved further. If army life was difficult, what could the army offer to compensate? Soldiers' desires were fairly prosaic

Why are you staying in?

- ☐ I like my job.
- ☐ The bonus helps.
- ☐ I'd like to live in Europe for a while.
- ☐ I've made some great friends in the Army.
- ☐ I can go back to school. Even get a degree.
- ☐ The PX and Commissary discounts save me money.
- ☐ I'm allergic to doctor and dentist bills.
- ☐ I like the free housing. No real estate tax. No monthly bills.
- ☐ I'd like to take the Hawaiian tour.
- ☐ I want a chance to do something different.
- ☐ The service clubs are getting livelier these days.
- ☐ I like the recreation facilities.
- ☐ I like the tax break.
- ☐ I like the idea of retiring at 38.
- ☐ There are never any moving expenses.
- ☐ I like the low-cost travel, especially when it's free.
- ☐ It's a chance to do my bit for my Country.
- ☐ The 30 days vacation with pay.
- ☐ I get the best life insurance deal anywhere.
- ☐ It's easy to get a VA and FHA housing loan.
- ☐ I like staying close to home.
- ☐ I like Army life.

Army advertising encouraged soldiers to reenlist by emphasizing benefits and support programs. In this ad from 1973, they are evident in two-thirds of the reasons for "staying in." Courtesy of CECOM Historical Office archive, Aberdeen Proving Ground, MD.

expressions of the hope for a decent standard of living for their wives and children: they wanted security, protection, health care, a family-friendly environment, and job training for the future.[89] One survey at Ford Ord, California, for example, reported that soldiers most wanted three things from the army—variable housing allowances keyed to a local index, dental and vision care for families, and more vocational and educational courses after hours.[90] Soldiers also wanted opportunities for education and training, a source of long-term earnings and potential upward socioeconomic mobility.[91] Soldiers wanted the army to take care of them.

Subsequent experiments conducted at several posts around the country echoed the importance of social and economic supports not only to soldiers, but also to their wives.[92] Benefits and programs determined much of the spouses' sense of family security and standard of living. Between 69 and 77 percent of wives of enlisted personnel reported, for example, that the army's educational programs exerted "some or strong influence" on them to recommend husbands staying in the army, allowing husbands to increase their earning potential.[93] In addition, 55–65 percent of enlisted personnel's wives reported that the army would be "much or a little better" by expanding programs like family housing, medical benefits, and educational benefits. If these benefits were upgraded, wives said, they would be more inclined to have their husbands reenlist.[94]

Soldiers and wives voiced their expectations that the army should take care of them. In 1975, Staff Sergeant D. L. Manley wrote a letter to *Army Times*, the service newspaper whose letters-to-the editor section vented the spleen of discontented soldiers and their families, complaining of being "subjected to the high cost of civilian dental care for my dependents." Though the military authorized seventy facilities to provide dental care to dependents living without accessible services, because Manley was posted to a "highly populated area with extensive civilian dental service available," he was sent into the civilian dental care system—to the private sector. In his unhappiness, he rebuked army leaders, throwing back in their faces the family-based social compact that they had articulated to lure soldiers. "When I entered the service . . . I assumed that I would serve the military and they would look out for my basic needs and welfare. The first responsibility of a leader is to accomplish the mission and to protect the welfare of the men." But instead, in forcing him to bear the burden of the $3,000 in dental costs that his wife was likely to incur, the army was "turning its back on the service

"Today's Army is a family of families."
Today's Army means many things to many people. Here's what the Wheelers and the Carnleys had to say about it.
"I like the shopping," said Mrs. Mary Wheeler. "I couldn't believe the difference in prices, the first time I shopped in the commissary."
Mrs. Vanessa Carnley liked the medical benefits. "I think the Army's facilities are excellent. I'm never worried about getting good care for me and my family."
Private First Class Harold Carnley liked the cost of Army medical care, as compared to civilian expenses. "Our baby only cost us $7.50. I almost said, 'I'll take two.'"
"To me, it's more than the obvious benefits," said SP/4 George Wheeler, Jr. "I feel that today's Army is a family of families. And I'm proud to be a member."
Why are you staying in?

The army advertised itself as a family that took care of soldiers' families. 1973. Courtesy of CECOM Historical Office archive, Aberdeen Proving Ground, MD.

members' needs." "If a sergeant can not afford the basic needs of his family now," he asked, "what is to be expected in the future?"[95]

Beyond the realm of enlistment and reenlistment, a paternalistic army provided benefits that a market-based army could not. At a practical level, army leadership pointed out that a military system of benefits and supports for soldiers and families was safer, politically speaking, than reliance solely on income incentives. When debating the free marketers of the Gates Commission, General Westmoreland had argued that even if the administration or Congress stalled military pay increases, they "would be receptive to expenditures of lesser amounts of money that would improve service attractiveness," such as benefits. Even more important, Congress would have a more difficult time cutting benefits than pay raises.[96] Benefits were complicated structures, tied into powerful bureaucracies. They were also tangible experiences that soldiers and their families lived each day and would miss immediately: shopping at the PX, visiting the doctor, settling into a house or apartment, dropping off children at a child care center. Deeply invested in these benefits, military personnel, soldiers, and families would protest more vociferously their reductions.

For army leaders, an Army Family model in which the army "took care of its own" also promised to enhance the public image of the army, an image crucial to the long-term success of any volunteer force. As the army entered the volunteer era, a spate of books reported on the "anguish" of the army with its "tarnished shield," and even forecast its death as a viable institution. Alongside the many public reports of shocking and unseemly army actions in Vietnam, these books reduced the legitimacy of the army.[97] Its leaders were acutely aware of "the extent to which the Army's public image had declined." Its surveys revealed that even among its own soldiers, the army had a bad reputation: "70 percent of Army veterans advised prospective volunteers to join services other than the Army."[98]

The Army Family model of the volunteer force played an important role in army leaders' efforts to relegitimize the army as an institution. For one, the respectable image of an Army Family taking care of its members contrasted with the perceived chaos of the Vietnam-era army, with its lack of accountability, insubordination, and discord. This framing was evident later in the 1970s as the army pushed for paid accompanied tours for soldiers with families. Commanders noted that the new family-friendliness of the army quelled all manner of bad soldier behavior. "At three dozen major U.S. military bases in West Germany," the presence of "dependent families" served as "a moderating influence" on soldiers. "Married men," *Time* quoted General John W. Pauley as saying, "tend to be more stable and much less subject to the dangers of alcohol, drug abuse and sexual adventures with the locals, provided family are with them at these overseas posts." An army of families, in which one overarching Army Family took care of them all, was a more professional, obedient, responsible, and honorable army. These were characteristics that the public—and even soldiers and lawmakers—had found lacking in the army during Vietnam, and that the army took pains to promote in the new era of the volunteer force.[99]

Family rhetoric—as well as actual wives and children—provided a moderating, even disciplining effect on soldiers. The Army Family that took care of its own reinforced the internal hierarchy of army life by modeling the patriarchal gendered relations of the traditional male breadwinner family. In the Army Family, the army assumed the highest place at the top of the ladder—as the symbolic head of household. The army took care of its "dependents" below, providing authority but also sustenance. The soldier stood one rung below the army, serving and obeying, but also caring for his own family. His care for them—as breadwinner—was supplemented, but not supplanted, by the army's supports for the family. And below the soldier stood the family—wives, essentially—dependent on both soldiers and the army for their care, yet serving both husband/soldiers and the army through their loyalty and care work. The Army Family model exemplified military hierarchy, but set it in a human context.

The Army Family model provided precisely the symbolism and metaphor for the kind of institutional goals the army was at pains to promote in the new era of the volunteer force: unity, cohesion, commitment, and loyalty. These goals worked internally to increase soldiers' sense of connection to the military, a connection army leadership hoped would translate into the decision to make a career of military service. But they also worked externally to represent the military as an institution epitomized by these virtues, virtues partly associated with traditional male-headed households. The army's paternal model—its marked contrast to the pecuniary, market-based model envisioned by the free marketers who hatched the plan for the volunteer force—helped assure the success of the nascent volunteer force of the 1970s. Within the army, the traditional family model served mostly an institutional purpose, representing relations between soldiers and the army as well as central values of the volunteer army's relegitimation. Outside the army, the soldier-breadwinner and the Army Family model helped lift the army's reputation from its depths and revived its social and political standing.

MOST MEMBERS of Congress found the Army Family model more convincing than the free market model. In direct contradiction to the proposals of free market economists to diminish the importance of non-cash compensation, army leaders worked with sympathetic members of Congress in the late 1970s to expand benefits and supports.

The prime targets of expanded army support constituted junior enlisted soldiers with families, those excluded from many of the traditional benefits granted to career soldiers and officers. Virtually every member of Congress concurred that these soldiers suffered hardships that the army's benefits and support services could assuage. In 1978 and 1979 army leaders and their congressional allies fought to bring all junior enlisted personnel under the umbrella of programs that previously only senior career personnel had enjoyed, an "officerization" of the army and its social welfare. The overall effort aimed to allow soldiers to have their families with them and to support those families at a better standard of living.

The most important proposed expansion of soldier benefits modified travel provisions for junior enlisted soldiers, what the army dubbed Junior Enlisted Travel (JET). The term "travel" was misleading, connoting, perhaps, vacation or airline tickets. In fact, "travel" denoted a host of payments and entitlements when soldiers and their families relocated to new posts—and support of families once there. The most significant of these were command-sponsored overseas tours, foreign billets in which a soldier brought his wife and children at the army's expense. Prior to the onset of the volunteer force, "accompanied" tours were viewed as the perquisites of long-term career service, necessary only for higher-ranking soldiers who both had families and had earned the privilege of the army's sponsorship. Only soldiers above the rank of corporal qualified. This left more than 40 percent of the army in the cold.

Though command-sponsored tours were historically a privilege of rank, leaders of the modern volunteer army of the 1970s redefined them as necessary to maintain soldiers' satisfaction. Commanders in Europe reported junior enlisted soldiers who refused to leave their families behind and brought them to Germany even without army sponsorship.[100] Living without command support "on the economy" cost more than first-term soldiers could afford. Forced to live off-post, sometimes without kitchens, heat, or appliances, they became isolated and disillusioned. "This type of situation," a member of the House Armed Services Committee pointed out, "is hardly conducive to force morale and retention and we are losing some very good people as a result."[101] As one staff sergeant put it, the rules precluding first-termers from bringing their families abroad could "single-handedly bring[] down the Army's volunteer concept."[102] "If we are to maintain a volunteer military," wrote an army wife to *Army Times*, "we must overcome the attitude that all first-termers are just kids." The entire army community, she insisted, "should be campaigning for the right of all military men to the same family care."[103]

The new entitlements would provide dependent travel, shipment of privately owned vehicles, storage of household goods, shipment of up to 1,500 pounds of household goods, and movement of a house trailer for service members in the ranks of corporal (with less than two years' service) and below.[104] "The long-range benefits of this action," promised Representative Bill Nichols (D-AL) who was chair of the Armed Services Compensation Subcommittee, "include potential better reenlistment rates, less attrition before completion of enlistment and longer overseas tours."[105]

Without a sense of army-provided security, soldiers and their wives might not reenlist. And without reenlistment, the new volunteer force might not succeed. The Army Family provided the logic for the extension of traditional officers' and career benefits to junior enlisted soldiers and families. The Army Family included all soldiers.

THE ARMY'S REFUSAL to abandon its benefits and its commitment to enlarge them deeply disappointed free market advocates. Beginning with Friedman in 1966, they had envisioned the military as an institution subject to the laws of the market. They had imagined a military purged of its inefficient benefits and programs, cut loose from its big-government appendages, lithe and flexible in drawing in the necessary manpower through measures and manipulations of the labor supply. But this was not what they got. They lamented how the DoD made so "little movement" to expand the free market's benefits into the military.[106] Corporate observers as late as the 1990s would refer to only "halting progress" of free market, private sector practices in the military.[107] A group of business executives and economists examining the role of the private sector in defense remarked that "DoD's support infrastructure has remained largely impervious" to the market.[108] Though free market advocates at the University of Chicago imagined in 1966 that the new volunteer military might serve as a full-blown model of a market-based, private-enterprise-infused government institution, the first two decades of the volunteer army proved otherwise.

Skeptical generals had rebuffed the free market modeling of the army. And for nearly twenty years after the establishment of the volunteer force, the generals more than the economists shaped its contours, even in the areas of manpower, benefits, and contracting that so engaged economists. As a model for the volunteer force, they invoked the decidedly nonmarket institution of the paternalist and patriarchal family. Westmoreland's personnel officers used it skillfully to press for a volunteer force lured and retained by promises of support, caring, and security, instead of money. And though free market advocates pressed cuts to benefits and contracting out of army services, the military's social service apparatus would only grow in the years that followed.

The paternalist model of the volunteer army that "took care of its own" would not, however, proceed without further challenges and difficulty. By the 1990s, new pressures from the post–Cold War cuts to the military's budget and new gambits from large corporations revived free marketers' vision of an army that contracted out or privatized its benefits. But there were more immediate challenges, too. Though the army's leaders fended off encroachment from free market economists, new groups eyed the army's benefits and social services. Over the course of the 1970s, federal employee unions turned their attention to the volunteer army. Though unions sat on the opposite end of the ideological spectrum from free market economists, their bid to unionize the army nevertheless struck again at the meaning and measure of the army's growing support structure. At stake was whether military service and civilian employment shared attributes that made the union, rather than the army, the institution on which volunteer soldiers should rely.

2

Is Military Service a Job?

IN LATE 1975, the *Wall Street Journal* broke the story that the American Federation of Government Employees (AFGE), an American Federation of Labor and Congress of Industrial Organizations (AFL-CIO)-affiliated union representing federal employees, was considering unionizing America's soldiers, sailors, airmen, and marines.[1] Half a dozen NATO allies had unionized their armed forces, so AFGE's bid was not without international precedent.[2] But in the United States, just after the dramatic end of the draft and the beginning of a volunteer force, the threat of a unionized military created an outcry. Pollsters anxiously registered public opinion on the matter; Congress demanded hearings; Presidents Gerald Ford and then Jimmy Carter weighed in; and military leadership became, in the words of one observer, "hysterical."[3]

At the moment AFGE made its bid, the army had just resisted the effort of free market economists on the Gates Commission to reshape the army as a more libertarian institution shed of its "big government" benefits and imbricated in the free market. But with nary a moment to rest, the army faced new challenges to its social welfare programs. In 1973 the U.S. economy declined into a deep recession that shrunk the gross domestic product, slowed growth, and instigated layoffs, plant closings, and bankruptcies. At the same time, rising inflation alarmed federal policy makers and threatened to rapidly and drastically increase the federal budget.[4] In the struggle to control costs, government spending of all kinds came under fire. And in this context, members of Congress and the public raised new questions about the costs and generosity of the military's benefits and social programs.

Rhetorically, the interrogations lumped together all military personnel and their benefits, skimming over the divergent status of new enlistees and career personnel and impugning the whole. While lower-ranked enlisted men, especially those with families, still lived perilously close to poverty and were only just beginning to fully enter the "Army Family" and receive its supports, their superiors received the full complement of military social welfare and enjoyed social and economic security that many civilians would envy. Amalgamating all military personnel into one category, and conjoining it with other government employment benefits and social programs, legislators and journalists called for equal cuts among all. As one of the lead critics of the military and its spending, Senator William Proxmire (D-WI) demanded, "the fiscal scalpels must be applied to both military and civilian programs."[5]

Union leaders at AFGE saw in the military benefits crisis a mirror image of the threats confronting its existing members—federal employees also facing the austerity of the economic downturn. Like so many workers across the country in the 1970s, they, too, suffered layoffs and pay and benefit cuts. Union president Clyde Webber insisted that AFGE was simply meeting the demands of career servicemen, whose thousands of letters to the union pleaded for help.[6] Not unlike working-class men in industrial jobs or blue- and white-collar public service, career military personnel felt they might lose the security undergirding their way of life. If the army and Congress would not stop this erosion and protect their benefits, about two-thirds of soldiers—even those who did not support a union—suspected that the union probably could. And between one-third and one-half of military personnel expressed full, clear support for unionization.[7] As soldiers surveyed the rocky transformation to the volunteer force and the dangers of the federal budget, some imagined that their security might require them to take actions similar to civilian workers. They imagined that even soldiers could join a union.

In the end, military personnel never signed union cards. After two years AFGE retreated and Congress outlawed military unionization. But AFGE's foray into military organizing profoundly shaped the future of the military social welfare programs on which the union bid was premised. During two years of intense debate in Congress and the media, military personnel, leaders of the uniformed services, defense policy makers, legislators, and the press were forced to ask and answer new and fundamental questions about military service and its rewards: Ought the military be considered an employer like any other? What would such equivalencies imply about the future of military service? Could military service and the benefits accorded it be compared to civilian jobs and their benefits? The proposed cuts to military support programs and the resulting bid to unionize the military tapped directly into deep questions of service, entitlement, and citizenship that struck at the heart of the growing military welfare state.

IN 1967, Congressman Mendel Rivers (D-SC), chair of the House Armed Services Committee, championed soldiers' pay by linking military pay hikes automatically to those won by federal employees, represented by increasingly powerful public unions. Though Rivers had never served in the military, he counted himself as "the granddaddy of the war hawks," the biggest supporter of the Vietnam War, and a guardian of military personnel.[8] He defended the notorious perpetrator of the My Lai Massacre, Lieutenant William Calley, and he framed his support of Calley as part of his wider commitment to honoring and protecting common soldiers, sailors, and airmen. He intended the Rivers Amendment to ensure honor and protection by guaranteeing military personnel the kinds of regular cost-of-living increases that civilian public employees received.

Rivers, no friend of organized labor, never intended that his bill would facilitate the first bid by a federal employee union to organize the American military. But the shared economic fate of soldiers and federal employees during the lean recessionary and inflationary decade of the 1970s drew the AFGE to the army in the mid-1970s. In early 1974, President Ford announced plans to bar the cost-of-living raises for federal employees, and hence military raises, citing fears of fostering inflation.[9] AFGE president Clyde Webber led the union in the fight for the pay raise in Congress. Fearing failure, Webber appealed to uniformed servicemen and women to write letters to Congress and the Ford administration in support of federal workers' pay rise—and thus their own. Servicemen and women responded and "conducted a heavy letter-writing effort" to try to resist cuts to the pay of both civilian federal employees and military personnel. They had not only their own linked pay hikes to consider, but also the prospect of one day themselves becoming federal employees. Since 1944, the Veterans Preference Act had given military veterans an advantage in securing federal government jobs. Despite the positive response of military personnel to AFGE's call to arms, the AFGE failed to win raises, and Congress actually repealed the Rivers Amendment in 1974.

Federal employees and military personnel faced an uphill battle in their quest to stay the budget scalpels because their pay cuts comprised just one element of the wide, intense scrutiny of government spending in a period of economic crisis. As the public absorbed the corruption of Nixon's Watergate scandal, federal spending was questioned with increased indignation and even desperation. Much of the outrage targeted the sheer size of the federal government, which was at a historic high. And the carping was not just among conservatives. Liberal senator Edwin Muskie (D-ME), in a speech to the New York Liberal Party, demanded to know "why can't liberals start raising hell about a government so big, so complex, so expensive that it's dragging down every good program that we've worked for?" Headlines warned of "BIG GOVERNMENT—BIG WASTE" and unearthed patently profligate spending—a "fleet of government automobiles . . . for 743 sub-Cabinet–level bureaucrats," in violation of the law; 71 separate energy commissions tucked away in various bureaus; cost overruns on construction projects; and research on supposedly spurious or unnecessary topics. Inflation and rising unemployment tore gaping holes in many Americans' budgets and fueled antigovernment fervor. One Boston man who'd seen his family income decline markedly returned his taxes to the Internal Revenue Service with tea leaves enclosed, to invoke the colonists' tax revolt against the British. And while "paying taxes through gritted teeth is nothing new," the *Christian Science Monitor* pointed out, "what is new in the last half of the 1970s is the growing feeling on the part of millions of Americans that, inflation aside, they are paying more yet getting less of their money's worth out of their federal government."[10] Stories of federal profligacy flourished, greedily absorbed by a restive public.[11]

Calls for cuts to federal government spending fueled assaults on federal employee and military benefits. In 1976, Congressman Les Aspin (D-WI) took the lead in the congressional effort to reign in benefits spending for federal workers and the military. "Everybody should get some fringe benefits," he told his colleagues on the Hill, "but there's a point at which they get out of hand. Federal benefits and military benefits are way past that point."[12] Aspin worked under the tutelage of the senior senator from his state, William Proxmire (D-WI), who had taken the notorious Joseph McCarthy's seat after his death in 1957. Proxmire made his political reputation battling government waste, issuing "Golden Fleece" awards for the most wasteful government spending projects. Aspin worked on Proxmire's staff and then joined him in Washington in 1970 as a member of the House of Representatives. Aspin possessed an impressive defense background. As a graduate of the Reserve Officers' Training Corps and with two years as an aide to Secretary of Defense Robert McNamara, he would eventually rise to chair of the House Armed Services Committee in the 1980s and later secretary of defense under President Bill Clinton.[13] With Proxmire's tutelage, Aspin became a formidable foe of what he called excessive defense spending—including funds for the military's benefits and social services.

Aspin joined Proxmire in public crusades against defense spending and his focus reached every corner of the defense budget. With Proxmire's help, he led an attack against the Department of Defense (DoD)'s budget proposal in 1976. The historically high budget proposal of $112 billion was based on estimates from the Central Intelligence Agency (CIA) of the Soviet Union's military strength. Aspin charged that the CIA had exaggerated the Soviets' defense capabilities as well as used faulty calculations when demonstrating that the United States would supposedly have to spend many billions to meet the Soviet challenge.[14] Yet he also dogged the Pentagon lunchroom operation, whose annual $1 million budget he called "grossly inefficient," with nearly as much vigor. Employing 87 staff people to serve only 330 meals each day, the cost per lunch ran to about $13.50 each, the equivalent of over $50 in 2015 dollars. Yet top brass only had to pay $1.50—the rest constituted a "taxpayer subsidy." Over a year, Aspin pointed out, that amounted to "$1,030,476 and 73 cents." As the *Army Times*, the newspaper serving the army community, put it, Aspin "generally bedeviled the military."[15]

By 1976, Aspin's critical gaze fell upon on the system of pay and benefits for soldiers. Even before the volunteer-era expansion of benefits to enlisted soldiers and families, the figures in that category were staggering. Between 1964 and 1973, manpower costs grew from 42 percent of the total DoD budget to 56 percent, more than operations and maintenance, procurement, and research combined. Pay and allowances alone increased by $22 billion. The growth continued after 1973, even as the size of the army shrunk by about a million soldiers.[16]

Such figures provoked a flurry of proposals to cut military benefits in Congress. Aspin himself aimed specifically at health care, which he described as excellent care at mere "bargain basement prices." "Essentially, the taxpayers are providing free insurance benefits for active-duty members," who, he claimed, should also be willing to pay premiums just as civilians did.[17] Representative Paul Findlay (R-IL) wanted to halt cost-of-living increases for all military pensions. Senators John Culver (D-IA) and Henry Bellmon (R-OK) fought to "strip the commissary subsidy from the FY 77 Defense appropriations bill" because it did not contribute enough to basic military readiness.[18] Others proposed cutting the small federal subsidy that paid store clerks and baggers in the commissaries and Post Exchanges (PXs). Still others suggested increasing military families' copayments for select medical services through the military's health care insurance.[19]

The cost-cutting proposals left little doubt as to the congressional critics' verdict on military benefits: they were generous, perhaps excessive. "I don't see how in the name of patriotism those serving the country can milk the Treasury in this way and not [expect to] have something done about it," roared Senator Charles H. Percy (R-IL) when examining the military pension system.[20] Senator Jake Garn (R-UT), a reserve member of the National Guard and thus a recipient of military pay and benefits, insisted, "The changes . . . in working conditions, in privileges, in pay and a fringe benefits I doubt has been matched anyplace in the private sector or in other government areas. It is unbelievable."[21] With rising inflation and a swollen federal budget, military benefits looked to some like a boondoggle, part of an out-of-control defense budget that created needlessly high costs for taxpayers.

Army leaders viewed the timing of the attacks on military benefits as a tragic coincidence, with the decision to give up the draft occurring almost precisely at the moment that the U.S. economy entered the worst economic downturn since World War II. The army needed manpower funds to support the recruitment and retention of volunteer soldiers—to support the "Army Family" and its ability to "take care of its own." But the budget cuts threatened the army's success. "There could not have been a more challenging time in recent history," lamented Deputy Chief of Staff for Personnel of the Army (DCSPER) General Harold Moore, "in which to develop a volunteer army."[22]

To some degree, the army was a victim of its own successful advertising in the 1970s. The army touted its good benefits to potential volunteers and the public. Advertisements mentioned education programs, housing allowances and new family housing, free medical care, and even social services like child care. Media outlets picked up on these stories, generating a broader public understanding that life in the new volunteer force was solid, secure, and comfortable. The *New Yorker* reported on the army's new "commodious and attractive quarters."[23] *Time* magazine displayed a hip-looking designer's sketch of new army housing with mod light fixtures and creature comforts.[24] *U.S. News and World Report* in 1973 highlighted the army's new education programs for active-duty soldiers that would allow them "a free education," ranging from high school equivalency to a college degree before they got out of the army.[25]

Stories of good pay and high benefits appeared in magazines that targeted potential recruits. *Mechanix Illustrated* published the army's entire pay and allowance scale. Adding up the pay, allowances, benefits, and recreation, the author concluded, "Uncle Sam is making military life so attractive that he wants *you* to say to *him*, I Want You!"[26] *Essence* magazine, directed at African Americans, carried a section on the "Working World" with a story about the benefits in the armed forces: "free training and job placement, free or low-cost degree, free medical and dental care, free legal assistance, free housing and food or allowances for such, a month's paid vacation, all expense paid relocations, availability of cut rate merchandise and low cost entertainment, retirement at half pay at the end of 20 years."[27] *Mademoiselle* magazine for young women highlighted how "free dental and medical care for you and your dependents, small housing and food allowances, and the opportunity to shop in the low-priced commissaries and post exchanges can bring the effective worth of your pay to almost double."[28]

Even as job prospects dimmed in civilian life, the proliferation of stories of the army's benefits and services fostered an image of army life as good, even flush. Statements in the media equated the army's compensation and benefits to a middle-class standard of life, what with the "allotment for his wife and child, . . . half price purchases at the PX, socialized medicine for the family, and excellent insurance coverage. . . . All that plus foreign travel and retirement after 20 years." *Esquire* magazine projected this view of the easy military life in its July 1977 issue, which was themed around the troubled economy:

> If all else fails [in trying to find a job], Tell it to Your Uncle Sam. All your medical needs will be taken care of. You'll be paid a quarters allowance. . . . Married men live with their families either in government housing or places they find themselves. You'll get a food allowance, too. And if you're married your wife can shop at the commissary, where every day is bargain day. You'll get thirty days' paid vacation every year. . . . Put in your twenty years [and] . . .

> pretty soon you'll have more time in the chow line than most of those recruits got in the service. Then you can hang it up. Tell 'em to take that green uniform and put it where the sun don't shine. You'll get fifty percent of what you made on active duty. If you enlisted at seventeen, you'll only be thirty-seven. Which is not too old to be: Looking for a Job.[29]

In other words: live on the largesse of the army, retire, take home a huge pension—and you can still work another job. It all looked quite generous, insisted an editorial in the *Richmond Times-Dispatch;* "mighty fair," echoed a WBTV editorial in Charlotte, North Carolina; "vastly improved," insisted the *Milwaukee Journal.*[30]

With the fraying economy, some observers and reporters asked whether soldiers were receiving "too much."[31] James Davidson of the National Taxpayers Union referred to the benefits as the military "gravy train." And *U.S. News and World Report* questioned whether the army had become "too soft a life?"[32] The stories focused on the fringe benefits, repeating the long lists of military supports as self-evident over-indulgence: "allowances for food and housing, tax exemptions, enlistment and re-enlistment bonuses, free medical care that includes families, subsidized food stores, and retirement pay after 20 years of service." Members of the military might even be "overpaid."[33]

The threat to benefits was not lost on soldiers. A congressional study of the army reported that enlisted personnel devoured "newspaper articles, television specials and information provided by local base [*sic*] newspapers regarding proposed changes in military pay and benefits."[34] In case soldiers missed the news of Congress in the regular press, the *Army Times* covered developments in the battle over benefits every week. *Army Times* reported so heavily on benefits that they actually advertised to soldiers by playing up their benefits coverage: "Benefits—What's the latest word? Find out by reading *Army Times* every week."[35]

Army Times editorials repeatedly critiqued the suggested cuts to benefits and the members of Congress who proposed them. Targeted legislators appeared as bloated plutocrats, blithely partaking of their own perquisites while simultaneously questioning the comparatively modest benefits of simple, honest soldiers. The newspaper skewered Congress in cartoons, which ran on the first page of the editorial section each week. In one, army benefits were contrasted with the lavish, all-expenses-paid, "fact-finding" tours taken by members of Congress to destinations across the globe. It pictured two bulging members of Congress with young, smiling women by their sides, their suitcases packed and labeled as "congressional overseas tour." They spoke over their shoulders to a small, wan-looking serviceman holding a paper saying, "benefit changes." "When We Return," the caption read, "We'll Look into How Much We Can Afford for You."[36] In a similar vein, another cartoon portrayed an overweight member of Congress holding a soldier's uniform trousers and shirt with the words "fringe benefit losses" on them. The soldier stood thin and humiliated in his boxers, hat, and shoes. "He Still Has His Shorts," *Army Times* observed dryly.[37]

Soldiers' letters to the editors echoed these images. Many contrasted the purported fancy lifestyles of members of Congress with the simple, often difficult, lives of soldiers. "Is it fair of Sen. Nunn (D-GA)," asked a staff sergeant, "who recently received a nice $13,000 raise to tell 62,000 military

Army Times depicted the fleecing of soldiers' benefits by Congress. 1975. "He Still Has His Shorts." John Stampone. From *Army Times*, October 1 © 1975 Gannett-CN. All rights reserved. Used by permission and protected by the Copyright Laws of the United States. The printing, copying, redistribution, or retransmission of this Content without express written permission is prohibited.

and their families who may qualify for food stamps that they are over paid?"[38] Or they compared the ease of work on the Hill with the challenges of military service: "I doubt that Sen. Dewey Bartlee (R-OK), author of the bill passed by Congress [to reduce unemployment benefits for retired service personnel] has ever experienced the traumatic transition from military to civilian life and a completely new work situation."[39] "When some fat cat sapsucker in Washington, D.C. sits on his duff and says he's going to take away my pension it burns me up," a noncommissioned officer wrote. "Well let him fight the next war."[40] Congressman Aspin faced particular scorn for his critiques of soldiers' benefits. Sergeant First Class (Ret.) Steve Reed wrote, "Aspin is at it again, attacking 20-year retirement for servicemen. He gets another raise in October—two in one year—and more money in one raise than some enlisted get in wages in four years. Will this man ever stop to take care of his own store before he goes after the military?"[41]

Letters often asked whether members of Congress even merited special perquisites, especially in comparison to soldiers' hard work and sacrifice. A letter from Captain Daniel Shaw made this case in piercing detail:

> In an August 9 issue article REP. Thomas Downey (D, NY) is quoted as saying 'We cannot afford the military establishment we have today.' Well, Mr. Downey, let me say something about that and maybe enlighten you. "You talk about costs: well let me run over just what I cost the good old taxpayer, in terms of dollars in my pocket. Last year my pay was a little under $15,000 and subsistence allowance was a little over $600. . . . Ah, but one can hear this gentleman calling down from the Hill, don't forget all those other benefits, like the PX, commissary, health care and so on. Well, sir, if things are so good on our side of the fence, then why don't you trade places with me so you can cash in on the benefits? I'd be more than happy to rough it on the Hill. . . . Wouldn't it be great if we could all mail our letters for free? Wouldn't it be nice if we all had over a hundred free trips home during every two-year period? Or wouldn't it be exciting to take the wife on a free round-the-world trip—all in the name of fact-gathering? When it comes to fringe benefits, the military can't hold a candle to the Hill.[42]

Senator Barry Goldwater (R-AZ), a staunch defender of military benefits, became the darling of soldiers when he delivered a speech scolding his colleagues for "nit-picking" over military benefits. "It's hypocrisy," said Goldwater, "for congressmen who are enjoying so many tax-subsidized extras to begrudge the few left to service people." According to *Army Times*, "what delighted military people was Goldwater's saying out loud what so many can't—that members of Congress live too well themselves to be sniping at commissaries and health benefits."[43]

Similar analyses led many soldiers to demand parity in federal budget cutting between soldiers and members of congress. An *Army Times* cartoon pointed out the blindness of members of Congress to their own benefits even as they sought to cut the military's: A little owl sitting on a tree branch asks innocently, "Ever hear a congressman or a senator say: 'lets [*sic*] leave the military alone and reduce our pay and benefits?"[44] A group of soldiers and civilian army workers wrote in from Fort MacArthur, California: "We propose that each time our earned benefits are under study for cutback or elimination, that congressional benefits be considered for cuts or elimination equally by law." Their closing sentiments might have stood as a slogan for the soldiers and their families in the face of congressional criticism: "The active military, retirees, and civil service personnel are tired of having to be sacrificial goats for the nation's ills."[45]

THE AFGE OBSERVED the growing rancor of military personnel and recognized an opportunity to build on the letter-writing alliance that had united federal employees and military personnel around pay and benefits in 1974. AFGE's Webber explained to Congress that federal workers and soldiers continued to see their fates as linked, so he recommended to his national executive council that the union "consider offering membership within AFGE to members of the uniformed military."[46] After having floated the idea of unionizing the military in the fall of 1975, in fall 1976 at AFGE's national convention in Las Vegas, the union officially voted to change its constitution to allow organizing of soldiers, sailors, and airmen.[47]

At that moment, AFGE occupied the apex of its influence, which had been growing for more than a decade alongside that of other public unions. In the ten years before 1970, active membership in AFGE had soared by 362 percent.[48] Public employee unions had been growing in power since 1961, when Democratic president John F. Kennedy signed Executive Order 10988. It provided protection for any federal employee "to form, join and assist any employee organization."[49] The order shored up the status of the public employee unions that had operated with only limited protections and participation since their origins in the 1920s and 1930s. Unions such as the Building Service Employees International Union, a forerunner of today's

Service Employees International Union, handed out flyers with a smiling picture of President Kennedy informing janitors, window washers, and maintenance workers that Executive Order 10988 gave them the "right to join a union."[50] By 1975, on the eve of its bid for military unionization, AFGE represented nearly 350,000 federal employees.

Their growing militancy created a "turbulent state" in public sector employment that leveraged the power of growing numbers.[51] That turbulence had increased since early in the decade, marked by signposts such as the 1970 postal worker strike, the first national federal strike. Approximately 200,000 postal workers from New York to California walked off the job. In the same year air traffic controllers left the job in a "sick-out" over Easter, paralyzing spring holiday travel. Emboldened by the abandonment of no-strike clauses among these workers, local teachers, firefighters, nurses, and many other employees walked off their jobs.[52] In 1975, public unions called 478 strikes.[53] Such crusades catalyzed a new effort to win collective bargaining rights and other protections for public sector unions.[54]

They also emboldened AFGE in its bid to unionize the army. While AFGE portrayed military unionization as aligning the interests of persecuted workers, it also acknowledged the usefulness of the union gambit as a political threat. "What is important to the government and to our own status within the labor movement," said the national secretary "is that we have this weapon in the holster."[55] The AFGE hoped that rattling its saber at the military would help its leadership pressure Congress and the Ford administration to raise pay and benefits for the hundreds of thousands of civilian federal workers it already represented.[56]

In its military bid, the union moved skillfully within the larger political and economic context facing workers—especially male workers—in the mid-1970s. AFGE's effort to unite soldiers and federal workers exploited fears of the erosion of male breadwinning and the difficulty facing working-class and lower-middle-class families—the group from which most federal workers and soldiers originated. In the 1970s, the lives of the working classes were widely perceived as having descended into, as the title of Lillian Rubin's 1976 classic analysis of working-class families put it, "worlds of pain."[57] Declining economic indicators hit working-class and lower-middle-class men hard, with unemployment rates as high as 10 percent in industrial states like Massachusetts and New Jersey and layoffs growing among state and municipal governments.[58] A spate of scholarly and journalistic investigations of the "forgotten man" described his seeming downward trajectory, his inability to support his wife and children, and his accompanying loss of self-respect and dignity.[59] The perceived crisis generated fear among some Democrats that they might lose the loyalty of white, male working-class men, and resulted in a host of national policy proposals to shore up a male-breadwinning ideal.[60] Unions led the way in pushing for new legislation to help male workers, the most important example being the failed Full Employment and Balanced Growth Act (or the Humphrey-Hawkins Bill).[61]

AFGE's leadership astutely linked the threats to military benefits to the wider vulnerability felt by male workers. Its leaders understood the dangers to pensions and perquisites as deeply destabilizing for military personnel. AFGE leaders validated the worry and anger of soldiers, sailors, airmen, and marines. Webber, speaking to *Army Times,* explained how "We hear from military people toward the end of their career . . . , and they are just red hot. They talk about the loss of commissary privileges . . . about possible changes in health services." He cited the sense of betrayal soldiers felt; the government refused to "carry . . . out the promises made to them." And they turned to the union for help.[62] When called to testify before the House Armed Services Committee, Webber's successor, Kenneth Blaylock, shamed them "for the continuous attack on their [military personnel's] fringe benefits."[63] When some members of Congress like Les Aspin reprimanded Blaylock by pointing out that no cuts had yet been made—only proposals to cut—Blaylock warned, "you can take the position that the idea [of benefits erosion] is ridiculous, but I am telling you those military members out there don't think it is so ridiculous."[64]

Military personnel felt shaken at the prospect of losing the benefits they relied upon, and the perceived menace pushed some career soldiers to consider unionization. Many believed the union promised possible protection from the loss of their benefits and status. In terms similar to those used by civilian male workers losing their jobs, a retired soldier described his trajectory toward embrace of the union: "It has been with considerable interest that I have followed the military union story. At first, I ridiculed the idea, then slowly began accepting the idea after watching our retirement system erode. Today, I would join, endorse, and pay dues to a union that would represent me. Why not? We, the silent majority, require some way to influence the decisions that will affect us. Let's face it, if a union will protect our rights, then let's get on with it. Where can I sign up?"[65] Military personnel were the persecuted "silent majority" overlooked by society, forced finally to seek for themselves their fair share of protection. Sergeant First Class Henry Jennings explained his embrace of the union in the same terms: "The Secretary of Defense, Congress, and others. All these people speaking out on stopping service people from joining or forming their own union. . . . Well where were they when commissary subsidies were in trouble? Where were they when they put a five percent cap on our pay raise last year? Where were they when they cut back on CHAMPUS [the military's medical program]?" Left to fend for themselves, career soldiers had no choice but to turn to the union to protect their status. "I would really hate to see the services in a union," Jennings continued, "but I don't like being a second-class citizen."[66]

Amidst what they perceived as serious threats to their military benefits and security, then, many soldiers, sailors, airmen, and marines willingly listened to AFGE's appeal. By mid-summer 1977, over 10,000 service personnel had contacted AFGE inquiring about joining the union. AFGE president Blaylock recounted his own anecdotal experience meeting with an army unit in which "as many as 800 people in one battalion . . . want us to come on in and sign them up."[67] Evidence from outside the union also corroborated soldier interest. Citizen Soldier, a pro-union advocacy group run by Todd Ensign in New York City, determined through a direct mail survey that 52 percent of the enlisted ranks of the military favored unionization.[68] Although the military services and DoD declined to systematically survey the broad spectrum of servicemen and women, several small surveys by air force and army personnel, in addition to several studies by nonmilitary scholars, painted a portrait of significant interest in the union.[69] In a service-wide survey of 800 enlisted personnel, air force researchers found that 35 percent of enlisted airmen favored joining a union. Another survey of randomly sampled army personnel at Fort Benjamin Harrison reported the startling result that 54 percent of enlisted soldiers would join a military union, and 22 percent of officers "indicated interest" in union membership.[70] Though the numbers varied, they registered a real possibility of military unionization.

As the soldier backlash against proposed benefits cuts suggested, the "lifers"—career military men—evinced the greatest interest in the union.[71] Initially this surprised many in the military community. "When we first heard of the issue of unionization," said the national secretary of the Fleet Reserve Association, which represented enlisted seamen in the navy, coast guard and marines, "we thought the first termer would be the one who would respond and join." After all, they were freshest from civilian life, least acculturated to the military, youngest, and at the bottom of the military hierarchy. But they had miscalculated: "after a field trip that I made in December of 1975, I learned to my surprise that it wasn't the first termer but the second termer, in fact the career designated personnel. When I studied on that for a few minutes it didn't take me long to realize this would be true because first termers by and large at that time had not experienced any erosion of benefits."[72] The career cadre's openness to unionization heightened fear about its likelihood. "I think that is the frightening thing about the unionized pitch," explained the Fleet Reserve secretary. "It might be a little easier to handle if we thought it was just first termers, but it is the career people, the leaders in the enlisted branch."[73] The people with the deepest investments in the military and the most to lose formed the backbone of support for the unionization bid.

But if some career soldiers believed AFGE's effort might help them, most other observers believed a unionized military spelled disaster. Newspaper editorials scorned the notion of a unionized military. "Idiotic," insisted the *Richmond Times-Dispatch;* "makes no sense," said *U.S. News and World Report;* unionization would produce, according to the *Spartanburg, SC Herald,* "a paralysis of America's armed forces in a moment of grave peril." "Short of full-scale nuclear attack or devastating plague," Charlotte, North Carolina's WBTV news editorial alleged, "hardly anything could be so disastrous to this country as for its armed forces to go on strike."[74] The unionized military provided hearty feed for political cartoonists. In a *Kansas City Star* cartoon, a staff sergeant bellows "Soldier—Peel them spuds—that's an ORDER," to which the private, clutching his "Union Facts" booklet, replies, "Sorry, Sir—the K.P. Local has Jurisdiction."[75] An *Army Times* cartoon featured a soldier calling out in the middle of pitched battle, "Quitting time, Sarge—or else we go time and a half overtime."[76] A *Chicago Tribune* cartoon depicted the famed marines of Iwo Jima lifting the flag of "Local 151, Brotherhood of Amalgamated Grunts and GIs."[77]

Many Americans also seemed opposed to unionized soldiers. The antiunion Public Service Research Foundation conducted a national survey and found, for example, that 82 percent of American opposed military unions. If results from the notorious antiunion activist David Denholm would not convince union supporters, a Gallup Poll in mid-1977 basically confirmed the data. Of those polled, 74 percent opposed unionization of the military and only 13 percent supported it.[78]

Uniformed military leaders voiced alarm about a unionized armed forces. Marine Corps brigadier general William Flemming told senators: "it would be chaos. . . . You cannot run a combat unit by committee." General George S. Brown, chairman of the Joint Chiefs of Staff, told the House Armed Services Committee, "unionization and the operation of the military forces are totally incompatible."[79] CSA General Bernard Rogers said that the unionization of the army would prove "disastrous."[80] Another army general at the Pentagon expressed "sheer horror" at the thought of a unionized military.[81] Influential retired military personnel weighed in against the union, too. Retired navy admiral John S. McCain Jr. (Senator John McCain's (R-AZ) father) contended that the union would doom the United States, and "would lead to defeat of our way of life."[82] Former chief of staff of the army (CSA) General William Westmoreland insisted, "the Congress and President Carter have a duty to wipe out any prospect of military unionism."[83] Military service associations like the Fleet Reserve Association, the American Legion, the Association of the U.S. Army, the Air Force Sergeant Association, and the Reserve Officers Association all balked at a unionized military, too. They professed to advocate for service members "within the system," while unions transferred representation outside the boundaries of traditional military hierarchy, endangering discipline and morale.[84]

Most members of Congress who spoke on the issue also portrayed a unionized military as a threat to military discipline, and further, to national security. In hearings called by Senator John Stennis (D-MS), chair of the Senate Armed Services Committee, senators took turns to decry unionization of the military. Stennis himself warned, "Unless we meet this [unionization] with firm legislation, [the volunteer force] is going to go downhill fast and prove to be a failure."[85] "It will be a disastrous day for this Nation," Senator John Tower (R-TX) agreed.[86] Similar sentiments prevailed in the House, as Congressman Sonny Montgomery (D-MS) charged, "If the time came when a military commander's decision was subject to a union vote, you might as well not even have armed forces."[87] Back in the Senate Strom Thurmond (R-SC) led the drive for legislation barring unionization. A decorated veteran of the army who participated in the invasion of Normandy during World War II, he stood as a powerful advocate for the military in Congress. He also functioned as a committed foe of organized labor, defending the South against union encroachment.[88] He denounced the union as "a real and imminent threat" to the military, insisting, "Unionization of the American armed services would cause the enemies of freedom to rejoice all over the world."[89] In late 1975, he sponsored a bill to ban military unions outright. Most of the Hill agreed with him; his initial bill had thirty-seven cosponsors.[90] At least eighteen other members of Congress introduced similar bills outlawing unions in the military.[91]

Even AFGE's parent organization, AFL-CIO, concurred with Congress. AFL-CIO's president, George Meany, a committed cold warrior and defense hawk, had ridiculed the ad-hoc military unions during the Vietnam War–era GI movement. One of Meany's lieutenants, when questioned about AFGE's bid, replied incredulously, "I don't see how you could have the shop steward intervene when a sergeant says, 'Over the top.'"[92] Other AFL-CIO stalwarts chided military unions, too. Teamsters president Frank E. Fitzsimmons, in an unusually restrained tone, declared military unions "neither . . . desirable nor feasible."[93]

IN THE TWO years after AFGE's bid to unionize the military hit the press in late 1975, deeper questions loomed about what accepting a union meant for the definition of military service. Would accepting unionization equate soldiering to "work"? Was military service equivalent to civilian employment? What would such comparability imply about the meaning of military service and its future?

From the union's perspective, the answers to such questions were clear: military service was a job like any other. AFGE president Blaylock referred to soldiers as "employees" and the services as "employers," and told Congress he foresaw a fully unionized military in the near future. "History shows," he explained, "that if any work force has serious enough problems it will organize."[94]

But for most of the additional participants in the discussion, answering the question proved more complicated. Determining whether the military could be organized required evaluating the nature of military service in comparison to civilian employment, and obliged value judgments about each. Uniformed military leaders spurned the conception of the military as a job, as did many regular military personnel. Even though significant numbers of soldiers, sailors, airmen, and marines sympathized with the union bid, they nevertheless feared the consequences of unionization for the meaning of military service. They agonized about whether union membership required them to equate military service to any other civilian occupation, and whether such an equation might ultimately undermine rather than elevate their status, and increase rather than reduce the vulnerability of military benefits.

Questions about the meaning of military service in the union debate gained added weight because they were being broached outside union quarters as well. Several years before, the economists of the Gates Commission had advocated for the purely economic, free market model of a volunteer force in which military service would be induced by pay, just as civilian employment drew workers through paying the "price" for labor.[95] Shortly thereafter, longtime scholars of the military observed that with the end of the draft, the volunteer force seemed to shift to an employment model. In the early 1970s, respected military sociologist Charles Moskos explained that the small, pre–World War II army had always been seen by its career cadre as a "calling," or a vocation. But, he argued, the volunteer army's emphasis on recruiting soldiers based on their economic desires or their hope for upward mobility presented a new model of military as an "occupation."[96]

The employment question also arose in the context of calculating military pay. The 1967 Rivers Amendment, though repealed in 1974, had established a connection between the pay of civilians employed by the federal government and military personnel. Civil service pay raises were based on an elaborate "comparability" process in which certain occupations in the private sector were surveyed and then compared to the salaries of federal employees in the General Schedule. Based on that comparison, federal pay—and hence military pay—was raised in order to ensure "comparability." Even without the Rivers Amendment, the principle of comparability still stood as the major guidepost in setting military compensation fairly and competitively.[97] Many in the military endorsed the technical process of comparability since it promised regular raises without subjecting each annual pay raise to the legislative process in Congress.[98]

But the issue of pay comparability took on different connotations when it bled from technical discussion of pay into a wider discussion of the meaning and value of military service, and its relationship to other jobs. In the mid- and late 1970s, Congress and the public began to use the term less technically, outside of the specific pay process mandated by the Rivers Amendment, and employed a much less precise notion of "general comparability."[99] Secretary of Defense Donald Rumsfeld noted the "attempts . . . made to expand its [comparability's] application to the armed forces" and use a "colloquial rather than technical meaning to the term 'comparability.'"[100]

Within this everyday notion of comparability lay the assumption that soldiering was "comparable" to civilian jobs with analogues in the military, whether private sector clerks, communications workers, or police officers.[101] In spring 1977, the Senate Appropriations Committee circulated charts comparing "annual pay and benefits for civilians" and "annual compensation and benefits for Military."[102] These compared average salaries and benefits for military personnel to averages for private sector workers. To the shock of military personnel, the results showed that "military pay is actu-

'It's Not Confusing If You Know What You're Doing. Now, Where Are We?'

Army Times lampooned the pay comparability process as wrongheaded and impossibly complex. 1976. "It's not confusing if you know what you're doing. . . ." John Stampone. From *Army Times,* September 13 © 1976 Gannett-CN. All rights reserved. Used by permission and protected by the Copyright Laws of the United States. The printing, copying, redistribution, or retransmission of this Content without express written permission is prohibited.

ally higher than that of civilians who do comparable work in private business." "When fringe benefits to both the military and civilians are added to salaries, the average military employee receives $4,257 per year more than the civilian employee," a staggering figure considering median income in the United States in 1975 was only $11,000. Observers also made comparisons to nonmilitary government workers, where again military personnel came out on top. Pointing to the upper-level enlisted men and their officers, they noted that "from the rank of sergeant up through major general, military personnel were receiving anywhere from $3,610 to $13, 465 more in over-all compensation and benefits than civilian employees in comparable grades in the Civil Service."[103]

Soldiers denied the figures in the reports. Some pointed out that the comparisons focused too much on the career soldiers compared to junior enlisted men, who earned less. Others explained that the comparisons "exaggerated the [monetary] value of military compensation and benefits," somehow tallying numbers that seemed too high.[104] A soldier at Fort Jackson, South Carolina, insisted, "We make a hell of a lot less than the public thinks, in fact less than the minimum wage and much less than I'd make if I was working outside the Army." Soldiers and their families reported in interviews and surveys, "the quality of Army military life for soldiers and their dependents is . . . lower than that which exists in the public sector."[105] A survey of military personnel conducted by the DoD in 1976 reported "almost half of the military people contend they could make more money in civilian employment."[106]

More than the figures in the chart, the threat to soldiers stemmed from the assumption that military service could or should be compared to civilian employment. CSA General Rogers insisted no basis existed for comparison: "People should stop talking about the comparability of pay between military and civilians. I want to insure that it is recognized that a soldier is different from a civilian." Offering tautology in place of evidence, he railed, "I don't see a civilian counterpart because there is no counterpart to a soldier."[107] Civilian workers and soldiers inhabited mutually exclusive categories that prevented any and all comparability.

In the view of military leadership, no civilian endured the unique burdens of military life. The chairman of the Joint Chiefs of Staff, General Brown, in a speech before the Retired Officers Association in 1976, enumerated the "special costs of military life" with which most of his audience were familiar: frequent moves, family separations, personal risk. "When these freely given contributions are considered, it is obvious that there's more to military service than employment."[108] His predecessor had said much the same thing: "I wonder if the pay of the marines who were wounded, and who died in the Mayaguez incident is comparable to a young worker's pay in industry? Or even broader than that, is there any comparable pay to that of any of our soldiers?"[109] On the occasion of the DoD's Third Quadrennial Review of Military Compensation in late 1976, Secretary of Defense Donald Rumsfeld raised both the AFGE bid and the issue of comparability, observing that military personnel abhorred the comparisons between civilian jobs and military service. "Can a combat infantryman possibly be compared with a computer programmer? . . . It is insulting and demeaning to compare a combat soldiers, on duty call for 24 hours a day and potentially subject to death or injury with a '9 to 5' civilian."[110] Uniformed military leaders and their civilian counterparts resisted the union bid by insisting on a sharp differentiation between civilian occupations and military service.

Enlisted military personnel and officers assented, and accentuated the partition between military service and employment. While a few acknowledged similarities between federal workers and military personnel and questioned, "Are we so very different?" most generally rejected the implication that they "worked" for the government.[111] Military personnel and families pointed to the sacrifices and difficulties of servicemen when they questioned comparability measures: "We would like them to name civilian jobs which demand the hours or working conditions of a military job, or the ever present possibility of relocating on short notice, with or without one's family. How many civilian jobs can ask at any time for an employee to put his very life on the line? Not to mention that a soldier cannot simply say, 'I quit!' when he has had all he can take; he must live up to his commitment to his country."[112]

Soldiers sometimes demanded that civilians comparing their pay and benefits to soldiers' should trade places with the soldiers. "If they think we are being paid too much," a soldier at Fort Hood told Congress, "then let them fight for us."[113] "Who," demanded a master sergeant, "would like to take our places?"[114] He implicitly assumed that few, if any, civilians would accept the challenge. As *Army Times* summed up the views of soldiers, "Service members need no reminding that the conditions of life are different for the military community" from civilian employment.[115] The distinct challenges of military life seemed obvious. "This 'X' factor" marked the "chief objection" of soldiers to the comparisons with civilian pay.[116]

Contesting associations between military service and civilian employment necessitated value judgments about the worth of each. As servicemen and women demarcated the unique elements of military service, they disparaged civilian employment. Lieutenant Colonel Dennis J. Morrissey penned a blunt letter to *Army Times:* "It is really rather simple: either soldiering is honorable, useful work with wages commensurate with the effort and working conditions the government requires, or it is soft work like shuffling paper in the U.S., eight hours per day and the current clerical wages will do."[117] The contrast was clear and unequal: soldiering was demanding and honorable while civilian employment was undemanding and inconsequential.

Military leaders contended that soldiering deserved more esteem than civilian employment. The army's DCSPER, General Harold Moore, insisted, "The Army is . . . a way of life," connoting a totally enveloping mode of existence far more significant than just day-to-day employment.[118] His boss, CSA General Fred Weyand, repeated as much to Congress and disparaged civilian work at the same time. "The Army is a way of life, based on service to our Nation," he explained. It was "not just a working place."[119] Secretary of the Army Martin Hoffman told the El Paso, Texas, chapter of the Association of the U.S. Army that "the ideal that military duty is a unique public service and that national defense is more than an eight-hour-a-day job must be reinforced."[120] What else could he mean except the eight-hour-a-day job constituted "less"?

Military leaders took pains never to disparage unions or union members in their public comments—they depended too much upon unionized civilian workers and upon the blue-collar, union backgrounds of so many soldiers to risk offense.[121] Still, direct attacks on unions by others during the debate amplified the distinction military leaders and military personnel drew between military service and employment. Driven by an increasingly influential anti–public union movement, opponents of military unionization highlighted the greed and self-interest of unions, qualities deemed anathema to military service.[122] Senator Thurmond, the loudest congressional critic of the unions, accused union "bosses" of self-interest in contrast to the public interest that characterized soldiers. He chided AFGE president Blaylock for admitting that the union sought "to get a piece of the pie" before "other unions might attempt to organize the military." "Mr. Blaylock's 'pie,'" he scolded, "consists of the 2 million members of the uniformed military" who ought not fall prey to such selfish machinations.[123] The secretary of the Fleet Reserve Association also portrayed unions as selfish swindlers. "I think they are looking after the enlisted man's dues and muscle of his number to increase their effectiveness, but I fear it is going to increase their effectiveness for their civilian employees and not the military man. I think it is a rip-off of the military man."[124] Other union critics condemned unions' unruly and seemingly illegal actions of recent years. Senator Jake Garn, a former vice president of the National League of Cities, recounted his battle with the firefighting union, whose audacious exploits in the early to mid-1970s generated so much publicity. The unions, he explained, "did not have any concept of following the law."[125] Public unions had shut down police, fire, sanitation, and transit services in cities across the country, he reminded his colleagues. "That union militancy . . . might be extended to the military" was "down right alarming."[126]

Some military personnel echoed antiunion organizations and politicians. A telling cartoon in *Army Times,* for example, reflected a host of negative union stereotypes. It features the union as a four-armed, lantern-jawed behemoth with a dunce cap perched on his head, grabbing at soldiers' benefits.[127] Slow-witted but powerful and greedy, union bosses took advantage of servicemen and women. With such images in mind, soldiers often qualified their support of a military union. "I am not talking of a union that would rip off soldiers," wrote one soldier about his support of a union, "but a strict military union that would be comprised of military people."[128] This distinction not only revealed beliefs about pervasive union corruption but also suggested the natural "strictness" and uprightness of military personnel. The Fleet Reserve Association used similar negative assumptions about unions to distinguish between "bad" unions and "good" sailors who nevertheless expressed support for unions. Comparing the natural composure and integrity of sailors to union members, they implicitly tarnished unions by saying that the enlisted personnel who spoke in favor of a union were "not abrasive or radical. Their sincere, straightforward manner reflected their . . . perception that no one in Washington DC was looking out for their interests."[129] If they had not been abandoned, sailors would not have been forced to consider the dangerous union.

Antiunion rhetoric bled back into the debates about military service versus employment. The negative stereotypes of unions that dominated this discussion stood as implicit or explicit opposites of military service. And public sector unions emerged as a kind of nightmare scenario resulting from the encroachment of the employment model into the military context. Military service assumed a more powerful, vaunted position as something different from and more significant than "a job" that could be unionized. The union debate separated and elevated military service to a category of its own. Unionization implied an employment model of military service that threatened to degrade or at least dislocate the vaunted model of military service.

In the end, military personnel were never compelled to decide whether or not to sign a union card. As opposition to unionization mounted from 1975 through 1977, AFGE's leaders broke. Since they had begun the effort to unionize the military as part of a political strategy to increase their power, they began to fear a significant political backlash. Rather than abandon the campaign, they saved face by deferring the decision about military unionization to a referendum by its members.[130] At the end of the summer of 1977, the results were in. The *AFL-CIO News Service* reported, "AFGE locals decisively rejected a proposal to expand the union's jurisdiction and organizing efforts to the armed forces."[131] For their part, the hundreds of thousands of AFGE members said they overwhelmingly wished to focus on "organizing a larger percentage of the federal civilian workforce," less than half of which were actual dues-paying AFGE members.[132] But they, like their leaders, had probably come to fear risking their status by delving into the controversial territory of military unionization.

Though the union had folded, none of the antiunionization members of Congress acknowledged the fact. Quite the opposite occurred. The House Armed Services Committee dragged AFGE's and other unions' leaders to the Hill to testify, even though they had announced the end of the unionization bid.[133] Nearly one full year after AFGE had voted against unionizing the military, bills outlawing military unions were still working their way through Congress, accompanied by heated rhetoric.[134]

The union had morphed into a useful political object against which the military could define itself. The effort to defeat the union allowed military personnel, military leaders, and elected officials to differentiate military service as unique and fundamentally dissimilar from employment, and thus requiring unique consideration in the matter of benefits and the federal budget. Fighting off the danger of unionization became a tool to assert the noncomparability of military service to civilian work and life. Battling back the union simultaneously asserted the distinct and elevated status of military service.

Ironically, the union threat gave soldiers, sailors, airmen, and marines the leverage to force Congress to increase spending on military benefits and protect them in the future. As Lieutenant Commander John M. Kutch Jr., wrote to *Army Times*, "I fear, that if further erosion of military compensation is permitted by the Congress, and if the professional organizations (of active duty or retired military personnel like Association of the U.S. Army or the Fleet Reserve Association) are unable to protect service members' compensation benefits, then (and justifiably) the union should and will be given an opportunity to present the collective concerns of military personnel. I am not pro-union, but I can see the handwriting on the wall if further erosion occurs."[135] Even as they had told their stories of abandonment and reluctant embrace of the union, soldiers had usually offered up an alternative to the union: the military and Congress should fulfill the army's promise to take care of its own by protecting and enlarging military benefits. "If the Army was really taking care of its own," one soldier wrote to *Army Times*, "I believe soldiers would not feel that a union would do a better job of hearing grievances and protecting their interests."[136] Another insisted, "The only reason, and the moving reason, why we in the active military are being forced to not just consider unions but to move toward them is the virtual abandonment of use by our traditional 'father.'"[137] These soldiers offered a simple solution: we will drop the union idea if you meet your patriarchal duties as head of the Army Family and guarantee the growth of our benefits.

Military leaders welcomed this solution to both the union problem and the issue of benefits. It dovetailed perfectly with their case against the union and against equating military service with employment, and their claim for the essential uniqueness of military service. General Weyand linked this unique "way of life" directly to the need for robust, assured benefits: "The soldier often faces duty that is dangerous, distant or dirty," he told Congress. "It is not an easy or a certain way of life, and its compensation should not be measured by the standards of civilian life—normally just pay alone. There must be more; we take pride in saying that the Army takes care of its own, and by reaching out to help the families of those who serve . . . and to assist our men and women in other ways, we try to live up to that standard. . . . I hope you [Congress] see fit to grant us the resources to take care of our men and women."[138]

FROM 1978 through 1980, soldiers' fortunes reversed, as the military's benefits and social welfare programs expanded anew and criticism of their excesses evaporated. Though military benefits and services had never actually been slashed—and had in fact increased—the rhetoric of austerity vanished in the final years of the 1970s. Few at the Capitol spoke of overly generous military benefits. None demanded cuts. Nor did any insist on the comparability of military service to civilian jobs. The defeat of the union corresponded with the rising status of the military and its benefits before Congress. Even as legislators and the Carter administration pressed continued austerity measures on civilian workers and their benefits, they expanded military benefits. As Senator Thurmond put it, "While the obligation of the Congress to prohibit unions in the military is clear, there is an equal obligation to address and settle the issues which have brought this matter to a head."[139] That meant recognizing a system of social and economic supports as the reward of a unique military lifestyle. By the late 1970s, even stalwart detractors of excessive military spending and military benefits like Congressman Aspin advocated new and expanded benefits for soldiers. Aspin headed the drive to extend to junior enlisted personnel many of the benefits, special pays, and privileges designated solely for senior enlisted personnel and officers.[140] In 1979, several new bills providing extensive improvement in military benefits—nearly twenty new or upgraded benefits and allowances—made their way through Congress.[141] Highlights involved 11.7 percent increases in pay targeted at the career force—the senior enlisted personnel so frustrated by "benefits erosion" and so tempted by the prospect of unionization. The laws also created the Variable Housing Allowance to reimburse soldiers posted to high-rent locales, increased substantially the reimbursement rate for military personnel's costs for permanent change of station moves, increased temporary duty per diem reimbursement, and raised the reenlistment bonus from $15,000 to $20,000.[142]

The sentiment behind this generous support of military service grew directly out of the discussions and debates over unionization. Emphasizing the unique nature of military service, President Jimmy Carter, who signed the bills into law, proclaimed, "I fully support the military pay and benefits authorized by this bill for I share with the Congress its concern for assuming a level of compensation for our service men and women commensurate with their considerable contribution and sacrifice."[143] Carter's statements adopted nearly verbatim the lines that the uniformed military and soldiers had developed in the several years during and after the union threat, emphasizing the ultimate sacrifice that the "military way of life" required.

As Congress agreed to expand military benefits, those benefits began to reach a changing soldier population, raising new questions for the army about the programs it defended and the new ones it created. Soldiers from different backgrounds joined the army as it struggled through the 1970s, transforming its demographic profile. The career men who had fought the benefits battle and grappled with union membership were but one group of soldiers—older ones, largely white, career men with families. They were augmented by younger, less educated soldiers. And they were joined by an increasing proportion of African Americans and unprecedented numbers of women. These new soldiers were not the participants in the union debate. Nor were they soldiers peopling the imaginations of participants in the union debate: no one pictured a young African American woman as they went to battle for soldier pensions or the PX. Created largely for a white male soldier breadwinning population of professional soldiers, the benefits expanded in the 1970s came to serve a demographic that was increasingly feminized and associated with the nonwhite and poor. The transformations tested once again the army's sense of itself as an institution, and of the growing collection of benefits and programs provided to sustain soldiers and their families.

3

The Threat of a Social Welfare Institution

IN 1977, as the army battled the American Federation of Government Employees for the loyalties of soldiers, its leadership faced a new trial. Congressman Robin Beard (R-TN) announced to Congress and the public that the volunteer army, only four years old, had failed. Beard arrived on the Capitol Hill as a former Marine Corps officer and the sole member of Congress to serve as a member of the military while holding office—in the Marine Corps Reserves. He positioned himself as a steadfast right-wing Republican, fighting liberalized immigration policies and, as he put it, "the insanity of busing" children to integrated schools. But colleagues recognized him above all as an authority on national security; his seat on the House Armed Services Committee cemented his power over defense matters.[1] Beard accused Secretary of the Army Clifford Alexander, the first African American to hold the position, of "the biggest cover-up I've seen in my eight years of government." Alexander, he alleged, was "literally not telling the truth," about the army. While Alexander defended it as successful, it was actually a failure; "and he knows it," Beard reproached.[2] Borrowing a military staffer from the Department of Defense (DoD), Jerry Reed, Beard conducted a study of the effectiveness of the volunteer army that he then presented to Congress and the public. Based on dozens of interviews with soldiers of various ranks in posts throughout the world, the "Beard Study," as it came to be known, painted a portrait of an army in crisis "fighting for a future."[3]

Though Beard found much lacking in the volunteer army, his most dire assessment—the one Senator Sam Nunn (D-GA) pressed first when

Beard testified at Nunn's hearings on the status of the volunteer force in Congress—was that the army was being reduced from a war-fighting organization to a social welfare institution. The army, the Beard Study alleged, was "plagued by social welfare problems to the detriment of its mission," and could not survive the onslaught.[4] Rather than weapons training or war-gaming, Beard contended, the army resorted to "teaching kindergarten" to the under educated and poor, babysitting the children of female soldiers, and managing the dysfunction of new recruits who had entered the army for no better reason than they could not make it in civilian life.

Beard's comments laid bare growing and complex tensions within the army over the rapidly changing demographic composition of the enlistees in the new volunteer force. When Beard impugned the "social welfare" functions of the army, he referred not to the career soldiers—the upper-level enlisted men, noncommissioned officers (NCOs), and officers—who fought for their pensions, Post Exchanges, and housing allowances during the unionization bid. Beard's fears about social welfare problems sprang from his worries about the newly recruited junior personnel, whose characteristics in education, class background, race, and sex did not meet Beard's expectations. "When the draft ended," Beard explained, "a new composition in the Army was begun. More women, more blacks, lower income groups, and lower mental group personnel are joining the services."[5] Beard cast new recruits almost as members of an underclass, a term that would gain wide usage in the early 1980s with reference to mostly minority poor people and those reliant on public assistance programs. His study chronicled behaviors among newly recruited soldiers redolent of critiques of the poor: soldiers demonstrated ignorance, ineptitude, violence, debt, drinking and drugs, and family problems. Worse, these problems compelled the army to provide social, economic, educational, and psychological assistance, diverting the army's limited resources from military training and readiness to social welfare. Beard also criticized the growing contingent of female soldiers for sidetracking the army from its war-fighting tasks because of their supposedly unique "family" needs. For Beard the rapidly altered demographics of the volunteer army of the 1970s came to both symbolize and cause a hazardous diversion of the army mission from waging war to waging a war on poverty.

Beard's charges carried extra danger in the context of the 1970s, as social welfare programs of the New Deal and Great Society eras—and the clients who used them—came under sustained political attack from the right. His accusations made national headlines, prompted congressional reports, inquiries, and hearings, and fanned concern among the army retiree community. Army leadership in the Office of the Chief of Staff of the Army, its manpower and personnel offices, recruitment, and the secretariat understood the stakes in the negative assessments of the army as a last resort for the dregs of society: an army functioning as a social welfare institution and drawing from the margins could not garner respect.[6] If the volunteer army carried the stain of welfare, it might not survive.

THE 1970S did not mark the first such calamity regarding the respectability of soldiers and the fears of the army as a welfare institution. In the long history of the U.S. Army, enlisted soldiers had often occupied a tenuous social position. Soldiers were regarded as the lower order, rabble, or even dangerous. Class and status conflicts punctuated the Revolutionary War; the American Civil War featured more dramatic class conflicts, including the New York City draft riots. Even after wars ended, soldiers were often considered threatening. Demobilization always brought potential social disruption, and unappreciative local communities bemoaned the burdens of veterans' physical and mental disabilities. Common soldiers and veterans were seldom seen as the "better sort."[7]

Efforts to legitimize soldiers gained traction in the early and mid-twentieth century in large part due to the nascent social engineering applied to soldiers in World War I and full-blown social uplift provided during World War II and the subsequent GI Bill.[8] With a more comprehensive selective service system and the mass mobilizations of the two world wars, a wider swath of Americans served, which also validated soldiers. But during the Vietnam War, the legitimizing trend reversed, as soldiers and the military fell back into a less reputable status. With reported instances of insubordination, fragging, and mass killings of civilians, soldiers' reputations declined dramatically.[9]

As frightening as the degraded reputation of soldiers was the tainted image of the army as a social welfare institution, another consequence of the Vietnam War. In 1966, President Lyndon B. Johnson's administration drew an unwilling military into a social welfare venture called Project 100,000. Part of Johnson's War on Poverty, the program aimed, in Secretary of Defense Robert McNamara's words, to "salvage the poverty scarred youth of our society," by waiving the military's education and testing requirements, and accepting 100,000 low-scoring men for military service in Vietnam.[10] Admitting men who scored as low as the 10th percentile on the Armed Forces Qualification Test (AFQT), over a third of whom were unemployed, and read at or below the sixth-grade level on average, commanders were ordered to provide compensatory education, health care, and training to allow them to succeed in the military, and, ostensibly, upon their discharge.[11] In the end, the military assigned more than half of the new men to combat specialties, where some personnel referred to them as "a moron brigade." Commanders pointed out the risks of utilizing soldiers with staggering educational deficits, and protested that they sullied the reputation of all soldiers.[12] Congress acceded to the armed forces' critiques and ended the project in 1971. But the changing demographics of the volunteer army of the 1970s reprised the perceived perils of Project 100,000, this time with the burden of intense scrutiny and high stakes that accompanied the transition to the volunteer force.

To be sure, the revolution in army demographics was real. To a degree unmatched in the other services, the end of the draft decisively altered the army's composition. For one, the new enlistees came from poorer families and had less education than soldiers during the draft era. Though the DoD denied that the new volunteer force constituted a "poor man's military," their own statistics belied that claim.[13] Compared to the draft era, when even with the educational deferments that lasted until 1969, middle-class men were regularly inducted into the army, the volunteer force was noticeably poorer. While the new soldiers did not constitute the poorest of the poor, the army's new active duty enlistees fell toward the bottom of the income scale. "Today's volunteers," one scholar of military service explained, "are more disadvantaged economically than their counterparts who elect not to join the military."[14] Journalist James Fallows put it decidedly more emphatically. The army, he argued, had been "contracted out to the poor."[15] Data from 1975 confirmed that while only 5 percent of American families had incomes under $2,900 per year, nearly double the percentage of army enlistees came from such families. And while 40 percent of American families earned under $10,999 per year, 53 percent of army enlistees' families did. In 1976, moreover, the numbers of recruits from low-income families grew sharply, from 16 percent from families earning less than $5,000 per year to 30.2 percent. Representative William Steiger (R-WI), an early supporter of the volunteer force, admitted that "the Army tends to draw significantly more troops from lower income families than any of the other services."[16] A defense manpower task force conceded reluctantly, "Enlistees in the Army come from a somewhat less favored socio-economic background."[17] Just as telling, the army had one-third fewer soldiers from the middle class than were represented in the general population.[18] Esteemed military sociologist Charles Moskos told Senator Nunn, "In my stays with Army line units I am most impressed by what I do not often find—urban and suburban white soldiers of middle class origins." He fretted about an army reliant upon "recruiting at the margin" of American society.[19]

The lower-income backgrounds of the recruits correlated with lower levels of education. The number of enlisted recruits with college degrees or even a year or two of college education became "almost extinct" by the mid-1970s.[20] During the draft era, between a fourth and a third of soldiers had attended college or received their bachelor's degrees, but in the volunteer force of the 1970s, the percentage decreased sharply, to a mere 5.3 percent of total enlisted accessions in 1975 and a miniscule 3 percent in 1979.[21] In addition, high school graduation rates dipped several times in the 1970s to as few as half of all new enlistments.[22] Even more troubling, the high school graduation statistics were artificially bolstered by the army's decision to count as high school graduates those recruits who scored a 35 on the national high school equivalency exam, the General Educational Development (GED) test, a score that would not merit the awarding of a high school diploma in many states.[23] Recruiters confessed routinely to admitting soldiers at "the third or fourth grade level."[24] Moskos summed up the trends for Congress: "We have a situation today where the volunteer Army is going contrary to the national trend, recruiting lesser educated people when in society as a whole more people [are] finishing high school."[25]

A more remarked-upon change among the new volunteer cohort was their altered racial composition. Hispanics increased their representation in the army by only 1 percent to comprise about 3 percent of the service in 1977; even sixteen years later, in 1993, they constituted only 4 percent of the army. Asian Americans and Native Americans did not join the army in noticeably increasing numbers.[26] The changing face of race in the army derived from the choices of African Americans, who joined the volunteer army in very high numbers. African Americans constituted about 14 percent of enlisted accessions (entrances or enlistments) into the army in 1970 under the draft, in close proportion to their representation in the population. By 1977, they constituted 30 percent of enlisted accessions.[27] The number of black officer accessions increased 500 percent in those same years.[28] High enlistment rates combined with lower attrition levels and higher reenlistment rates than whites meant that African Americans constituted nearly one-fourth of the total army by 1977 and one-third by 1980.[29] In the ranks of E1–E3, the lowest-ranking soldiers and first-time recruits, nearly 37 percent were African American.[30]

African Americans' spectacular accessions resulted directly from the persistent racial discrimination they faced in the civilian world. African Americans with equal or higher education levels than whites nevertheless found that they could not gain comparable work opportunities to whites. In the army, by contrast, they could. One result was that African American soldiers, as Moskos explained to Congress in 1978, had higher educational achievement than white soldiers on average.[31] Whatever the problems the volunteer army faced with low levels of education among new recruits in the late 1970s, it was not due to the influx of African Americans.

As more African American soldiers signed up for the volunteer army, so too, did more women. And because Congress and the army subjected women to different recruitment standards, accepting no women without bona fide high school diplomas, female soldiers on average were better educated than male soldiers. Women's higher level of educational achievement in the army also resulted from labor market discrimination that they, like African Americans, faced in the civilian world.[32] Unable to enter sex-segregated professions on equal terms to men, and still earning about two-thirds of what men earned, some women saw the army as providing an attractive prospect. *Working Women* magazine noted the new opportunities for women to use military benefits with the switch to the volunteer force: "the military has provided a way for poor men to obtain education and job benefits and improve their social status. The same opportunities should be available to women. . . . And now they are."[33]

Rapid increases in women's enlistments demonstrated the army's reliance on women to cover shortfalls in male manpower. On the eve of the volunteer force, women constituted only 1.3 percent of active duty enlisted soldiers, about 12,000 total. By 1978, that number had increased over four times to more than 50,000, with women constituting 6.6 percent of the enlisted soldiers.[34] And by 1980 they represented nearly 9 percent of the army.[35] African American women became the most overrepresented group in the army: soon, one half of all women in the army were African American.[36]

THE ARMY'S changing faces fomented the Beard-led sense of crisis, and the keyword of that crisis was "quality." In the military's technical vocabulary, "quality" was a manpower term that referred to a measure of the test scores of army enlistees on the military's Army Service Vocational Battery (ASVB) test along with the enlistee's level of education. Though the test ostensibly aimed at measuring intelligence, its results were phrased in terms of "mental categories." And these mental categories were then correlated to the term "quality." Higher ASVB scores in the top mental categories of I and II along with completion of high school and some or all of college correlated with higher quality, while scores of III-B (mental category III being divided between a higher A and a lower B category) and IV on the test and/or the lack of a high school diploma correlated with lower quality. With the onset of the volunteer force, the army increased its number of lower-scoring category III-B personnel rather dramatically at the same time that it decreased its representation in the higher categories I through IIIA. Groups I and II decreased by 26 percent.[37] Even worse, in 1980 the army admitted it had incorrectly categorized the quality measures of a huge number of soldiers in the late 1970s through an erroneous calculation of ASVB test results. As a consequence it accidentally admitted many of the lowest-category soldiers—huge numbers of category IV recruits, a group normally screened out. When the army discovered the mistake and recent enlistees were retested, an astonishing 50 percent tested in category IV.[38] In the army's measures, half its soldiers constituted low-quality recruits.

Soldiers with lower quality ratings often performed poorly in the army. At the time, it was common knowledge that enlistees with higher education levels had better chances of successfully completing their enlistments than soldiers with low scores. Poorly educated soldiers thus proved more likely to cost the army money in wasted training when they failed to complete their terms of service. Low levels of education also correlated with poorer performance in military occupational specialties (MOSs).[39]

Chief of Staff of the Army (CSA) General Bernard Rogers, joined Secretary of the Army Alexander, who defended the army before Congress, protesting that despite the changes in official "quality" measures, soldiers without high school diplomas could "acquit themselves creditably; indeed, they have been and are some of our best soldiers."[40] Deputy Chief of Staff for Personnel (DCSPER) Lieutenant General Robert Yerks likewise insisted that the army's "selective enlistment process is working when considering" that only 6 percent of new army enlistees read at a fifth grade level or below, as compared to "a Health, Education and Welfare (HEW) study that established that 21 percent of Americans over 17 suffer the same lack of reading skill." The comparison was hardly fair considering the HEW study included adults of all ages, encompassing functionally illiterate elderly adults born into poverty or in foreign countries at the turn of the century or before, whereas the army took in 18–24 year olds.[41] Still, the army claimed that unlike college-educated soldiers or high school graduates, undereducated "enlistees want to learn even more. Over 50 percent enlist for the Army's education opportunities, especially vocational and technical training."[42] The army seemed to argue that poorly educated soldiers' desire for further education rebutted the arguments impugning their performance.

But the evidence of lower performance remained powerful. At the same time that General Rogers and Secretary Alexander defended poorly educated soldiers, other army commanders reported, "many recruits are unable to adequately understand training manuals and other written material."[43] Soldiers scoring in the military's categories III and IV proved "unable to operate the sophisticated components of the army's air defense systems or even such basic individual weapons as the Redeye missile." One study "demonstrated that more than a fifth of those serving in Germany (and more than a quarter of those serving in the United States) in the late 1970s did not understand the procedure for aiming their battle sights."[44] Army officers and NCOs reported that their new recruits were "not scholastically very bright."[45] An officer's wife complained that her husband's unit forewent necessary military training while her husband "has to teach kindergarten" to his troops.[46] A *Washington Star* editorial surveyed the educational data and concluded, "the general level of aptitude and adaptability of recruits has become appalling."[47] ABC News similarly concluded in a report entitled "The American Army: 'A Shocking State of Readiness,'" that low-quality army personnel were "significantly different from their civilian contemporaries" and rendered the army "incapable of meeting America's national security needs."[48] Their lack of education and intelligence translated to a lack of readiness that could doom the army. The Beard Study lamented that the army had to "downgrade the training manuals, rewriting them, downgrading them from the 11th grade to the 8th grade; in many cases in the form of comic books." "Are we to be combat ready?" Beard asked, or "are we to be an educational system?"[49]

The quality crisis in education and testing was real and involved legitimate worries about what dismal test scores and low educational attainment spelled for the army's readiness. But the conversation about quality often reached beyond these specific gauges and far afield of test scores and education measures. When many critics of the army's new soldiers talked about quality, they also talked about the army's new demographics—poorer soldiers, plus more overall numbers of African American soldiers and female soldiers. The class, race, and sex of new soldiers operated as a powerful auxiliary to the seemingly education-based "low quality" critique, sometimes becoming the animating force of an argument that concerned more than military readiness—the very fabric and purpose of the institution.

Politicians on both the right and left used the occasion of the quality debate to express concern about disproportionate numbers of African Americans joining the army. Senator John Stennis (D-MS), a longtime segregationist, seemed never to have abandoned his Southern distrust of arming African Americans even within the army, particularly after the civil rights movement and the rise of Black Power. He and others claimed that an all-volunteer force would lure too many African American "militants" who, once trained, might "form a domestic revolutionary force," and take up armed insurrection.[50] Congresswoman Shirley Chisholm (D-NY) countered that these critics so feared African Americans that they "shudder[ed] at the idea of a whole army of black men trained as professional soldiers."[51]

Other critics of the disproportionate numbers of African Americans in the army drew their references from Vietnam. African Americans' overrepresentation in the volunteer force constituted a carryover from the draft era, when during the early years of the war, African Americans faced higher casualty rates than white soldiers. Senator Edward Kennedy (D-MA), for example, asserted that the new volunteer army still lured too many African Americans as a result of their disproportionate poverty and lack of opportunity. In his view the army remained a form of conscription for African Americans, who chose the army only because of the dearth of opportunities in civilian life.[52]

The army tread carefully through the discussion. It relied heavily on African American enlistment and reenlistment, and its leaders did not want to jeopardize success with African American recruits by any admission that their positions in the army posed problems. African American leaders like Ron Dellums of California and Secretary Alexander believed that questions of overrepresentation derived too often from pure racism.[53] Beginning early in the volunteer era with Secretary of the Army Bo Calloway in 1973, army leaders met "very frequently" with members of the Congressional Black Caucus, and assured them that the army continued to work to "enhance . . . [equal opportunity] everywhere we could."[54]

In its public pledges to equal opportunity, army leaders skillfully turned the purported "problem" of overrepresentation into a "solution." The army used the overrepresentation of African Americans as an argument for the superiority of the army as an American institution. Secretary Calloway cited the army as "the best opportunity for a minority, particularly blacks, to really be able to proceed entirely on their merits with absolute equality. I thought it was as close to that as I saw anywhere in America."[55] During Senator Nunn's hearings on the Beard Study, DCSPER General Dewitt Smith told Nunn and Beard the same: "the reason that we have this disproportionate number of [black] young people coming in the U.S. Army today is that they get a fair shake; . . . they have equal opportunity. . . . That is not at all bad."[56]

In this vein, the army turned the tables in the public debate, pressing critics into a corner where they either had to articulate racist understandings of the problem or, if that proved too dangerous, to drop the subject. Assistant Secretary of Defense for Manpower John White, for example, emerged triumphant in defending the racial composition of the army by refusing to engage Congressman Beard, whose study condemned the overrepresentation of African Americans in the army.

Beard: "If current enlistment trends continue as they are, . . . in the 1980s, 45 percent or more of the Army will be black, and if present enlisted trends continue as they are, that 65 percent of those career soldiers in the Army who have been in 7 years or longer will be black. Do you see a problem here?"

White: "I don't know whether there is a problem or not. Why do you think there might be a problem?"

Beard: "Is that representative of our society? . . . I am just asking. Is there reason to be concerned here?"

White: "I don't know if there is a reason for being concerned with black versus white per se, no."

Beard: "In other words, that is the answer?"

White: "I just don't understand, Mr. Beard, what you are getting at. . . . I don't understand the problem per se."[57]

Beard dropped the subject rather than explain that black overrepresentation per se constituted a problem for him. White had forced him into an uncomfortable position where the only option was to fully articulate his fears about African American soldiers. It was a strategy used repeatedly by other army officials to counter the charge of overrepresentation.

Despite confident army tactics, the critics of African Americans' overrepresentation could not be quieted. The most influential critique argued that the "nonrepresentativeness" eroded long-term success of the army and its role in American life. In 1974, sociologists Charles Moskos and Morris Janowitz contended that the army would eventually reach a racial "tipping point." At that time white soldiers would see the army as a "black" institution and refuse to enlist, thus accelerating the unrepresentativeness of the army. Moskos and Janowitz saw nothing inherently wrong with African American soldiers—indeed Moskos went to great lengths to make sure the army understood that he spoke solely about race, not quality, repeatedly explaining that African American soldiers were, on average, better educated than whites of similar backgrounds. But they argued that civilian–military relations would suffer with an "unrepresentative" army.[58] Sociologist David Segal of the University of Maryland conveyed the problem not as the overrepresentation of African Americans but more as "the nonrepresentation of the white middle class" in the army. Moskos, Janowitz, and Segal worried that the white middle class would soon find itself increasingly isolated from the military, resulting in a worrisome "distrust and lack of interest" from this "large segment of civilian society."[59] This argument seized the attention of army and military officials. Both Donald Rumsfeld, who in late 1974 was serving as the military assistant to President Gerald Ford in the White House, and Secretary Calloway discussed the "tipping point."[60] In a "perfect" world, Calloway conceded, "a representative army . . . would have exactly the same percentage of rich and poor, black and white, of north and south, of all the demographics, exactly the same as America is." While perfect representation might be impossible to achieve, Calloway believed the army should come close, if it could. "If you [the army] are going to be prepared to fight," he explained, "we [*sic*] do not want an all poor army, an all black army, an all anything." America wanted, instead, "an all American army, an army that we supported."[61] Calloway's ambiguous "we," used in the context of worries about various "thems," underscored the complexity of the concerns surrounding changing demographics in the army.

The increased number of female soldiers offered another vector by which worried discussions of new soldiers took place. For those like Beard who believed the army was failing, the problem posed by women in the army related not to them being low-quality, lower-class soldiers: again, because of recruiting rules, they were by definition higher educated than their male counterparts. The perceived problems with female soldiers derived from the perception that women had intrinsic feminine vulnerabilities and needs that allegedly threatened the overall function of the army.

Though high-level military leadership ostensibly welcomed women into the ranks, significant sectors of the army and many of its allies equated their arrival with the downfall of the institution. The social and cultural markers of women were antithetical to war-fighting. Feminine associations with nurture, dependency, delicacy, and passivity allegedly undermined the independence, leadership, strength, and bravery associated with a masculine army. In addition, reports proliferated about the practical costs in money, unit cohesion, and readiness caused by women.[62] When women entered 55 percent of traditionally male MOSs, and when women undertook integrated training and entered the military academies, the demise of the army's status as a world-class fighting machine seemed assured.[63]

The feminization critique equated "female soldiers" with "mothers" and placed responsibility for new and difficult "family issues" in the army at the feet of these women. "Increasing numbers of women soldiers," DCSPER General Robert Yerks wrote, "have brought new challenges." He cited "pregnancies, joint domicile for in-service-couples and single parent families, and . . . dependent care [child care]."[64] Congressman Beard concurred, and insisted that because of women, "more social issues are predominating" on army posts.[65] Some contemporary scholars of the military quickly recognized the core assumptions behind such statements: "The issue of women in the military is directly related in the minds of many, with family responsibilities."[66] The army had long discriminated against women with husbands or children; until the early 1970s it forced them out if they married or had children. And the army of the late 1970s and early 1980s still required women with children to demonstrate that they had a plan to care for their children if they were deployed, a rule that did not apply to male soldiers.[67] In 1979, *Time* magazine featured a story of army sergeant Elayne Venema and her son Stephen, asking "If Mom's a G.I., who babysits?"[68] *Newsweek* noted that "women stationed overseas have missed maneuvers because they couldn't find baby-sitters, or brought their children along. In a real emergency, some experts fear that soldier-parents will stop to worry more about their children than their duties."[69]

While the media fretted about female soldiers' child care needs, male soldiers were actually far more responsible for bringing family issues into the army's purview. In the mid-1970s the army was between 90 and 95 percent male, and over 50 percent of them were married. Indeed, their wives and children were so numerous they outnumbered soldiers two to one.[70] In addition, the army's roughly 40,000 single parents were not mostly female but overwhelmingly male, a fact not well known outside the military. "Although there are proportionately more female than male single parents," scholars of military manpower policy explained, "there are numerically more males than females in the armed forces with sole responsibility for dependent children, because there are so many more men than women in uniform." Though many divorces in the 1970s resulted in the mother's custody of the children, some men in the 1970s won primary custody, and military personnel were among them. Clearly "the family issue" was "not just a female issue," or even mostly a female issue, but critics nevertheless consistently portrayed it that way.[71] Jim Webb, former Marine Corps officer, secretary of the navy under Ronald Reagan, and recent Democratic senator from Virginia, played up "family problems" that women supposedly caused as part of his broader agenda to remove them from the armed forces. Focusing on the bogey woman of the single-mother soldier, he asked, "what do we do to assure [military] readiness? Do we turn the Army into a baby-sitting service?"[72]

CRITIQUES OF the new soldiers amalgamated worries about race and gender along with education, class, and performance in ways that drew both enlistees and the army into the orbit of wider civilian discussions about the poor and welfare. Observers both outside and inside the army expressed fears of new soldiers that echoed the incipient "underclass" discussion of the poor in American society. Though stigmatization of the poor and welfare clients dated to the founding of the nation, the 1970s featured a notable retreat from government commitments to care for the poor. Framed by a conservative attack on the New Deal—and Great Society–era welfare programs—and infused by the sociological theories of Oscar Lewis in the 1960s claiming the existence of a dysfunctional "culture of poverty," policy makers cast aspersions on the poor as pathological members of a pathological social group.[73] They also blamed the programs that served them. Combined with growing political resistance against the African American Civil Rights

Movement and the welfare program Aid to Families with Dependent Children, a host of writers and researchers painted portraits of an individualized, highly psychologized culture of poverty among poor Americans.[74]

Public discussions of the army's new soldiers bore more than passing resemblance to the antipoor and antiwelfare discourse writ large. They referred to the new soldiers as poor and worthless. They had chosen the army because they could not make it in mainstream civilian life. "'Why do people enlist?'" a soldier answered a *Los Angeles Times* reporter covering the story of perceived weaknesses of the army. It was not patriotism, the soldier explained, nor a sense of service, nor even a desire for upward mobility. Instead, the soldier said, soldiers in the new volunteer force joined for "'two basic reasons: Food and shelter.'"[75] Secretary Calloway remembered that in the mid-1970s, the other three services—the air force, navy, and marines—creamed off the best individuals, thus forcing the army "to take all the dregs."[76] In 1978, the DCSPER lamented the growing public perception that the army functioned as "the last poor refuge of those unwilling or unable to participate in any other way in achieving the goals and values or our nation."[77]

If some of the new recruits of the 1970s seemed to represent a lower order of American society, people who fundamentally couldn't make it in real life, then they might depend on the army the way a welfare client might depend on public assistance. One soldier, for example, wrote to *Army Times* characterizing the typical soldier as "someone who is lazy, has low intelligence, is dishonest, and wants to generally 'get over.'"[78] Congressman Beard agreed. "There are a lot of people out there who are not even thinking of going to the Army because there is something else out there. But for the poor kid who can only read up to the third or fourth grade level, that Army has something for him; the Army is a good deal."[79] Here Beard followed the common wisdom reported in the press that the "lower-class origins of most volunteers" made them likely to see the "free meals, lodging, and other benefits provided by the Army" as a "significant increase in their standard of living."[80] "For the high school dropout," another article echoed, "the military offers an immediate paycheck and a second chance."[81] This theme bore resemblance to critiques lodged against low-income civilians who utilized public welfare programs: the army attracted people who needed to rely on the largesse of its support programs.

Some army commanders at the unit level also associated new volunteers with the kinds of problems welfare clients were believed to exhibit, referring to the "dysfunction" and "serious family problems" of young, low-income soldiers and their families.[82] They cited a litany of troubles—"family indebtedness, child abuse, and family desertion." A colonel at Fort Hood, Texas, noted that "married kids in the enlisted ranks are plagued with all kinds of problems: abandoned children, wife beatings, bad debts, and in many cases these kids are very troubled people." The problems "required counseling, administration and help."[83] The wife of a career NCO in the army for twenty years complained about the new soldiers in an *Army Times* feature that questioned the army's decision to extend support to troubled enlisted personnel. "Must the Services Take Care of Everybody?" her article was titled. These young, poor, troubled families, she argued, constituted "an extra added burden on the community."[84] The wife of a warrant officer in Germany concurred, reporting to the author of the Beard Study: "My husband . . . has been in the Army for 22 years. He is totally disillusioned with the Volunteer force. . . . Many people cannot read, write or even manage their own checkbooks."[85]

The new soldiers of the 1970s did not just remind many observers both within and outside the army of welfare clients, some actually *were* welfare clients.[86] Just a few years earlier, upon the transformation of the draft army to the volunteer army, some members of Congress had pointed to welfare and food stamp use among soldiers to shame colleagues into supporting an across-the-board pay raise for the new volunteer soldiers; such a raise was crucial to the successful recruiting and retention of the new volunteer force. In the late 1970s the stories about welfare use still caused discomfort, but they offered the potential for additional interpretations, too, coming at the same moment as wider critiques about the dysfunction and "low-class" behavior and habits of enlisted soldiers. In Congress, the discussion revolved in part around the excessive consumption of government resources that soldiers used—both army benefits and civilian benefits. The army, in fact, often pointed its low-income families to the federal food stamp program to help them survive. At Fort Carson, Colorado, for example, army personnel pledged to "explain the [food stamp] program and make an appointment" with the local welfare office.[87] In 1978, the CSA and the secretary of the army admitted to Congress that soldiers were heavily reliant on food stamps. "In FY76," they explained, "food stamp redemptions in commissaries reached $5.5 million. Dividing this amount by the national average of $1500 worth of food stamps per year redeemed by food stamp households indicates that approximately 3,600 families used them in the commissaries in

1975, an increase of 8 percent over the previous years." Though sympathetic to poor soldiers, the army described the phenomenon in passive terms, not blaming meager DoD or army support, but rather "the adverse financial situation of some military families."[88] The stories of welfare reliance among soldiers had the potential to reinforce connections between soldiers and the images of welfare use.

Associations of soldiers with welfare clients rankled members of an institution who thought of themselves, at least ideally, as very nearly the opposite of welfare clients. By the end of the 1970s, there was no denying welfare's connections to stereotypes widely associated with blackness and femininity.[89] These stereotypes did not sit well with many soldiers and the values associated with their own avocation.[90] The soldier, with his masculinized imagery of bravery, independence, strength, and sacrifice, ought not fit into a demeaned, racialized, and feminized landscape. "Soldier" and "welfare client" existed as mutually exclusive categories for members of the army.

Many soldiers and their families actually hinged their identities on the contrasts they drew between themselves and welfare clients, so implied correlations between soldiers and the welfare poor insulted them. One soldier told *Newsweek*, "I'm tired of being looked at as a third-class citizen—as someone who can't cut it on the outside, who joined up as a form a welfare."[91] Army leaders noted to Congress that soldiers took umbrage at being discussed as if they were problematic, dysfunctional, or generally low-quality. DCSPER General Dewitt Smith explained he had been "told by young people and some older people that they resent being discussed in terms of [low] quality."[92] The Beard Study surveyed NCOs who described welfare clients as "individuals who often 'never work,'" and contrasted their own "ethic of service."[93] Letters to *Army Times* sometimes echoed soldiers' investments in their status as the opposite of welfare clients.[94] Critiques of soldiers constituted, according to one author, "nothing less than a hostile and envious assault on a selected segment of our populace [soldiers] who scorn welfare and other public handouts in favor of gainful employment."[95] An army wife echoed such sentiments, writing to demand that "more money should be spent on defense and I feel that the money should come from HUD [Housing and Urban Development], welfare, Medicare, and food stamps, to name a few programs. Millions and probably billions, of dollars are wasted on these programs."[96] Though accusations of growing civilian social welfare spending were wrong—social welfare programs endured cutbacks in the 1970s—that was not the point for soldiers or their wives.

Simply being discussed in the same breath as welfare clients repudiated their honor.

The growing associations between welfare, poverty, and soldiers may have insulted some soldiers, but doubters of the army's new enlistees worried less about the soldiers and more about the army itself. Critics of the new class, race, and gender demographics of the army like Congressman Beard warned that the new personnel added a heavy welfare burden to the army. The army, he charged, was being forced to become a "social welfare institution" in order to meet the needs of problematic soldiers.[97] When it should have been training and preparing for war, it was instead providing social services.

Whether it was having to "teach kindergarten," the "social work" required to handle family needs, or the "baby-sitting service" for female soldiers' children, the implications of the changing demographics and supposedly changing functions of the military were clear: a venerable war-fighting institution faced the ignominy of becoming a safety net for the least advantaged, least able, neediest, and most demanding groups in the United States.[98] The DoD's own report on the volunteer force characterized "army leadership" as being "swamped by social welfare problems."[99] The army commanders interviewed in the Beard Study complained, "we have become babysitters. We have become social welfare workers"—a clearly unwelcome development in these officers' eyes.[100] Even a levelheaded observer of the army like sociologist Charles Moskos admitted to "the accompanying organization and economic costs" of the army's marked social change.[101] Military sociologist David Segal paraphrased the critiques he observed at the time: "The force was and is becoming increasingly unrepresentative of the American socio-demographic population. . . . The services are also increasingly dependent upon female personnel . . . that cause special deployment problems." According to critics, Segal said, "All of these factors are thought to add up to a military force incapable of meeting American's national security needs."[102] The summary finding of the Beard Study highlighted the link between shifting demographics and the army's perilous transformation into a social welfare institution. Beard stated bluntly: "The Army is becoming too involved in social rehabilitation programs. . . . Officers and NCOs pose the question to Congress: 'Is the Army a fighting machine or just another social institution?' It can't be both."[103]

But the army could not simply choose one or the other option. It had to be both. The volunteer army of the late 1970s had no choice but to accept less-educated, poorer, and fewer white and more female soldiers. It did so simply to fill its ranks and survive. Manpower chiefs could not suspend the intake of soldiers with their supposedly less desirable demographic profiles. While observers and army insiders might bemoan the specific "quality" problem of low test scores and education levels, others fretted over the more diffuse, wider demographic questions and the connections to social welfare. No dictate from above could arrest all this. The changes in demographics and services of the late 1970s brought the military, soldiers, and popular perceptions of welfare closer than the army and its supporters liked, without an easy solution.

THE NEW DEMOGRAPHICS and the more prominent role of social welfare programs in the volunteer force threatened the army's survival. The perceived problems of quality and the association of the army with a social welfare institution created an existential crisis. The period from 1977 through 1981, a colonel in the army's Recruiting Command remembered, was characterized by "large controversy . . . about 'whether or not the All Volunteer force was working.' "[104] Whether it worked depended on where one sat.

Some welcomed the crisis. Longtime skeptics of the volunteer force, a diverse group from across the political spectrum and inside and outside Washington, DC, and the army, seized the opportunity to articulate the perils of the volunteer force for national security. Robin Beard and Sam Nunn used the crisis in demographics and the "quality" and social welfare issues to press for a return to the draft. Nunn's 1978 hearings in which the Beard Study played a feature role, were called precisely to examine the viability of the volunteer force given the "quality" and "social welfare" problems supposedly plaguing it. And Beard's study constituted nothing if not a direct assault on the volunteer concept. Outside of Congress, in late 1979, the Hoover Institution at Stanford University also held a worried conference on the fate of the volunteer force.[105]

Print and television journalists produced daily reports of the army's failings, alarming army leadership who rightly viewed the stories as a public referendum on the volunteer force.[106] Though they could publicly discuss it only sparingly, many army leaders feared the imminent failure of the volunteer army. Colonel Robert Phillips, tasked by the army's Recruiting Command to study the available data, concluded that the "data . . . illustrated conclusively the contentions of the opponent school. In my words, the volunteer concept works for the 'Armed Forces' but not for the Army."[107]

Failure of the volunteer force proved unthinkable for the economists and the defense manpower specialists who had hatched the plan for it in the first place. They understood that the volunteer army might not survive. But they saw the problems as caused not by the concept of a voluntary military, but by the lack of support provided by policy makers. The low quality, the shifting demographics, the social welfare needs of soldiers, these were all problems created by policy makers who did not sufficiently manage and support the force. Just after Ronald Reagan took office, economist Stephen Herbits, a participant in the Gates Commission, wrote to Reagan's chief policy advisor, Martin Anderson, to warn him about the danger of the "current atmosphere and issues surrounding the AVF." He offered to help the Reagan administration defend the volunteer force, promising, "I can get you any additional information on specific issues that may be helpful" in quieting or contextualizing the perceived problems.[108] As a free market advocate who had helped found the volunteer force, Anderson and his staff were convinced that "finding the most cost-effective method to solve current recruitment problems will help eliminate the threat of a draft."[109] At the same time, Milton Friedman wrote Reagan to reaffirm continued support for the volunteer force amidst the overwhelming critiques. "Your friends," he wrote, "remain ecstatic about your actions and your persistence in sticking to the long and principled view."[110]

But it proved increasingly difficult to take the principled view, even for some conservatives of the free market persuasion. The conservative magazine the *National Review* published a column laying out the "confusion of American conservatives" caused by the difficulties of the volunteer force. "For conservatives and for many liberals the draft represents a crisis of ideology. In the past thirty years, conservatives like Barry Goldwater have been sincere and heroic opponents of conscription. Yet at the same time they have been staunch defenders of U.S. military might and troop commitments. What happens now, when choice between these two predilections is becoming inevitable?" If quality did not rise, and if dysfunctional, special-needs soldiers compromised the army, could conservatives continue to stand by the principle of a volunteer force? Could they risk U.S. national security?[111] The perception of the army as "the last poor refuge" for America's least capable, and as a safety net for a poor, racialized, and feminized force, pushed even volunteer force supporters to the brink of reviving the draft.

Whether the army's critics and the army agreed about the new demographics and their social welfare implications proved less important than the debate itself. The demographic shifts of the army obscured boundaries between civilian social programs and military social programs. Just as the lines demarcating military benefits from other kinds of federal spending were beginning to blur due to the budget cutting in Congress, the rapidly shifting demographics of the army smudged the lines further. The inclusion of more African Americans, women, and lower-income people, and the army's social welfare programs, added new dimension to the ongoing questions about the relationship between the military and civilian society, and social entitlements for each.

THIS MOMENT of convergence between the army and welfare never faded from the collective memory of the army, but the army recast it. The episode became part of official military history and military lore. Stories of the dangers of the 1970s—to soldiers and to the army itself—were widely retold within the military as part of the larger narrative within military and defense circles that contrasted "the dark days" of the army in the 1970s to what would soon become the story of the restoration and honor of the Reagan years in the 1980s. In the 1970s soldiers and the army were under attack from without and within, the story went. From without, Congress weakened the army by failing to adequately prevent the decline in soldier quality. The army's official history referred to "serious and stubborn problems . . . in personnel and manpower" due to "a decade of neglect."[112] From within "low quality," burdensome recruits undermined the army. As a result, the laudable nature of military service and the army itself was almost destroyed. After those years, the army and soldiers remained wary of allusions to both the "quality" of soldiers and to the army's connections to social welfare.

Army leaders of the 1980s and 1990s would make special efforts to clear the army of associations with social welfare. But it proved a challenging task. Though the education levels of recruits would rise in the 1980s, the class, race, and sex of soldiers generally persisted along the trajectories set out in the mid-to-late 1970s. In the army of the 1980s and beyond, African Americans would remain overrepresented. The volunteer army would remain intransigently non–middle class. And the number of female soldiers would, after a pause, rise, doubling between 1980 and the end of the century. Added to this was the growing number of soldiers' wives, whose increasingly vocal participation in the army would accentuate fears about the feminization of the service. And while in the 1980s and 1990s the army took new steps to quash the "quality" question and to sever associations with social welfare, worries about the race, class, education, and sex of soldiers and their families did not die. They reappeared again, in different forms, and shaped debates about benefits and services within the army—and social welfare outside the army—in years to come.

4

Supporting the Military in Reagan's America

IN MAY of 1981, two months after the attempt on his life, President Ronald Reagan gave the commencement address at the United States Military Academy at West Point. Six months earlier, Reagan had swept into office promising to rebuild the military, whose weapons budget and force size had declined since the early 1970s even as Reagan believed the nation faced new threats from the Iranian hostage crisis and the Soviet Union's invasion of Afghanistan. Though defense cuts had occurred largely under Republican presidents Richard Nixon and Gerald Ford, Reagan nevertheless pinned the blame on Democratic president Jimmy Carter, and a Democratic Congress, overlooking their defense spending increases, raises in military pay, and expansion of military benefits.[1] "For a time," Reagan lamented, "it seemed that there was an erosion of respect for the honorable profession that you have chosen. . . . In much of the seventies there was a widespread lack of respect for the uniform."[2] Then Reagan moved to his campaign theme—the dark days were over, both for the military and for the nation: "I'm happy to tell you that the people of America have recovered from what can only be called a temporary aberration."[3] Defense would grow, and the army—like the nation as a whole—would recapture its rightful glory. "There is . . . a hunger on the part of the people," he assured, "to once again be proud of America—all that it is and all that it can be."[4] Invoking the new army recruiting theme of General Max Thurman—"Be All You Can Be"—as the theme of the entire nation, Reagan linked the aspiration of the army to the resurgence of the United States.

After a decade of bruising assaults culminating in a crisis comparing the army to a welfare institution for America's poor, army leaders grasped at Reagan's pledged redemption. They would soon spend Reagan's enormous defense budget on cutting-edge technology, a massive arsenal, and a bevy of civilian defense employees and soldiers. But they also seized upon Reagan's promise to restore the esteem of the army, whose image now dangerously blurred with those of civilian social welfare programs and the dysfunctional poor. Army leaders hoped to reassert boundaries and draw sharp lines around the military. One tool the army used in this effort was a reinstitutionalized GI Bill, the entitlement that provided veterans with paid post-secondary education.

In its first iteration after World War II and through the Vietnam era, the GI Bill had functioned as a social policy tool to reward draftees for service and ease them back into civilian life. After the Vietnam War, Congress suspended it, citing high costs as well as the lack of wartime necessity. As the army called for a new GI Bill, its leaders redefined the historic benefit. The new Montgomery GI Bill of the 1980s, named for champion Congressman Sonny Montgomery (D-MS), aimed to help the army as much or more than the veteran.[5] It aimed to lure back to the army the demographic that disappeared with the end of the draft—upwardly aspiring, college-bound youths, young people perhaps whiter and more seemingly middle class than those the army of the 1970s had attracted. The GI Bill held the promise to transform the army's image from a social welfare institution of last resort to a foothold for a potential, if not actual, middle-class America. The irony of utilizing a social welfare program—the GI Bill—to erase the stain of the army's association with social welfare programs apparently went unnoticed, and in any case did not diminish the army's zeal for the strategy.

The political alchemy of the GI Bill was laid bare by the special role it played in the Reagan administration. Reagan's support for the GI Bill derived from his own desire to restore the legitimacy of the army, but it also served an equally important political goal—to discredit the social safety net for civilians.[6] Reagan coupled his advocacy of the bill with his attack on the nation's higher education programs for civilian youth—the Guaranteed Student Loans and Pell Grants. From 1981 through 1985, Reagan's domestic policy team, his Department of Education, and some members of the Department of Defense (DoD) promoted the GI Bill as leverage in their fight to cut federal aid to college students. In the political calculus they drafted, only Americans who volunteered for military service deserved the fulsome assistance of the federal government.

Through the policy debate over the GI Bill, Ronald Reagan and his domestic policy team honed a national political strategy of a militarized domestic politics: champion the military function of government while dismantling the social welfare functions of government. Reagan's military and domestic policies intertwined in an effort to rebalance the scales of government spending, citizenship, and social welfare in favor of the military. During his West Point address, in the same breath that Reagan lambasted President Carter's purported "neglect . . . [of] one of its (government's) prime responsibilities, national security," he disparaged liberals' "social experimentation" funded by "an ever-larger share of the people's earnings that it took by taxation."[7] Reagan envisioned liberals engaged in a zero-sum game in which they cut support of soldiers' "honorable profession" in order to increase "benefits to those who were not serving their country."[8] Reagan set out to reverse the flow.

FIRST CREATED in 1944 as the Servicemen's Readjustment Act, the GI Bill became a symbol of postwar American life, a way in which the military prowess of the United States intertwined with economic and social mobility for everyday Americans. The bill operated as a veterans' benefit program providing qualified former military personnel with a range of support programs, including most notably education loans and stipends. Subsequent versions provided veterans of the Korean War, the peacetime Cold War military, and the Vietnam War with similar, though less generous, benefits. The program transformed American life by raising the overall level of educational achievement among American men, and providing real socioeconomic mobility for millions of American families. Both recipients and observers lauded it.[9]

In 1974, as the Vietnam War ended and its draftees left the army, President Ford proposed ending the Vietnam-era GI Bill.[10] Many in Congress agreed that given the cessation of hostilities and the switch to the volunteer force, veterans no longer needed the benefit. And the GI Bill cost too much in an era of austerity: the program provided expensive, across-the-board benefits for all who served, and such a generous program to reward wartime conscripts and ease their adjustment to civilian life seemed unnecessary in a peacetime, volunteer setting, where presumably more soldiers would make careers of the military and all soldiers chose to serve.[11] After December 31, 1976, enlistees would no longer qualify for the benefit.

Even as Ford and Congress were making the decision to end the GI Bill, the army fought to preserve it. As the largest and least popular service, the army had rightly predicted a steep recruiting challenge with the switch to the volunteer force. As recruiting numbers dwindled, the army performed a frantic calculation of the GI Bill's worth. "The recommendation to eliminate the education benefits may have a serious impact on the All Volunteer Force according to youth surveys and other data now available."[12] The army reported to the DoD that its end would threaten the very existence of the volunteer force. "Elimination of the GI Bill could adversely affect recruiting efforts by as much as 50%," reported Carl Wallace, assistant secretary of the army. "My Deputy for Military Personnel Policies and Practices stated that in conversation with 51 recruiters in the past week, 49 stated that the GI Bill was one of the most essential sales factors in recruiting personnel. A division commander," he reported, went even further, insisting that "'without the GI Bill my unit would be decimated.'"[13] Though the assessments evinced hyperbole, the intense fears about manpower shortages fueled alarm over losing the GI Bill just after the army lost the power to conscript.

Secretary of the Army Bo Calloway, in overseeing the transition from the draft to the volunteer army, fought to retain the GI Bill. Throughout 1974, he trudged across the Pentagon from his army office to his superiors in the DoD offices over and over to beg for reinstatement: "I reclama'd and reclama'd [military slang for requesting reconsideration of policy] and went on and on," he recalled, "until finally, I just had to be told [by the DoD], I don't want to hear any more about it. And that was a real blow." He fumed at his Pentagon superiors that he could not be held responsible for the results. "I told you I could make the volunteer army work, but I never told you I could make it work without a GI Bill."[14]

Calloway's dire assessment emphasized the material effect of the end of the GI Bill, but it also revealed just how much his quest for the bill intertwined with his worries about "low quality," representativeness, and the demographic fate of the volunteer army. Calloway needed the GI Bill to augment what came to be called the "Calloway Shift," his efforts to redirect recruitment to more middle-class, white areas of the country. When Calloway entered his position in 1973, army recruiters reeled in most of their enlistments from central cities.[15] In African American enclaves, like "Harlem and the black sections of Birmingham, Atlanta and similar cities," Calloway noted, the army had "three, four times as many recruits per person in that area as we had in some suburban areas."[16] Though Calloway would fight the trend, even until the late 1970s recruiters peddled the army "downtown where the pool halls were, where the type of people that hung around in pool halls were, the non-grads or the lower quality people," explained a recruiter out of Fort Sheridan, Illinois. Its recruiting centers sat "where the recruiting is easiest . . . , where the unemployment's the highest; . . . where the jobs are hardest to find."[17]

Calloway pushed recruiters to the malls that lined suburban throughways across the nation in search of a more educated, less impoverished, and presumably better "quality" soldier. And this was where the GI Bill became important to Calloway. If the army was at least talking to "not necessarily the upper class, but at least the middle class, the higher caliber person," Calloway believed the GI Bill would be the necessary enticement to pull that person into the army.[18]

Calloway's enthusiasm for the GI Bill as a tool for middle-class recruitment carried racial significance when the malls of the suburbs were white and the pool halls of the center city were more likely to be African American. Calloway's thinking mirrored the thesis of sociologist Charles Moskos, who had first made the argument about the army's need for a GI Bill with his colleague sociologist Morris Janowitz in their influential 1974 "tipping point" article about "representation" in the army. At that time, the authors were concerned with overrepresentation of African Americans in the army, and had proposed several ways to increase white enlistment. Their suggestion that garnered the most interest among army manpower experts was the creation of a new GI Bill.[19] The "major outcome [of a GI Bill]," they claimed, "would be the reintroduction of white middle class males" into the army's combat forces.[20]

Four years later, in 1978 and 1979, Moskos had more fully developed the idea of education benefits and promoted them before Congress and in writing.[21] By that time, three years had elapsed since the program's demise, and the army had reached the nadir of its crisis over "quality," bedeviled by the polarizing charge of the "near-total failure" of the volunteer army.[22] Moskos captured the promise of the GI Bill by framing the problem as the "absent middle class." He lamented that "recruits . . . from the least educated sectors of the white community" had replaced the white middle class.

To lure back "better qualified young men," Moskos argued, the army should offer them a generous "quid pro quo"—four years of college education in return for two years enlistment in one of the combat arms.[23] Both the army and Moskos wanted the white middle class back.

Moskos's arguments for a GI Bill bolstered the hopes of rather desperate army leadership. Several months after publishing his piece in the *Wilson Quarterly,* Moskos met the new commander of army recruiting, General Max Thurman. A small, meticulous man, Thurman reveled in analytics, and "loved the operations research" in the army. He enjoyed quantitative analysis and sought models of organization and management from both military and nonmilitary planners.[24] Like Calloway several years before, Thurman made the quality of the new volunteer army his mission. He is often credited with saving the volunteer force, and these assessments derive largely from his perceived success at "vastly improving the quality of the average soldier," as his obituary at Arlington National Cemetery recorded.[25] Though Thurman is best known in army manpower circles for his long-running, successful "Be All You Can Be" advertising campaign, his main goal, of which the ad campaign was part, was procuring higher-quality, upwardly aspiring soldiers.

Thurman had just been named to the army Recruiting Command, at the height of the army's image crisis, when he travelled to a conference on the volunteer force at the Hoover Institution at Stanford University, where he met Moskos. The army, Moskos told Thurman, could use educational benefits to capture "college-oriented . . . youth who might look for a short hiatus between high school and college," a hiatus that could be taken in the army, and that would grant them a free education afterward.[26] As he had in his writing and testimony, Moskos argued that the GI Bill would entice the elusive middle-class white recruit whose scores and statistics would raise the army's quality level. General Thurman, of course, already believed that the army needed a more educated, more middle-class force. But now he came to see that a GI Bill—some kind of an educational incentive program—was necessary to accomplish that goal. Thurman was so "super keen on the . . . GI Bill," as Moskos later recalled, that the two became fast friends, and together pushed along the proposals for a new GI Bill.[27]

When General Thurman left the Recruiting Command to become deputy chief of staff for personnel, he enlisted Moskos to work on the army's version of educational benefits developed in the gap left by the defunct GI Bill.[28] Back when the sun began to set on the GI Bill, the army had created and funded its own educational benefits program to lure "quality" soldiers.

The Army Education Plan cobbled together and expanded existing education and training programs that might compensate for the loss of the GI Bill. The plan emphasized to recruits the opportunities for both vocational and technical training on and off duty. It also included the Predischarge Education Program (PREP), "a high quality education program designed to be responsive to soldiers who have not completed high school or need preparatory, remedial instruction." Finally, the army offered off- and on-duty opportunities to work toward high school, college, and graduate degrees.[29] The Army Education Plan sent education and training costs soaring. A large part of this compensated directly for the loss of GI Bill benefits. Once Congress eliminated the GI Bill in 1976, the Army Education Plan's costs reached $6.3 billion.[30]

In the late 1970s, Congress surveyed these programs and agreed to directly fund limited educational benefits for soldiers, creating the Veterans Education Assistance Plan (VEAP). VEAP operated as a contributory program in which soldiers socked away funds for education that were matched at a 2:1 ratio by the services, and limited by a modest ceiling. In 1980, Colonel Robert L. Phillips of the army Recruiting Command undertook a study of the VEAP at the Army War College to examine its power to increase the quality of army recruits. Using a data set containing information on the general population and military recruits, he found "a higher percent of individuals in the Armed Forces who aspired to become college graduates than in the labor market." So there seemed like a natural desire for educational benefits within the recruited population. Even more important, the study showed that the young men and women who had considered enlisting but decided against it stated as their main reason pursuing postsecondary education. For Phillips, this data suggested that the army could compete for these people given the right lure, and that the lure ought to take the shape of "special educational benefits."[31]

Phillips then drew up a plan that he presented to the highest levels of leadership in the army, including the chief of staff of the army (CSA), for enhanced educational benefits. For the army, Phillips recommended an "Ultra VEAP" program, more generous than the existing one, and an army "kicker," an additional extra sum, between $6,000 and $8,000, to be provided for high-quality soldiers enlisting in needed specialties. Army leadership assented, and Phillips's program eventually became the Army College Fund (ACF), which, Phillips happily reported, provided the army "a new market of quality graduates."[32] The college funds seemed to promise a solution to the army's thorny "quality" problems.

Army leaders jumped at the seemingly positive results of the testing of educational benefits. They concluded that educational programs decisively aided the recruiting of more educated and more upwardly mobile soldiers. Several sociologists who studied the army and recruitment agreed that the educational inducements would provide measurable gains in recruits, projecting the "greatest gains . . . among college-bound youth, who would enter the military with above-average mental aptitudes."[33]

By 1980 and 1981, the army took the evidence from its test cases to Congress to press for a fully funded new GI Bill. It found a largely receptive audience there among those who favored the volunteer force, but who had been worried by the drastically reduced educational levels of new recruits. By 1981, Congress demonstrated solid support for educational benefits, with eight bills that approximated a new GI Bill introduced in the Ninety-Seventh Congress.[34] Congressional supporters agreed with Representative Bill Armstrong (R-CO), who argued that the army's precipitous decline in recruits' capabilities took place "after Congress terminated eligibility for the GI Bill education benefits in 1976." If Congress enacted a new GI Bill, the benefits were likely to bring into the military "at least 50,000 additional high quality recruits a year, enough to eliminate present shortages, and to replace 15,000–20,000 volunteers in the lowest mental category with volunteers from higher mental categories."[35] If others on the Hill weren't as precise about the numeric improvements promised by a new GI Bill, many nonetheless professed the faith of army leaders that "many young people—though not necessarily careerists—are willing to serve the Army and the Nation in exchange for benefits leading to a college education."[36] Representative Montgomery championed the GI Bill more than anyone on Capitol Hill. Montgomery's family had a long history of service, and he attended college at Mississippi State College on a Reserve Officers' Training Corps scholarship. A veteran of World War II and a member of the National Guard after the war, he assumed the chair of the House Veterans Affairs Committee in 1981.[37] He would work closely for several years with Moskos to craft a bill and push it through Congress for the approval of the president.[38]

By that time, President Reagan had assumed office, and his personal politics augured well for the reinstatement of the GI Bill. A deep patriotic militarism infused Reagan's campaign for the presidency in 1980, in which the Cold War and the military took center stage. Reagan's campaign speeches had repeatedly underscored his overall commitment to the military and to the GI Bill program specifically. Reagan promised in a televised speech a few weeks before the election to ask Congress to reinstate the GI Bill. He also promised veterans groups specifically that "we must restore the GI Bill." Reagan's campaign rhetoric never mentioned the dire recruitment and retention problems of the volunteer army as a reason for reviving the GI Bill. Rather, Reagan cast support for the bill as part of a just compensation package for honorable soldiers, following arguments that army leadership had begun making about their benefits in the debate over comparability and employment during the union bid in 1977. "Our country must provide our service personnel and their families," he told the voters, "with the security, the incentives, and the quality of life to compensate for the sacrifices they make on our behalf."[39] For Reagan, a revived GI Bill served his strategy for restoring the legitimacy of the military, an institution that Reagan considered one of the most important—perhaps the single most important—in American life.

Despite Reagan's personal commitment to a restored GI Bill, his administration in the first year and a half struggled to determine an official stance on it. Reagan populated his administration with economists and businessmen pledged to cutting the federal budget and the size and function of government. Many of the manpower economists in Reagan's Pentagon retained personal connections to their colleagues who had served on the original Gates Commission that created the model for the volunteer force. As part of their "small government," free market ideology, they had opposed the use of military social welfare programs, such as the GI Bill, to lure and retain soldiers. Just as they objected to the general growth of military benefits at the outset of the volunteer era, they voiced skepticism about the efficiency and effectiveness of an educational benefits program in the 1980s.

Many economists doubted the army's sunny forecasts for the results of a GI Bill. Their worries were intertwined with the existential crisis facing the volunteer force, a force many of them had personally helped to craft. Former Gates Commission member Stephen Herbits, now an executive at Seagram's, worried that the high cost and low returns to the GI Bill would divert precious defense resources away from targeted recruitment strategies based on cash incentives. He cited the work of University of Chicago educated manpower economist Christopher Jehn. "The services are pushing 'quick fixes' for the AVF [All-Volunteer Force] without the analytical back up," Herbits wrote Martin Anderson, now Reagan's chief domestic policy advisor and point person on the volunteer force. He insisted the army's proposal for a "restoration of the G.I. Bill" rested upon "test data . . . not yet sufficient to permit a choice among various alternatives." Blindly supporting the program "could divert expenditures away from programs of greater value to the AVF," like cash bonuses.[40] Cato Institute economist Roger Nils Folsom—a member of the free market Foundation for Economic Education and the Ludwig von Mises Institute—also called the GI Bill "an inefficient way to recruit a skilled military." Referring back to the original Gates Commission proposals to eliminate expensive military and government support programs for soldiers, Folsom suggested a turn to free market principles. "The point is *not* that educational benefits should be restored to earlier levels: The demise of the GI Bill should have been accompanied by a real increase in cash pay."[41] For free marketers, cash bonuses or pay offered a simpler, market-friendly solution to military manpower problems.

Reagan's assistant secretary of defense for manpower Lawrence Korb echoed the doubts of economists when he told Congress that the GI Bill represented a blunt and costly manpower tool. He worried that an educational entitlement program for members of the armed forces might cost anywhere from $2 billion to $5 billion each year. Korb conceded that such huge "sums might be well spent if they contribute to the recruitment and retention goals for a viable and healthy all-volunteer force." But he doubted that they would "help us recruit and retain the personnel we need." Utilizing the Reagan administration's anti-tax rhetoric, he phrased his objections as "fiscally responsible to the taxpayer."[42]

Korb also worried that the GI Bill would perversely create a disincentive, rather than an incentive, to military recruitment. Noting a distinction between military service and a military career, he asked, "How can we encourage young persons to perform military service to earn special educational benefits and then, only a few years later, discourage them from leaving the service in order to use these benefits?"[43] The Cato Institute's Folsom had also expressed this worry. Educational benefits "discourage military careers because to be a full-time student and obtain the maximum benefit, one must usually leave military service."[44] Reagan's Office of Management and Budget (OMB), headed by the former Michigan congressman and budget hawk David Stockman, in outlining its concerns about the GI Bill, insisted that the costly educational incentives "act as a retention disincentive in some cases."[45]

Many economists and manpower experts advocated for what they saw as the proven cheaper methods to bring more bodies into recruitment offices: signing bonuses—cash paid to enlistees upon signing enlistment contracts. Studies by the Congressional Budget Office (CBO) showed that cash worked better than education benefits to lure people into the army. If soldiers wished to use the cash for educational purposes, they could be referred to existing programs of the Departments of Health, Education and Welfare, and Labor.[46] The CBO also suggested that the army target raises and benefits toward those specialized areas in which recruitment and retention was most difficult. The GI Bill, they argued, took an inefficient and costly blanket approach, needlessly giving away precious defense dollars to all military personnel without consideration of manpower needs.[47] The high costs of education programs simply could not be justified by the small increases in recruitment that a GI Bill might provide. Assistant Secretary Korb fought the GI Bill by advocating enlistment bonuses, which he called "the most cost effective way we know to get people."[48]

The army persisted in its quest to revive the GI Bill, explaining that the protestations of economists missed the point of educational incentives. Manpower economists focused too narrowly on "getting people," on the pure numbers of soldiers required to meet manpower objectives. But the army's interest in the GI Bill derived not from a fear of too few soldiers overall, but too many "low quality" soldiers. Back when Ford and Congress canceled the GI Bill, they had fundamentally misunderstood its importance, explained former secretary of the army Calloway. The policy makers had always "looked at it as entirely numbers. I said it's got nothing to do with numbers."[49] Given the public's negative impression of the soldiers of the new volunteer force, it was not quantity people like Calloway worried about, but quality.

Thus from the start of their campaign to revive the GI Bill in 1974, army leaders had always rejected the proposal that offering large cash bonuses could help with its recruitment problem. Cash bonuses alone could not compensate for the lack of upwardly aspiring, better-educated, "quality" recruits. Calloway had argued that the army aimed not for "the guy that couldn't get a job anywhere else." That man would be easy to recruit, and a bonus would do the job: "He'd get a combat arms bonus and buy a car. That sort of thing motivated him."[50] The army wanted the guy with better prospects, the guy who was planning for either a good job or postsecondary education. For that soldier, Calloway and subsequent army leaders argued, the educational benefits were essential. GI Bill advocate Charles Moskos put it succinctly at the end of the 1970s: the bill "would attract new people to the recruitment pool—particularly higher income/status youths—instead of simply drawing more people from the pool."[51] Army leaders felt desperate for "bright, young people," and they insisted that the GI bill would allow the army to "compete successfully for college qualified youth."[52] The GI Bill, former army secretary Calloway insisted, "was powerful. . . . That's where you got the good ones."[53]

"The good ones" promised the army not only higher education levels and test scores. The "high quality" soldier constituted a more committed, responsible, upstanding soldier, one who would fulfill personal obligations to the army first and foremost, but in other areas of their lives too—family, community, citizenship. Having both a high school diploma and the desire to pursue postsecondary education, "these credentials," the CSA explained, "clearly identify people with the determination to fulfill personal obligations."[54]

The economists at the CBO allowed that the GI Bill might let the army capture a few more technically high-quality recruits than it could otherwise. "Improved military education benefits," they explained to Congress, "could help recruiting . . . of high school graduates with high test scores." Indeed, in a definitive study of the GI Bill much later in the 1980s, Secretary of Defense Frank Carlucci would show that the GI Bill offered a very modest increase of 4–5 percent of enlistments of high-quality personnel.[55] Keying in on what would be the army's deepest reason for demanding the revival of the GI Bill, the CBO conceded that the bill might also "enhance the image of the military as a desirable place to serve before continuing in school."[56] But CBO critics of the GI Bill would not agree to spend vast sums of money for small increases in quality accessions or a better "image."

For army leaders who felt the volunteer force faced a crisis of low education levels as well as a reputation of recruiting from the margins, the cost calculation over the GI Bill worked differently. The "good ones" that education benefits might entice, though admittedly they might be few, seemed worth the cost if they helped dislodge the "dummy" and the "dregs" images plaguing the army. Education benefits offered the army the possibility of rechristening itself: the army could be an institution that offered soldiers with more than solid army test scores—soldiers with ambition and drive—a possibility to make lifelong improvements in their education, skills, and earnings. Army leaders expected the GI Bill to lure soldiers and capture the promises of aspiration and opportunity to benefit the army's public image.

For the army, even if the GI Bill failed by the numbers—which its leaders did not concede—it nevertheless succeeded as symbolism. No data ever showed that the educational benefits produced more than minor gains in recruiting higher-quality soldiers, nor that the bill was cost-effective. The army nevertheless pressed harder than ever for the GI Bill as part of a broader program to shift public perception. The few good men that the program might snare represented a good army, and the program itself—an upwardly aspiring program of higher education—would stamp itself on all soldiers, not only those who actually earned and used the program. The army's ad campaigns of the early 1980s explicitly linked the positive imagery of the ambitious soldier and the army. N. W. Ayer crafted advertisements that wove the army into the aspirations of college-bound young people and their families. "The Army Has Helped Send More People To College Than There Are People in College Today," one ad headlined.[57] In others, eighteen-year-old white adolescent boys wore letterman's jackets, held books in their hands, and sat with their parents, learning how they could "start college two years older, two years wiser, and $15,200 richer."[58] For army leaders, the GI Bill represented a new image that decisively countered the prior image of low-quality soldiers using the army as a handout. For the army, the cost of the GI Bill was worth it.

In the midst of the Washington debate over the fate of the GI Bill, the army's recruiting numbers budged upward. In 1981 and 1982, the army reported that its use of bonuses and educational benefits through the VEAP program then under testing had helped "reverse . . . a previously unfavorable situation." For the first time in years the army met both quantitative and, more importantly, qualitative recruitment targets.[59] From 1982 to 1983, the army actually exceeded its recruitment objectives for enlisted personnel. By this time, over 80 percent of new soldiers were high school graduates, a significant improvement over the mid-1970s, when only half held a diploma.[60] The army heralded it as "a refreshing reversal from the days when we could not be as selective."[61]

Though top army leaders touted the education programs' responsibility for the turnaround when reporting to Congress, more important was the sluggish economy of the early 1980s, which pushed some young Americans to choose the military over poor labor market options. In 1980 and again from 1981 to 1982, the United States officially fell into recession, and this coincided nearly exactly with the army's increases in quantity and quality of accessions. In the last several months of 1982 the official unemployment

THE ARMY CAN HELP YOUR SON OR DAUGHTER SAVE $8100 FOR COLLEGE OVER THE NEXT THREE YEARS.

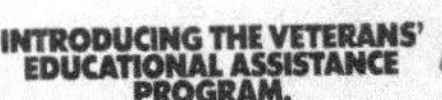

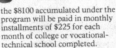

INTRODUCING THE VETERANS' EDUCATIONAL ASSISTANCE PROGRAM.

Now your son or daughter can accumulate up to $8100 for college or vocational-technical school during just 36 months in the Army.

Under the Veterans' Educational Assistance Program, they can save from $50 to $75 each month, with their savings matched 2 for 1! And that adds up.

FOR EVERY DOLLAR THEY SAVE TOWARD COLLEGE, TWO WILL BE ADDED.

By participating in the program, a young person gets three dollars back for every dollar saved toward college or vocational-technical school—the dollar saved plus the additional two dollars of matching funds.

If the maximum of $75 a month is saved ($2700 over 36 months), $5400 will be added for a total of $8100. If the minimum of $50 a month is saved ($1800 over 36 months), $3600 will be added for a total of $5400.

HOW DO THEY COLLECT?

Assuming your son or daughter has finished the 36-month enlistment in the Army and has deposited, for example, $75 to the educational fund each month, the $8100 accumulated under the program will be paid in monthly installments of $225 for each month of college or vocational-technical school completed.

If they decide not to continue schooling after the Army, they get back all the money saved. The matching funds will be paid only if used toward completing up to four years of college or vocational-technical school. The extra $5400 matching amount becomes a strong incentive for a young person to continue with school.

THEY CAN ALSO GO TO COLLEGE WHILE IN THE ARMY AND WE PAY UP TO 75% OF THE TUITION.

If your son or daughter enlists in today's Army, all kinds of educational opportunities are open for earning college or vocational-technical credits right on post with the Army paying up to 75% of the tuition. Under Project AHEAD, for example, a young person can enlist in the Army and start a college or vocational-technical school program at the same time. Nearly 1400 colleges and universities around the country now participate in Project AHEAD. It's a great chance for a young person to get a jump on the future.

YOUR LOCAL ARMY REPRESENTATIVE IS THE PERSON TO TALK TO NEXT.

The Veterans' Educational Assistance Program, along with all of the other educational benefits the Army offers, will help your son or daughter serve their country better as soldiers now, citizens later. There's no better time to start getting that education than now. Your local Army Representative has full details on all the educational and other opportunities for young people in today's Army. Or, if you'd like us to send the information to you, just write: Commander, U.S. Army Recruiting, 1000 Liberty Avenue, Pittsburgh, PA 15222. Or call 800-242-0605 toll free, day or night.

Join the people who've joined the Army. It's an education, too.

Before the revival of the GI Bill, the army advertised its postservice education benefits to represent itself as an institution for upwardly aspiring young people. Courtesy of NW Ayer Advertising Agency Records, Archives Center, National Museum of American History, Smithsonian Institution.

rate neared 11 percent, with higher unemployment reported for youths and nonwhites. The CSA and the secretary of the army admitted to Congress that "the success derives . . . from economic and social factors" as well as the army's trial education benefits.[62] Indeed, the army's Historical Summary for 1982 did not mention educational benefits at all when noting the improved recruitment numbers. It emphasized "the influence of a depressed economy."[63] Senator Sam Nunn (D-GA) made the point in sharper partisan terms. Better recruiting, he argued, resulted from Reagan's poorly crafted economic policies: "Supply-side economics is working," Nunn cracked, "it is supplying the military with volunteers."[64]

Even as the army's recruiting and overall manpower situation improved, the army nevertheless continued to advocate for a new GI Bill. It needed the GI Bill as a long-term symbol of the increasing quality of the U.S. Army.

AS THE PRESS for the GI Bill continued in the early 1980s, the Reagan administration found itself in a bind over the bill's passage. Though Reagan's economists and manpower experts doubted the efficacy and principles of the program, Congress, the army, and, most importantly, the president supported it. Above all, the GI Bill reinforced the entire Reagan administration effort to legitimize the military and recognize its personnel. Even Assistant Secretary of Defense Korb, who doubted the efficacy of the GI Bill, generally supported robust new programs benefiting military personnel. "We must," he warned Congress, "raise the morale and self-image of the military." Korb and Secretary of Defense Caspar Weinberger had pledged to transform military personnel from "second class citizens," as the political leaders of the 1970s had supposedly cast them, to first-class citizens of the Reagan era.[65] And the two had willingly raised defense spending to unprecedented highs to support the effort, following Reagan's dictum that "defense is not a budget issue."[66] The Reagan administration raised military pay by 14.3 percent in the fall of 1981.[67] And Weinberger embarked on a hiring spree: active duty military personnel strength rose from 2,050,000 to 2,189,000, an increase of 7 percent, and the reserve component rose to its largest number since 1959: 1,190,000. He increased civilian hires in defense by 130,000, a nearly 15 percent increase, many of whom went to work in the growing support programs of the army.[68] With the president committed to a GI Bill and a defense team generally committed to restoring the military through high spending, Reagan's administration found it difficult to maintain opposition to the GI Bill on grounds of cost, efficiency, or effectiveness.

As the man with the most intimate history with the volunteer force, Reagan policy aide Martin Anderson was forced to smooth out the administration's contradictory statements on the GI Bill. In contact with Korb and his office at the Pentagon as well as Stockman and his staff at OMB, Anderson became a clearinghouse on the GI Bill.[69] He gathered Reagan's public statements on the bill, media coverage, administration memos from the various cabinet offices, and tried to create a degree of "interagency coordination on [the] GI Bill." With conflicting messages coming from the Pentagon, OMB, and the White House, Reagan's advisors needed to definitively "ascertain policy in this area, so that [they could] begin working out how to accomplish the President's wishes."[70] The "president's wishes" had generated considerable traction for GI Bill advocates in Congress. As Sonny Montgomery pointed out to Korb during the latter's tepid testimony on the GI Bill, "The President of the United States told me on two different occasions what we need to get going again is the GI education Bill. So I hope you are telling him what you are doing in the Defense Department because the Commander in Chief is telling me he wants the GI education Bill."[71]

Reagan's administration eventually lined up behind the GI Bill, as the president wished. But not for exactly the same reasons—or at least not only the same reasons—as the army did. How Anderson, and later others, came to the decision revealed how important the GI Bill's imagery and implications were to Reagan's military politics and his overall domestic political agenda in his first term as president.

As advocates for a renewed GI Bill pressed forward, they gained traction with a new argument that reached beyond the army and its recruitment problems, and into the world of civilian social welfare programs. Back in 1979, when sociologist Charles Moskos had advocated for the GI Bill, he ruminated on the seeming lack of "dedication to equality of sacrifice," meaning military sacrifice in the United States. He pointed to the federal student aid programs—government loans and grants to college students—as an example. "It is surprising," Moskos argued, "that given the extensive discussion of financial relief for families with children in college, no public figure had thought to tie such student aid to any service obligation, civilian or military, on the part of the youths who benefit."[72] Whereas a GI Bill would provide federal aid to education as a reward for military service, civilian college students were being furnished college loans and grants on the basis of economic need, without any reckoning of duty to country.

Moskos referred to the Guaranteed Student Loan (GSL) program and the Pell Grant program. Sputnik inspired Congress in the late 1950s to institute the first student aid, forgiving up to 50 percent of loan costs to certain students who used their degrees in desired fields. But the large student aid programs had begun under President Lyndon B. Johnson as part of his Great Society. The Higher Education Act of 1965 provided grants to colleges and universities to pass on to needy students and guaranteed student loans for middle-class families for whom the cost of college exceeded their savings. In 1972, Congress authorized the Basic Educational Opportunity Grants (which came to be known as Pell Grants) that provided aid directly to needy individual students. Together, the federal grants and loans grew into a major source of support for American students. In 1972, about 1 million students used the GSL program, but by the 1980s, 2.5 million had signed up.[73]

When Reagan entered office, this program landed in the sights of Reagan's government-cutting domestic policy agenda. Reagan had long campaigned against the encroachment of "big government" and social welfare programs both as governor of California and as a candidate for the presidency. One of his first major legislative wins as president consisted of nearly across-the-board social welfare spending cuts along with new rules for means-tested programs in the 1981 Omnibus Budget Reconciliation Act. Overall, Reagan sought to shift burdens of social and economic support away from government and onto families and individuals.

Beginning in late 1981, Reagan's Department of Education, as well as his domestic policy advisors in the White House, attacked student aid as one front in Reagan's general assault on social welfare. It was not an easy battle as Americans of the middle classes were by this time relying upon student aid and endorsed it. But his administration nevertheless pursued it. They aimed to exclude higher education from the purview of government responsibility, and instead cast it as the private responsibility of individuals, families, or private sector donations. In the words of one critic, student aid cost the government both the price of grants and loans and the additional "waste . . . [of] hundreds of thousands of dollars spent on the bureaucracy that managed them." In comparison to scholarships or grants from private organizations, corporations, or individuals, federal student loans represented "a very inefficient way to support our Universities."[74] Reagan's Department of Education proposed a "definitional change" through which the administration could "reassert the appropriate role of the family as the primary focus of responsibility for meeting the costs of postsecondary education for their children."[75]

Reagan's administration argued that the system of government loans and grants was suffused with fraud. Like other recipients of government aid, recipients of grants and loans were not often truly needy in the administration's view. Reagan's aides cited cases of middle- or even upper-middle-class families who falsely presented their children as financially "independent" students in order to qualify for federal aid. Though estimates of the numbers of such families never exceeded more than a couple percentage points of overall recipients, the Reagan team nevertheless emerged with a campaign featuring them: it sought to "highlight . . . the moral issue of working taxpayers supporting rich kids who don't need the help."[76]

To build its case for cutting the programs, the White House sought "'horror stories' in federal student aid."[77] Some Americans responded, writing Reagan directly to decry federal aid to higher education as wasteful and undeserved, even for low-income students. A woman employed at a public college in California cheered Reagan's attack on the "flagrant use of such programs as Financial Aide to the College student [*sic*]." She encouraged Reagan to monitor "the extravagance in the Equal Opportunities Program [by which she meant the Pell Grants]." Drawing on Reagan's anti-tax theme, she cited her status as a "property owner, a single woman owning my own home." "I have always paid my own way," she concluded—unlike the college students depending upon government grants or loans.[78]

Reagan's policy team proposed alterations to the programs that took various forms. New regulations and rules cut overall spending and increased stringency. They pushed more college students into the labor market to fund their own educations, redefined eligibility rules, raised income qualifications for guaranteed student loans and grants, and required graduate students pay higher interest rates for loans.[79]

Reagan's campaign against federal aid to higher education entered the policy debate about the GI Bill in early 1981, just after he took office. The two policy proposals—one to cut civilian aid to higher education and one to augment military aid to higher education—developed in tandem. Few at the time or since noticed the correlation. Indeed, when universities rose in protest against the cuts to federal student aid, they cited the benefits of higher education by invoking the boon to America from the World War II,

Korean War, and Vietnam-era GI Bills. The general secretary of the American Association of University Professors wrote President Reagan to decry proposed cuts and referred to the earlier GI Bills as enormously beneficial to generations of Americans and to the strength of society as a whole. He intended the reference to the GI Bill to strengthen the case for maintaining and expanding federal aid to civilian higher education. But he did not realize that the current incarnations of the GI Bill before Congress were crafted not to dovetail with or reaffirm federal student aid to civilians but to oppose such aid. As the GI Bill and federal student aid entered the same discussion, the new GI Bill of the 1980s was being built in part on the backs of civilian students who would be deprived of federal education aid.[80]

The argument to limit federal student aid rested partly on the assertion that it deterred military enlistment and competed with the hoped-for GI Bill, but the data were murky. The CBO reported to Congress that federal college loans and grants did seem to offer at least some small disincentive for potential enlistees in the army. When the CBO had critiqued the GI Bill's efficacy, it had not only pointed to the inefficiency and minimal cost-benefit of the GI Bill, but also to the competition presented by other government programs that offered young people free or subsidized education. "Youths today can use numerous federal and state student aid programs that do not require military service," CBO directors explained to Congress in a hearing before the House Budget Committee. Generous military education benefits thus "might be relatively ineffective as a recruiting incentive."[81] The Cato Institute performed a military manpower analysis that asserted with greater certainty that "Congress had compounded the difficulty of recruiting by greatly expanding educational grants and loans available to civilians (Federal Guaranteed Student Loans and Parent Loans, Basic Supplementary Educational Opportunity Grants, National Direct Student Loans, and college work-study programs), with no requirement for military service."[82] At almost the same time, however, the Center for Naval Analysis, the navy's research arm, conducted its own study of deterrents to enlistment. It reported several variables that affected enlistment, including compensation, the rate of unemployment, quality of recruiters, and the existence (or not) of education benefits like the proposed GI Bill or the army's VEAP program. However, the report concluded that that the one variable they studied that had no effect on enlistment was government student aid programs for civilians.[83]

The actual impact of student aid on recruiting numbers, however, was not the main point the Reagan administration made in linking federal student aid and the GI Bill. Their connection of the two policy issues did not aim to solve a military manpower problem so much as to symbolize the priorities of the Reagan administration: cutting federal student aid using the justification of the GI Bill allowed Reagan to demonstrate his commitment to the relegitimation of the military and soldiers in American life and his delegitimation of government social welfare and aid. The federal student aid programs symbolized the undeserving civilian users of government social welfare programs and the GI Bill represented just recognition of worthy soldiers and a revered military.

Reagan carried the banner for the GI Bill on precisely these terms, folding support for the GI Bill into a broader set of domestic policy priorities that sought to recalibrate the meaning of deserving and undeserving in the realm of entitlements. "A few years ago," Reagan told the army, "the GI Bill was eliminated and replaced with a program having fewer benefits." Reagan linked this cut directly to expansion of spending in other areas: "At the same time we were expanding Federal aid to college students. The Federal Government, in effect, provided more benefits to those who were not serving their country and reduced them for those who were."[84] Reagan thus coupled his support for the GI Bill with specific reductions in federal loans and grants for civilians. For Reagan, the GI Bill both served soldiers and punished those who sought government loans without sacrificing through military service. Reagan's vision of the GI Bill sharpened his promilitary, anti–social welfare state politics.

Back in 1981, even as Reagan gave his West Point speech, Anderson had already begun working on gutting the Pell Grant program using this reasoning. Anderson's aide, John McClaughry, explained to him, "There is sentiment for limiting the BEOG [Basic Educational Opportunity Grant] program only to those who complete a military service requirement." McClaughry pointed out that Pell Grants were "available to millions of 'needy' college students, in effect a GI Bill with no GI requirement." Reagan's policy team called into question both the true "need" of Pell Grant users and the lack of stipulations applied to the grant itself. In their view, as in Reagan's, the federal government would not give way money for education without extracting military service in return.[85]

The army came on board with this view. CSA General Shy Meyer made this argument explicitly to Congress a year later. In congressional testimony on the GI Bill and student loans, he explained that the "$4.4 Billion worth of federal programs for which the individual does not have to pay back through [military] service" seemed unfair. Meyer proposed a direct relationship between the two in which support for one unfairly eliminated the possibility of the other. He advocated cutting all federal grant and loan aid and redirecting all that funding to the GI Bill, "so that the country was in effect getting back service for the use of these." The GI Bill would cost nothing new in the federal budget, he explained, as the funds taken from federal grants and loans would go "straight into funding the GI Bill."[86] The bill would rectify the "equality of sacrifice" and save money at the same time.

Supporters of the GI Bill in Congress joined the army in coupling student aid to the GI Bill. Sonny Montgomery called the federal student aid program "kind of a GI Bill without service." In pushing for the GI Bill he stated, "at least we [advocates for the GI Bill in Congress] are getting some obligation from somebody." Montgomery, like General Meyer, proposed funding the GI Bill by "cut[ting] back on some of these student loan programs, grant programs."[87] Congressman Ed Bethune (R-AK) proposed to "slow the rapid growth and cost of student assistance programs" by funding a GI Bill that allowed student aid only to those who volunteered as a "quid pro quo."[88] Congressman Duncan Hunter (R-CA) held local hearings in his heavily military San Diego district on the GI Bill, which also raised the perceived inequality between civilian students and military personnel. Though he exaggerated the differences between the two programs, he nevertheless made his point: "We have this tremendous student loan program for people who don't want to serve the country, and you have this miserable little VEAP program." The inequality, in his view, demeaned military service. There was a "certain psychology," a negative psychology for military personnel, he explained, "in having such a dismal program for the service people. . . . I think that it [the GI Bill] is going to allow the service person to hold his head up."[89]

These arguments held the day, as Reagan initiated two additional changes to federal student aid. Reagan's administration promoted successful bills that altered student aid rules to include selective service registration, which remained a national requirement for men even after the advent of the volunteer force. Though not directly related to the GI Bill itself, the rule changes—the result of two pieces of legislation supported by Reagan in 1982 and 1983—limited federal student aid to those men who registered for the selective service.[90] Opponents of the reform insisted the rules persecuted conscientious and principled objectors to the selective service.[91]

Reagan's response demonstrated the links the administration sought to make between federal aid to students and military service. He answered critics: "if a young man is enjoying all the rights and privileges associated with living in this great country of ours, he should also willingly assume the obligations of membership in that society."[92] Without assuming those obligations, no federal aid to higher education would be available to men. The rules requiring selective service registration for student loan qualification reprised the long simmering controversy over the Vietnam War and its protesters. Reagan's hostile relationship with antiwar college students at Berkeley in the 1960s perhaps colored his choice to require selective service registration. The rules also scored points with veteran organizations seeking to punish citizens who in the past either burned draft cards or refused to serve when called—"young men who flout the law by refusing to register for the draft," as Brigadier General Theodore Mataxis (Ret.), president of the Philadelphia Chapter of the Military Order of World Wars, put it. He wrote Reagan urging him to "keep up the fire!"[93]

Reagan combined the selective service requirement with bills cutting the federal student aid programs. From 1981 to 1986, the Reagan administration reduced funding for financial aid and altered programs to emphasize loans instead of grants. In the mid-1970s, grants had constituted 80 percent of the federal assistance package, but by the mid-1980s, they constituted only 50 percent. The effects of student aid cuts were exacerbated because the price of enrolling in even a state college or university rose faster than the general cost of living.[94] The student loans and grants programs took severe hits, and many college and university officials decried not only the bad outcomes for students, whose "lives and hopes" were "disrupted" by the changes, but also for the institutions themselves, whose viability was threatened by the "disastrous" and "dramatic" alterations to the law.[95] Members of Congress reported details of harm to students, colleges, and universities they represented.[96]

As the cuts to federal student aid took effect, Reagan's administration resolved their differences and expressed united support for the GI Bill. Having quieted the concerns of his economists and budget hawks about the program's weaknesses, the administration developed its own proposal for the GI Bill. In 1984, Congress passed a first temporary GI Bill, providing full benefits to all qualified military personnel, a program far more generous and thoroughgoing than the army's stopgap VEAP education benefits. When the GI Bill came up for renewal in 1986, Reagan signed it in a special ceremony in the Rose Garden.

Reagan's cuts to federal educational loans and grants alongside his support of the GI Bill functioned as two sides of the same coin—a rejection of government support for civilians and an embrace of soldiers, a rejection of civilian government programs and a championing of the military as the most legitimate function of government. The harshest edge of Reagan's GI Bill politics proved effective for the army in that they honed right in on the issues of legitimacy and respect called into question by the putatively "low quality" army of the late 1970s. Reagan's canny interpretation shifted the blame to "big government" programs that rewarded the undeserving.

The reinstatement of the GI Bill capped the efforts of the army to dispel the previous decade's image of an army of dregs. Reagan's shrewd politics elevating the GI Bill and discrediting civilian student aid helped the army in its effort to tamp down the charges from the late 1970s of being a social welfare institution. Instead, the army replaced those images with nearly its opposite: the army as a place where independent, ambitious youth—youth who serve rather than rely on the government—go to get a leg up, not a handout.

The fact that the GI Bill appeared only after the army's several-year effort to alter its recruitment and recast its public image, and after Reagan had elevated the military to a new political position, signaled its symbolic rather than substantive significance. Though many soldiers within the army subsequently used the GI Bill—more than in any other service—the bill did not accomplish what the army promised on the recruitment front.[97] An official DOD retrospective report on the enhancement in military manpower during the Reagan administration does not even mention educational incentives or the GI Bill—the program simply did not bring in the numbers, as its critics had always said.[98] What the bill did do, however, as army leaders well knew, was mark the army as a legitimate institution free from the stain of social welfare while tainting civilian student aid programs as handouts.

The timing of the passage of the GI Bill proved the symbolic importance of the program. By 1984, the army had already been recruiting far more high school graduates for three and a half years. As early as 1981, the CSA and secretary of the army asserted the army's "quality" and readiness in their annual reports to Congress. That year, as the year the army commemorated the two-hundredth anniversary of the Battle of Yorktown in the Revolutionary War, the chiefs issued a positive report about "steady improvement."[99] "From the perspective of reports and personal visits to the field, we can highlight many positive strengths in today's Army. The core is strong," they assured. "We're mid-stream in tightening up our standards." A year later, their report stressed readiness, with the chief and secretary insisting that the army now had "competent Soldiers with an understanding of our national traditions and the desire to serve their Nation proudly."[100] Their more assertive statement in 1983 led with a quote from famed French military leader Maurice de Saxe, the marshal of France (when American military officials still dared to quote French soldiers): "It is not the big armies that win battles; it is the good ones." And the U.S. Army was once again one of the good ones.[101]

"It's a great time to be a Soldier," General Meyer wrote in the Association of the U.S. Army's annual Green Book that same year. "Today's Army," he explained, "is headed . . . toward a quality Army—well trained, disciplined and combat-ready. . . . Years hence I want each of you to be able to look back with pride at what the Army was able to accomplish together."[102] From 1981 to 1983, the army's official statements projected the sense that the worst had passed. The army's Historical Summary for the year celebrated the "Spirit of Victory" and noted "a renewed sense of confidence in the future." The "chronic problems and worrisome deficiencies" of the mid-to-late 1970s "were finally beginning to yield."[103]

The army's redemption in the early 1980s registered in national public opinion, which showed "revived prestige for the military" after the era of the Vietnam War.[104] The army reported "a palpable shift in attitudes away from the predominantly negative feelings toward the military which had characterized public opinion since the end of the Vietnam era."[105] Weinberger opined, "The members of the Armed Forces, and the youth of America, quickly recognize that dignity had been restored to military service. . . . Today, more than ever, we have every right to be proud of our people in uniform."[106] In 1982 the National Opinion Research Center found that 59 percent of Americans agreed that the volunteer military "was working well or fairly well."[107] By 1986, 63 percent of Americans reported in a Gallup Poll that they had "great confidence" in the military.[108] The GI Bill capped and symbolized the army's turnaround.

IN 1988 the Pentagon, then under the leadership of Secretary Carlucci, wrote an analysis of the defense turnaround that Ronald Reagan and members of his administration had effected. It reflected on the steps the administration had taken to realize enormous gains in skills, ability, and personnel quality. Nowhere did the report mention the GI Bill. Congressmen Sonny Montgomery noticed the omission and penned a sharp objection to Carlucci. "Not one time is there any reference to the New GI Bill and its effectiveness in recruiting and retaining bright young men and women." Montgomery did not cite any recruitment statistics, but instead invoked the general feeling that he and leaders in the army had about the importance of the program. Carlucci's team, Montgomery insisted, had to "get out in the field" and talk to "enlistees . . . recruiters . . . those who command the troops . . . and the Service Chiefs of Personnel." Bonuses and pay, what Montgomery saw as throwing money at the problem, had not been effective. "Bright young men and women . . . want an education above all else," he explained.[109] The GI Bill had tapped into that hunger. Carlucci dutifully apologized. "We clearly missed an opportunity by not making particular note of the Montgomery GI Bill." He called it a "vigorous and successful initiative" for "countless individuals who have and will become better people in uniform and better citizens."[110]

Despite Carlucci's mea culpa, he and his Pentagon team perhaps overlooked the GI Bill because in fact it did little to concretely alter military recruitment. Despite the army's enormous faith in the program, and despite its widespread support in Congress and from Ronald Reagan, the program never did deliver the many middle-class and white recruits the army had so desperately sought since the mid-1970s. Though more high school graduates did join, the sought-after white middle-class stayed away. The high school graduates who joined were working class, and enlisted in large part because of the increases in pay, enlistment bonuses, and the downturn in the economy, which spent nearly two years in recession between 1979 and 1982 and created persistently high unemployment. Though the enlistees of the latter 1980s held high school degrees, they were not fundamentally different from a socioeconomic and demographic perspective from the supposedly problematic ones of the 1970s: they remained poorer than average Americans, disproportionately African American, and women continued to join in larger numbers.

But as Bo Calloway had insisted back when he pressed the Pentagon not to let the Vietnam-era GI Bill lapse, the numbers were not the point—not for the army and not for the Reagan administration that had supported it. For the army, the revived GI Bill quieted the charges against its supposedly low-quality, poorly educated soldiers from the dregs of society. That it did so even when the class, race, and sex demographics did not fundamentally alter testified to its power. The new GI Bill helped the army recast its soldiers, and it became a centerpiece for the upwardly mobile image of the army in the 1980s. For the Reagan administration, the GI Bill symbolized its militarized domestic politics. The administration used the bill to recalibrate what constituted legitimate versus illegitimate government spending. Reagan's effort to discredit student aid as underserved welfare marked a salvo in his larger attack on the welfare state and a simultaneous upgrade in the military's social welfare benefits and their legitimacy.

Yet military benefits and their legitimacy grew in other ways in the 1980s, too. Just as Reagan swept into office, an increasingly vocal group of army wives would successfully press the army to expand its family supports. At almost the same time, the ascendant conservative Christian right lent its support to the army and its benefits, embracing them as a political symbol of "traditional values" in the 1980s. The growing collaboration between the army and spouses, as well as the army and the Christian right, spurred additional military social welfare programs and secured their legitimacy in the late 1980s.

5

Army Wives Demand Support

ON A FULL page of a 1975 issue of *Army Times,* appears a photograph of a neatly coiffed woman holding a child on her lap. "Want your soldier to re-enlist?" the boldface copy queries the presumed commander. "Ask his wife what she thinks about army life."[1] In the late 1970s, approximately six of ten members of the armed forces were married—over 80 percent of the officer corps, about 50 percent of enlisted personnel, and 78 percent of career enlisted personnel. Ninety-five percent of army spouses were women.[2] As army leaders of the 1970s extended traditional military benefits beyond the career and officer cadre to all soldiers, they presumed that they had met the needs of army wives and their families. With access to housing and allowances, and sponsored tours for enlisted families to points across the continental United States and Europe, army wives were believed to have assumed happy roles as members of the "Army Family." "Chances are," the advertisement ventures, "his wife may like Army life a lot more than he knows."

In fact, most army wives, including those long admitted to the Army Family, held more conflicted emotions about army life than army leaders understood. Even into the flush years of President Reagan's early 1980s, young wives of junior enlisted personnel faced hardships despite the increasing access to traditional career personnel's benefits. Sent abroad to expensive posts, they encountered a lack of decent housing—sometimes a lack of any housing. And the relatively low pay of junior enlisted men did not meet the high costs of living in many locales. Few support programs of any kind assisted them in their moves. Officers' wives who faced less in the way of economic challenges nevertheless also faced difficulty. They detailed family disruptions from deployments and frequent moves, a lack of services for acclimation and adjustment, and pervasive housing and child care shortages.

Equally frustrating for army wives was the fact that some of the social supports that the army touted—child care, emergency financial programs, family recreation—were not in fact provided not by the army, but by the volunteer labor of army wives themselves. Army wives still functioned in the shadow of the traditional "Army Wife," crafted from customs of domesticity, gentility, and sacrifice codified in guides such as the classic 1941 *The Army Wife* by Nancy Shea. They still organized wives clubs, hosted lunches, teas, and dinners, provided informal counseling and advice to junior wives, managed the post "lending closet," ran recreation programs, operated the libraries, and created volunteer "nurseries" for child care, among many other services. Until the early 1980s, promotion reviews for soldiers often considered the behavior, attitude, and voluntary duties of wives. The ideal army wife lived as part of a family in the army and also in the Army Family. She was an essential component of the army's "support."

Just as the Reagan administration and top army officials were pushing through the new GI Bill in the early 1980s, a grassroots movement of army spouses—mostly the wives of officers and noncommissioned officers (NCOs)—coalesced in a new movement to expand and redirect the army's growing welfare state to serve the needs of army wives. They drew inspiration not from the militarization of the Reagan administration but from their own changing impressions of their roles in society, the workforce, and the home—sometimes fueled by the atmosphere, if not the movement, of second-wave feminism. Their demands coincided with the Reagan-era commitment to military benefits, and the resulting financial largesse allowed the army to acquiesce to wives' demands. Yet army wives' awakening challenged an institution that had already been ambivalent about the creation of new social programs as well as the presence of women in its ranks. Together, organized army wives contested their subordinate position within the Army Family; rather than simply serving the army, they demanded very nearly the opposite—that the army aid and support them.[3] They called for basic assistance in meeting the challenges of army life. And many sought to renegotiate the expectations that they perform unpaid labor for the army.

If the army wanted wives to counsel their husbands to reenlist, and if wives were to be part of an Army Family, then wives asked to be served equally by the army's growing welfare state.

THE WIVES of the volunteer era entered an institution bound by tradition, but in the midst of profound change. In 1975, just after the armed forces ended the draft and converted to the volunteer force, 920,000 women lived within the military as wives of military personnel. The majority of them made the army their home.[4] A small minority—about 18,000—were actually female soldiers in what the military called "dual service couples," but the overwhelming majority were civilian women.[5] They were young. Soldiers and their partners married earlier than their civilian peers, partly due to the youth required of soldiers, but also due to social mores and practices of men inclined to join the military. The median age of army wives rested in the twenty-year-old age group in contrast to civilian wives, whose median age reached forty years. Over 75 percent of military wives were under thirty years old.[6] One study of army wives showed that only 40 percent of them lived on post, while the rest lived off post, mostly in suburban areas.[7] They were recent imports from civilian life, with ties still binding them to communities outside the military.

While the army had difficulty recruiting men with high school diplomas, most army wives had completed high school. Forty percent of officers' wives held college degrees, with 5.4 percent finishing advanced degrees. Even those who hadn't finished college had pushed into postsecondary education, with nearly four-fifths pursuing some kind of formal education after high school.[8] "Today's young wife," a senior army wife observed in the mid-1970s, came "from a campus setting," in which she brought "with her dynamics which call for maximum community use. She belongs to a 'caring generation' and she wants to be . . . using her talents to the fullest."[9] Many did not know how army life might match their expectations.

Though fresh to the volunteer army, they entered a long history of women who had worked with and for the army. Indeed, armies have rarely gone to war without women. Soldiers' wives and companions followed armies along marches, into battles, and through defeated territories. They lived off the meager pay or bounties of their male companions, from the profits of plunder, or off the pay from the army itself for duties such as cleaning, nursing, cooking, laundry, or sewing.[10] In the American Revolutionary period, the

20,000 "women of the army," as they were known, performed just such duties. Some also handled weapons—carrying ammunition, loading muskets, and even firing them.[11] Military success necessitated women's work.

Despite the importance of women to armies, U.S. law beginning in 1847 banned soldiers with wives from enlisting. Still, the tradition of camp following continued, even through the Civil War.[12] Though the wives of officers were often spared the most arduous tasks of army support, they were still essential. They "served as nurse, seamstress, counselor, confidante, hostess, and friends of those in need, whether they were officers, enlisted personnel, wives or children, servants, regimental animals, or personal pets!"[13] The wives of enlisted men continued to perform the physical support labor of cooking, washing, mending, and sewing—if they were lucky, in the direct employ of the army. The labor of both types of women supported especially the remote Western outposts with few comforts and more than their share of sickness and danger. As two historians have described women's frontier life with the army, "Some died; many survived under harsh circumstances" but all helped "create in the isolated, male outposts of the West a vestige of civilization of the East."[14]

In the first half of twentieth century, although the U.S. military continued to discourage marriage, it was not uncommon among officers and senior career enlisted men. During the early part of the century, some received from Congress the first official "family support" of housing, access to dispensaries, and a subsistence allotment.[15] In the modern, twentieth-century army, wives' labor turned more toward social than material support. Officers' wives clubs performed benevolent functions for enlisted men, in addition to providing social and moral support for one another.

The number of army wives grew enormously during the massive mobilization of World War II.[16] The manpower exigencies—16 million men needed for the duration of the war—forced the military to alter its policies toward women "with" the army. Congress rescinded the ban on married enlisted military personnel in 1942, and millions of military wives materialized almost overnight: nearly half of all soldiers, sailors, airmen, and marines were married. Wives often had close contact with the army. With mandated family support from Congress, 40 percent of all military wives chose to accompany their soldiers on or near post. There, private support from the newly created Army Emergency Relief Fund, the United States Organization (USO), or the Red Cross provided additional short-term assistance of various kinds. Still, the army disrupted and complicated the lives of most wives, with resources such as pay and housing allowances falling short and stresses such as frequent relocation and deployment running high. Many wives, especially those with children, eventually moved in with relatives.[17] Some took paid jobs to augment their husbands' earnings. "Sockin' it in the savings," wrote one wife to her husband, "so's we'll have something when our sweet Daddy comes home."[18] A few career soldiers' wives formed "waiting wives" groups for mutual support until the war's end.[19]

In the postwar period, the large standing Cold War army with its peacetime draft continued to admit married men. The question was no longer whether there would be families but what to do with them. As the United States occupied territories after the war, the military made the decision to sponsor the families of officers and senior career enlisted men to foreign posts in Germany and Japan. As "unofficial ambassadors," army wives represented and fostered domestic order within the rebuilding societies of war-torn Germany and Japan.[20] But they were also central to an orderly American military. "Families presence overseas was thought to stabilize soldiers, boost troop morale, and keep skilled men in the service who might have left if separated from loved ones."[21] By mid-1946, "30,000 wives and children had crossed the Atlantic on former troop transports to be with husbands and fathers."[22] And by 1960, 327,446 wives and children made their home in Europe, and 462,504 total lived with husbands posted outside the United States.[23]

As the Cold War continued and the conflict in Vietnam escalated, military wives continued to increase in numbers, and by the 1960s, wives and children—all 3.73 million of them—outnumbered military personnel.[24] Though officially accepting of families, the military had not prepared to serve large numbers of wives and children. In 1955, the National Committee on Social Work in Defense Mobilization undertook a study of military families that alerted the military to brewing problems. A leading figure in welfare policy circles, Elizabeth Wickenden, warned military brass, "of all the social welfare problems confronting military community [*sic*] none are more difficult than those falling in the general area of child and family welfare." She acknowledged that the military was overwhelmed: "the military establishment, while prepared in terms of tradition and organization to care for its own personnel, has only recently become—on any large scale—a family affair." If the military did not catch up to the civilian world, which, since the New Deal, had "seen a vast elaboration in the civilian community of laws and agencies designed to safeguard, strengthen, and supplement the successful functioning of family life," both military families and military performance would be affected.[25]

Ignoring Wickenden's warning, the army continued to imagine army wives as the readers of Nancy Shea's *The Army Wife.* Marketed for years in various editions as the bible for women marrying soldiers, the book provided a touchstone for many army wives in the decades to come. Doris Durand, an army wife who later studied army families, remembered that when her husband joined the army in the 1960s, her "role was explicitly spelled out" in the book.[26] Shea infused her guide to military life with the domesticity permeating American life in the postwar period. The "army officer's wife is not only necessary, honorable, and good, but also the epitome of womanhood."[27] Like a middle-class, white wife from the pages of *Ladies Home Journal,* she "finds satisfaction and fulfillment in her home."[28] Incorporating civilian postwar domesticity, the army wife smoothed the rough edges of military life with the comforts of decoration, home management, and neighborly socialization. Shea's classic featured chapters covering army weddings, social events, and housekeeping ("if you can possibly afford it, buy sterling silver," and "never buy faddish furniture or something made for the particular house you are occupying. Remember, you may move tomorrow!").[29]

The ideal army wife provided more than June Cleaver-esque domestic service to her husband, however. She also supported his career—and the army—directly. "When a man enters the service," the magazine *Mrs. NCO* explained in 1969, "the government has gained not one, but two—the man and his wife." *Mrs. Lieutenant, Mrs. Field Grade,* and other advice magazines for army wives were likely to concur.[30] The army's own guide for officers' wives told a woman she, too, could be a "good soldier" for the army. Like a soldier, she would uphold the virtues of duty, honor, and country, and "in these things she will find enough of glamour, interest, satisfaction, life."[31] Army wifedom required full commitment, according to Shea. "Our husband's Army career," she explained, "will reflect his life at home, your attitude toward the Army, your interest in his duty, and your adaptability. It is your responsibility to create the right background for your husband and your ability to do so can make a subtle, but important contribution to his advancement."[32] Army wife Durand recalled that she "followed Shea's guidance by belonging to the Officer's Wives Club (OWC) and attending every commander's wife's coffee. I worked at the local military community thrift shop to help raise funds for military social welfare activities on base, and

prepared cookies and casseroles for unit gatherings." Durand, like most other army wives, endured enormous pressure to participate in army support activities. "I believed that if my husband were to be promoted, I had to do what the Army expected of me." And she was right, since soldiers' annual efficiency reports commonly included comments concerning a wife's achievements, or lack thereof.[33] As a result, Durand found herself totally enveloped in army life. "I was unquestionably part of . . . the 'two person career,' a pattern where formal and informal demands are placed on both members of a married couple, but only one spouse, generally the man, is employed by the institution."[34]

The "two-person career" provided essential physical and social support for a postwar army challenged by the presence of hundreds of thousands of army families for which it was not fully prepared. Though the army categorized soldiers' wives, like children, as "dependents" upon both soldier and the army, they were, as Shea observed, "independent dependents."[35] Within the confines of supporting husband and army, they had to show pluck, hard work, and organization. The army came to depend on army wives' commitment and labor for social and economic supports that it did not provide directly to soldiers and their families. The wives clubs were mobilized for aiding enlisted soldiers and their families, who lived at the margins of army life. They provided used clothes, housewares, and furniture. They organized babysitting and afterschool programs. For families with more extensive needs, they sent wives and children in the direction of the charities like the Red Cross or Army Emergency Services, or to chaplains, or medical professionals.[36] Army wives' clubs operated as both direct help and a clearinghouse for further information.

In the mid-1960s, both army wives and brass sought to rationalize and organize the essentially piecemeal, uneven volunteer programs created and run by army wives by establishing the first official army family support program, Army Community Service (ACS). ACS grew out of the work of activist volunteer wives like Joanne Patton, married to General George Patton III, the son of the famed World War II commander. A highly involved, dedicated volunteer, Patton viewed the creation of ACS as advancement for the army wife. Affiliation with an army-wide organization, with higher standards and professional employees, would, she hoped, help "professionalize the volunteer" and raise esteem for the essential, unpaid work of army wives.[37]

Patton and other well-placed officers' wives collaborated with army leaders whose work brought them into contact with military families.

Colonel S. G. Davis in the Office of the Surgeon General of the Army first proposed a comprehensive social welfare agency for the army in 1963. As the directorate for all of the army's medical services, the office's employees received thousands of referrals from families with problems each year. "Many social problems of military families," the surgeon general explained, "are referred to medical channels for lack of an appropriate Community Service Facility." Working with the director of Army Morale, Welfare and Recreation, the office recommended that the Department of the Army integrate and organize the various social welfare operations at posts around the world, and then hire professionals and create a social work agency run from the Office of the Deputy Chief of Staff for Personnel (ODCSPER). "The need for sound planning and professional guidance in the area of meeting the complex social needs of military families is acute," the colonel explained.[38]

The surgeon general cast the effort to create an army wide social welfare program for families as part of the long tradition of "an officer's responsibilities towards his men."[39] But ACS actually partook of the tradition of officers' wives caring for soldiers and their families, and "the volunteer participation of dependents was the heart of this particular program."[40] Army Regulation 608–1, which created the ACS program in 1965, explicitly outlined the crucial role of volunteer wives. "The foundation of an effective ACS Program," the army explained to commanders, "is a volunteer corps composed primarily of Army wives." Commanders were ordered to "actively encourage the recruitment, training, use and retention" of volunteers.[41] And a literal small army of volunteer women constituted the backbone of the ACS program from the beginning, transferring the work they already performed individually and as small groups on individual posts to an army-wide agency. By 1979, the army noted of ACS that "5,667 volunteers (plus 190 volunteers in Child Support Services) . . . donated a combined total of 791,523 recorded hours of services to 162 ACS-sponsored community projects." Three years later, in fiscal year 1983, the army relied upon 7,822 volunteers, the vast majority of whom were military wives, to staff ACS. They donated a staggering collective 1,827,451 hours of their labor to the army.[42]

Without the wife volunteers, the army's ACS program could not have functioned. Though army wives worked both with and under the supervision of paid professionals, mostly social workers, the wives' womanpower dwarfed the professionals'. The total paid staff for ACS in 1983 consisted of 985 employees, less than one-seventh of the number of volunteers.[43] The army occasionally acknowledged the economic value of an army organization run mostly by unpaid volunteers. "At one of our larger army installations, with a total population (military, civilian, retirees and dependents) of 187,000," ACS reported, "100 separate volunteers" made a collective "dollar value . . . contribution" of approximately $90,399 per year.[44] Had ACS extrapolated from that example the total dollar value provided by the more than 7,000 volunteers in 1982, the result would have been an astounding $6,329,000 in services that army wives provided for free to the army.

Valuable voluntary labor gave pride to many army wives. Joanne Patton reported with evident satisfaction to a national social work convention that the ACS volunteer operated as "the central figure upon whose numbers and efficiency . . . [ACS] almost entirely depend[ed]."[45] The army created an "ACS volunteer Awards Program" including an "ACS pin" and "ACS year guards" that could be attached to ACS volunteer uniforms, both of which acknowledged women's service and fostered pride among volunteers, like the awards and decorations of soldiers.[46] And many women proudly attached their year guards to their khaki smocks, attesting to their many years of service.[47]

As ACS developed in the 1970s, army wives performed increasingly important tasks for the army. No longer confined to handing out used pots and pans though the "lending closet" or providing reliable referral services for families in need, they volunteered to support vital direct services for families. ACS volunteers worked alongside professionals in anti–domestic violence and child abuse programs, child care programs, financial counseling and literacy programs, and programs for disabled children and other family members.[48] As the frontline workers in the army's organized social welfare programs, army wife volunteers made a difference in the everyday lives of hundreds of thousands of soldiers and their family members. They were poised, even in the eyes of army leadership, "more than any other group, except perhaps commanders, to increase the career satisfaction and influence career retention."[49] In the early 1970s, Joanne Patton proposed that the army sponsor social work education for ACS volunteers, encouraging them to truly professionalize their voluntary activities.[50] She did not want the army wife volunteer "to relinquish her role as a program innovator and activist to her professional colleagues," but rather to assume the mantle of professional volunteer.[51]

Though the army had begun to formally recognize the importance of volunteer wives, some army wives of the 1970s increasingly questioned the expectations placed upon them. Even in Patton's most professionalized slant on voluntarism, volunteer work still smacked of Nancy Shea's guide and remained rooted in the traditions of domesticity and support for husband and the army.[52] There was little question that the army still preferred a traditional, volunteer wife. Scholars hired by the military in the 1970s to study wives explained that from the military's perspective, the "most desirable [role] . . . for the military wife to adhere to" was "the woman who fully participates in the duties and activities surrounding her husband's formal occupation. She . . . responds to the organization's needs rather than to her own personal or family needs."[53] That kind of sacrifice had made the postwar army a much better place for the hundreds of thousands of families joining its ranks. But for the many army wives of the coming volunteer era—more numerous, younger, and of a different generation—the role of the army wife, both at home and with the army, looked different.

CAROLYN BECRAFT helped construct the new role for the army wife. Unlike most army wives, she had entered the army as an officer. After graduating from the University of North Dakota, she joined the army for five and a half years, serving as the head dietician in a 1,000-bed army hospital and reaching the rank of captain. In 1969, she became one half of one of the new "dual military career" couples, marrying a fellow army officer. In 1971, shortly after rising to the rank of captain, she found herself pregnant. The army offered to let her remain in service, but with a hitch; following its discriminatory rules for female soldiers in place until 1973, it imposed a terrible choice: as a female soldier, she could not remain in the army with a child unless she signed over official legal custody of her child to her husband, who at the time was doing a tour in Vietnam. She chose instead to quit her army career, and she began a new life as a woman with, rather than in, the army. She gained a new vantage point on the army and army wives.

After several years stateside, she and her child accompanied her husband to Germany for three years, where she learned a great deal about the trials of being an army wife. In 1978, *Time* magazine reported on the "the tough fight in West Germany," where "G.I.'s with families" were the "worst off" of all soldiers. That year, Congress was still debating expanding junior enlisted travel benefits, and so "the army still d[id] not pay transportation costs and living allowances nor d[id] it provide them with low-cost housing." The results were disastrous, *Time* reported: "as many as 70% of the young G.I.s are married and thousands of them are living in poverty."[54] A young army wife interviewed by *Time* in a follow-up story in 1980 described how she had to "wash all our clothes by hand because the base launderette is too expensive." Despite the hardship, she wanted to remain in West Germany. She just wanted more assistance from the army.[55]

Families who remained stateside found challenges similar to their peers in Europe. In the mid-1970s, the difficulties boiled over into the pages of *Army Times*, creating a forum for army wives' grievances. Letters to the editor, for example, began to openly criticize the army's lack of respect for wives and families. In 1976, one wife writing under the name "Concerned" wrote about "what so many at Fort Hood [Texas] have felt [about army leadership]. . . . Are families such nonentities that their needs are just relegated to the bottom of the heap?" She questioned whether army leaders understood "the tensions caused by these less-than-ideal conditions" for families. Another army wife from Fort Benning, Georgia, calling herself "Disgusted," concluded that military apathy meant her family had suffered "the complete loss of family life and the end of a promising career."[56] Another wrote to question the army's commitment to its own motto: "I've been hearing for years how the Army 'takes care of its own' and it's about time steps were taken to live up to that phrase."[57]

Social and economic issues assumed primacy for army wives. One described her struggles upon her husband's deployment: "When he left unexpectedly, I found myself in a motel, in an unfamiliar town, waiting two more months before I could move into our newly purchased home—with three babies still in diapers, a new puppy that Daddy had bought them, emotional turmoil, and physical exhaustion."[58] While this army wife could afford to purchase a home, most could not. In fact, with quickly rising inflation, young soldiers at the bottom of the pay scale struggled to meet the needs of their families. The army knew enough of the struggle to embark upon a campaign of money management for its lower enlisted personnel. At Fort Eustis, Virginia, the "How to Make Ends Meet" fact sheet covered the basics of how to "live within our incomes." "Young couples," it explained, "find it hard to come out even, both in the Army and out, unless they made a budget and make their dollars count."[59] The army directed soldiers and their wives to low-cost housing where rent comprised "one-fourth of soldier's income." The waiting list, though, was two years.[60] The army also advised soldiers and their families to reduce their food costs by shopping only after meals. "When you're hungry," the army explained, "you tend to buy more than you really need." The literature also recommended carpooling to "save gasoline money."[61]

Money problems left many young soldiers and their wives short well before the end of the month, and as a result, many of them were plagued by indebtedness. Some entered the military with debt and then, trying to survive with a family on a relatively low income, took on more debt. Others went into debt after enlisting. The army studied its soldiers' financial problems in the late 1970s, conducting surveys at one of the army's largest basic training posts, Fort Leonard Wood, Missouri, where it could research a range of ranks. Over one-fourth of soldiers surveyed were in debt, owing an average of about $2,200 each. Married soldiers owed greater debt, with an average of nearly $3,400 each. Most owed money not on stereos, TVs, or other consumer goods to make life comfortable, but on the basics. They had debts to banks, credit unions, and finance companies—mostly car finance companies like GMAC—for house or car loans. Almost 30 percent of the debt derived from other high costs of living—medical bills, overdue rent and utility bills, school loans, back alimony payments to previous wives, or legal fees surrounding divorce or suits. The army concluded that these soldiers' families had "debts in sufficient amounts, which could pose significant hardships if they were to be paid from military income alone." It created a debt liquidation program to help guide soldiers through bankruptcy or other loan reduction programs.[62] Young, married, and trying to make ends meet at isolated posts made army wives' existence stressful.

As a participant in and observer of army wives' lives, Becraft registered these widespread economic difficulties, but also sensed a broader dissatisfaction among the women, even the more privileged wives of officers like herself. She felt she was experiencing second-class treatment as a new army wife, in which her husband had to sign a slew of forms giving her permission to take care of family finances, their child, and to have use of army facilities. Undertaking her master's thesis (from afar) at the University of Southern California, she made her army wife peers in Germany the focus of her research.[63]

Like many young, educated women of the era, Becraft was familiar with the women's movement. By the mid-1970s, the National Organization for Women (NOW) was nearly a decade old, and its Legal Defense Fund had brought women's equality before the courts and Congress, challenging a raft of gender-specific practices in education, employment, and government. The media in the 1970s covered the rise of feminism—indeed feminists had their own media outlets like Gloria Steinem's *Ms.* magazine. Becraft set out to understand the effects of the movement—if any—on the wives of army officers.

By that time, several observers had concluded, "overall, military wives have demonstrated minimal involvement with the Women's Movement."[64] Two scholars in the feminist journal *Signs* speculated about the relative unpopularity of feminism among army wives. They hazarded that the relative isolation on army posts where "military services . . . accommodate their every need" rendered army wives "relatively unavailable for recruitment to a [feminist] movement."[65] Hierarchy and compulsion characteristic of military life seemed to tamp down feminism's appeal, at least open support of the movement, especially among young wives who could not afford to "behave more independently."[66] As one woman reminded them, "Being a military wife one must be most careful when expressing an opinion because the outcome can be unhappy results for the husband."[67] The power of the Nancy Shea ideal of the army wife remained significant, and mitigated against entertaining or engaging in feminist action.[68]

Though feminism faced obstacles among army wives, by the mid-1970s the women's movement had begun to influence some. *Army Times* featured columns and letters to the editor about feminism and "women's lib." Not unlike civilian women, the more educated and middle-class among army wives were more likely to espouse ideas of the women's movement. "Officers' wives," one author explained, "parallel more closely the civilian feminist attitudes." On the other hand, "the older, unemployed women who hold the more traditional orientations toward women's roles" were unlikely to endorse any feminist ideas.[69]

Capturing a definitive snapshot of the women's movement's effects on army wives proved elusive, as it did in the civilian world, since so many women (and men) held differing understandings of feminism. Many military wives endorsed the women's movement when they considered its calls for equity in economic terms and the labor market. Military officers' wives who were asked to rate their support for the women's movement cited equal pay for equal work as the "central and common point of positive evaluation, personal significance, and explicit movement support."[70] Indeed, for many military wives, equal pay for equal work represented the sum total of their understanding of feminism.[71]

Some military wives found the social and cultural goals of feminism, as they understood them, to be unappealing, however. "Most commonly rejected were putative tendencies to define self as important (selfish), to sacrifice children, to be overly sensitive to society's view of women, and to adopt the 'hate and blame men attitude.'" By the mid-to-late 1970s, with the rise of an active antifeminist movement, including the influential Phyllis Schlafly's STOP ERA (the Equal Rights Amendment) campaign, negative portrayals of feminism emphasizing such themes abounded. Some military wives reported as "objectionable" feminism's purported support for "'bra burning,' 'the rush to do too much too fast,' and 'causing unrest in women who previously enjoyed being housewives.'"[72]

The sense that feminism upset the calm waters of military wifedom did indeed trouble some army wives, even some of the most active achievers like ACS leader Joanne Patton. Patton, like other civilians critical of feminists, expressed the sense that the "Women's Liberation Movement today" portrayed "the image of the housewife-community volunteer" as "archaic." With NOW's emphasis on women's employment and feminists' critique of patriarchal family structures and roles, some women who worked inside the home as mothers or outside the paid labor market as volunteers did not find a message that resonated with their desires. They might even have felt the NOW agenda insulted them. Joanne Patton explained that an army wife trying to achieve a more "professional" volunteer status might wonder what feminism meant for her. When the 1973 "NOW GOALS" defined "traditional service-oriented volunteerism directed at alleviating social ills as an on-going *exploitation of women's labors*," it seemed to reject their actions as illegitimate. For Patton, army wives' voluntarism spelled achievement and pride, "practicing women's lib in its most constructive and non-militant form," as she quoted admiringly from a magazine article about women's voluntary work.[73] If army wives perceived feminism as denigrating their roles as caregivers for home or for the army, they would not gravitate toward it, especially if they engaged willingly in such work.

Still, even Patton understood and perhaps endorsed certain aspects of feminism. At the very least she recognized that that those who hoped to help both army wives and the army itself must reckon with the influence of the women's movement. "One must in fairness acknowledge . . . Women's Liberation's . . . strong influence on the young Army wife—and thus the potential ACS volunteer—who is joining us during these years." Shea's model of "delicate habits and modest manners," she admitted, "could hardly be said to describe with justice the young, well-educated Army wife of 1973."

Even more traditional army wives now wanted to function "in positions of 'real importance,' not just in 'supportive roles.'"[74]

Many wives of all ages pointed to the "roles of real importance" that army wives had always played and their resonance with feminism. Given their husbands' long and unpredictable hours, their deployments, and many moves, they were often independent and accomplished. They ran their households solo for long stretches. In considering their own attitudes toward their roles, some wives reminded scholars, "Tinker, tailor, merchant, nurse, cook, financial manager, gardener, father, mother . . . I feel I have to do it all."[75] The army wife operated in a paradoxical relationship to autonomy and power: "The military wife has been expected to place her husband's and the military's needs before her own or those of her children. Ironically, the military system simultaneously requires an independent, self-sustaining, liberated woman if it is to accomplish its own mission most efficiently."[76] An army wife version of feminism, if there could be said to be one, centered less on political, social, and cultural feminism and more on liberal individual feminism's economic planks. It featured less of a critique of patriarchy, family roles, and service and more celebration of independence, coupled with advocacy for voice and recognition for women in a military context. It did not identify as feminism per se.

Carolyn Becraft's study confirmed a similar portrait of army wives' views of themselves and their roles with the army. Her survey of approximately eighty army officers' wives in Germany revealed the mixed emotions army wives held toward the army, feminism, and their changing place within the army. Many women felt as disillusioned over the army's treatment of them as she did. In particular they perceived that they were locked out of productive engagement with the army on their own terms—unable to use their education and expertise to lead the army to better treatment of wives and families. Many of the wives wondered how to build an independent and fulfilling life for themselves and their family amidst the demands of army life.[77]

Becraft's findings were echoed in additional venues, suggesting a wider recalibration of traditional roles and the realities they encountered. "One is not an individual when married in the service, only an extension of one's husband," one army wife explained. "But being an adult, I like to be responsible for my own doings."[78] Another reported this as a trend, with "more and more military wives . . . seeking their own identity."[79] The wife of an army colonel explained how she was "ignoring her obligations at teas and receptions," instead spending her time "very aggressively seeking changes in discriminatory on-base housing patterns" for nonwhites. Another had embarked on a campaign against strict codes of dress for army wives on post.[80] Some wives' rejection of their traditional roles and embrace of greater activism forced base commanders to order "'rap groups' in response to increased restlessness manifested by wives and/or in anticipation of such restlessness."[81] "Wives," one scholar concluded, "are no longer responding to orders from the top."[82] An editorial by army wife Lucy McLean from Fort Riley, Kansas, pushed wives to seize power for themselves. She urged wives to take matters into their own hands to solve the many problems facing army families. She argued for "an organization composed solely of military dependents, the U.S. Army Dependents Association," that would include all dependents, regardless of rank, and whose purpose would be to educate and agitate. "It is time," she summed up, "that the dependent becomes more independent and is given the opportunity to use, in some measure, his or her rights."[83]

Carolyn Becraft had concluded the same after finishing her study. When, to her surprise, the commanding general's wife at the post in Baumholder asked her to present her findings to the OWC, Becraft recommended creating an organization specifically to address wives' questions and dissatisfaction, one outside the confines of the "wives' clubs." As a model of autonomous action she offered the Junior League, a national women's organization that grew out of the late nineteenth- and early twentieth-century women's club movement, one whose educated, upper-class character might appeal to officers' wives. The Junior League operated independently for the causes its members felt were important. By the 1970s, these included women's political participation and action, generally speaking. Junior League members, not unlike army officers' wives, balanced gender and class propriety and traditionalism with independence and action. Though Becraft's Junior League suggestion hardly seemed radical, within the constricted army setting and against the press of long-held tradition, the claim to more autonomy was bold. To her astonishment, the commanding general's wife and the audience proved receptive.

BECRAFT'S POSITIVE reception signaled change. In 1980, she moved back to the United States when her husband was posted to Washington, DC, and there she met an organized group of wives already engaged in the effort to reform the roles of army wives—the venerable Army Officers' Wives' Club of the Greater Washington Area (AOWCGWA). The leaders of the effort were married to senior officers posted in Washington, DC, mostly at Fort Myers or the Pentagon. Some, like the longtime professional volunteer advocate Joanne Patton, had married generals. Other generals' wives included Joyce Ott and Barbara Schneider, women with decades of intimate experience with the army. Most were a bit younger and wed to colonels, but they had all lived the army life for many years.[84] The women were college-educated and some had their own careers.[85] Bettie Stieger's career, for example, arguably outshone her husband's army career. She worked as a top executive at a pioneering information technology company in Virginia.[86] In roles of influence and responsibility, the officers' wives had become increasingly aware of the challenges facing not only themselves but also army wives and families in general. They felt a "need for a gathering of family members from all levels of the Army in order to communicate and discuss issues facing the Army family."[87]

In late 1979, the AOWCGWA found a modest sum to begin the process of planning for an army family gathering, with a one-day seminar that operated as a pilot project for the larger symposium they desired. Five months later, the club's board of directors voted to provide $3,000 for the creation of the first-ever Army Family Symposium, as they called it. The Association of the United States Army (AUSA), a private membership organization that followed army affairs, agreed to match the AOWCGWA funds, and cosponsor the symposium. The organizers, however, consisted solely of the army officers' wives in Washington. They sent out invitations to nominate delegates "to all wives clubs (Enlisted, NCO, and Officer's) throughout the world; all Brigade Commanders; all ACS chapters; all AUSA . . . ; and Army Chaplains offices." Delegates had to pay their way to the conference and a $70 registration fee. This was a very high price for many potential delegates, especially wives of enlisted personnel, but the club's modest budget would not allow for a cheaper rate.[88] Carolyn Becraft, who could not afford the registration fee, found a less expensive way to participate. She took a position as an official facilitator at the symposium, a job for which the fee fell to $10.[89]

In October of 1980, the Army Family Symposium got underway, designed, led, and facilitated by army wives who determined the agenda, the debates, and the recommendations that emerged.[90] Approximately 200 delegates from various army wives' organizations around the world participated, with about two-thirds representing officers' wives and one-third enlisted wives.[91]

They recruited the highest levels of army leadership to participate. Through their connections with one another and through their influence over their husbands, they had worked the back channels to secure the attendance of army leaders. The wife of the chief of staff of the army (CSA), Carol Meyer, smoothed the way for the symposium by hosting a tea at her house for symposium organizers, a tea at which her husband, General Edward "Shy" Meyer, stopped by. It signaled an unofficial blessing by Meyer, and he agreed not only to send army staff to the event, but also to give the opening remarks himself.[92]

The symposium results proved to be a watershed in the army's relationship to wives and families by facilitating two revolutions in the army's dealings with families: first, recognition that army wives constituted neither passive nor dependent extensions of their husbands or the army itself; and second, creation of concrete services to support wives and children. Gaining recognition of their independence meant chipping away at the centuries-old role of women "with" the army and its most recent incarnation, the decades-old Nancy Shea "two-for-one" model of the army wife. "Women," the delegates informed the army that day, "are asking that there be a reappraisal of their role in the military community." For too long, they had suffered "second-class citizenship," subject to the capricious demands of military life with "few effective avenues by which . . . [to] participate in those decisions that affect them and their families." Relocations, changes in work shifts, deployments—all with little notice or sensitivity to the impact on wives and families—left wives feeling "powerless to make decisions." The army's official nomenclature for them—"dependents"—accentuated this sense of impotence, and they demanded instead the terms "family members" or "spouses."[93]

To augment their independence from the army, the symposium delegates challenged the army to operate within "a reciprocal relationship . . . between the Army and the families of its members."[94] The army could not expect acceptance from wives without also hearing their needs and ideas. The most fundamental goal of the symposium was finding a voice, and having that voice heard. Above all army wives sought an "opportunity to be heard by and to hear from [the] official Army."[95] In a hierarchical institution, wives needed "*two-way* communication," even though there was little precedent for it.[96] Discussion of hierarchy foregrounded the tension-filled and unequal relationships that normally existed between army wives and families and the army.

The delegates balanced their calls for autonomy with affirmations of their alignment with the army and their desire for participation, not rebellion. The leaders and most of the attendees were, after all, longtime army officers' wives practiced in the arts of protocol. Shrewdly positioning themselves—as most of them were—as patriotic, pro-army wives, they invoked a "spirit of cooperation," and added that they were hopeful that "the goals and objectives of both the Army and the family will be achieved."[97] The polite, respectful tone affirmed the army as a valuable institution, but required that wives and families be accorded the same esteem. As evidence of their value, the women offered themselves as "dedicated, caring, intelligent delegates who had done their homework." They also emphasized their representativeness, reminding army observers that they did not come as individuals, but as representatives of their widely varied peers from posts and clubs around the world. Likewise, the issues they brought to discuss did not dip to the "personal or petty," but rather represented generally observed patterns of problems and unmet needs among all wives.[98]

Wives' claims of unmet needs served as the basis for the second significant result of the Army Family Symposium—the demand that the army create programs to meet wives' and children's needs. Delegates at the symposium asked not how they could care for the army, but whether the army of the volunteer era had met its promise to "take care of its own." Delegates identified twelve areas in which army families had struggled, and the army had not done enough to help. Many concerned basic financial difficulties: compensation for service personnel and allowances for families were too low; medical care copayments were too expensive; and the army provided no dental care so army families who could not afford totally private care did without. Other concerns centered on quality of life issues. Women described inadequate and rundown housing stock. They told stories of poor care from barely qualified physicians. They expressed concern over lack of resources in Department of Defense (DoD) schools and the resulting declining quality of teachers for their children.[99]

Delegates voiced repeated concerns that families simply were not given the support necessary to withstand the unusual pressures of military life. They outlined the many problems, for example, that resulted from sudden reassignment of soldiers to new installations. Wives who already had to do much single parenting were ripped out of social networks they relied upon for help with child care and daily socialization. Wives and families arrived at new installations with little or no orientation, no effective buddy or sponsor program, and no description of the family services (if any) available to them or their children on the new base. Wives who wanted careers or an education, meanwhile, were torn from their jobs and classes repeatedly, making it virtually impossible to develop a meaningful professional life, much less earn needed money.

Deployments produced similar stress, also unattended to by the army. Delegates enumerated a litany of problems exacerbated by deployments: "alcoholism, drug abuse, divorce, spouse abuse, delinquency, intergeneration conflicts, and child abuse." These problems were frequently overlooked because of "a serious shortage of professional personnel available." Even where the services were available, wives were "often reluctant to use available services because of fear that such use will reflect adversely on the service member's efficiency report." The army had done little, the delegates noted, to assure army families and soldiers that using mental health services would not harm a soldier's record.[100] Deployment also underscored the acute need for child care services. When a father left for months during deployment, even nonemployed wives needed child care to take care of provisioning, medical appointments, and other necessities. Parents who lived in a dual military career family or were both employed were especially desperate for quality, reliable, flexible child care.

This last issue, spousal employment, emerged multiple times as a conundrum during the symposium. Though not all wives worked or wanted to work, the question of paid employment went to the heart of wives' dissatisfaction over the army's expectations that they play the traditional army wife role: wives working for pay could not easily volunteer for unpaid labor for the army. The call for the army to recognize wives' needs and desire for employment also constituted a call for the army to quit relying on—even expecting—voluntary labor from women. Even women who did not work for pay outside their home might not want the army to demand their labor as part of the two-for-one deal. The question of women's employment underscored the army wives' fundamental case at the symposium: "the Army spouse is an individual and not an extension of the service member."[101]

The portrait of army wives' voluntary labor in the late 1970s revealed new patterns. Among officers' wives, 45 percent still volunteered for the army, and nearly a quarter volunteered in more than one venue. Those who lived on post were more likely to volunteer than those who lived off post, embedded in more distant communities. Without data, no one could know how many enlisted wives volunteered, though the numbers were undoubtedly lower. Enlisted wives were likely to be younger, and women with young children proved least likely to volunteer. Women with children in school or out of the house had more time and energy for volunteer work.[102]

Yet even those army wives who chose to volunteer increasingly expressed some dissatisfaction. Some of this derived from the mismatch between the education and skills of new army wives and the limits of voluntary activities. Fewer than 14 percent of officers' wives actually used their formal education in their work as volunteers.[103] In an increasingly social-service-providing ACS, professionals were more likely to hold the degrees and perform the hands-on counseling and assistance services, while wife volunteers "supported them." Joanne Patton bemoaned the declining voluntarism she observed as a result of the gap.[104] Some ACS volunteers watched the professionals with dismay, one offering, "This year's work with ACS has suddenly made me dissatisfied with myself. . . . How much more satisfying it could be if I were properly educated."[105] Still others simply resented the expectation that they should volunteer. An *Army Times* story on "service slights" against wives reported a revolt against volunteer expectations. "No longer are all military wives content just to raise children, stay at home, and perform volunteer work."[106]

The necessity and opportunity for paid employment among army wives underscored voluntarism's flawed premises and fueled resentment over volunteer expectations. A study of military wives by an employee at the Bureau of Labor Statistics (BLS) outlined sources of the change. At the beginning of the 1970s, wives of military personnel were markedly less likely to labor outside of the home than the wives of civilians, in keeping with the pressure to perform domestic and volunteer labor. Less than a third worked in paid employment. Over the course of the decade, however, labor force participation among the wives of military personnel "skyrocketed." By 1979, military wives' labor force participation rate had increased by 20 percent, reaching 50 percent of all military wives, a proportion equal to civilian wives.[107]

Officers' wives were lured into the labor market by many of the same opportunities that lured middle- and upper-middle-class civilians. Military wives with high levels of education and skill, the BLS reported, "are apparently hesitant to limit themselves to traditional volunteer work when they can earn money in private enterprise."[108] Those who worked took jobs in "educational institutions (33%), medical services (21%), government (12%), or retail and wholesale trades (11%), or self-employ[ment] (10%)." Not unlike army wives of the nineteenth century, "half of those who were employed by the government worked for the Army." Many, in fact, worked as professional social workers or nurses in army facilities.[109] Still, officers' wives—indeed all wives of husbands with higher ranks—chose paid employment less often than their enlisted sisters; the proportion of employed wives declined as the rank of their husbands rose.[110] As in civilian life, women married to men of higher incomes and means were more likely to stay out of the labor market.

Among army wives who worked outside the home, personal growth and achievement often came in second to the need for financial security, just as it did in civilian life. Officers' wives reported working to improve their already stable standard of living, and wives of young enlisted men took jobs "primarily to meet basic living expenses."[111] Families needed more resources in the late 1970s, as increasing inflation eroded military pay raises to some degree and forced many wives into the labor force.[112] Army wives, the BLS found, were even more crucial to protecting their families' finances than civilian wives, on average. For the wives of lower-paid enlisted men especially, their wages "contribute[d] a larger proportion of their families' income than do their civilian counterparts."[113] Army wives also carried the burden of a higher likelihood of widowhood than civilian women, and being "thrust into the role of primary breadwinner." Some women said they worked to make sure they were skilled and financially secure in the event of tragedy.[114]

Army wives of all ranks, not just officers' wives, worked at a variety of jobs similar to their civilian counterparts. Most worked clerical jobs as secretaries, then the number one women's occupation in the nation. Many others worked in professional-technical or service jobs, including a variety of paraprofessional aide and assistant jobs. They also took jobs in stores and restaurants.[115] Wives who had higher educations, and wives who lived in or near major metropolitan areas—the minority, to be sure—had an easier time finding work than their less educated or more geographically isolated peers.[116]

But even those army wives who had college degrees or the good fortune to live near a city nevertheless faced enormous difficulties in sustaining steady employment, much less making upward progress on the career ladder. The peripatetic life of the soldier meant leaving jobs behind over and over. An employment survey of army officer's wives revealed that over half had lived at their present location for less than one full year. Almost half of them had actually just moved within the preceding three months, as army families relocated regularly.[117] Army wives told stories of employers who turned them down once they learned they were married to soldiers because of their roving lifestyle. They found it difficult to finish occupational certifications or degree programs because of frequent relocations and the residence requirements for tuition at many schools.[118] Even those who managed to complete certifications and degrees found "that state employment qualifications and requirements were not uniform," so they faced the need to requalify with each move. Above all, the frequent transfers meant that army wives often restarted at the bottom rung of the career ladder at each new post. They lost seniority, fringe benefits, and the possibilities for advancement.[119]

Economically, the results were grave. Unemployment among army wives reached heights above those of civilian women. They suffered unemployment rates ten points higher than women not married to military personnel. In 1978, unemployment among military wives reached nearly 20 percent.[120] The salaries for many wives, especially the wives of enlisted men, also fell "substantially below those of civilians." For enlisted wives, lower education and skill levels left them restarting relatively low-paid jobs in the pink-collar ghetto—clerical work, services, or retail. There was no room to rise up the relatively paltry pay scale in these sectors.[121]

Many army wives felt that the army's attitude toward their employment made for more difficulties. As one scholar summarized the situation, "Although the economic need of families, especially in the lower pay grades, is readily apparent, the recognition of any military wife's need to work to supplement the husband's income has been, for the most part, unrecognized by the military."[122] Working army wives reported negative perceptions about themselves from the army. They felt the army was "viewing wives in general as 'problems.'"[123] The pressure to volunteer rather than work for pay remained significant. The army wife advice guides of the era still endorsed the more traditional Nancy Shea-esque role of the army wife, either refusing to endorse or merely ignoring work outside the home. As a result, an amazing 18.6 percent of full-time employed army wives still made time for unpaid volunteer labor for the army. And 55 percent of part-time workers—more than even the nonemployed wives—made the time for army volunteering.[124] But resentment often resulted. Wives who either worked or wanted to work viewed the army as "a constraint to their involvement in the work world." One fed-up navy wife pledged to resist: "No one can convince me it's my duty to make layettes for Navy Relief when I need to work to help make our own house payments."[125]

Army wives at the symposium took a slightly more diplomatic tone than their navy sisters, but they nevertheless proposed that the army adopt a new attitude about wife employment. They asked that the army create " 'Job Opportunity Centers' for civilian spouses" that could offer job counseling and a list of employment opportunities in the area.[126] They even stepped into broader military manning policy, asking that the army consider spouses when making decisions about manpower, duty stations, and personnel tempo. "Assignment policies," the women suggested, should take into account "spouses' career, [and] educational needs."[127] They confronted head on the still powerful ideal of army wife voluntary labor. The army, they explained, needed to eliminate once and for all the "semiofficial pressure to volunteer." In the place of volunteers, the army would need to hire paid professionals—an actual staff.[128] Proposals to support army wives' paid employment asked the army not only to reject the tradition of "two-for-one" soldier and wife, but also acknowledge and facilitate the individual, separate achievement of army wives as central to the well-being of the soldier's family, and hence the army itself.

Having raised concerns regarding their status in the army and their needs for support, army wives followed up with a second symposium, this time organized by Carolyn Becraft herself along with Emily Cato, another officer's wife. The success of the second begat a third symposium, and in 1984 they convinced the army to sponsor the process itself, a sponsorship that continues to this day. Sitting around Becraft's kitchen table, Becraft and Cato, joined by peer Bunny Smith, drew up plans for the process still used by the army today. They dubbed it the Army Family Action Plan (AFAP).[129] The AFAP mandated an annual army-wide review process to determine family needs and how to meet them. Local installations sponsored family symposia at which local members of the community raised problems and concerns, and outlined policy goals to address them.[130] By 1987, 270,000 army family members were attending them.[131] After the local meetings, installations commanders, along with their newly created local Family Liaison Office (FLO), would then review the problems and policy goals to see which could be remedied on post, and which required action at the level of the Department of the Army. Department of the Army leaders would themselves then meet each year for their own family symposium, along with representatives from various wives' groups and the army family bureaucracy, and determine which problems to address and how. Final recommendations requiring new law and appropriations were forwarded to Congress as formal army requests.

Army wives gained greater voice and power as the army began to extend its social welfare apparatus directly to wives and families. For the first time, the army created permanent administrative structures designated for army family programs and policies.[132] The army organized a FLO within ODCSPER, then headed by General Maxwell Thurman. The army charged this initially small, overburdened four-person administrative unit with a huge array of tasks. These included being an "army proponent for family program resources and plans," an "umbrella agency to integrate and unify family helping services and volunteer organizations," coordinating "Army family program research" plans, the "development of policy," as well as outreach and public relations to make families aware of programs that did exist.[133] The army also established a Community and Family Support Center that handled program implementation.

Army wives and children receive their post identification cards from family liaison officers, photographed as part of the army's outreach effort to spouses. Ca. 1983. Courtesy of Harriet Rice Photograph Collection, U.S. Army Heritage and Education Center, Carlisle, PA.

The institutional power of wives spurred tangible enhancements to the social welfare of army wives and children. In 1983, General John A. Wickham Jr., became CSA. In this role he was responsible for all aspects of the internal workings of the army. However, he placed the problems of army families "up front" in his vision for the service.[134] His "Army Family White Paper" laid out this commitment, and in 1984 funding for army family programs began to grow enormously. "For the first time, resources were programmed specifically for many family programs designated as high-cost/high payoff."[135] Over the next ten years, 200 policy issues went through the AFAP process and produced new rules, offices, and laws, all of which translated into new programs for army families.[136] These included major programs identified by wives as crucial from the beginning of the process: housing, wives' employment, and child care. It also included a collection of counseling, acclimation, and orientation programs to keep families informed and safe.[137]

THE ACTIVISM of army wives transformed the relationship between the army and the wives of soldiers. And it spurred what would become the largest growth in the army's history of social programs for soldiers, their wives, and their families. The active army wives of the late 1970s and early 1980s disputed the assumption that wives had to work solely for the good of the army. Instead, they voiced the reverse demand: that the army work for the good of army wives and families. Little wonder then that Carolyn Becraft looked back on her work with army wives with pride. After her experiences with the Army Family Symposium and the AFAP, Becraft eventually went on to work for the Pentagon on behalf of family issues from 1993 until 2001. She took her first position as deputy assistant secretary of defense for military and community support—the Pentagon-wide post responsible for families. And in 1998, she became assistant secretary of the navy for manpower and reserve affairs—the effective head of all navy personnel issues. Despite the many achievements of her august career, she cited as her single greatest achievement the plan she and her army wife peers crafted over her kitchen table, the AFAP. It forced the army into an annual dialog and negotiation with wives, and altered the way that the army addressed the wives of its soldiers.[138]

As important as it was, that moment of transformation did not guarantee the power of army wives nor instantiate their exact vision. There were still significant sources of resistance in the army to both the nontraditional army wives and their autonomy. Even General Wickham's 1983 "Army Family White Paper," heralded as a groundbreaking recognition of the importance of soldiers' wives and children, expressed ambiguity. On the one hand, it affirmed the "equal" status that wives had demanded in the family symposia by speaking of "a partnership between the Army and the Army Family." It also clearly stated that the army valued the families of soldiers and would work to recognize and serve some of their needs. But on the other hand, though the army pledged to "develop a sense of community; and strengthen the mutually reinforcing bonds between the Army and its families," it remained unclear what "bond strengthening meant." In a document that articulated no official acknowledgment of wives' autonomy or their voice, it might mean bending wives to the army rather than the other way around.[139]

In fact, as time went on, the army would resist and attempt to contain wives' influence. After issuing his white paper, General Wickham guided new army family programs toward conservative Christianity. With active guidance from a growing civilian and army evangelical community, new family programs shaded toward Christian right models of family life that resuscitated conservative "traditional" gender roles for women. In the 1990s, amidst the budget pressures of the post–Cold War drawdown and the growth of ideologies of independence and self-sufficiency across American life, army wives would find the army a decidedly reluctant partner in the Army Family. Defined in new ways, a version of the Nancy Shea army wife would rebound. In 1993 an *Army Times* article would warn: "Wives Still Hostage to Volunteerism."[140]

And there remained questions about whether the family programs demanded by women were accepted. If it wasn't enough that army wives had demanded voices and moved out of voluntary army support roles, they also demanded the army become, as James Webb had put it a few years earlier, "a babysitter," spending vital defense dollars not on training or weapons, but on services for families and, in particular, women. Wives' demands for paid personnel and material services for themselves and their children seemed to fan the fears of the late 1970s that the army had transformed into a feminized bastion of social welfare provision. Some commanders complained to evaluators about the new family programs, saying that they "served no useful military purpose" and even undermined military effectiveness. One commanding officer of the 1980s echoed the late 1970s fears of the "social welfare-ization" of the army: "Child care money is coming out of defense for babysitting," something the military had no business doing.[141] Throughout the 1980s, the army resisted, albeit unsuccessfully, congressional mandates "fencing" appropriated funds for use in family programs. The army preferred to have the money appropriated without stipulations that it be used solely for family support.[142] Queasiness over the new voice of women in the army coupled with suspicion of new family support programs continued to nurse ambivalence within the army about its social welfare programs.

6

Securing Christian Family Values

THE U.S. ARMY proclaimed 1984 as "The Year of the Family."[1] Following army customs, the newly hatched family administrative office, the Community and Family Support Center, garnered its own insignia and flag. Glossy brochures touted, "The Army Family—A Partnership," describing the "services for your family" on most army installations throughout the world.[2] A new series of advertisements aimed to retain career soldiers by promising, "It not getting any easier to be a soldier. But it is getting easier to be a soldier's family." The Year of the Family symbolized the rapid, massive, and historic growth in family support programs that characterized the 1980s. The army raised compensation, hired more support personnel, and constructed family housing. It built new child care centers and created a raft of military family support programs that ranged from counseling to after-school programs to a growing chaplain program. Between 1984 and 1989 the army developed a family social welfare apparatus costing well over $10 billion.[3] While the growth of the army family programs was fueled by the Reagan administration's recalibration of citizens and entitlements to favor the military, and by the successful demands of the army wives movement, it also gained support from a new constituency in the 1980s—Christian conservatives.

Beneath the new catchphrase and the secular policies of the army family programs a transformation in the army's conception of the "Army Family" was in progress. As the family programs multiplied, many of them fell under the influence of conservative evangelical Christian leaders who drove the rise of the religious right in the United States. Evangelical leaders such as

Dr. James C. Dobson of the influential Focus on Family established relationships with evangelical Christian army leaders, whose numbers grew in the 1980s. Most notable was Chief of Staff of the Army (CSA) General John A. Wickham Jr., who oversaw the expansion of evangelical Christian-inspired programs. A born-again Christian, Wickham welcomed conservative Christian influence over the growing military social welfare system. He often framed his family programs in religious terms, seeking ways to "increase the influence of the church in the Army." Wickham purchased from Dobson counseling and programming materials for army-wide use in family programs. And the army chaplain's office took an influential role in family counseling programs at many posts, especially in the army's new marriage and family counseling, and family and deployment support. The 1970s rhetoric of the Army Family that "took care of its own" tilted in the 1980s toward a more conservative traditional family and Christian values.

There were limits to the reach of conservative Christianity on army families, however, and Dobson never became a household name among most soldiers. Conservative Christian values did not directly influence basic benefits like family housing or child care. And for some enlisted personnel, the chaplain's office or Christian-infused counseling programs rarely, if ever, touched their lives. In addition, many army families lived a messier reality of divorce, single parenthood, substance abuse, and family violence than the ideal depicted by the army or the Christian right. Still, increasingly conservative ideas about families shaped the way the army talked about and portrayed families. They colored the army's programs and changed their feel. And conservative Christian influence on army family programs pressed the army into the wider conservative "family values" politics of the decade. Army leaders' views reflected the Reagan administration's larger conservative family policy agenda of antipornography efforts, opposition to federal day care programs, antiabortion stances, and, of course, cuts to social welfare. Decades before President George W. Bush pressed faith-based social welfare programs, Reagan and the Christian right stamped them onto the growing military welfare state.

CSA GENERAL John A. Wickham Jr., served as architect of the army family programs built in the 1980s. Wickham grew up in upstate New York, graduated in 1950 from the United States Military Academy at West Point, and was commissioned as an infantry officer. A pedigreed service took him from

IT'S NOT GETTING ANY EASIER TO BE A SOLDIER.
BUT IT IS GETTING EASIER TO BE A SOLDIER'S FAMILY.
A soldier's job is tough enough without having to worry about the well-being of his or her family. That's why the Army is taking steps to make the soldier's family feel more at ease.
The Army Family Action Plan is a total program to deal with Army family problems on a systematic, long-term basis. It includes improved child care, housing, health care, and many other services and facilities.
The Chief of Staff, General John A. Wickham, and Sergeant Major of the Army Glen E. Morrell are totally committed to supporting this plan.
Construction has already begun on over 2,500 Army family housing units; 250 child-care facilities have been improved. Many new child-care facilities are on the way.
A Health Facility Modernization Program has begun.
And employment resource centers are being established to help expand employment opportunities for Army family members.
Your family's lifestyle problems won't be solved overnight, but they *will* be solved.
Every day, you prove what you can do for the Army. The Army wants to prove what it can do for your family.
ARMY FAMILY.
BE ALL YOU CAN BE.

THE ARMY'S JOB HASN'T
CHANGED IN OVER 200 YEARS.

BUT OUR WAY OF LIFE IS CHANGING FOR THE BETTER.

The job is still to defend American liberty, but the Army's attitude toward the soldier's family has changed dramatically.

The Army Family Action Plan is a demonstration of today's commitment to the human and material needs of Army family members.

The plan is designed as a total program to deal with a wide range of Army Family problems on a systematic, long-term basis. It includes measures to improve housing, child-care, medical and dental care, and many other services and facilities for Army families.

The Chief of Staff, General John A. Wickham, and Sergeant Major of the Army Glen E. Morrell, are totally committed to this plan and have pledged their full support.

The construction of over 2,500 Army family housing units has already begun. Many new child-care facilities have been approved for construction; 250 have already been improved. A Health Facility Modernization Program has also begun. And presently, employment resource centers are being established to help expand employment and priority placement opportunities for Army family members.

Your problems can't be solved immediately, but they *will* be solved. The Army has always had the responsibility of defending the nation. Today it has another important responsibility – to continue to improve the lifestyle of the Army family.

ARMY FAMILY.
BE ALL YOU CAN BE.

Two print advertisements from N. W. Ayer represented male soldiers and their wives and children, part of a campaign to retain soldiers through the expansion and extension of programs serving soldiers' families. Courtesy of NW Ayer Advertising Agency Records, Archives Center, National Museum of American History, Smithsonian Institution.

the Korean War to Harvard University, where he earned two master's degrees, and then back to West Point again, where he taught in the vaunted social science department. After West Point, he commanded a battalion in Vietnam, where he was gravely wounded, and later went on to lead the lauded 101st Airborne Division in the late 1970s. In the 1970s, he amassed considerable military policy experience in the Pentagon as military assistant to Secretary of Defense Donald Rumsfeld during the transition of the army to the volunteer force. Just prior to his appointment as CSA, he led U.S. Army forces and the Eighth Army in Korea.[4]

When Wickham assumed his new post after General Edward "Shy" Meyer departed in 1983, the army stood on firmer footing than it had in two decades. General Meyer and General Max Thurman, commander of the Recruiting Command and then vice chief of staff of the army, had taken advantage of the poor economy and the flush Reagan budget, using new recruiting techniques and advertising to turn around the army's manpower problems and, just as important, its image. The army Wickham inherited no longer wobbled on the brink of collapse.

Wickham had the luxury to turn his attention beyond mere institutional survival and pursue what he considered a moral regeneration of the army. As he led soldiers in the Vietnam War, he had witnessed firsthand the declining discipline and morale among troops in the latter years of the war. He had also survived the turmoil accompanying the switch to the volunteer force, when education levels plummeted and the volunteer force teetered on the brink of failure. Now as top commander, Wickham feared a "morally empty Army" and sought to build a moral atmosphere in army units by "ensuring that every soldier knows and understand the values that are central to the Army." He emphasized loyalty both to the institution of the army and to the unit, but also "personal responsibility" and "selfless service."[5] Like all chiefs of staff, Wickham developed an official "Army Theme" for his tenure, and his was "Values."[6]

For Wickham personally, values meant conservative Christian values and a sense of "biblical integrity."[7] He had become an evangelical Christian during the Vietnam War, when his grievous wound left him dying in the jungle, praying for his men and his family until help reached him.[8] A man of "great faith, but quiet faith," he welcomed army leadership with "a sense of thankfulness and a prayer." He laced many of his speeches to military audiences with stories from the Bible and references to God.[9] He insisted that "most soldiers can and do possess a faith in God," and that "a soldier's adherence to Judeo-Christian values points him in the direction of duty, dedication, and service" necessary for the army.[10] Over the years, Wickham developed close ties to civilian leaders of the evangelical religious world. He exchanged letters with the Reverend Billy Graham and gave an interview about his faith to Graham's Christian magazine, *Decision,* in 1984. He also corresponded with Bill Bright, the founder of Campus Crusade for Christ, and the Reverend Billy Kim, an influential leader of the Christian evangelical movement in Korea, where Wickham had served in command.[11]

By the 1980s, Wickham achieved public recognition as leader of a growing evangelical Christian movement in the army.[12] The movement had begun during the Vietnam War, when civilian evangelicals began to proselytize among army officers and converted many, like Wickham.[13] After the war key flag officers and other high-ranking members of the officer corps, and leaders at West Point helped spread the growth of evangelical Christianity, especially its more conservative varieties. These were what conservative Christians would call Bible-based movements, including nonliturgical evangelical, fundamentalist, and Pentecostal movements. The men who led them created officers' prayer groups at the Pentagon, West Point, and the command schools such as Fort Leavenworth.[14] Evangelicals also began to dominate the regular officer corps. At West Point, whose cadets would later become the army's most influential officers, mainline Protestantism had declined. *Christianity Today* remarked upon the dramatic change, noting that while "for a century, it sufficed morally at the Point to be a Christian gentleman," now "you had better be a 'born-again' Christian."[15] Among the 53 percent of army officers who identified as Protestant, the officer corps developed ever more rapidly into a base for conservative evangelicals with conservative politics.[16] By the mid-1980s, a national poll revealed that more than 85 percent of the officer corps defined themselves as "political conservatives," an identifier that in the 1980s referred in large part to the political surge of conservative Christians. Social science research found that by the early 1990s, only 3 percent of officers identified themselves as "liberal."[17]

At the same time that army leaders tacked toward conservative Protestant Christianity, so, too, did the army chaplaincy, the official religious leadership and service providers to the army. Chaplains were trained to provide religious services to all soldiers and their families, regardless of religious affiliation. Military chaplains of the 1980s employed 3,488 chaplains who represented 205 faiths. Almost 20 percent of chaplains were Catholic, and 1.28 percent identified as Jewish.[18] But 70 percent of the chaplaincy identified as Protestant. And among them, conservative and evangelical Protestantism predominated. The conservative National Association of Evangelicals noted approvingly in 1983 that "Evangelicals populate[d] the corps to a greater degree than ever."[19]

Civilian conservative Christians welcomed the rise of evangelicalism within the army. Since the advent of the Cold War, they had entered the fight against communism with a deep faith in the military's ability to defeat the Soviet Union. Many of the most conservative among them supported both aggressive anticommunist militarism and fringe militarist Christian groups such as the John Birch Society. Conservative evangelical leaders provided some of the staunchest support for the U.S. war in Vietnam.[20] One of the leaders of the National Evangelical Association, Harold John Ockenga, published numerous pieces in Christian magazines underscoring the moral importance of American military action against the North Vietnamese.[21] As evangelicals and fundamentalists entered formal politics under the charismatic leadership of men such as Jerry Falwell in the 1970s, they embraced the military even more tightly. Many were inspired by Ronald Reagan's hawkish military buildup, and by his interventions in Latin America, where they viewed the rise of antidictatorial leftist regimes through the lens of godless communism. Conservative Christian leaders nourished closer ties with the military, seeing it as an agent for Christianity in U.S. foreign policy.[22] They were also inspired by Reagan's commitment to the Strategic Defense Initiative (SDI), also known as Star Wars. The Religious Coalition for a Moral Defense Policy, a collection of conservative religious leaders and organizations including televangelists Jimmy Swaggart and Jim Baker along with Jerry Falwell of the Moral Majority and Bill Bright of Campus Crusade for Christ, officially endorsed SDI, with a "day of prayer" to "seek God's intercession" in its favor.[23] In the 1980s, meetings such as the Christian World Affairs Conference, sponsored by the Faith America Foundation, regularly featured civilian Christian right leaders alongside evangelicals in the army, including Secretary of the Army John O. Marsh Jr., who served with General Wickham. In the words of one attendee, these meetings were "pervaded" by "an undercurrent of militancy, jingoism, and aggressiveness" that made plain the links between the Christian right and the military. Civilian Christian leaders joined military leadership to discuss such foreign policy issues as the SDI, the Sandinistas and the Contras, the Soviet Union, and terrorism.[24]

In Wickham's years as CSA, politicized evangelicals drew closer than ever to the military, reconceiving it as crucial to the decades-old battle against communism, and also, newly, as an agent for Christianity within the United States—an actor in the so-called culture wars. As early as the late 1960s, conservative Christians had found the army comfortable as an institution that shared "a common ground of upright moral conduct" with Christians.[25] By the 1980s, the church and the military together comfortably shared the top two positions in annual Gallup Polls registering Americans' trust in national institutions.[26] More and more, as the army fulfilled the will of the Christian right in foreign policy, conservative Christians came to believe its example could also operate in domestic policy.

Wickham tried to sculpt the army into an image of Christian values and morality. He endeavored to eradicate what he viewed as "vices" from the army. One campaign took up smoking and drinking.[27] Wickham tried "to deglamorize alcohol and reduce its use for health reasons," but he also viewed alcohol reduction as central to his values campaign. [28] *Army Times* described his effort as "discourag[ing] the macho drinking environment" in the army.[29] In 1983, "the Army prohibited all Army Club sponsored events, such as Happy Hour, which offered reduced pricing or unlimited alcoholic beverages."[30] The next year, the army began plans to phase out the enlisted and officers' clubs entirely. Wickham also forbid soldiers to purchase alcohol while on duty (consuming it while on duty had never been allowed). Some soldiers perceived the crackdown on alcohol as "coercion" and many interviewers raised the subject with the general, suggesting that new rules faced questions.[31] Wickham acknowledged that the idea might seem "sort of heretical." But he worried that "NCO [noncommissioned officers'] clubs and officers clubs have tended over the years to become places where you do a lot of drinking." In explaining the bans, Wickham stated that the army sought to "create an environment that pulls families together rather than . . . splits them apart."[32] Overall Wickham's plans may have worked, as the army reported that army culture came to "frown upon" excessive drinking as a result of his efforts.[33] The general evinced pride in the sharply declined rates of alcohol consumption and related problems in the army on his watch.[34]

At the same time Wickham launched a war on pornography in the army, a campaign that closely mirrored civilian evangelicals' efforts against pornography in the 1980s. Just as Reagan's attorney general, Edwin Meese, worked with evangelicals to conduct a national inquiry into pornography, Wickham and evangelicals in the army's chaplain corps also developed arguments against pornography in the army. They contended that the wide availability of pornography in the army and its voracious consumption by soldiers profoundly contradicted army goals promoting moral values and family values. To justify this they cited evangelical social science research on pornography.[35] Overall, Wickham created a culture among the leadership that frowned on pornography. In terms of policy, though, he did not outright ban pornographic materials. He forced the army's Post Exchanges to cover them and make them harder for minors to obtain.

Wickham's push for conservative Christian values achieved greatest force in the family programs he nurtured for soldiers and their spouses and children. Wickham pledged a new era for army families after admitting the "studied neglect" and "ambivalent and selective inclusion of families" in the army in the past.[36] In 1983, he issued his "Army Family White Paper," the first army strategy paper ever to focus on questions of family and support. Then, in 1984, his office initiated his "Year of the Family," and, more importantly, compiled the first "Army Family Action Plan" (AFAP), the policy agenda first generated by army wives.[37] In the first year after the AFAP, "sixty-seven initiatives were undertaken" to improve the lives of soldiers' families.[38] Wickham established a corresponding "Army Family Budget" to fund those initiatives and every other facet of soldier and family support.[39]

Much of Wickham's Army Family Budget expanded basic support programs without any direct links to religious content like housing and child care.[40] But the new army family programs also offered extensive hands-on social services that connected more closely to Wickham's religious leadership—counseling, intervention, prevention, and recreation programs. In 1985, the army administered eighteen distinct family programs constituting a web of nearly comprehensive social welfare services for soldiers and families:

Family Support Centers
Individual Counseling/Therapy/
Marriage and Family Counseling/Therapy/Enrichment
Chaplain Services/Religious Opportunities
Parent Education
Youth/Adolescent Programs
Financial Counseling/Management Education

Single Parent Programs
Pre-Marital Programs
Programs for Families with Handicapped Members
Services for Families During Separation
Crisis Referral Services
Spouse Employment Services
Recreational Programs
Spouse/Child Abuse Services
Alcohol treatment/Drug Abuse Programs
Rape Counseling Services
Legal Assistance[41]

The growing social services programs, particularly the new counseling and support programs that the army provided to families, became the site upon which Wickham folded evangelical beliefs into the Army Family Programs. Not unlike civilian megachurches, whose emergence joined ministry with social welfare activities, the army fused conservative Christianity with its wider family support programs. Many of these programs revolved around family counseling of various kinds—counseling for spouses going through relationship difficulties, counseling for children, and counseling for entire families who might need assistance during or after deployment or during other crises. Other counseling programs concerned information and support provision, such as support groups mobilized during deployments. In these services, army families became directly entangled with the emerging Christian right politics of "family values."

Wickham's new counseling and support programs were guided in part by one of the major evangelical figures of the late twentieth century, Dr. James C. Dobson. Dobson studied to be a pediatric psychologist and had worked in Southern California in the 1960s and 1970s, developing what he called a "Christian psychological perspective" that sought to assist people in psychological distress through the invocation of Christian beliefs and behaviors.[42] In 1977, he left medical practice and founded the influential Christian nonprofit organization Focus on Family in the air force town of Colorado Springs, Colorado. He dedicated Focus on Family to the "preservation of the family and the propagation of traditional, pro-family views." He rose rapidly as one of the stars of the Christian right, and began to consult at the national level on public policy matters in the Reagan administration.[43] In the early 1980s, two Christian evangelical congressmen with whom General Wickham was friendly through Washington prayer groups, Dan Coats (R-IN) and Frank Wolf (R-VA), introduced Wickham to Dobson.[44]

Dobson and his organization began specializing in the treatment of military families, perhaps because of their location in Colorado Springs. According to Focus on Family's own analysis, military personnel and their spouses contacted the organization for help handling the pressures of military life on their families. Over 50 percent of those who wrote to Focus on Family were wives of military personnel. "Family separations" topped the list, with "both husbands and wives . . . apprehensive about how this will affect their marriage relationship." Another great concern constituted marital problems of conflict resolution and infidelity.[45] Dobson's organization responded to these requests for assistance by developing a range of counseling-related materials "directed specifically to a military audience . . . from a Christian psychological perspective."[46] Focus on Family conducted a brisk military business in mail-order reading materials, radio broadcasts, videocassette sales, and magazines.

In 1984, Wickham invited Dobson to his Task Force on Soldiers and Families to advise the army how to better serve families. Dobson was joined by other less well-known conservative Christians such as David Edens of Stephens College in Missouri, who closed his task force letters with the reminder to "keep the faith and share the light."[47] Wickham asked them to determine how "we can strengthen the role of the Church in the Army."[48] At Dobson's suggestion, Wickham and Deputy Chief of Staff for Personnel Robert Elton agreed to incorporate a "spiritual dimension" into the soldier and civilian surveys conducted by the Army Research Institute in order to plan for how to use "chaplains, religious counseling, and religious communities to strengthen families within the Army."[49] But Wickham hoped Dobson would do more than invigorate the chaplaincy. Wickham welcomed him as, in Dobson's words, a "partner . . . in strengthening the institutions of marriage and parenthood for those serving in the military." Wickham wanted the help of the conservative Christians in crafting an army with "family values." So impressed by Dobson's work on the task force, Wickham invited Dobson to address the spring Commanders Conference at the Pentagon, where Dobson gave a speech on "the importance of traditional home-life values." In his growing advisory capacity to the army, Dobson steered army family services toward Christian right notions of family.[50]

The army embraced the religious right by purchasing materials from Focus on Family for use in army family programs. The army bought books and videotapes by Dobson about family problems.[51] The best known was the video *Where's Dad?* about the importance of fathers' leadership and participation in the lives of their families.[52] In its original form, it contained overt references to Jesus and the Bible, but the army purchased the "cleansed" version that met the army's regulations regarding the use of religious materials in nonreligious settings. Still, the video retained its affinity with biblical notions of family.[53] Wickham announced to army commanders in March 1985 that he had approved *Where's Dad?* for distribution within the army. "I encourage you," he said, "to show this thought-provoking film to your soldiers and their spouses together." *Christianity Today* reported that "all active duty soldiers are expected to see Dobson's film."[54] The army briefly investigated Dobson for potential conflict of interest in both advising the army on family issues and selling his wares to the army. But it quickly cleared him of any impropriety. Indeed, it seems that Mr. Dobson had no need to use special influence to sell his perspective to army leadership. It already pervaded their ranks.

While Dobson's materials moved freely through the secular army family programs, overtly religious family programs developed through the U.S. Army Chaplains Office, which played a growing role in army family programs. These were part of what Dobson and other evangelicals had meant when they had hoped to "strengthen the role of the church" in army family programs. The chaplaincy had always been an important component of the army, providing religious guidance and support to soldiers according to their sectarian needs. Over time, as families grew more numerous, the chaplains engaged more in day-to-day family issues. And as Wickham crafted his Army Family Budget, he included funding for expansion of all chaplains' activities, including the Chaplain Family Life Centers.[55] The army had established these centers "on various Army installations since the early 1970s" and army family programs encouraged their growth and coordination. Like the army's secular family supports, the Chaplain Family Life Centers were aimed at family wellness, but they "operated from a theological base" and used ministry to reach those goals.[56]

Though chaplains had always provided spiritual counseling, in the 1980s they developed a family counseling model of their own, one that they marketed widely in ostensibly nonreligious contexts. Chaplains became particularly involved with support to family members of deployed soldiers, generating guidebooks, talking points, handouts, and audio/visual materials to help families survive deployment.[57] Chaplains began working directly with the spouse and staff leaders of the nascent Family Support Groups, the volunteer groups that families relied on during deployments. Chaplains were directed to "maintain active involvement in the family support group process, to include training of family support group leaders, rear detachment personnel, and the welcome process for newly arrived soldiers and families into the unit."[58] At Fort Bragg, North Carolina, where the 82nd Airborne pioneered Family Support Groups, the chaplain's office actually provided the sole and direct financial aid for the support group.[59] Chaplains coordinated closely with the newly created army Family Liaison Office (FLO), later called the Community and Family Support Centers (CFSC). The office listed the chaplaincy under a host of army programs for "Children/Youth," "Spouse," "Self-Improvement," "Crisis," "Education," "Self-Help," and "Health."[60] The FLO and CFSC national newsletters highlighted the Chaplain Family Life Centers in articles explaining that the programs existed "to meet your needs and help you maintain strong family ties." The army emphasized how the chaplaincy met essential army family program goals and advised soldiers to "take advantage of these unexpected benefits."[61]

It made a difference that more chaplains were conservative evangelical Christians than ever before, and that their numbers exploded from the 1980s onward. The leaders of family life programs were not as likely to be "mainline" Protestant ministers or mainstream Catholics, but more likely conservative, nonliturgical, charismatic, even fundamentalist pastors, including Pentecostals, Church of God in Christ, "Full Gospel Church" groups, and Southern Baptists.[62] These Christians pursued their faith work in the army with vigor, pressing lawsuits against the army to allow them to practice the specificity of their fundamentalist beliefs even when assigned to serve soldiers who did not share them, and allowing them to "proselytize," even when the army prohibited it.[63] Indeed, in countersuits pressing cases against the army's conservative Christian activities, witnesses testified that army worship "tilt[ed] heavily in favor of non liturgical Protestant modes of expression" favored by conservative evangelicals and fundamentalists.[64]

With the increasingly Christian conservative bent among the chaplaincy, the Chaplain Family Life Centers fostered a Christian conservative approach to matters of the family. Fort Bragg, North Carolina, the army's largest post, for example, represented the stronghold for conservative Pentecostal chaplains. Its Center for Family Life and Religious Education aimed to handle what it called "the complexity of family problems" facing the thousands of soldiers and spouses posted there. The Pentecostal chaplaincy's close interconnection with official army family programs there spelled a particularly strong conservative Christian, even fundamentalist, influence on the way Fort Bragg families were envisioned and how they were advised to function.

For example, conservative religious messages infused representations of army marriages used by the army's counselors, both secular and religious. Materials in both settings bore striking resemblance to biblical notions of marriage and gender roles. This view portrayed God and Jesus as spiritual leaders of the family with fathers and husbands as the lead executors of their will in everyday life. Fathers and husbands honored and respected wives, but men alone led and made decisions. Wives were not partners, but assisted in the leadership of husbands; they were deputies who deferred, or "submitted" to, husbands' authority. The cleansed *Where's Dad?* video, for example, emphasized dire need for male household leadership during a time of perceived crisis in the status of the American family. It referred to such leadership as "a God-given responsibility."[65] Similarly, an army lieutenant colonel visiting a post in Guam noted with dismay a chaplain's poster about "a class to make wives 'better.'" To his shock, it advised them to become more submissive.[66] Many of the messages may not have been so blatant, but they nevertheless reinforced female sacrifice. A favorite "Prayer for the Army Wife" circulated in the army's Community and Family Support newsletter. Merging religious themes about creationism with traditional gendered notions about military wives, it offered a story about the "good Lord . . . creating a model for military wives." The Lord tells an angel assistant, "we will give her an unusually strong heart so it can swell with pride in her husband's achievements, sustain the pain of separation, beat soundly when it is overworked and tired, and be large enough to say I understand, when she doesn't, and say, 'I love you,' regardless."[67] Just as God had ordained a two-parent, male-headed family, He had ordained the submissive nature of an army wife, whose many virtues and skills were to be directed toward making her husband's career and their marriage work. This Christian take on gender and family intensified the army's already existing emphasis on traditional gender roles—the male soldier-breadwinner (at the expense of the female soldier) and the supportive wife—to create powerful messages about men and women and the relationship between them in the army.

Religious conservatism shaped not only the programs for army families but also the public presentation of army families. *The Times Magazine*, a bimonthly supplement to *Army Times*, regularly featured articles on spouse and family issues, and these frequently paired portrayals of healthy families with religious behaviors. Family counselors wrote articles like "What makes for a good Marriage?" In one, they concluded that in addition to secular skills like communication and making time for each other, "those who see the marriage bond as sacred or sacramental are much more willing to change their behavior."[68] Stories of family problems, by contrast, often featured deviations from religion and church as a path to family discord and strife. A set of detailed first-person narratives from abusive male spouses, for example, addressed family violence within a religious framework. Several men referred to the church as a mooring from which they had sprung loose, thus unleashing their violence. One described how he "withdrew from the church," as a first slip toward violence toward his wife. Another lamented his abuse as not merely hurtful to his wife but destructive of their religious bond. His abuse, he said, drove his wife to abandon their previous life, including her church, for her safety, thus severing "a child of God from the church and her religion." Another soldier articulated his hope that his Chaplain Family Life Center programs would help him recover.[69]

Despite prescriptive Christian messages, the lived experience of army families in the 1980s did not conform to a conservative Christian family ideal. In sectarian terms, most obviously Jewish, Muslim, Hindu, and other non-Christian soldiers, though their numbers were small, clearly lived apart from the practices and beliefs of conservative Christianity. So, too, did the many agnostic and atheistic soldiers who peopled the army. Many Catholics and mainline Protestants also eschewed the conservatism and fundamentalism of the Christian right.

Regardless of religious affiliation, the lived experiences of most soldiers and their spouses proved far more complex than the Christian right might have wished. Many army families underwent the same trials as many civilian families. Some lived difficult and even troubled lives that hardly conformed to a Christian ideal. The discrepancy, however, did not dissuade Christian efforts so much as spur them while at the same time demonstrating their limits.

Between 1960 and 1990, the divorce rate in the United States more than doubled, and army families were not immune. Divorce rates increased among military personnel at roughly the same rate as civilians.[70] From 1975 to the 1990s, at any one moment in time, between 4 percent and 8 percent of army personnel were single parents. While that number might at first seem small, army researchers noted that because soldiers' statuses altered often through remarriage and divorce, between 12 percent and 24 percent of all army personnel had been single parents in the recent past.[71] That meant that anywhere from a sixth to a fourth of army personnel had been or were single parents in the 1980s.[72]

Divorce and the difficulties of single parenthood took center stage in discussions of army families in two venues in the 1980s, belying the ideal of a Christian army family. First, the divorced wives of service personnel organized a new movement pressing for their rights to military health care and a portion of their husbands' pensions after their divorces. Ex-Partners of Servicemen (Women) for Equality (EXPOSE) drew members whose divorces had severed them from all of their benefits, even if they had devoted their entire adult lives to supporting a soldier, sailor, or airman. EXPOSE noted that "95% of our members were surprised to find that their marriages ended right before his retirement or shortly thereafter . . . most of our members were caught off guard (left in the lurch)."[73] They lobbied Congress, with receptive hearings by Patricia Schroeder (D-CO), David Durenberger (R-MN), Bob Packwood (R-OR), Mark Hatfield (R-OR), John Burton (D-CA), and Dennis DeConcini (D-AZ).[74] The women's stories of late-in-life abandonment directly contradicted the ideal of military marriage promulgated by the Christian right and army leadership, in which men provided for women. It was particularly notable that the organization was formed by the wives of career men, most of whom retired as commissioned officers or NCOs. "Christine Langtry," a pseudonymous author, wrote in *Army Times Magazine*, which covered the EXPOSE spouses closely, about her divorce from an air force master sergeant to whom she had been married for nineteen and a half years, and her fight to retain a share of his pension when he retired six months later.[75] Their stories of callous husbands who had started new families and then discarded their former spouses and children on the verge of retirement cast the army family in a very different light than the conservative Christian family with its "traditional family values."[76]

Stories of divorce among army families also surfaced when soldiers failed to pay child support to ex-spouses. Several years after Congress passed new laws providing for the garnishment of soldiers' salaries for failures to pay timely child support, the army's Community and Family Support Center newsletters for families reminded soldiers of their obligations: one out of four yearly issues of the newsletter featured an injunction for soldiers to pay child support. So many soldiers failed to support their children that it constituted the number one question directed to the army's family hotline for several years running. As a result, the army wrote its own regulation on soldiers' failure to pay child support (Army Regulation 608–99) and issued its own publications for ex-spouses and lawyers, "The Key to Collecting Child Support from U.S. Army Soldiers and Civilians." "The Army expects soldiers to be aware of what is required of them," the army's newsletter repeatedly exhorted soldiers, "and to fulfill their financial responsibilities to support their families."[77] Soldiers' abandonment of their financial responsibilities to their families and children did not portray soldiers as moral patriarchs protecting their families, as the reigning Christian family ideal suggested.

Violence among army families even more significantly challenged this ideal. As several officers candidly told a *New York Times* reporter, "Child abuse is but one product of the stresses of military life today. . . . Repeated moves, long separations and inadequate housing have led to violence, alcoholism, drug abuse," and a host of other problems.[78] Several stories about child abuse in the army, one at West Point and another at the Presidio in San Francisco, hinted at wider physical abuse and sexual violence.[79] The army noted in 1985 that reported incidents of violence and abuse in military families increased by one-third compared to the year before. Army spouses suffered 3,255 cases of spousal abuse that year, and children 3,672 cases. Three children of soldiers were killed by abusive soldiers as were two women. More worrisome, the reporting system created in 1983 did not capture all the abuse the Department of Defense suspected, with as many as "one out of every two cases . . . never reported." A staff member at the military's Family Resource Center, the office in the Pentagon tasked with addressing service-wide issues of abuse, suspected "the rate we are hearing from officers is low." "It may be," she stated, "that they [the officers] are better at keeping it quiet."[80] The crisis of family violence appeared regularly in the *Army Times* and its supplement *The Times Magazine* throughout the 1980s, painting a portrait of "violence in the families."[81] Whether it was divorce, desertion, failure to support families, or abuse, there was no denying substantially different lived experience among some army families than the Christian right ideal prescribed.

Though some army families exhibited behaviors that fell short of the Christian right ideal, conservative Christians did not lose faith. Critics of Christian families values often cited the failure of putatively Christian individuals to live up to their ideals as evidence of hypocrisy or an actual lack of faith. Even today they point to areas of the country that have strong correlations between high rates of divorce, out-of-wedlock births, and addiction, and, at the same time, adherence to conservative Christian beliefs. But for conservative evangelicals, it was not the human failing—something from which few escaped—that marked a fall from grace, but a tolerance of the failing. As long as sinners acknowledged the sin and asked for redemption, conservative Christians accepted sinners. General Wickham, for example, never denied the serious problems of divorce, desertion, or abuse among army families. But his faith compelled him to try to prevent them, and to represent them as falls from faith that demanded assistance and redemption. Army leadership strove to meet the ideal, setting a path for army families toward the redemptive power of traditionally religious family values. That all or even most families did not meet them did not diminish the virtue of the army carrying the banner for a conservative Christian ideal.

The army carried this banner through its public embrace of the symbol and rhetoric of the Christian family, and sought opportunities to deploy it. In 1983, President Ronald Reagan created the "Great American Family Awards" as part of his "National Family Week" initiative. The awards were putatively secular, but embodied Reagan's embrace of the family values agenda of the right "to recognize the central importance of the family in American life and to honor the most fundamental unit of our society."[82] Reagan and his wife Nancy, honorary chairperson of National Family Week, structured the awards so that one military family was always chosen among the winners to represent the highest ideals of the American family; Army Services YMCA joined seven additional organizations as nominators of families. The judges, who included "marriage enrichment" pioneers David and Vera Mace, authors of *Sacred Marriage*, as well as devout Mormons Donny and Marie Osmond, evaluated dozens of "strong families."[83] The "Army Family" came out of the competition as "One of America's 9 Best."[84] The first army family to receive the award, First Sergeant Raymond Oeth and his wife Nadine, were Mormons. Though Mormons had been viewed warily by many Protestant evangelicals, their conservative theology nevertheless increasingly aligned them with the Christian right in the 1980s. The Oeths had "held nearly every office in their church from church secretary to Sunday

School leaders." Following her husband to posts around the world, Mrs. Oeth had volunteered for Army Community Service programs as well as her church.[85] The next year, Colonel William Xenaskis and his wife Nancy received the award from Nancy Reagan. Colonel Xenaskis, Nancy Xenaskis explained, "is head of the house." Their "church functions" provided a basis for their community service activities and their marriage.[86] Army families like the Oeths and the Xenaskises represented an ideal type of traditional Christian family that strengthened the symbolic connections between the army and conservative Christian politics.

Evangelicals singled out the army as "an enclave of virtue" apart from—and above—other American institutions and other American families.[87] Conservative Christians in the civilian world applauded the worldview of General Wickham and other Christian evangelical army officers who had crafted the programs and held them up as contrasts to civilian programs. As the story went, in a society drifting from the values of the traditional family, the army had chosen to emphasize the conservative Christian family. As General Wickham noted, he had "tried to foster the ideas of family cohesion and family values within our military community," and in doing so offered a model for the rest of the nation: "There is a dimension of the American dream, the notion of strength," he explained, "that is tied to the military family." Wickham felt that the army was uniquely situated to spread family values. "We have a great opportunity," he explained, "to influence and perpetuate that dream."[88] Army officers increasingly trumpeted their family values as exceptional compared to civilians', and proclaimed their moral superiority.[89]

Conservative evangelicals boasted their success in the army as a crowning achievement. Billy Graham's *Decision, Christianity Today,* and Focus on Family's magazine and radio show all began to praise the army in the mid-1980s for its embrace of Christian family values. Focus on Family's magazine, which went out to 650,000 evangelicals according to Dobson, featured Wickham and the army in its August 1984 cover story: "Today's Army: Advancing on the Home Front." Subsequent issues praised Wickham specifically for taking up the use of Focus on Family's *Where's Dad?* video. Dobson "thanked the Lord for these breakthroughs" of the Christian community into the army. Anne Loveland, a scholar of evangelical Christianity and the army, explained that because of the mutual embrace between the army family programs and Focus on Family, "Wickham's name became a household word within the evangelical community." Wickham publicly embraced Focus on Family, telling a meeting of the organization in Washington that "you and your organization help us [the army] to ensure that we have those values," the values associated with strong army leadership and strong families. For this, conservative Christians recognized Wickham publicly as "a committed Christian," and his papers reveal the many evangelicals who individually wrote him to thank him personally for "his Christian witness and influence."[90]

Members of the civilian Christian right community viewed successful evangelization within the army as an advance in a wider political campaign to gain influence in Reagan's administration. Ever since Reagan had pledged to evangelicals during the 1980 campaign, "I endorse you," he had built ties with evangelical leaders of an active Christian right like Jerry Falwell of the Moral Majority and Pat Robertson.[91] Once in office, Reagan incorporated evangelicals in his administration. Secretary of the Interior James Watt and Surgeon General Everett Koop were born-again Christians who served at high levels in the administration. So too was Attorney General Edwin Meese, who led Reagan's antipornography effort. Evangelical Christian Gary Bauer, who went on to run the conservative Christian Family Research Council, worked as domestic policy advisor to Reagan in his last years. He penned "The Family," Reagan's executive order pledging to strengthen traditional family values across all of his cabinet offices.[92] Evangelicals tightened their hold on the national policy agenda through their influence in the army.

One of the most important, but least recognized, ways this occurred was through the public contrast made by conservatives both within the army and outside between a supposedly moral army family and a putatively immoral, decaying civilian family. The support accorded the army and its family programs reinforced the opposition of the Reagan administration and the Christian right to government spending on social welfare programs outside the military. Reagan had been cutting social welfare programs since his first days in office. The signal reductions took place in the 1981 Omnibus Budget Reconciliation Act, which included a series of tax and social spending cuts and more stringent means testing for assistance programs such as Aid to Families with Dependent Children. The cuts continued in subsequent years with food stamps, Medicaid, and an effort to reduce Social Security. The conservative Christian family agenda growing within the White House invigorated the opposition to social welfare. In 1987, Gary Bauer's "White House Working Group on the Family" issued a fulsome critique of civilian social welfare's corrosive effects on the family.[93] "The fabric of family life has been frayed by the abrasive experiments of two liberal decades," Bauer warned.[94] The final report cited income assistance, child care, and even medical care for poor parents, single mothers, or two-parent, mother-at-work families as harmful to the traditional family.[95] President Reagan's Executive Order 12606—"The Family"—issued in the wake of the report forced executive agencies and departments to review all programs and policies to guard against incursions by the government on the power and responsibility of the family. It specifically asked agencies to "help the family perform its functions" on its own rather than acting to "substitute governmental activity for the function." And it warned against any new programs that might "erode the authority and rights of parents in the education, nurture, and supervision of children." All of the injunctions aimed directly at the web of civilian social welfare programs cited by Bauer as dangerous.[96]

The Reagan conservative family agenda did not identify the expansion of army social welfare programs as dangerous substitutions of government programs and the greater government control over military families. Programs very similar to civilian social welfare aided soldiers' families with child care, financial troubles, and health care. Indeed, the programs offered to army families covered far more than material and health needs, entering into the areas of financial, legal, and psychological counseling—programs that few civilians could hope to access through the government. Social welfare programs that conservatives rejected in the civilian world were not only accepted, but supported, when offered to soldiers and their families by the army.

The growth in army family programs underscored the Christian evangelical impact on the Reagan-era recalibration of citizenship and entitlement. Army families existed in opposition to a putative degenerating civilian family structure. They stood as lauded opposites arrayed against the other types of families who did not merit government support. A similar equation attached itself to the programs serving army families: government benefits and services were legitimate when they served traditionally constituted families, but not when they served less traditional civilian families. If aimed at nonmilitary single parents or nontraditional families, government programs were cast as downright dangerous. In contrast, families connected to the virtuous U.S. Army could be trusted with government support.

GENERAL WICKHAM'S Army Family Programs prospered through close connections to the conservative Christian right. New family services and benefits expanded alongside the popularization of an image of army families comporting closely with conservative Christian ideals: a male-headed "traditional" family that either implicitly or explicitly structured itself or functioned as Christian, and embraced "family values." And this image strengthened political support for both the military and its soldier and family programs among conservative and evangelical politicians. During the 1980s, soldiers and their families occupied one of the sole legitimate sites that Reagan's politics reserved for government support. The massive army family support apparatus grew at the same time that Reagan's administration opposed similar programs—housing, child care, and income support—for civilians. The history of the expansion of the army family programs amidst the politics of general retrenchment of the civilian welfare state underscores the Christian right contours of the Reagan politics of social welfare. And the army family welfare state grew not only despite the cuts to civilian social programs, but also to some degree on their backs.

As powerful as these military family programs and politics were during the Reagan years, they were not invulnerable. In 1989, the Reagan administration's defense spending would give way to the austerity of the end of the Cold War. The resulting drawdown, as both the personnel and budget cuts were named, would reshape profoundly the army's commitment to its families as well as their relationship to civilian social welfare. The army shed nearly 40 percent of its soldiers in the decade between 1989 and 1999, sending hundreds of thousands of personnel and their millions of family members back into the civilian world. The Christian right lamented the downsized military, fearing a degradation of the country's defense capabilities, and a weakening of a politically allied institution. But it also espied a potential windfall. As the army began to downsize in 1989, evangelical Christian groups hoped to recruit exiting soldiers for positions in ministry and mission work. "[C]hurches, missions, and parachurch organizations can turn this 'peace dividend' into new ministry workers," a *Christianity Today* author promised. Just as after World War II, when "mission efforts grew dramatically . . . as service people returned from a foreign war, were inspired to take God's word to the world . . . the current downsizing may represent another strategic opportunity." Evangelical Christians began "thinking and strategizing about how these people [soldiers] could be mobilized for a new mission," serving God instead of only country.[97]

The nearly half million soldiers who remained in the army endured an exile from the flush, politically protected realm of the Reagan era. In the early 1990s, the army and its programs for soldiers and families entered a new era. The exceptional status reserved for army family programs would end, as budget pressures and the advent of new discourses of "self-sufficiency" in civilian social welfare circles created a totally new context for support. Despite continued public lauding of soldiers and military families by the political leaders of the 1990s, and despite the still growing influence of evangelicals in the smaller army, soldiers and their families confronted new challenges. A growing consensus on social welfare demeaned "dependencies" on the government and demanded "self support" and "self sufficiency." The army's decade-old worries about providing too much social welfare, about being a "social welfare institution" were revived, worries that the Christian right years of Reagan and Wickham had largely obscured. In the decade to come, the army attenuated its commitments to soldiers both rhetorically and materially. The tight connections to the Christian right of the 1980s benefited soldier and family support programs during the Reagan administration but did not necessarily guarantee long-term political protection.

7

A Turn to Self-Reliance

IN EARLY JANUARY 1991, the United States mobilized for its first large-scale war since the conflict in Vietnam. The previous summer, Iraqi leader Saddam Hussein had amassed his army on the boundary with its small Persian Gulf neighbor, the kingdom of Kuwait. After a decades-long border dispute aggravated by years of war with Iran, Hussein ordered three divisions of his elite Republican Guard across the border to take possession of the disputed land and resources.[1] A coalition of thirty-four nations, led by the United States, condemned the invasion and mobilized to protect nearby Saudi Arabian oil fields, flush the Iraqis out of Kuwait, and punish Hussein through an invasion of Iraq. The war in the Persian Gulf, known as Operation Desert Storm/Desert Shield or the Gulf War, thrust the army into high gear, as it deployed the 82nd Airborne division followed by 120,000 more soldiers, and shipped 700 tanks and 1,400 armored vehicles to the Persian Gulf.[2] As the first test of the volunteer army in a major combat operation, the Gulf War operated as a referendum on the status of the U.S. military. President George H. W. Bush hailed the war as a military triumph before a joint session of Congress two months later: "This victory belongs to the finest fighting force this nation has ever known in its history. We fought hard and, with others, we won the war."[3] The war was widely viewed as a vindication of the volunteer military nearly two decades in the making.

The war also functioned as the first wartime test of the support functions that the army had built for soldiers and their families since the end of the draft, and on this count the verdict proved ambiguous. On the one hand, the army hailed their success. The Gulf War and its aftermath called into action a range of family supports that by the army's account served the function of promoting military readiness. Family support groups, counseling, extra day care, and after school programs all kicked into high gear. And as a result, families and soldiers mobilized fast, survived the deployment with ease, and turned back to a peacetime footing quickly.[4] But on the other hand, and paradoxically, the programs' successes caused some members of the army to question them anew. The tens of thousands of wives who joined support groups, called their rear detachment commanders, turned to counseling, or asked the chaplains for help unsettled some close observers of the programs. The army had perhaps provided too much support and in the process "generated unrealistic care expectations," as one report would later explain it.[5] The war raised the questions: Did soldiers and their wives expect the army to literally "take care of its own" during deployments? What about afterwards? Were these expectations acceptable? The post–Gulf War inquiries opened a wider review by the army of its two-decade-old social and economic support system. Did the army of the 1990s still owe its soldiers and families what it promised twenty years before?

Beneath concerns about soldiers' and families' reliance on the army lay worries that reprised the dark days of the 1970s when the army was threatened by the close association with welfare and the attendant feminization of the force. Army officials reviewing family support in the wake of the Gulf War evinced considerable ambivalence over women and the army's support system. These concerns had been papered over during the years of growth and support for the military and its benefits in Reagan's 1980s, but the Gulf War revived them. Since the mid-1980s, wives had occupied a more visible and influential space in the army, taking part in the Army Family Action Plan (AFAP) process each year, and continuing to press the army for more fulsome spousal and family support. The Gulf War magnified their presence as army wives scrambled to a war footing and demanded active engagement from the army. That they were joined by the largest ever deployment of female military personnel only magnified concerns that women played too large and too demanding a role in army life. Resurgent concerns about the effect of women on the army's war-making capabilities drove the reevaluation of the army's support programs.

The post–Gulf War period also revived anxieties of associating the army with social welfare after a decade's hiatus in which the army's programs had been cloaked in the glory of the Reagan defense buildup and the glow of the Christian right. It was no coincidence that the army's hesitation concerning its support system emerged at the same time that President Bill Clinton promised to "end welfare as we know it." A bipartisan consensus for cutting welfare and setting stricter rules for recipients set the context for the army's own reevaluation of its social welfare programs. In the same years as the Gulf War and its aftermath, in the civilian world a policy discourse geared to "reducing dependency" on social programs like public assistance or food stamps took center stage in states like Wisconsin, and rose to the national level through a bipartisan "welfare reform" agenda.[6] Though seemingly worlds apart, concerns about dependency within the army drew from the same context as those in the civilian world—from scholars in sociology, social work, and psychology. These researchers undertook studies inquiring into dysfunction and reliance on public institutions both among low-income families and among military families. In an era marked by demands for American citizens to display "independence" and "self reliance," the army's top family researchers and its uniformed leadership tried to decouple the army from any association with welfare.

The army's doubts about its social and economic supports could not be separated from the cuts to military budgets and personnel that accompanied the end of the Cold War. The drawdown remarkably altered the material structure of the army's support programs, and that story, told in Chapter 8, forms a twin to the story of ideological change told here. Intertwined and mutually reinforcing, the reevaluation occasioned by the Gulf War and the fiscal constraints of the drawdown together contributed to new philosophies and practices within the army's welfare state. After nearly two decades of building an "Army Family" that "took care of its own" during the 1970s and 1980s, senior leadership now questioned the system.

WHEN PRESIDENT BUSH announced on January 16, 1991, "allied air forces began an attack on military targets in Iraq," the army had mobilized both for the invasion it knew would follow, and for the support of its soldiers and families.[7] As 100,000 troops amassed on the border of Iraq, the army promised to "extend . . . a hand to the families left behind." The U.S. Army Community and Family Support Center (CFSC) promised "24-hour family assistance centers to provide all types of support to waiting families." The army prepared "child care plans," "briefings and outreach initiatives," "on-post transformation for needy families," and other possibly necessary services.[8] "Don't be afraid or embarrassed to ask for help if you run into problems," the army assured spouses. "If the Family Support Group members cannot meet your needs or help you resolve problems that arise, the staff at Army Community Service can either help you or get you to the right place to get the help you need." The army would be "there to help you survive the separation."[9] With the initial deployment, the army promised to fulfill its commitment to "take care of its own."

Family Support Groups (FSGs) operated as the featured vehicle of family support during the war, and the army monitored their performance closely. The groups had first emerged from the efforts of army spouses in the early 1980s at the first Army Family Symposium in Washington, DC. Army wives had requested formal assistance in establishing and running programs to build relationships among army spouses and assist them with relocation and deployment.[10] Though the army did not immediately respond, beginning in that same year, and spreading slowly and steadily thereafter, army spouses began to organize their own support programs. Their growth demonstrated the persistence of the army's reliance on wives' volunteer labor even after the army wives movement. The 82nd Airborne Division, based at Fort Bragg, North Carolina, for example, "operated Family Support Groups to provide an information and assistance network which reduced demands on the force deploying to Grenada."[11] So, too, did the 7th Light Infantry Division at Fort Ord, California, which deployed to the Sinai Peninsula in 1982.[12] These nascent FSGs prepared families for deployments, helped them cope for the duration, and assisted them in adjusting to the soldier's return. The groups provided a network to share information about deployed soldiers and the unit, and the services available to spouses and children that remained at home. They also addressed crises among families as they arose—providing support and referral to services if bills went unpaid, someone fell gravely ill, or if problems erupted between mothers and children at home.[13] In 1987, it became the official policy of the army to promote FSGs for all army units.[14] The army lauded their growth as "the most important" development in family policy that year.[15]

In the lead-up to the war in the Persian Gulf, the army tasked FSGs to provide mutual support and referral to needed family services during the conflict. Volunteer spouses, usually the wives of the highest-ranked commissioned officer and the highest-ranked enlisted soldier of the unit, led the

FSG. They were aided by an officer—part of the rear detachment of the mobilized unit—and by other support providers on post: the Chaplain's Office, Army Community Services, and the CFSC. The FSGs offered camaraderie, information, and access to services to assist families through deployment.

According to the army's initial assessments, the wartime FSGs triumphed. The early results of studies of Desert Storm families suggested that families "involved in an active family support group" or "hav[ing] a military resource like a rear detachment or a family assistance center to help them in solving problems" survived the deployment better than those who did not.[16] The chief of staff of the army (CSA) and the secretary of the army thanked FSGs' volunteer efforts for "making family support groups an extra dimension of readiness."[17] The army's postmission self-assessment—the after action report—published immediately after the end of the war in May 1991, underscored how "Family Support Groups played a key role in sustaining families by providing information and social and emotional supports." Rear detachments worked well with the army's Family Assistance Centers and the FSGs, and together comprised, in the army's words, "a total community effort" for family support. As a result, families felt the army cared. Most importantly, "soldiers' morale and unit cohesion increased after learning that the Army was caring for their families." The FSGs and related family supports seemed to serve their purpose of giving both spouses and soldiers the sense that the army cared for them.[18]

Yet the same after action report also produced more critical conclusions, in which the army cited negative consequences of family support. The problem lay not in providing *too little* support to army spouses but in providing *too much*. Brigadier General Raymond Roe, commander of the CFSC, told army audiences in Germany that during the war the army went "overboard" and fulfilled what he saw as unreasonable requests. "We got [ourselves] into a box of mowing lawns, providing transportation, babysitting, rides to the commissary and delivering groceries."[19] Postwar reports described army wives who had come to expect too much support from the army and its FSGs during the war: "Unrealistic family care expectations," one report explained, "were often reinforced . . . when commanders, rear detachment personnel or family support group leaders promised to help families with any problem that would arise."[20] The FSGs, the army concluded, had fostered impractical expectations among army wives. Promises of support "led to family frustration when the Army did not deliver," as spouses came to expect the army to help them.[21]

The perception that army spouses demanded too much from an indulgent army pervaded the internal army folklore of the war. Entries in the Gulf War Army Cartooning Contest, a competition meant to foster soldier morale in the Gulf, featured several entries concerning spouse and family support. First Sergeant Edward Quay, whose pen name was "The Mad Bomber," depicted interactions between spouses and the army during the war, including the demands made by army wives on army officials. In one cartoon, he drew a frazzled male rear detachment commander fielding three ringing phones and cringing beneath screaming spouses. One shrieks, "I need a bus schedule" while another complains "my car won't start," and still another asks "where's the babysitter?" Their cacophony of questions represents a litany of the various and—in the minds of some army leaders—excessive demands for assistance.[22] It seemed that the army had promised to care too much for its own during the war, and the spouses, in turn, had demanded too much from the army.

In the aftermath of the war, the army surveyed the wives of unit commanders who had run the FSGs, and they, too, issued pessimistic assessments of the FSGs as well as some of the wives who joined them. "I don't know if there's anything that can be done . . . ," one FSG leader responded, "[but] there needs to be some work or some focus on the enlisted ranks. . . . For us, that seemed to be where most of the problems came from."[23] Tensions over comportment had always existed among the wives of officers and the wives of enlisted personnel, but the critiques of the Gulf War drew on the particular class context of the volunteer army in the 1990s. Commissioned officers' spouses had higher incomes and more education than most enlisted army wives, and were usually older than the rest of the army wife population. Wives of commissioned officers had for decades observed the traditional rules against "fraternization" among the ranks, and developed their own social and informal support groups apart from enlisted wives. The volunteer force undermined this separation, as the army extended family supports to all ranks, and wives of all backgrounds met at child care or recreational facilities. Both the army wives movement and the AFAP aimed to empower all wives, and as a result they also dissolved some boundaries between middle-class officers' wives and their working-class enlisted peers. But the remnants of class hierarchy remained embedded in the army. Because officers' wives played a crucial role in FSG leadership, that hierarchy entered the FSGs.[24] Enlisted army wives as late as the early 2000s still accused officers' wives of "socially segregat[ing] themselves" and retaining separate activities within the FSG such as "senior leader spouses activities" of various types that they alone attended.[25] In the eyes of some enlisted wives, these activities set the officers' wives apart, proving that they were "snobbish."[26] As the FSGs switched into high gear during the Gulf War, recurrent contacts between officers' wives and lower enlisted ranks' wives exacerbated tensions.

The FSGs often created a sort of surveillance system for enlisted wives. Many FSG leaders maintained comprehensive rosters of the wives in the units. For officers' wives, such information facilitated problem solving in times of emergency. Yet it also served as a detailed record of the wives of enlisted soldiers in the units, including their personal behavior and family difficulties. "We had fact sheets on all the wives," one FSG leader reported, including where they lived and with whom, where they worked, hometowns, and other basic information. Even when enlisted wives refused or failed to provide information to the FSG leaders, those leaders nevertheless collected data about them in other ways. Personal behavior and problems were noted in the information sheets. During the Desert Storm deployment, one FSG leader collected notes on all 268 families in the battalion. As she described, "when . . . we had some real major problems we would make notes on these and the date. If something came up and we needed to know, we listed it."[27]

These "major problems" troubled some FSG leaders. Collecting the data, one officer's wife recalled, "we got some crazy details" about enlisted wives' lives. "You really had to wonder after they left what they were thinking when they filled out the papers," reporting information that revealed particulars of personal lives, unusual employment, debt, and legal problems.[28] The leaders of FSGs were called on to handle some of the very intimate difficulties of the wives in the group, and this responsibility magnified the sense among officers' wives that the enlisted wives were either hapless or perhaps foolish. During the Desert Storm deployment, for example, leaders of FSGs regularly complained of the "financial problems" of enlisted personnel's families.[29] One FSG leader stated that she "felt . . . some of these things should have been handled before deployment" but were neglected by enlisted wives who failed to plan wisely.[30] Instead "I would . . . end up closing down apartments, impounding cars, getting after the wives for unpaid bills."[31] Enlisted wives, they pointed out, didn't have joint bank accounts, they didn't know how to write checks, and didn't know how to read pay stubs.

In addition, they squandered what money they had. "They spent too much time in the Geissen club playing BINGO," one FSG leader complained. "Thousands of dollars were spent doing that."[32] The wives and girlfriends of lower-level enlisted personnel were sometimes depicted by FSG leaders as ignorant or profligate.[33]

A year after the after action report, commanders' wives posted to the Army War College at Carlisle Barracks, Pennsylvania, while their husbands spent a year on professional education, created their own independent report on FSGs. In their document, which they used to brief the vice chief of staff of the army in 1992, they painted a distressing portrait of the FSGs and the army wives who relied on them. The army's family support programs were hindered, they told him, by "dependency," "ignorance," and "demands" among enlisted spouses. It was time for the army to do something about "family-member trouble makers," as the officers' wives dubbed them.[34]

The critique of enlisted army wives during the Gulf War was magnified by the fact that they were not the only women in the military deemed troublesome. In 1993, Marine Commandant General Carl Mundy Jr., announced a new Corps policy: the Marines would no longer allow marines with wives to enlist.[35] For his part, General Mundy said his order reflected genuine concern that, as the news paraphrased it, "marriages among young marines were . . . a cause of a low re-enlistment rate. . . ." A concurring senior staff sergeant added bluntly: "Marriage detracts from readiness. A marine's mind can't be back home, wondering if his wife has a roof over her head."[36] A shocked and alarmed secretary of defense, Les Aspin, immediately reversed the order, "to the general's great embarrassment." Aspin characterized Mundy's order as out of step with long-accepted military policy acknowledging and accepting wives. But in fact, the commandant's aborted order reflected an extreme expression of the army's increasing skepticism concerning army wives and family support.

That skepticism was amplified by negative assessments of female soldiers deployed during the Gulf War. Just as the war served as a referendum on the volunteer force's combat readiness and its social supports, it also represented an opportunity to render a verdict on female soldiers and their widespread incorporation into the volunteer military beginning twenty years before. Although reporters and critics framed the discussions of female military personnel as pertaining to military readiness, they also bled into the question of dependency and neediness that framed the debate about family support groups. Critics of the feminization of the military revived arguments from the 1970s about female soldiers making unique and even dangerous demands on the military. The dozens of media stories about the so-called Love Boat represented the most sensational take on this theme. After the war, a reporter learned of the navy vessel USS *Acadia* stationed in the Persian Gulf that purportedly had an exceedingly high number of pregnant sailors.[37] Though the statistics were later proven to have been both incorrect and reported out of context with comparisons to civilian pregnancy rates, the story fueled a broad discussion of how potential pregnancies threatened military readiness.[38] The "Love Boat" reports accompanied additional stories of women who purportedly got pregnant in order to avoid deployment, could not deploy due to pregnancy, or refused deployment because of children. The reports identified women who demanded extra time to make child-care arrangements and women who could not focus on combat because of worries about their children.[39]

Such reports opened into a wider debate about whether women associated with the military constituted a "weak link," in the words of one critic—a dangerous feminization of the military in which female dependence and demands reduce military readiness.[40] For female soldiers, the reports threatened their persistence in the military. Former service women pointed out that the military began to monitor its numbers of women in the service, using the opportunity of the general drawdown of personnel in the wake of the end of the Cold War to stabilize the number of women in the armed forces rather than continuing to grow it to a more representative number.[41] For wives of soldiers, the question was less about their numerical presence than about their own behavior and their relationship to the army's family support system. The Gulf War assessments of army wives and their use of the army family support system raised concerns that the army coddled demanding and difficult women.

AS THE WIDER question of feminization of the military unspooled in the wake of the Gulf War, the army's doubts about the enlisted wives and its family support programs made their way up the chain of command, and through new army offices. Among the most influential was the Army Family Research Program, whose studies of army wives and army family support would contribute to a striking philosophical redefinition of the army social and economic support system for soldiers and their families.

In the aftermath of the war, the army tasked its family sociologists and psychologists with formally assessing the anecdotal evidence of difficulties caused by wives in the FSGs. Military family sociology was by then an influential and established subfield of family psychology and sociology, having grown from a few dozen studies in the 1960s to hundreds if not thousands by the 1990s.[42] The army itself performed some family research through its U.S. Army Research Institute, but scholars at research institutions like RAND Corporation or universities carried out the bulk of it. The very first study of military families was published after World War II, when psychologist Reuben Hill inquired into wartime traumas among families.[43] But the emerging field of military family research in the 1970s unified inquiry around questions of individual psychology with respect to everyday events rather than devastating shocks. The new research embraced widely popular and accepted notions of family functioning and individual and group adjustment, typified in the structural adjustment theory of figures like Talcott Parsons, which had gained influence beginning in the 1950s.[44] In the field of military family studies, the military context framed the notion of "adjustment": "adjustment to separation" during deployment; "adjustment [in the family] to reunion" after deployment; "reintegration [of the deployed soldier father]" into the family; and "adjustment to loss" in the case of the soldier's death. Military family sociologists and psychologists focused on how the military could promote wives' "adjustment" to the unique contours of military life—long hours, shift work, frequent relocation, separation, and worry about loss of life or limb.[45] Much army family research revolved around how the army "could build . . . family commitment to the Army mission."[46] Researchers were not always sanguine. As Hill wrote in the foreword to an influential text on military family psychology in the mid-1970s, "the military has little understanding of the stubborn resistance that families can build up to sabotage . . . military expectations."[47]

After the war in the Gulf, military family research explored the "sabotage" caused by the problematic behaviors of army wives during the Gulf War, and, as the 1990s progressed, during additional deployments such as those in the Balkans. In ways few recognized at the time, the post–Gulf War analyses of army wives mirrored analyses of civilian welfare clients. Military family psychologists and sociologists gathered various critiques of army wives into unified theories of military family dysfunction, slotting army spouses into categories similar to those used to characterize civilian welfare clients.

Army research psychologist D. Bruce Bell led an influential study in the 1990s that formally articulated several versions of "difficult families" that were encountered during the Gulf War and in subsequent deployment in the mid-1990s in Bosnia.[48] One was "the multi-problem family," a categorical term in common usage among civilian social workers and psychologists since the early postwar period. Used in the civilian world to describe families with multiple contacts with public assistance agencies or the courts, Bell pulled the multi-problem family analysis into the military setting, noting that some of the military families with problems during deployment had in fact always had problems and were "well known to [military] family agencies . . . even before the soldiers left" for the Gulf. These families functioned poorly under regular circumstances, requiring repeated intervention due to health, financial, child welfare, spousal violence, and other problems. Under deployment conditions, the problems worsened.[49]

Individual wives also posed difficulties, and Bell and his colleagues transformed the informal general observations about dependency among army wives during the Gulf War into a categorization of army wife "types" and the obstacles they posed to the army. They identified the "overly dependent spouse" as one specific problem. This woman proved to be a "type" whose predicaments, like the multi-problem family's, predated deployment. She was a wife "who does all right while the soldier is present but does not have the will or skills to cope when the soldier leaves." Excessively passive, dependent on the guidance of her soldier husband, she reached for the army's hand when the soldier deployed.[50]

The "overly dependent spouse" closely related to "the overly demanding spouse." The latter "would often state that their soldier performed these services when he/she was home and since the Army had taken him/her out of the home, it was up to the Army to fill the gap." One wife, the researchers explained, demanded that her "FSG leader should get out of bed at midnight . . . [and] drive her husband back to his Bosnia-bound plane," since she had a bad case of stomach flu. Another example involved "a spouse whose household goods had arrived after the deployment had started" and who felt "soldiers should come and assemble it." And yet another woman whose car had broken down upon arrival at a German port demanded, "a soldier should come with her, start it, and help her drive it back!" The "overly demanding spouse" clung to expectations that "someone would call these spouses on a regular basis to check to see how they were doing."[51]

She had come to rely on the army to such an extent that her dependency became not only a burden to the army, but also a pathology in itself.

The emphasis on dysfunction and dependency among enlisted army wives bore resemblance to studies of low-income civilian women, whose attitudes and actions came under increasing scrutiny from family psychologists who studied welfare programs and clients in the same period. It was not a coincidence that some of the most prominent military family scholars also studied welfare clients and low-income civilian women. Professor Gary Bowen of the University of North Carolina, Chapel Hill, conducted research both on military wives and on welfare families and single mothers. In 1993, Bowen published back-to-back studies on welfare clients and military families, one inquiring into services that "promote welfare independence of mothers on AFDC [Aid to Families with Dependent Children]" and one on "family adaptation of single parents" in the army.[52] Emerging on the other side of the Gulf War, military psychologists' assessments of army wives and the army family support system shared similarities with assessments of civilian welfare clients. Working off of a conjoined research agenda and a powerful language of dysfunction and dependency, military family researchers would, alongside civilian family researchers, provide the knowledge base for policy makers who aimed to reduce the dependency of women and families on government support programs and reduce their putatively dysfunctional behavior, both in the civilian world and in the army.

That specific agenda took shape in the 1990s. By 1994, both the newly elected Republican Congress of Newt Gingrich and the Democratic Clinton administration were working on welfare reform bills that aimed to eliminate perceived dysfunction and dependency among low-income women through a reimagining of the purpose of welfare. Drawing on the work of political theorists like professor Lawrence Mead of New York University and political polemicists like Charles Murray of the Heritage Foundation, policy makers proposed conditional requirements for receiving government support. Mead in particular developed a theory of "social obligations" for welfare that included avoiding child bearing, performing work, and seeking heterosexual marriage.[53] The new welfare reform agenda demanded that clients achieve "independence" and "self-support." Army wives were not far behind. As a result of the many evaluations and studies of army spouses spurred by the Gulf War, army spouses—and soldiers—would soon be enjoined to "take care of themselves."

As early as spring of 1991, the army began to readjust its philosophy for supporting both families and soldiers. The Operation Desert Storm after action report on family support sounded a coming change. The army's longtime family motto, "The Army Takes Care of Its Own," promised too much.[54] In subsequent deployments, the report explained, the army needed to carefully "instruct soldiers and families on what services they can" as well as cannot "request when a soldier is deployed."[55] The army ought to focus on "teaching families self-sufficiency not fostering dependency."[56] Instead of promising to "care for its own" the army needed to "redefine how the Army supports and assists families by emphasizing self-sufficiency and training." Army leaders had to "make soldiers responsible for family readiness" rather than the army.[57]

The first step toward "self support" emerged in a new program called Army Family Team Building (AFTB). As the word "team" suggested, AFTB proposed that the army alone did not hold responsibility for families—family readiness and support combined the efforts of soldiers, wives, and the army. And the word "building" suggested that family support was a process in which families must participate in order to reap benefits. AFTB operated on the metaphor "basic training for Army families." The program offered classes taught both by army staff and by seasoned army wives. Senior spouses would advise junior ones how to understand, navigate, and enhance readiness in the army. Elementary-level classes explained the basics of army life while more advanced courses advised spouses on how to improve their volunteer performance, access army networks, and use financial resources to enhance readiness.[58]

AFTB drew directly on the adjustment psychology developed by the Army Family Research Program and extended it in new ways. It endorsed the perspective that army wives served the army as part of the army family, and that anything that supported their adjustment benefited both them and the army. But it took the proposition further by suggesting not merely that the spouse adjust to army life, but that she do so to avoid dependence upon the army. AFTB enjoined families to "understand better what the Army expects of families" in order to "be able to function successfully" when soldiers were deployed.[59] The program's creators suggested that AFTB knowledge would help spouses "contribute to their military community, thus become part of the Army team."[60] "The program," its promoters promised, "will provide training to family members so they can do all the things that they did in the past faster, easier, and more efficiently," and thus rely less on the resources of the army itself. Above all, the army designed the AFTB for "teaching families self-sufficiency not fostering dependency."[61]

AFTB pioneered the policy turn away from the army taking care of its own and toward self-reliance, but similar changes in policy and rhetoric spread throughout the army. Morale, Welfare and Recreation (MWR), which housed AFTB alongside most of the army's family support programs and which represented the public face of the army's social welfare apparatus, officially altered its philosophy regarding family and soldier support in 1995. As the 1996 welfare reform, the Personal Responsibility and Work Opportunity Act, wended its way through congress, MWR pioneered a strikingly similar redefinition of the army's support programs. Harriet Rice, the civilian public affairs director of MWR, took to the road that year to discuss the new approach. She talked to the army's family service providers, unit and post commanders, leaders of FSGs, and AFTB trainers around the country and the world. The highlight of her PowerPoint presentation consisted of a newly defined and markedly altered army support motto. Since the advent of the volunteer era, of course, the army had promised, "The Army Takes Care of Its Own." It was the pledge that helped build the volunteer army. But now, in the mid-1990s, the army revised its vow. In its place, Rice offered audiences a "changing Army philosophy": an enormous American eagle swooping down over the word "SELF-RELIANT." Below the patriotic eagle appeared the new philosophy: "The Army Takes Care of Its Own by Teaching Its Own to Take Care of Themselves."[62] The rather long and infelicitously phrased motto demonstrated how the Army Family, not unlike a family receiving welfare, now had to take responsibility for itself.

The army pressed its new philosophy to the media, which expressed renewed interest in army support programs on the occasion of the twentieth anniversary of the All-Volunteer Force.[63] Nolan Walters, a reporter from Knight-Ridder, a news syndicate with over 300 outlets, contacted the MWR for a story on how the volunteer army had evolved toward a system of social supports for soldiers and families in the more than two decades since its origins. Walters wanted to explore "the increased importance . . . that social services have acquired as the All-Volunteer Army has matured." Though completely accurate, his inquiry set off alarm bells at MWR, where Harriet Rice "read something between the lines about the Army needing more of this [social services] as late and his wanting to make a story of that."[64]

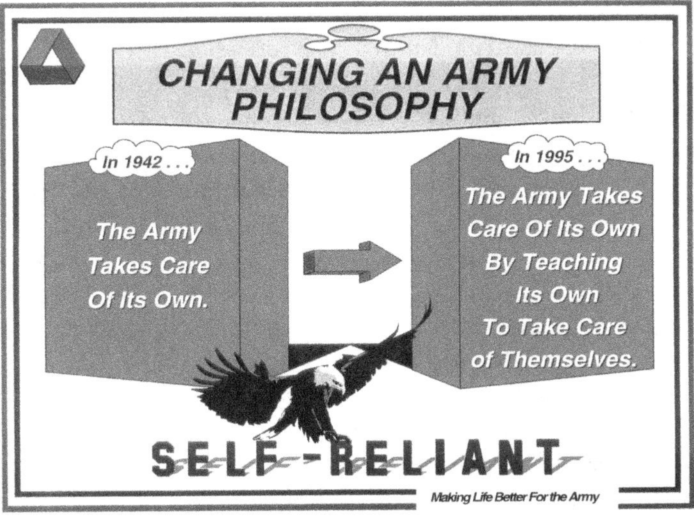

Morale, Welfare and Recreation's Harriet Rice announced the new army philosophy of self-reliance for soldiers and families in a PowerPoint presentation for army posts around the world. Courtesy of Harriet E. Rice Papers Collection, U.S. Army Heritage and Education Center, Carlisle, PA.

MWR agreed that the staff would communicate a clear message in response to Nolan's and other such inquiries: "FOCUS ON PREVENTION, SELF-RELIANCE."[65] The army's programs for soldiers and families were "not social services," which meant to "'help people when they're down'. But rather [a] 'preventive approach.'" Soldiers in America's army, a colonel at MWR told the reporter, "must be productive."[66] MWR staff touted the "fundamental change in philosophy from 'The Army takes care of its own' to 'the Army teaches its own to take care of themselves.'"[67]

Up the chain of command, the MWR's self-support mantra wove itself through new programs and into new offices. In early 1996, the CSA incorporated self-support philosophy into formally articulated army family policy. General Dennis Reimer recalled one of the original documents of army family policy, the "Army Family White Paper" written in 1983 by then CSA General John Wickham Jr., even as he called for changes. In a memorandum sent to every command in the army, guard, and reserve, Reimer made the case that the increasingly stressful context of army life in the 1990s, with its repeated deployments and scarcer resources, required revisiting the original philosophy of the Army Family. He wrote reverently of "the genius of the original white paper" and its "principles of partnership, wellness, and a sense of community." But while the white paper provided a foundational text for the army, it was time to revisit it in order to be sure that "the principles . . . contained in the original Army Family white paper, still provide the foundation required." In Reimer's view, they did not. They required a "rounding out" that reflected the conclusions about the Gulf War, army research on wives, and the new army motto. Reimer proposed a new principle of self-reliance. "We must teach soldiers and families to care for themselves." Though self-reliance reversed the original promise to "take care of its own," Reimer voiced no reflection on the contradiction and ordered, all "Future family programs must be reshaped to assist in creating self-reliance in our people."[68]

As the order descended through army commands, officers recast their family support functions as promoting the independence of soldiers and their families. The leader of the U.S. Army Special Operations Command (USASOC) at Fort Bragg, for example, interpreted self-support as an injunction to produce military readiness among families: "This command is committed to improving the quality of life for our soldiers and family members. This can be done by creating a proactive family readiness training program."[69] A year later, Special Operations Command's Human Resources Directorate laid out a more detailed vision of family readiness for its soldiers and families that emphasized self-support to a higher degree: "VISION: Highly adaptive, self-sufficient, resilient USASOC families, integrated into America's Army; ready and capable, today, tomorrow, and always." And: "MISSION: Promote programs and advise on services that engage soldiers and families to enhance their level of confidence and self-sufficiency."[70] Even the spiritual leaders of the chaplaincy, ahead of the curve, disseminated new proposals for family ministry to assist families in developing "the skills associated with self-reliance."[71]

Not surprisingly, given the pivotal role the FSGs had played in causing the army to reevaluate its approach to family support, the army redefined them with a new emphasis on self-support and self-reliance. It touted their goals as improved "performance, readiness, retention, [and] self-sufficient families." "A Family Support Group," the army warned, "is not baby-sitting or taxi service, coffee group or club, surrogate parent or spouse, financial institution, professional counseling service."[72] At Fort Leavenworth, Kansas, home of the Command and General Staff College and the post where all battalion commanders received training before taking command, commanders were taught the proper definition of family support under the new regime. According to a staff member from the CFSC, FSGs still functioned to "reduce soldier isolation, provide mutual support, distribute information, establish a sense of community," but they now also aimed to "enhance self-reliance."[73]

At the turn of the millennium, the army capped its redefinition of its family and soldier support by changing the name of FSGs. At the annual Commander's Conference at Carlisle Barracks, Pennsylvania, a CFSC leader explained the name change and the rationale. While the army had already been officially encouraging self-reliance for five years, the symbolism of the new name communicated the decisive break from earlier notions of army support for soldiers and families. "There is a sense throughout the Army," he explained, "that the present Family Support name may foster a dependency mentality among some family members and could encourage the use of the program as a crutch instead of encouraging self-reliance." The information paper tellingly referred to the "stigma of family programs as being too support-oriented," referencing the increasing stigmatization of all forms of reliance on social welfare in the 1990s, in both civilian and military life. Changing the name "from 'support' to 'readiness'" would "help eliminate" the danger of this stigma. "Many Family Support Groups," the paper reported approvingly, "have already transitioned to the new name."[74] On June 1, 2000, four months after the conference, the Department of the Army renamed the FSGs Family Readiness Groups "to emphasize the need for readiness and self-sufficiency among Army families in the modern Army."[75]

IN 1994, as the army began to undertake its revolution from "caring for its own" to making its own "care for themselves," transformations in the army's social and family supports registered in the press. That year *Army Times* published a five-page story, the first of an ongoing series that rendered a harsh verdict on the change. The cover quoted the official line from the leadership, that "the army cares about families," but the story queried, "Does Anyone Believe It?" The resounding answer, the article suggested, was no. Apparently, the army's retreat from full-throated support for families had filtered down to wives, informing their perceptions that the army did not, in fact, care for them. The reporter described the bleak life of Cathy Pigott, who lived in "a rundown family housing complex at Fort Campbell, in Kentucky" and the frustration of "parents at Fort Bragg, N.C., who after months on a waiting list, still can't find spots for children in an on-post child development center." It highlighted a couple who had sought marriage counseling and been "placed on a two-month waiting list instead" and the "young wife of a specialist who recently made her first visit . . . to apply for food stamps" because her husband's pay did not meet their needs. "Somewhere along the route between Army headquarters and Army installations," the reporter concluded, "the message [that the army cares about families] has lapsed into lip service."[76]

The army's increasing failure to take care of its own worried the man who had staked part of his career on building army family programs. General John A. Wickham Jr., the former CSA who oversaw many of the army's expansive family supports of the 1980s told *Army Times* that his married son, who served in the army, observed numerous shortfalls in army family policies and programs. Seemingly unaware that the army support programs he had created were under attack for fostering dependency, Wickham warned that the army's commitment to "strong families and programs that strengthen their quality of life . . . will have to be more than lip service." At almost the precise moment of his warning, the army was actually no longer officially giving "lip service" to taking care of its own. Quite the contrary. While Wickham warned the army "to prove it cares," the army was setting the condition of self-reliance on any programs for care.[77]

The effects of the army's new ideology of self-support were compounded by its increasingly straitened finances during the post–Cold War drawdown. In the depleted budgetary terrain of the 1990s, the army's well-developed and costly support programs for soldiers and families proved vulnerable not only to ideological reorientation but also to new economic configurations. According to longtime scholars of army family programs, the growing budget concerns about "the national debt and . . . defense spending" made "current military community facilities and programs . . . likely targets for . . . defense budget cuts."[78] Concrete services to help families—health, housing, child care, education, social services—carried a high price. In this context, the army's emphasis on building self-support among soldiers took on political-economic characteristics as the army pursued new methods of privately contracting, or outsourcing, and privatizing soldier support. Ideological retrenchment worked hand-in-glove with the army's turn to the private sector. The army of the 1990s would teach soldiers and families to take care of themselves, and hire private firms to provide much of the care that soldiers themselves could not.

8

Outsourcing Soldier and Family Support

SHORTLY AFTER the fall of the Berlin Wall, President George H. W. Bush spoke to the venerable Commonwealth Club, a business group in San Francisco, California, about his cuts to the defense budget. The contrast to the Reagan-era military largesse was stark. With evident satisfaction, Bush informed the audience that "in 1986 defense expenditures consumed 6.3 percent of our gross national product." But the budget he had just submitted to Congress held "down defense spending . . . to just above 5 percent of gross national product." While Bush was no dove and cherished no romantic notion of a windfall from a "peace dividend," he and his defense secretary, Richard Cheney, nevertheless began slashing defense expenditures.[1] Over the four years of his presidency, Bush reduced defense spending by 17 percent.[2] The reductions targeted every area of the defense budget. He cut the Operations and Maintenance and the Research and Development budgets. He also sliced procurement by 40 percent. Bush eliminated personnel, with some 300,000 soldiers, sailors, airmen, and marines exiting the services. And finally, he shuttered military installations around the world.[3] The Bush-Cheney cuts to the military, referred to widely as the "drawdown," ushered in an unprecedented era of austerity for the army.

Bush's successor, President Bill Clinton, matched Bush's cuts and added his own burdens to the army—the mandates of his National Performance Review, commonly called the "Reinvention of Government." Occasioned by a slumping economy and federal budget cuts as well as "New Democrat" faith in business, the Reinvention of Government introduced into the federal government boardroom practices such as cutting overhead, outsourcing, increasing efficiencies, and improving "quality management" as coping mechanisms for a sharply reduced spending regime. Led by Vice President Al Gore, the Reinvention of Government embraced corporate influence on the military, bringing a Wall Street financier to lead a new outsourcing and privatization office in the Pentagon. The initiative pressed the army into close relationships with private sector firms.

The drawdown and the advent of contracting out facilitated the long-sought victory for free market and corporate leaders who had called for the end of the army's institutional support structure since the birth of the All-Volunteer Force. They chafed in the 1970s and 1980s—especially under the putatively business-friendly Reagan administration—as the army and the Pentagon built its own substantial architecture of support covering everything from health to housing, child care to counseling. But with the straitened military finances after the late 1980s and the concurrent Clinton-era embrace of corporate methods, economists and corporate advisors to the federal government and the Pentagon realized their long-held goals. Contracted military support services grew steadily in the 1990s, increasing from about 30 percent of all military contracting in the late 1980s to nearly 45 percent by 1999, when they matched or exceeded total military spending on products (weapons, materiel), traditionally the bulk of private military contracting.[4] The overwhelming proportion of services contracted fell into the broadly defined realm of "soldier support," the banal necessities of running a military—managing military property, cooking and serving food, cleaning facilities and uniforms, generating strategic planning, consulting on new military doctrine, performing public relations and public affairs activities.[5] Within this category, some of the biggest service contracts emerged in military social welfare—providing soldiers and families with health care, housing, social work, counseling, and more.

This shift in the army's political economy from public to private began a year prior to the war in the Persian Gulf, and thus before the army had begun is ideological retrenchment from its promise to "take care of its own." Yet the two phenomena—the embrace of "self-reliance" and of the market—developed simultaneously and buttressed one another. As the drawdown unfolded, the commanders of the army's soldier and family support system shuddered, realizing that the ax was poised not over "the fighting units" but "on the support side of the house," already deemed suspect for promoting dependency within the army.[6] Lodged in the unglamorous offices and commands that coordinated the army's vast array of support functions—logistics, installations and housing, community and family support offices—the men and women who managed the "non-core competencies," the corporate term for support services, were pressed by political and economic circumstances to transfer the army's welfare state from public to private hands. They were a new generation of officers, some with bachelor's or master's degrees in business and more open to the private sector than the generals of William Westmoreland's generation who had resisted the free market model of the military. Struggling to manage their budget cuts and meet their reform "benchmarks," they pioneered the new business methods that eventually shaped army-wide policies in favor of outsourcing and privatizing the army's social welfare system.[7] As they chipped away at the support system of the "Army Family," the army no longer literally "took care of its own" but paid others to do it.

AS THE ARMY endured cuts to its budget, personnel, and physical infrastructure, the Army Materiel Command (AMC) may have suffered most. Though AMC did not provide direct support services to soldiers, it did provide across-the-board materiel support for the army. As one army saying had it, "if a Soldier shoots it, drives it, flies it, wears it, communicates with it or eats it, AMC provides it."[8] The command managed the entire acquisition process of "stuff" that soldiers used and then made sure the stuff got to soldiers and was properly maintained. AMC radically restructured and downsized between 1987 and 1991, as it faced a force reduction of 5,200 jobs, including a 30 percent reduction at headquarters, and the closure of many of its installations through the Base Realignment and Closure (BRAC) process.[9] "By 1995 . . . AMC was reduced to a size operating with less than half of the strength it possessed during the 1980s. There were 40 percent fewer maintenance depots, no supply depots, and a major reduction in management overhead."[10] Surveys of employees in AMC conveyed an attitude of "hopelessness" and a telling feeling of "emasculation."[11] As one of the most enormous units of the army involved in most aspects of army life, its fate proved decisive for other army functions, particularly the support services.

The leaders at AMC looked to corporate America and business schools, whose methods they hoped would help them manage the drawdown and survive budget cuts. AMC had always functioned in close relationship to the private sector. Its logisticians worked every day with corporations through the procurement process—obtaining the uniforms, the guns, the tanks, the food, and everything else the army needed. Over the years, AMC's staff had accrued knowledge about contracting with the private sector. Pressed by the federal policies created first by Eisenhower and Johnson that mandated federal reliance on the private sector for commercial services, policies that took on new urgency in the fiscal crisis of the 1970s, the army's logisticians became more familiar with contracting out not only for materiel but also for commercial services. They advanced new ways of contracting, like the now well-known Logistics Civilian Augmentation Program (LOGCAP) first created in 1985.[12] Logisticians took courses in business management and tested contractor-provided supports in everything from food service to payroll to preplanning for overseas mobilizations. In the late 1980s and early 1990s, as they shredded their own functions to meet budget cuts, they rapidly increased their knowledge of the private sector and began applying corporate management methods and philosophies.

AMC guided its cuts and closures using the practice of "Total Quality Management" (TQM) borrowed from the private sector. TQM constituted a management process that proposed the enhancement of a firm's goods or services through rigorous, constantly evaluated measures of "customer satisfaction." It originated in Japanese firms in the early postwar years of economic restructuring and growth and migrated to the United States in the early 1980s. It then spread throughout the corporate world in the late 1980s as management guidance for firms facing greater international competition and seeking greater efficiencies and effectiveness. It began its leap from the for-profit private sector to the not-for-profit and public sectors in the late 1980s and early 1990s.[13] In its iteration in the United States, it demanded total "buy in" in business terms, from both management and employees. Everyone agreed to use established methods of reflection and evaluation to try to meet evolving customer demands in evolving circumstances.

Adapting TQM to the military environment represented a profound challenge for a tradition-bound institution like the military. But beginning in 1988, General Louis C. Wagner of the AMC formally adopted corporate-style TQM to rebuild the command in the image of dominant Japanese corporations of the 1980s like Sony and Toyota.[14] His previous four years as deputy chief of staff for research, development, and acquisition had put him in contact with leading corporate defense firms already engaged in the corporate practice. He and his team introduced the terms "management" for commanders and staff, and "customers" for soldiers, staff, and Congress. Wagner began by using TQM principles to help the command undertake "detailed functional analysis . . . in order to determine what it [AMC] did, how it did it, and what could be done differently."[15]

The generals who followed Wagner faced the steepest cuts of the drawdown, and the task of adapting business practices to the context of rapidly diminished resources. General William Tuttle Jr., who took over AMC from Wagner in late 1989, struggled to "improve efficiencies" in several ways. A Harvard University MBA who later in life inaugurated an eponymous Award for Business Acumen in Defense and Government, Tuttle adopted methods used by downsizing corporations in the United States to fight increasing foreign competition.[16] He cut jobs, streamlined transportation, reduced inventories in storage facilities, implemented simplified acquisition and contract procedures, consolidated supply depots, and introduced automation to some support functions.[17]

It was not until General Jimmy D. Ross took over AMC in early 1992 that corporate methods fully blossomed, however. Ross was born in the tiny Northern Louisiana town of Hosston and attended Henderson State University, one of the many small Christian colleges that dotted the rural Ozarks combining evangelical Christianity and free enterprise curricula.[18] Ross had spent thirty-three years in the army, undertaking multiple tours in AMC and five years in the Office of the Deputy Chief of Staff for Logistics. Chief of Staff of the Army (CSA) General Gordon Sullivan warned Ross that he would "have to give up" swaths of AMC's functions and infrastructure. But he wanted Ross to avoid a "salami slice approach" in favor of strategic planning methods that would help "AMC . . . become a more efficient operation as it becomes smaller."[19] Ross, who in 1975 had earned a business degree from Central Michigan State University, threw himself into his task of bringing a "business orientation" to the AMC. He met with "industry CEOs and presidents to discuss their reduction strategies."[20] He then hired private contractors—consultants in "strategic management principles"—to help guide his transformation of AMC into a more business-like institution. (They constituted 80 percent of the personnel on his planning team.) Together they also visited "industry experts" and academics at Penn State, the Massachusetts Institute of Technology, and Syracuse University who

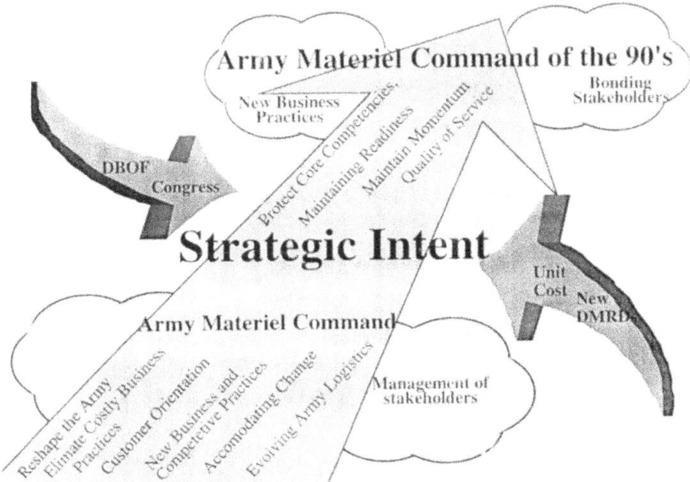

A PowerPoint slide from a presentation on the "Army Materiel Command of the 90s" illustrated the range of corporate methods, philosophies, and vocabulary used by General Jimmy D. Ross. Courtesy of the Army Materiel Command's Historical Office.

provided briefings on TQM and what they called the "strategic management process." Ross had no small task—cutting the size of AMC without losing any of its capability, while at the same time improving its "quality."[21]

Army leadership watched AMC's adoption of corporate practices closely and looked to its generals for guidance regarding the downsizing and reorganization of the army as a whole. Upon Ross's appointment, CSA Sullivan had admitted to Ross, "there is no question that AMC is out front in the development and application of TQM." And he asked Ross to "help identify those policies we must change [in the Army Staff] for the good of the Total Army."[22] AMC's adoption of TQM thus had implications far beyond the single command.

In 1990, the Office of the Under Secretary of the Army announced that the U.S. Army officially "endorsed the philosophy of Total Quality Management (TQM) as a strategy to increase quality, productivity, and efficiency throughout the Army."[23] The army rechristened the corporate philosophy and practice as its own, coining the term "Total Army Quality" (TAQ). In July of 1991, the army announced it would "rewrite Army management philosophy (AR 5–1) to align it with the principles of TQM." The army now formally described its institutional management in the terms used by corporations around the world.[24]

In 1992 Vice Chief of Staff of the Army (VCSA) General Dennis Reimer took over personal responsibility for the practice, a move signifying the centrality of the philosophy and process to the man occupying the position most intimately involved in managing the day-to-day army. Using AMC as a model for the entire army, he brought the TAQ process to the center of army planning for the drawdown. Before the end of the year, he made sure that the units outside AMC that also faced budget cutbacks would follow the TAQ process. He initiated new courses in TAQ "throughout the Army's training and educational systems."[25] All other army components that supported soldiers through either infrastructure or services or programs would be inculcated in corporate planning and practices to manage their cuts. One-, two-, three-, and four-star generals and army civilian leaders sat beside corporate leaders, management consultants, and scholars from business schools to discuss how TAQ could help the army survive the drawdown. "The Army is going to get smaller. The budget is going to be reduced," he explained. But TAQ "gives us hope."[26] Reimer's effort to push corporate practices throughout the army would soon be intensified by the transition to the presidency of Bill Clinton, in which corporate practices assumed pervasive influence on governance.

WHEN CLINTON first took office, his administration did not telegraph its intention to revolutionize the military's orientation to the private sector and thereby transform the volunteer force's commitment to "take care of its own." Clinton's first steps in defense merely followed the path of President Bush. Clinton, like Bush, pledged to cut defense, though his actual budget cuts proved more modest than those of the Bush-Cheney era, amounting to 5 percent over the course of his presidency.[27] Under Clinton the army's numbers fell to approximately 495,000 active duty personnel and only ten active army divisions.[28]

The Clinton-era growth of private contracting for military support partly resulted from these additional defense cuts, but it was also driven by a new federal government-wide initiative—the National Performance Review (NPR). More than any previous Democratic president, Clinton embraced the rhetoric that had for years characterized antigovernment conservatives:

he agreed that government might be "too big" and that too often it functioned ineffectively and inefficiently. Campaigning as a "New Democrat," he promised to reduce the federal deficit by cutting and streamlining the government—what his vice president, Al Gore, would refer to as "Reinventing Government."[29] After the election, Clinton and Gore announced that the vice president would lead the NPR's full-scale assessment of government activities. The reassessment embraced corporate ideology and practices and attempted to install them in the public sector. It spurred the transfer of military support functions to the private sector.

The NPR descended from previous executive-branch-led efforts to cut government through the application of corporate methods and power—the Hoover Commissions of the late 1940s and early 1950s and President Reagan's Grace Commission of the early 1980s.[30] Under pressure from the right due to the growth of government during both the New Deal and World War II, President Harry Truman had authorized former president Herbert Hoover to undertake two reviews of the "Organization of the Executive Branch of Government." Hoover's commissions recommended applying private sector practices to achieve cuts and efficiencies and eliminating entirely government "commercial activities," those "federal business enterprises in competition with private enterprise."[31] The Grace Commission thirty years later made similar recommendations, but with an even fuller indictment of the failings of the public sector and fuller praise for the virtues of the private sector. Its corporate authors promised there was "no surer way of ensuring that [government] economies will be realized than by turning to the private sector."[32] Though Clinton's NPR struck a more sanguine note about the importance of government than the Hoover or Grace Commissions, it nevertheless shared their assumptions about the inefficiency of the public sector and the efficiency of the private sector. Solutions to the thorny problems of governance lay in most every case in the private sector: imitating its can-do attitude, applying its models of market systems, or quite simply handing over government functions to it.

The intellectual inspiration for the reinvention of government came from a nationally best-selling book published in 1992 by David Osborne and Ted Gaebler, *Reinventing Government.* Clinton, who then hired Osborne as part of the NPR, endorsed the book as "the blueprint" for "every elected official in America." In a reprise of free market and contracting themes offered in the 1970s by free market advocates, the book instructed readers in how to apply "the entrepreneurial spirit" to "transforming the public sector." The chapters detailed "innovative" practices derived from the private sector and applied by exemplary government agencies: cutting and streamlining services and overhead, putting "customers" first, transforming management cultures, focusing on quality, and building partnerships with the private sector. The authors focused especially on "catalytic" government agencies, agencies that successfully achieved efficient, effective services. Among the most important characteristics these catalytic agencies shared was their willingness to "partner" with the private sector. Twenty-six of the thirty-six models the authors presented entailed public/private or entirely privately contracted provision of traditional government services. Provisos regarding the importance of governance aside, the book unambiguously celebrated the possibility that private sector practices would improve American governance.[33]

At the heart of the Clinton-Gore Reinvention of Government lay the corporate practice of "outsourcing," an updated term used to describe the contracting out of government functions to the private sector. In the corporate world, outsourcing referred to the process by which a firm ceased performing what its leaders defined as its "non-core functions." An aerospace firm, for example, might decide that since its "core competencies" lay in the research, development, and construction of satellites, it would hold onto the divisions and employees central to that process and cut other functions—say customer service, payroll, janitorial services—and send them out for bid with private contractors who themselves specialized in these areas. In the late 1980s and early 1990s, outsourcing resulted in millions of layoffs from American corporations as "non-core" employees dropped from salaried payrolls and were replaced by temporary or lower-wage workers from contracted firms. In government, outsourcing operated in surprisingly similar fashion. Government agencies were told to shed the activities that were neither inherently governmental—tasks that only government could perform to guarantee public safety, well-being, and democratic oversight—nor central to an agency's mission. Many of the same functions that the corporate sector outsourced were then targeted in government: administrative services, customer service, cleaning and maintenance all fell quickly to outsourcing.

The language of the NPR initially minimized the degree to which reinventing government would actually cut government and send its functions into the private sector. Vice President Gore always praised federal workers in his speeches.[34] He told an audience on the first anniversary of the performance review that he and his partners had simply pursued "a better way to do things" with the help of "state and local government or the private sector." But from the start, the NPR's mandates militated for outsourcing.[35] Economist Alice Rivlin, Clinton's director of the Office of Management and Budget, explained that the NPR would "shrink the size and intrusiveness of the federal government" and, perhaps most importantly, promised a "very serious rethinking of the essential role of the federal government." "Some activities," she explained, were "not appropriate for any level of government" and "would be performed more effectively by the private sector or by public entities subject to incentives and pressures of private sector competition."[36] True to Rivlin's words, many of the NPR practices led to outsourcing: its "decentralizing" stood for both devolutions of power to the states from the federal government, and also contracting out; "empowering people" meant not only changing management practices to allow more employee input, but also changing practices to allow outsourcing; "enhancing core activities of government" meant not only improving those activities but also cutting the activities deemed "non-core."

The NPR encouraged outsourcing of as many "non-core" functions as possible, and a great many fell in the area of social welfare programs and services. At the Department of Health and Human Services and the Department of Labor, for example, programs including child welfare administration, labor and employment services, child welfare (adoption, foster care), and Aid to Families with Dependent Children (AFDC, renamed Temporary Aid to Needy Families—TANF—in 1996) were contracted out to the private sector. Federal government private contracting in these areas followed the lead of contracting that had taken place at the state level in these and other programs. But the NPR encouraged further contracting with the passage in 1996 of the PRWOA, which narrowed the definitions of what constituted "core" government functions and therefore ceded additional terrain to the private sector. For-profit national corporations, such as Maximus, Inc., Affiliated Computer Services (ACS), Dyncorp, Inc., and Anderson Consulting, all entered the public social welfare sector. Several, including Dyncorp and ACS, were either active military contractors or were soon purchased by military contractors.[37]

In 1994 President Clinton created a new Office of Assistant (Under) Secretary of Defense for Economic Security in order to promote outsourcing in the military, and here, too, "non-core" social welfare services became targets. To the new post he sent Joshua Gotbaum, the son of famed New York City public union leader Victor Gotbaum. The younger Gotbaum was no union man, however. A partner at the Wall Street firm Lazard Frères, he had spent thirteen years engineering many of the biggest deals of the great merger movement of the late 1980s and early 1990s. As Gotbaum put it, Clinton told him, "we'd like a restructuring expert . . . to help us do it [national defense] in a more businesslike fashion." Gotbaum's orders were to "help private industry help defense."[38] Though a wide array of issues fell within Gotbaum's bailiwick, he prioritized the mandate to accelerate outsourcing and privatization of defense. "At a time when the Department must reconcile a smaller budget" to sustained military demands, "it seems natural," Gotbaum told the Senate, "to look for private sector help."[39] His office pressed the Department of Defense (DoD) to speed up and simplify outsourcing and privatization.[40]

Business interests close to the Pentagon, whose bottom lines also suffered from the drawdown, supported Gotbaum's outsourcing agenda to help them capture a new source of revenue from government contracts. With weapons and material procurement budgets slashed by as much as 40 percent, firms closed production lines, laid off workers, shuttered plants, and outsourced their own noncore functions.[41] But their problems were exacerbated by the Pentagon's refusal to contract out more of its functions. As the president of one influential defense trade organization explained, its members found themselves not only losing revenue due to diminished materiel contracts, but "competing against federal agencies" that were conducting activities that the private sector could, in theory, undertake.[42] Seizing upon the context of the NPR and the installation of Gotbaum at the Pentagon, defense firms pushed Congress and the Pentagon to place new swaths of military business in their hands. They chipped away at the rules, regulations, and practices inhibiting outsourcing and pressed the process to its furthest possible ends. They especially pushed the outsourcing of all the services they deemed "non-core" military functions.

They were helped in this by the Defense Science Board (DSB), an organization of military personnel, scientific experts, and defense contractors chartered by the secretary of defense that shaped the agenda for outsourcing defense services. Created during the Eisenhower administration to advise the Pentagon on weapons systems and technology, the DSB of the 1990s focused largely on finance and budget issues.[43] In 1996 a DSB report described which defense services should remain at the "core" of the military and which should be outsourced. With representatives of longtime military contractors like Bechtel, Boeing, and MPRI, Inc., as authors, the report argued that the military ought to finance a leap toward a leaner, high-tech force by outsourcing all of its support. "A revolution in business affairs is needed," the report explained, "to pay for the revolution in DoD military affairs." Handing over the support services to the private sector would "pay for" the fully modernized military of the twenty-first century by shifting defense spending from "soft" manpower and logistics supports to "hard" weapons and technology procurement. To that end, the report took aim at the same "government commercial activities" that anti-New Dealers, early free market advocates, and then defense manpower economists had battled—the "good[s] or service[s] that could be obtained from the private sector and that . . . [are] . . . not inherently governmental."[44] The DSB report recommended that every single government commercial activity performed by the military should be put out for competitive bid to the private sector.[45]

The DSB's recommendations were echoed almost verbatim by a second defense industry group, Business Executives for National Security (BENS). BENS operated as a private, nongovernmental organization established in 1982 to support the massive Reagan defense buildup, and played a key role in establishing the procedure for the BRAC process, the first round of which occurred in 1988. Having established a reputation for "eliminating inefficiencies" at the Pentagon through "applying . . . best business practice solutions," BENS moved into the 1990s with a sharp focus on privatization and outsourcing.[46] One year after the DSB issued its outsourcing report, BENS produced its own. As had the DSB's, BENS's report recommended near total outsourcing and privatization of all noncore functions. BENS warned that "if it wants the full benefits of privatization, the Defense Department must be willing to cede ownership and control" to the private sector.[47] Though the reports of both the DSB and BENS spelled prosperity for defense industries (as the business magazine *Barron's* put it, there would be a rush to get in "on the ground floor" of military privatization and outsourcing), the reports dwelled solely on the purported benefits for the military of outsourcing and privatizing its supports.[48]

Additional corporate interests endorsed the DSB's and BENS's agendas on outsourcing and privatization. Major trade organizations with connections to the military, including the Associated General Contractors of America, the American Consulting Engineers Council, the Contract Services Association, and the Professional Services Council, championed the efforts of congressional Republicans such as Representative John Duncan (R-TN) and Senator Craig Thomas (R-WY) to pass the Freedom from Government Competition Act. That bill, like the DSB and BENS reports, made the case that government activities could "be better done in the private sector," and sought to enhance profits in the private sector by "remov[ing] the competition of the Federal Government." The bill prohibited the federal government from conducting commercial activities and instead required contracting with the private sector. It targeted all the support functions of the military suggested by the DSB and BENS. Though the Freedom from Government Competition Act did not pass Congress, it united corporate interests around the outsourcing and privatization agenda.[49]

The pressures from government and corporations to outsource defense support functions accelerated DoD plans already under way. The Pentagon pledged to "embrace the principles of the National Performance Review to operate more effectively and at less cost." "Market dynamics," the DoD promised, "will replace reliance on internal monopolies" of public servants performing public services. "Outsourcing of non-core functions," the department explained in language that could have been pulled directly from Gotbaum's office or the DSB or BENS reports, "has been proven in both the private and public sectors to be a sound business tool." And the DoD would now do the same.[50] Secretary of Defense William Perry planned that "essentially all DOD 'commercial activities' should be outsourced . . . and all new needs should be channeled to the private sector from the beginning."[51]

AS THE PRESSURE to outsource grew within the Clinton administration, the army shed approximately half of its total support functions to the private sector.[52] Army contracts for services increased from $13 billion in 1990 to $23 billion in 2000. Its service contracts grew much more rapidly than its contracts for products (materiel) or for research and development. Beginning in 1993, total contract spending on services overtook contract spending on products and on research and development, a total inversion of the pattern that had prevailed throughout the postwar period in which the military has made its most expensive contracts in products—weapons and materiel.[53] Dozens of categories of services—maintenance and repair, education and training, social services, medical, management consulting, and more—resulted in thousands upon thousands of "contract actions."[54]

The army shifted its burden of services for "caring for its own" from its own shoulders to those of private, for-profit corporations.

The soldiers and civilians who managed the army's vast installations made one of the most significant transitions to outsourcing and privatization. Installation commanders were responsible for the day-in, day-out functioning of the posts where soldiers and families lived and worked. They managed services like child care, fire protection, and Morale, Welfare and Recreation services, in addition to support infrastructure like family housing and community centers. Like the soldier support services of AMC, the support functions of installations faced steep cuts in the drawdown of the late 1980s and early 1990s.[55] Since 1989, the army had diverted massive funds from its operations and maintenance and construction budgets and left installations struggling with "deterioration of infrastructure," "shortage in Army Family Housing Funds," and cuts to "quality of life initiatives" such as recreation, family support, and children's services.[56] Just as in AMC, installation commanders were told to experiment with private sector practices to downsize and reorganize the resource-starved installations. VCSA General Reimer ordered installation commanders to "critically examine which services we should provide, which we should divest [privatize], and which should be contracted [out to the private sector]."[57] Reimer hoped to "to reshape the installations' structure and business processes along more entrepreneurial lines."[58]

The army created a new entity to put installations on a business footing—the Office of the Assistant Chief of Staff for Installation Management (OACSIM). This proponent operated as the knowledge center and policy maker for all installations, gathering information and innovative management techniques and then promulgating them throughout installations. It developed "installation and sustaining base doctrine" for the army.[59] The OACSIM commander hired private contractors from Delta Research and RAND to help define its "vision," its "customers," its "goals," and its management "strategy."[60]

The new corporate-style strategic plan emphasized the need for privatization and contracting out noncore functions to the private sector. Installation commanders would now be "forming . . . partnerships for facilities and services to improve operations, customer service, and fiscal effectiveness and efficiency." And the command would give them "resource management flexibility" to "enable installations to operate as business activities and maximize the effectiveness and efficiency of resources."[61] Annual awards for the most effectively and efficiently run army community rewarded commanders who "had been able to incorporate private contractors and vendors" into the process.[62] Newly created courses for installation commanders in 1995 drilled them in outsourcing practices, devoting one of four total days to understanding, managing, and executing private contracts and privatization.[63] Outsourcing and privatization constituted the primary vehicle for installation commanders to survive the drawdown.

Housing represented the most important and costly program installation commanders contracted to the private sector. Historically the army had always struggled to meet its obligations to provide soldiers and their families adequate homes. Military construction and maintenance required enormous, long-term capital investments, investments often skimped on by Congress and military leaders in favor of force modernization or training. The army had long relied on a combination of government-built military housing and the private housing market—"on the economy," as soldiers put it. Through the 1960s, military housing consisted of government housing for career commissioned and noncommissioned officers, and for married career enlisted men, with barracks for single and low-ranking enlisted men. Soldiers who chose the private housing market made their purchase or, usually, rental agreements alone, in units rented or bought from private citizens.

This combination of housing sources periodically failed, creating crises that sometimes made front pages of national newspapers and magazines. Right after World War II, the editors of *Life Magazine* were scandalized by their pictorial exposé of soldiers and their families crammed into drafty trailers and shacks near Fort Dix, New Jersey. In the early 1970s, *Stars and Stripes* told stories of soldiers and families posted to Germany shivering in underheated, centuries-old housing an hour from their German post, the only apartments they could afford.[64]

In the 1990s, the housing crisis returned. Although the army spent hundreds of millions improving the army housing stock in the 1980s, the total amount of army housing still fell short in the 1990s.[65] The downsizing of the military in the 1990s aggravated the low housing inventory. Though over a million military personnel left or were forced out over the course of the decade, theoretically freeing up housing, base closures actually resulted in large concentrations of army personnel at fewer—and suddenly more populous—posts. Crowded onto fewer megaposts, army personnel faced sudden shortages of housing. The results were what one military housing researcher labeled "ghettos" in which the army functioned as "slumlord."[66] According to researchers, "approximately two-thirds" of military housing stock was "in need of repair or replacement."[67]

Surveying the tight budgets of the late 1980s and early 1990s, Army Staff in Washington, DC, "concluded that the Army did not have the money either to upgrade 40,000 of the 120,000 family houses it owned or to get rid of them and pay housing allowances to an additional 40,000 families."[68] Without the funds to build and maintain their own housing, Army Staff made the decision to use the private sector in a new way. Rather than just refer soldiers into the private housing market of rentals and purchases, "Army Staff decided that it would be necessary to privatize the army family housing program."[69] The army would enter contracts with real estate and construction firms to build, manage, and maintain housing for soldiers and families.

It was not the first time the army had experimented with large contracts to private sector developers to build houses and apartments for express lease to soldiers and families. The housing crises of both the 1940s and the 1970s had convinced the army to sign contracts with private real estate builders to construct and maintain army housing. In the late 1940s and early 1950s, the Wherry and Capehart programs, named after their congressional sponsors, produced 63,000 units for the army.[70] Then again in the early-to-mid-1980s, the 801 program, as Congress dubbed it, produced 4080 units for the army. All the programs were abandoned, the early ones cancelled by Congress because of alleged high costs and "windfall profits" to developers, and the later one abandoned by the private sector, which felt the more regulated deals resulting from the earlier experiments were not profitable enough.[71]

As the army's installation commanders struggled to reconcile their enormous budget cuts to the needs of the volunteer force in the 1990s, the context looked far more felicitous for a private sector solution to which the government could agree. In the era of downsizing and outsourcing, with the widespread adoption of corporate ideology and practices, large-scale, privatized military housing found support in the army, in Joshua Gotbaum's Pentagon office, and in Congress. Gotbaum's office had created a "tiger team"—an in-house, fast-acting task force—devoted to military privatization and outsourcing, and that team proposed legislation for military housing privatization. In Congress, the legislation passed easily in 1996.[72]

Housing privatization legislation allowed the army to create its own housing authority—the Residential Communities Initiative (RCI)—with the ability to contract with large real estate and construction corporations.[73] For each deal, the army formed a limited liability corporation (LLC) or limited liability partnership (LLP) in conjunction with a developer. The army served only as a minority partner while the developer served as the "managing member" who assumed "authority for day-to-day operations." What the army brought to the deal was initial "direct cash investments, loan guarantees," or "conveyance of land ownership," and then a guaranteed revenue stream from the long-term lease the army paid. These leases were longer than any in army housing history: a fifty-year term with another twenty-five-year option.[74]

The deal structure "leveraged," in the army's words, limited army dollars by ensuring profits for private corporations. Leases were paid from the "rent" that army families paid—their Basic Allowances for Housing (BAH); the allowances, however, bypassed the soldiers who signed them over to be directly paid from the army to the LLC.[75] The "rents" were set to guarantee a profit to developers: they covered the costs of design, construction, renovation, maintenance, and management. Developers risked only the possibility of shuttered army posts. But in that eventuality, the military promised to pay back four-fifths of the companies' debts on the projects.[76] The army praised the private sector deals for giving it the ability to "attract private capital and expertise."[77] It insisted early on that it would "invest only $380 million" but be able to "leverage nearly $7.2 billion (for the first 17 projects)."[78]

Though "leverage" was the term that the army, Gotbaum, and the private sector emphasized in government privatization, the enormous lure of the massive privatization of army housing almost certainly lay in the modest impact of the deals on the army's annual budget during a period of austerity. The low budget impact derived from the rules of "budget scoring"—the term used to describe the accounting rules of the federal budget—and the impact they made on an agency's annual budget. In previous military-private sector housing deals of the 1940s and 1950s and the 1980s, the army had only "scored" the annual payments of either leases or mortgages to private partners to their annual budget. That is, if a housing contract had cost $50 million for a twenty-five-year project, the army previously had only had to charge the annual $2 million lease or mortgage payment to its budget. The army, not unlike individual consumers or corporations, benefited in its annual accounting from what were essentially "installment purchases." Even an overly expensive project could seem inexpensive when broken into small annual payments. In the late 1980s and early 1990s, however, the rules of budget scoring changed dramatically to put an end to this particular fiction of cheaper privatization deals. The new rules forced federal agencies, including the army, to charge more of their large-scale capital projects to their annual budgets. With the new rules, the army now had to charge the full costs of its construction projects in the same year that the project began. Thus, the same contract for $50 million, executed over twenty-five years, was nevertheless charged in the first year of the contract deal, in order to make sure that the army—or any other federal agency—actually had the funds to pay for the long-term costs of the contract. The new budget-scoring rules transformed private projects from an accounting boon to a bust, one the army could ill afford in a time of deep austerity.

The 1996 housing legislation, however, permitted military services to circumvent the new budget-scoring rules by legalizing new deal structures that allowed the army to score absolutely nothing—zero—in their annual budgets. Unlike any other of the armed services whose budgets were not quite as crunched and which had lesser housing needs, the army used the conveyance of land and property to the private sector as a way to induce the private sector's partnership. If the army had offered firms subsidized loans or made direct monetary investments in the projects, these would have been charged in full to the army's annual budget. But according to the budget rules, land and property conveyance—even though it represented hundreds of millions of dollars—scored nothing at all. So the army simply transferred title to public land or existing housing units on its relatively large and ubiquitous posts to the private sector. The private sector firms built on or renovated the hundreds of millions of dollars of "free" property.[79] And the army charged none of the conveyance to its budget.

As the army privatized housing, its installation commanders developed close relationships with national and international real estate and construction firms. The firms were enormous, as only huge firms had the resources to commit to the fifty-year leases required by the project.[80] Some were established American construction firms. J.A. Jones, a firm working in both the private and public sector and based out of Charlotte, North Carolina, finished the first privatized homes at Fort Carson, Colorado. GMH Military Housing, created as an offshoot of GMH Associates, a Pennsylvania-based construction company that had staked its claim in dormitory construction at universities such as Penn State and University of Maryland, also entered the military housing market early on. J.A. Jones was later purchased by Centex, a Dallas, Texas-based construction firm created in the early postwar years that had over time moved into military housing. Centex had worked on the army's 1980s private housing in the defunct 801 program. Hunt Building Corporation also moved into the military housing market, and that corporation already had a long history with infrastructure projects in the army. Actus Corporation/Sundt Corp out of Napa, California, a single-family home construction giant, staked their claim too. At the tail end of the 1990s and the early 2000s, huge, foreign multinational firms moved into the U.S. market by buying up the large U.S. firms building military housing. In doing so, they expanded their already enormous portfolios of "public private partnerships" established in the much-privatized United Kingdom and Australia. Balfour Beatty, an international infrastructure and property firm based in the United Kingdom, bought out Centex and GMH Military Housing to secure a share of the U.S. military market. Lend Lease, an Australian multinational firm, also moved into the business, buying up Actus Corporation/Sundt Corp.[81]

Within five years, the army was contracting with these firms for tens of thousands of new housing units each year. The RCI program built typically suburban and exurban homes with the amenities middle-class civilians enjoyed and expected: Energy Star heating and cooling, two or more bathrooms, open floor plans, and full wiring for Internet and cable television. The developments also offered additional "exceptional amenities" including "new community centers, bike and riding trails, tot lots." The very first such community started at Fort Carson, Colorado, which "became the . . . RCI pilot program." There the installation leadership touted "double sinks in master bedroom, walk-in closets, ceiling fans."[82] To be sure, not all units featured such generous elements. But characteristically middle-class neighborhoods sprung up around posts across the nation: in one year alone, nearly 5,500 units at Fort Hood, Texas, 3,600 at Fort Lewis, Washington, nearly 3,000 at Fort Meade in Maryland, and just over 3,000 at Fort Stewart and Hunter Army Airfield in Georgia.[83] Ten years later, the privatized programs had built or renovated 87,000 homes at 44 army installations, constituting over 90 percent of all official army family housing in the continental United States.[84]

Army leaders spoke glowingly of the RCI program as an unqualified success, and many soldiers no doubt agreed. An official at a special briefing in

The army's Residential Communities Initiative partnered with real estate firm Balfour Beatty to build housing at Fort Carson, Colorado, in the late 1990s. Photo credit Hall Puckett Photography, courtesy of Balfour Beatty Communities.

2000 at Fort Hood invoked the now-defunct, but apparently still resonant army motto when he touted RCI as "all about taking care of our soldiers and their families."[85] While about half of soldiers in the continental United States continued to live "on the economy" in individually rented or purchased homes in the private sector, the RCI program began to fill the shortfall in army-provided housing stock, and the housing was evaluated as higher quality than previous army-built housing. Easing both the quantity and quality crisis in army housing, RCI provided soldiers and their families more and pleasanter housing than ever before. If the fact that private firms rather than the army built and managed the homes bothered soldiers, their dissatisfaction did not erupt as a notable groundswell. Most soldiers and families probably were not aware of the privatization, the details of who built their housing and why being less important than the improved housing stock itself.[86]

Those in charge of army housing occupied a better position to comprehend, or at least acknowledge, the consequences of privatized housing. One obvious result was that privatized housing moved outside the army's chain of command. The garrison, or installation commander, no longer had direct authority over housing matters. Soldiers facing maintenance issues, and the commanders who might try to assist them, had to rely upon the good graces of a corporation like Balfour Beatty or Lend Lease, with no recourse if their problems were not solved satisfactorily. About this or other results of privatization only a tiny minority publicly voiced even mild cautions concerning the changes. In 2004, a lieutenant colonel at the Army War College reported his slightly cautious conclusion that the RCI program lacked sufficient oversight. He warned, too, that the benefits of the fifty-year contracts might be outweighed by a loss in budgetary flexibility and potentially less expensive twenty- or thirty-year contracts. Overall, he reminded the army that the RCI program did not actually "decrease costs, expenditures or funding requirements." Yes, the programs leveraged private sector funds, and yes, they scored little or nothing in the federal budget process. But the army nevertheless handed over enormous sums to firms through lost real property and through the guaranteed BAH payments. Still, those worries were the author's own. In general, the lieutenant colonel remarked, "Almost everyone [in the army] with some knowledge of RCI speaks very highly of the program."[87] Though the communities embodied a new era of military-private sector combination in which the basic functions of everyday military life were now assumed by military outsiders, those involved in the deals comfortably ceded the responsibility.

BY THE LATE 1990s, the question for the army was no longer which support programs could be outsourced but which could not. The default setting switched from retaining military support services "in house" and making painful decisions about which to send out, to contracting out or privatizing all support activities. Only certain exceptions in military support services avoided outsourcing. The story of how one of the support sectors most likely to have been outsourced survived to stay within the army demonstrates the degree of this shift. Though the army's logistics and installation commanders handed over many of their services to the private sector through outsourcing and privatization contracts, the army element directly responsible for mundane day-to-day soldier and family support successfully resisted a great deal of privatization and outsourcing.

The Army Morale, Welfare and Recreation (MWR) program probably represented the least "core" war-fighting element in the entire army. It provided soldiers and families with everything from bowling to libraries, from snack bars to arts and crafts, from marital counseling to afterschool programs. Like all the other noncore support functions that had suffered deep cuts, MWR had too. Congress found it difficult to justify funds for the woodworking shop or ping-pong when it had slashed the procurement and ammunition funds by 40 percent. Indeed, MWR faced cuts of a far higher proportion than the overall army. MWR's internal reports noted that while overall army manpower cuts in the 1990s hovered around 21 percent, many of MWR's programs faced annual manpower cuts of 27 percent, 31 percent, and even 49.5 percent in the early 1990s. By 1993, even huge posts like Fort Bragg, North Carolina, and Fort Drum, New York, had no recreation centers; and the enormous Fort Leonard Wood, Missouri, had its MWR personnel cut from fifty-four to three employees.[88]

With all these vulnerabilities, MWR became a prime target for elimination and privatization. In 1993, a study by the RAND Corporation recommended that many if not most of the functions of MWR be cut and sent into the private sector. The authors suggested that the army could "maximize . . . soldier benefits in times of austerity" by taking the monies used for MWR functions and giving the "extra cash" to soldiers "to procure whatever MWR services they wish on the private economy"; that is, from the private sector. Echoing the initial free market proposals of the economists promulgating the volunteer force back in the late 1960s, RAND proposed that soldiers receive a sort of MWR allowance, as they did for subsistence or housing, and then use it to join, say, a volleyball league, seek family counseling, or to stay at a private hotel on vacation. The RAND authors portrayed MWR and the social services provided by the army as relics of another era—expensive, inflexible, superfluous institutions.[89]

Despite the pressure, however, MWR did not undergo outsourcing or sale to private vendors. Instead, MWR turned itself into a virtual private sector business, reinforcing the larger turn in the army toward becoming a corporate-style institution. MWR's survival derived from its unique fiscal operation. It had been funded by a combination of appropriated funds from the Congress and nonappropriated funds (NAFs) generated from the small fees that soldiers and families paid to use certain recreation services. For years, the army had collected the fees, saved them in an account for the year, and then turned them around to help fund activities for the next year.[90]

With the budget crunch of the drawdown, however, Congress sliced appropriated funds for all but those activities deemed central to soldier education and physical fitness. With the severe diminution in funds, the pool of fees collected through MWR activities—the NAFs—suddenly grabbed the attention of army leadership. The army determined that "these dollars could play a more significant role in the Army's future."[91] If the fees were raised, if the funds were soundly invested, and if the programs were run more efficiently, the army could make more money from MWR programs, and that money could cover the shortfall in congressionally appropriated funds, or eventually allow them to be reprogrammed entirely for weapons modernization.

The army retooled MWR along the lines of a private sector firm. The army created a board of directors to oversee strategic planning, investment, and spending. It created a new office at the level of the Department of the Army that oversaw everything that MWR purchased with NAFs. And it consolidated and changed the oversight of the account into which all the NAFs were deposited, handing it over to a new Army Banking and Investment Fund. Its managers sought to reduce cash reserves—money sitting around from year to year in various accounts—and invest as much as possible at the highest rate possible (in securities issued by the U.S. Treasury or by other government projects) to produce greater returns. In the first year, the fund "paid a compound interest of 7.02 percent to depositors, for a total of $46.2 million."[92]

Two years into the transformation of MWR into a business, the board decreed that henceforth MWR would "maintain and communicate a corporate image of value and quality."[93] MWR's first strategic plan highlighted its "guiding principles," which could have come straight from the desk of any successful corporation in the United States:

> MWR's customer is America's Army.
> The MWR program is customer-driven.
> NAFs will be returned to customers through provision of market-driven services, activities, and capital improvements.
> The MWR systems will be managed consistently with business-like practices.[94]

The board's chair, former VCSA General Robert RisCassi, told its members MWR's new "structure and policies are the most business-like and provide the greatest opportunity to cope with the challenges of these turbulent times."[95] MWR was thus transformed into a business entity.

Expanding established efforts to increase profits and streamline their management, MWR launched itself as if it were a branded corporation. In the mid-1990s, MWR opened its own restaurants on army posts around the world. The restaurants relied on only the funds collected from the NAFs, leveraged with private sector loans. The ventures were modeled on existing national franchised restaurants.[96] MWR's "Primo's Italian Restaurant," for example, was the army's version of Olive Garden. "Reggie's Beverage Company" had a "neighborhood pub atmosphere," not unlike the Houlihan's chain. "Sports USA" imitated any number of successful sports bar chains in the United States. And then specialty restaurants began to pop up in designated recreation centers: "Mulligan's" offered at army golf courses mimicked golf club restaurants and "The Strike Zone," in bowling centers across the world, functioned as a bar and snack bar. As MWR reported, "these restaurants function as businesses and must be, at a minimum, financially self-sustaining." Even better, they would be profitable with, "any remaining profits . . . reinvested in local MWR programs."[97]

At the same time that it entered the restaurant market, MWR launched a new advertising campaign to generate greater demand for MWR programs. Harriet Rice, the public affairs officer for MWR with over twenty-three years experience in recreation programs, helped direct the reorientation of MWR's message in the 1990s. As she crisscrossed the globe with her message of "self support" for families, she also exhorted local MWR directors to stop the "ever downward, revenue-losing spiral" of cutting little-used programs because of low "consumer demand" by soldiers. Instead, they should borrow ideas and methods from "Madison Avenue" and "create demand" for MWR programs. MWR, she explained, had to imitate corporate America. She suggested "reading trade publications like Advertising Age or American Demographics, . . . watching television commercials, studying magazine advertisements, and talking to business people." "Imitate whatever works," she implored. If MWR programs "aggressively mimic[ed] private sector programs" they could be "successful."[98]

Like a private corporation, MWR also established a brand appearance. "We want to create a new MWR corporate image," Brigadier General

Morale, Welfare and Recreation's new corporate-inspired logo was intended to sell its services to soldiers, families, and army leadership. Courtesy of Harriet E. Rice Papers Collection, U.S. Army Heritage and Education Center, Carlisle, PA.

John G. Meyer, commander of MWR and Community and Family Support Programs, explained. The corporate image should "communicate . . . our mission to deliver top quality programs to soldiers and their families." Its "logo launch" in 1995 featured a half-globe intended to represent MWR's worldwide reach, and the tagline "Serving America's Army." The MWR director at Fort Hood told the post newspaper that the logo launch would allow MWR "to build as much [brand] recognition as we can as quickly as we can."[99]

In 1994, Rice reflected in an interview with *Army Times* that MWR had learned the lessons of corporate America and applied them.[100] She swore that its efforts to fight off privatization were "not an effort to avoid taking [MWR's] fair share of . . . cuts" as the budget drew down. Rather, MWR, having rechristened itself as "a business," did not need the private sector to take over its functions.[101] It already was the private sector—inside the army.

What soldiers thought of MWR's new "brand" remained open to question, as MWR cut some services, raised fees, and took new tacks with some programs. In an effort to raise revenue, MWR cut those programs and personnel that did not fit into the "streamlined" MWR organization any longer. The board also raised the previously nominal fees that soldiers and families paid for recreational, child and youth, and other family and community programs. Now the army made sure that "soldiers paid their fair share," since, after all, the services were supposed to generate revenue. For some soldiers and families, particularly junior enlisted personnel, even small increases in fees spelled hard choices about participation and enrollment. The army also looked to some of its biggest moneymakers for increased revenue, and these might not have benefited soldiers' bank accounts either. MWR hunted for higher revenues by enlarging its Army Recreation Machine Program—the army's term for gaming. Operated outside the

United States, army gaming owned 5,000 slot machines and other gambling games. In 1992, right as the MWR transformed, army gaming reached its highest revenues in its history thus far—$102 million. Plans for expansion rested upon reaping even more gaming revenue. While soldiers might enjoy gaming, its odds favoring the "house"—just as in Las Vegas casinos—meant that overall the gambler lost and the owner won. Efforts to make MWR a financially self-sufficient entity thus preserved the organization but with some costs to the soldier and his or her family.[102]

WITH THE TURN to the business revolution, the army cracked one of the pillars on which the volunteer force rested—that the army represented a "family" that "took care of its own." Direct institutional connection to the individual soldier and family was supposed to build the kind of loyalty and cohesion necessary to sustain a volunteer army. While in the early 1970s, army leadership had roundly rejected the suggestion of free market economists to shed its support of soldiers, by the 1990s, with the cuts to defense and the advent of government "reinvention," the objection to the private sector dissolved. After 1990, the volunteer army began to contract out a significant portion of its responsibility to care for soldiers to private, for-profit entities. Corporations facilitated or conducted entirely the caring relationships on which the "Army Family"—that concept deemed so central to maintaining loyalty and commitment in a volunteer force—was premised.

In the years immediately following the privatization and outsourcing of the service functions of the military, some voices of caution emerged. In 1997, the General Accounting Office (GAO), which supported outsourcing and privatization along with other corporate management processes, nevertheless warned that promises to significantly reduce military costs through outsourcing and privatization were unlikely to be met. "There is reason for caution about whether the magnitude of hoped for savings can be achieved." Past outsourcing contracts of the 1970s and 1980s, few and modest though they were, did not produce expected economies. Feeble savings derived in part from erroneous models for cost savings, models that assumed contracts would be bid out in highly competitive markets; indeed it was a truism among private sector advocates that competition produced savings. However as the GAO pointed out, in the highly specialized, capital-intensive industries associated with defense, truly competitive markets rarely existed. In most areas of outsourcing, like housing, only a few firms had the size, capacity, and experience to handle enormous, long-term military contracts. Market dynamics militated against, not for, cost savings.[103]

Within the army, the transition from a public to a privatized support system provoked some critical evaluation among senior staff and officers. In 1996, the retired former surgeon general of the army, General Alcide LaNoue, expressed his doubts about the ability of the new privatized health care system, Tricare, to adequately serve soldiers and their families.[104] A year later, a program analyst at the Office of the Assistant Secretary of the Army for Financial Management and Comptroller published a critique of the general phenomenon of privatization and outsourcing in *Defense Acquisition Review*. J. Michael Brower's caustic evaluation echoed GAO's doubts concerning planned savings. Observing his colleagues in the army, he noted, "Many who have overseen some outsourcing and to a lesser degree, privatization projects, are discovering that these 'new ways of doing business'" produced economic loss rather than gain. "Contractors bid for outsourced work claiming substantial savings," he explained. Afterwards, "government employees are surplussed or RIFed [terminated as part of a Reductions in Force plan]. Then . . . the contractors run up the bill. Uncle Sam then has nowhere else to go." Brower concluded that the only conceivable purpose of privatization and outsourcing, then, was to deliver profits to a defense industry concerned about the effect of the drawdown on its bottom line. "Cuts in infrastructure, (i.e. military installations), personnel, and support functions will be required to ensure the health of large and small corporations. . . . Privatization and outsourcing," he predicted, "will be the purest expression of the sentiment to support those industries." Even in the army, he concluded, paraphrasing Calvin Coolidge, "the business of America remains business." Perhaps unsurprisingly, Brower left his position at the army secretariat for a position at the Department of Justice, where he oversaw a program monitoring contracting, outsourcing, and privatization.[105]

One of the army's in-house historians researching the effect of 1990s defense reforms reported that, like Brower, some senior army officials held "deep misgivings" about the mandate to outsource in the Clinton years.[106] In 2002, three officers—one from the navy, one the air force, and one the army—evaluated the attitudes of installation commanders toward privatization ten years into the process. The response rate to their questionnaire was not as high as they hoped, but the results confirmed skepticism among officers charged to oversee outsourcing and privatization. When asked if the DoD outsourcing and privatization policies were "headed in the right direction," just over half said no. Only 3 percent "strongly agreed" with current policy. Some commanders reported that it "was a terrible process" or that it was heedless of "broader strategic impact" for the military as a war-fighting institution. One insisted, "we need to cut this BS out!" The three study authors, who favored outsourcing and privatization, found the officers' responses troubling.[107]

Though some formal opposition appeared, the typical venue for discussion of army policy—the research papers at the Army War College where officers grappled with big issues—produced only moderate numbers of studies concerning the dramatic policy change. Between 1997 and 2006, officers at the Army War College conducted ten studies of outsourcing and privatization. Five endorsed the practices, seeking through their research either to document improvements to army functioning or to identify ways to expedite and fine-tune them. Five produced either mixed or negative conclusions concerning the turn to the private sector. Of these, the most negative concerned the question of private military contractors on battlefields, an issue that would dominate the discussion of military outsourcing beginning in the early 2000s with the wars in Iraq and Afghanistan.[108] Another critique addressed the outsourcing of the Reserve Officer Training Corps program. By handing over the training of its officers to the private sector, the army risked "a loosening of the control of the military's profession itself."[109] None of the critiques, however, addressed the area in which the bulk of privatization and outsourcing had taken place—the realm of soldier and family support.

The relative terseness of up-and-coming officers at the Army War College matched a lack of full or official reflection among senior army officers still in leadership roles. In an institution known for creating doctrine—a reflective guide to action—regarding even the most mundane of tasks related to military operations, the lack of acknowledgment concerning the shift from army-provided support for soldiers and families to privatized business-provided support was unusual. The term "contractors" began to appear in army statements as members of a "Total Army" community in relation to soldier support, but the army produced no new Army Family White Paper like the foundational text of the 1980s to address the advent of privatization and outsourcing. The army did not formally address what it *meant* to extend the notion of an Army Family to private corporations, nor what it *meant* to have those corporations actually do the "caring" that the volunteer army had originally promised to do. Army leaders did not address the implications of the transformation of its social welfare system from public to private. In place of doctrine and regulation there were only contracts—individual contracts with individual firms. Yet the contracts did not make firms accountable to soldiers and the public. They existed outside of the chain of command. They were not even open to the public. The army did not deeply examine what it meant for the army to "harness . . . the revolution in business activities" to "care for its sons and daughters."[110]

PERHAPS THE ARMY of the late 1990s and 2000s was not likely to broach questions regarding the historic transformation in soldier and family support. It was no longer the army of traditionalist William Westmoreland and his market-skeptic successors in the 1970s, and few original Army Family stalwarts remained. Twenty to thirty years on, army officers enjoyed an unprecedentedly close relationship to the private sector. By the late 1990s, senior army leadership relied upon business and management schools to educate and train its upwardly mobile officers in corporate philosophies and practices.[111] The army created new organizations to tighten the ties between its leaders and corporations, launching an annual "Captains of Industry Conference" with major defense firms, and an annual "Wise Person Seminar" with nondefense firms like WalMart and FedEx whose corporate practices the army wished to emulate.[112] Army leaders of the turn of the century considered the private sector as an ally, even a peer.[113]

Former CSA General (Ret.) Gordon Sullivan capitalized on the army's embrace of the private sector when he published a best-selling book, *Hope Is Not a Method: What Business Leaders Can Learn from America's Army*, which preached the lessons of the army's economic transformation from 1991 to 1995. As Sullivan knew, and his successor explained to Congress that year, the army had woven business practices "into the fabric" of the institution.[114] In fewer than ten years, the army emerged from the drawdown and government reinvention as a model of a creative, corporate-like institution.[115] General Sullivan argued, that although "the military took its survival cues from business, . . . corporate America could in fact learn a lot from the Army's transformative experience."[116] The army had so thoroughly embraced TQM and outsourcing and privatization that it could serve as a paradigm for corporate-style reinvention.

The army's decision to outsource and privatize its support functions did indeed represent an influential paradigm shift, changing the lived experiences of social welfare both inside and outside the army. In the decade to come, outsourcing and privatization would shape the day-to-day experiences of soldiers and their families. Some of the consequences of the army's privatization of its support structures—as well as its retreat from its philosophy to care for its own—would become clearer amid the urgencies and stress of the fifteen years of war that began in Afghanistan in 2001, Iraq in 2003, and continues today.

EPILOGUE

Army Welfare at War in the Twenty-First Century

IN DECEMBER of 2004, at a staging post in Kuwait, Secretary of Defense Donald Rumsfeld stood before a huge gathering of soldiers heading to the war in Iraq. One of the free market allies of Milton Friedman, Rumsfeld had helped dismantle the draft over thirty years before and then oversaw the volunteer force as President Gerald Ford's defense secretary. Now in his second appointment as secretary of defense under President George W. Bush, Rumsfeld guided the two-year-old war in Iraq, part of the Global War on Terror. That December the U.S. military faced a growing insurgency across Southern Iraq, and at that moment American troops were fighting the second battle of Fallujah, a brutal urban conflict considered the worst of the war in Iraq. At the town-hall-style meeting, a soldier stepped to the microphone and asked the secretary an unusually direct question about equipment failure: Why hadn't the Humvees they would drive north into Iraq been equipped with bullet proof glass and floor armor to protect military personnel from insurgent attacks? The soldier's query served as a proxy for larger questions about the preparation of Rumsfeld and the Bush defense team for the war: Why had so few troops been requested to fight the war? Why did they rely on so many contractors? Why were plans for the postinvasion so vague? Why had leaders not anticipated the ferocity and breadth of the opposition insurgency? In a much-quoted line, Secretary Rumsfeld answered the soldier with a touch of the condescension for which he was famous: "You go to war with the army you have, not the army you might want or wish to have." Rumsfeld meant to instruct the soldier on the practicalities of defense budgets and planning. But Rumsfeld's response undercut his own credibility and created a controversy. It suggested that the military had not been prepared fully for the wars unfolding in Afghanistan and Iraq.[1]

While most analysts of the war considered Rumsfeld's ruminations on the "army you have" versus "the army you might want . . . to have" with respect to weapons, materiel, strategy, and tactics, his comments also could have spoken to the status of the army's social and economic support structure, which went to war along with the rest of the army. The U.S. Army entered two open-ended wars in Afghanistan and Iraq after a decade of profound changes to its social welfare system. What would it mean to wage decades-long wars on two fronts with a support system that had contracted out swaths of its services to private corporations and officially endorsed self-reliance for soldiers?

THE SOCIAL WELFARE system that Rumsfeld and Bush took to war in the 2000s was not the one that the architects of the early volunteer force had built. With the end of the draft, army leaders had successfully pressed Congress to expand the army's traditional benefits and services once reserved for officers and career personnel to the entire volunteer army. A fully developed system of social and economic supports for all soldiers, they contended, provided not only the impetus for soldiers to enlist and reenlist, but also built the bonds of cohesion and loyalty necessary for a war-fighting institution. They constructed the army's social and economic support system in the image of a paternal and patriarchal "Army Family," with a commitment to "taking care of its own."

The system faced formidable challenges from outside and within the army. Free market economists like Friedman advocated ceasing all military-provided, government-run support for soldiers (and their families), from health care to housing to the Post Exchange, with some going so far as to call the army's supports "socialist." A federal budget crisis during the recession of the 1970s prompted members of Congress from both parties to question the growth of military benefits. The American Federation of Government Employees laid claim to the army in the name of protecting military benefits. And a vocal contingent of current and former military personnel cast aspersions on the military's growing social welfare function, especially when it seemed to serve recruits whose education levels, class, race, or sex did not conform to their ideals of soldiers. Despite the challenges, army leaders of the 1970s persisted. The army expanded existing social welfare programs, created new ones, and spent billions on soldier support.

The army's support system thrived in the 1980s, when the army and the Reagan administration drew sharper lines between civilians and soldiers. Reagan cut civilian loans and grants for higher education as he championed the revival of the GI Bill. Conservative Christians close to the Reagan administration and long sympathetic to the military allied themselves closely with the army and its support programs. Their equation of the army with Christian family values threw a protective cloak over the growing system of government social welfare. Army wives emerged as an organized group in this auspicious moment to successfully demand additional family support programs. The lavish defense budgets of the 1980s, the lauded status of military personnel, and the grassroots efforts of army wives fostered a historically unprecedented military social welfare system.

In the decade that followed, however, the army's social welfare system departed from the original pledge to "care for its own" and transferred support services from the army to the private sector. While Friedman and his acolytes had failed to transfer military services to the private sector in the 1970s and the 1980s, free market advocates in the 1990s succeeded. Members of the Defense Science Board (DSB) and Business Executives for National Security (BENS) used the occasion of the post–Cold War drawdown and the slumping economy to advocate corporate boardroom practices—cutting overheads, increasing efficiencies, and improving "quality"—in the military. Vice President Al Gore's "Reinvention of Government" endorsed these recommendations and encouraged outsourcing and privatization throughout federal agencies. President Bill Clinton then appointed a Wall Street financier to lead a special outsourcing office in the Pentagon. Together, the actions of the 1990s resulted in a historically unprecedented transfer of military support services from the public to the private sector.

The contracting out of the Pentagon's support coincided with efforts to encourage independence and self-reliance among soldiers and families. The army's new philosophy—"The Army Takes Care of Its Own So That They Can Learn to Take Care of Themselves"—telegraphed that soldiers and their wives should no longer "depend" on the army. As welfare-to-work programs gained ground in the civilian world, similar ideology took hold in the military. Military family sociologists, drawing in part on civilian studies of welfare families, embarked on efforts to reduce "dependency" among army families in the wake of the Gulf War. Every support element of the army, from Morale, Welfare and Recreation through the Chaplain: Corps rewrote their rhetoric and altered practices to encourage soldiers and families to "take care of themselves." Not unlike the civilian clients whose "welfare as we know it" was "ended" by the Clinton administration and Congress, soldiers felt the pressures of a polity geared toward reducing individuals' participation in and reliance upon the state.

WHEN THE WARS began in 2001 and 2003, the army went to war with a support system that had strayed some distance from its origins in the 1970s. The turn-of-the-century support system of private contractors and a support philosophy of soldier and family self-reliance proved ill-equipped to assist soldiers and families given the unprecedented hardships that emerged during the extended conflicts.

After a decade steeped in an ethos of self-support, army leaders underestimated the degree to which soldiers and families would need help surviving the deployments to Iraq and Afghanistan and their aftermaths. The small, post–Cold War volunteer force solved its personnel and resource shortages by sending many of its soldiers on multiple tours of duty to the war zones where they endured increased exposure to traumatic injury and mental stress. By 2011, 75 percent of all soldiers had deployed to Iraq or Afghanistan, with many clocking their second, third, or fourth deployments. Six or seven deployments were not unknown.[2] Over 53,000 service members had been wounded in action by 2014.[3] Between 17 percent and 19 percent of deployed military personnel reported post traumatic stress disorder (PTSD) with another 3–4 percent reporting other mental distress.[4] Soldiers suffered over 4,600 "severe or penetrating" traumatic brain injuries (TBIs) by 2014, with another 160,000 moderate or mild cases.[5] Army suicides began rising in 2004 and exceeded the rate of civilian suicides in 2008, with over 20.2 suicides per 100,000 members of the army population. In 2009, an average of almost two soldiers a day took their own lives.[6] On the home front army families struggled to cope with the absences of spouses and the physical and mental fallout from the wars. The volunteer wives who led Family Readiness Groups (FRGs) handled families who had been separated for multiple deployments. Soldiers' mental and physical problems had spilled over into the lives of wives and children with sometimes devastating effects. Though the military did not and still does not officially track the mental health diagnoses and suicide rates of spouses and children, spouse and family advocates insisted the situation for many army families was dire.[7]

Six years into the war in Afghanistan and four years into the war in Iraq, the army began to recognize the severe toll taken on soldiers and their families. In January 2007, President Bush named General George Casey to the position of chief of staff of the army, and Casey and his wife Sheila made the first formal efforts to reinvigorate the spirit of the traditional army pledge to "take care of its own." Within months, Casey announced an "Army Family Covenant" that allocated over $100 million to family support. He hired paid army and civilian defense staff to support leaders of the FRGs and provided additional child care and youth services. His five-year budget committed another $4 billion to soldier and family support. As Sheila Casey told a reporter, she and her husband wanted to send the message to army families that "we are listening and we're hearing and we're doing everything that we can to help. . . ."[8] In 2007, Congress created a program to fund and coordinate research on brain injury, and the army began its first formal effort to make unit leaders aware of the symptoms and first-step referrals for TBI.[9] In 2009, the army formally recognized the suicide problem and charged Vice Chief of Staff of the Army General Peter Chiarelli, with creating a comprehensive prevention and treatment program.[10]

But at the same time that the army recognized the growing physical and mental crises among soldiers and families, it continued to endorse the ideology of self-reliance through the newly adopted concept of "resilience." The American Psychological Association defines resilience as "the process of adapting well in the face of adversity, trauma, tragedy, threats or significant sources of stress. . . ."[11] Resilience research had become an influential new subfield in research psychology in the 2000s, though it was not without its critics.[12] In the army resilience emerged as a legatee of the 1980s research on adaptation and the 1990s concept of self-reliance. The army's Ready and Resilient program sought "to inculcate a cultural change in the Army by directly linking personal resilience to readiness and emphasizing the responsibility of personnel at all levels to build and maintain resilience."[13] Even as General Casey promised to help army families, he seemed to cling to the hope that even at war, soldiers could still be made responsible for their own self-care. "Even in this era of persistent conflict," he explained, "we'd like to give more Soldiers the skills to deal with stress so they are more likely to succeed."[14] Treatment and support programs across the army employed the concept of resilience. It was drawn into general training programs. Amidst drawn-out conflicts with increasingly serious consequences, the army continued to offer treatment and support programs rooted in notions of "self-reliance."

The emphasis on self-reliance permeated not only army programs, but also army culture during the wars. In 2006, a year after the most intense fighting in the war in Iraq, the army hired McCann Worldgroup to create a new advertising campaign to promote strength and self-reliance among soldiers and families. "There's strong," the campaign read, "and then there's Army Strong." Soldiers became "warriors," and even "wounded warriors" lost none of their toughness. Soon after the "Army Strong" campaign began, the army expanded it from soldiers to their families. Offered as both a paean and an exhortation to army families, the "Army Family Strong" campaign presented army families as warriors in their own homes. In 2009, the army hired acclaimed documentary filmmaker Lauren Greenfield to create a video for the campaign. Intimate verité footage of army wives and children enduring lonely deployments combined with stoic portraits and a soaring soundtrack to create a moving tableau of "strong" army families. The script never mentioned direct army support for families at all.[15] Families and soldiers were reminded that they were "Army Strong," relying on themselves to solve serious problems.[16]

If the army philosophy of "teaching soldiers to take care of themselves" made it harder for some soldiers and families to survive the wars, so may have the outsourcing and privatization of the army's support structure. Placing support programs in the hands of private contractors diminished the army's ability to address the serious problems facing soldiers and their families. The best-known case was the scandal at Walter Reed Army Medical Center in Washington, DC. From 2003 to 2007 soldiers wounded in Iraq and Afghanistan languished in leaking, moldy buildings, some infested with insects and rodents. Staff lost patients' paperwork, failed to give them appointments, and let soldiers with brain injuries wander the grounds without care.[17] In 2007, reports by the *Washington Post* spurred government inquiries that pointed to the role of private contracting in causing the problems at Walter Reed.[18] Many of those responsible for the poor care were contractors, employees of IAP Worldwide Services, Inc., a firm that had tried for more than five years to take over services at a privatizing Walter Reed. The long fight over privatization left the remaining government and army staffs demoralized and too small to oversee or even coordinate correctly with contractors.[19] As a result of the scandal, the army moved to hire

3,500 of its own employees to handle the growing medical caseloads of injured soldiers.[20] But it nevertheless continued to contract out large components of its Warrior Transition Program, Wounded Warrior Program, and other army medical programs.[21]

EVEN AS the war in Afghanistan continues and conflict in Iraq resurges, the defense establishment is planning for the military of the future, the army it "wishes to have," in Rumsfeld's words. Though the military social welfare system that evolved in the 1990s proved itself inadequate to meet key tests of the wars of the 2000s, the Pentagon is nevertheless continuing on this path and considering the rapid acceleration of both privatization and self-support for the future.

Beginning in 2011 the Department of Defense (DoD) entertained demands from corporations and free market advocates to privatize more of its benefits—this time a more radical privatization of health care and a total restructuring and privatization of pensions. Promulgated by the Heritage Foundation, corporate leaders on the DoD's Defense Business Board (DBB), and members of the private BENS, health care and retirement proposals sought to replace existing government programs with privately held, market-based health care and retirement programs that utilized vouchers and cash substitutes in place of defined and guaranteed supports. They closely mirrored free market proposals for Social Security, pension privatization, and health care vouchers in the civilian sector. Using the rhetoric of providing "choice" to military personnel, the programs decreased total benefits and increased private sector access to government funds and the money of military personnel.[22] Instead of using the existing government-contracted health maintenance organization/preferred provider organization model called Tricare, military personnel and their families would receive health care vouchers allowing them to either purchase whatever health care plan they chose from an array of private sector providers—or to purchase none. Instead of earning defined retirement benefits—pensions—soldiers, sailors, airmen, and marines would participate in "defined contribution plans" like privately held 401K programs—or simply take a lump sum of cash.[23]

Veterans' organizations and military professional organizations objected to the benefits reform proposals. But the history told in this book suggests that they may well lose the battle. The pension and health care reform proposals represent the end point of the logics of both privatization and self-reliance adopted by the military in the 1990s. Dispensing even with military contracting, the military proposals for cash and vouchers completely marketize the social provisioning in the army, signifying total victory of the free market once and for all over the paternal, government-provided support system of the 1970s and 1980s. Cash and vouchers will also leave soldiers and families truly self-reliant. Each will cast out into the private sector alone, entering separate relationships with separate firms for separate health or investment services. If soldiers receive poor or inadequate treatment they will face it unaided, without recourse to a chain of command and without recourse even to the pressure that one large contract from the military might bring to bear on a particular firm. Soldiers and their families will be dispersed. Ties to the military will attenuate.

The fight of veterans and military service organizations against further privatization and self-reliance will also be difficult because of the isolation of military personnel from civilians. During the recent wars military personnel often noted that civilians did not recognize their sacrifices because so few Americans actually served in the volunteer force. It was also true, however, that many civilians overlooked the needs of military personnel and their families because military leaders, presidents, and Congress had told them for years that their own civilian benefits bore no relationship to or equivalency with military benefits. Since the advent of the volunteer army in 1973, its leaders, with the support of Congress and the executive, have painted bright lines between military service and civilian employment and between civilian social welfare programs and those serving military personnel. The army cleaved itself from the civilian world, and the resulting segregation of soldiers and their benefits from civilians has diminished civilian awareness of the army community and its needs. For many years, both army leaders and many soldiers themselves followed a cautious, narrow path toward special recognition and support in Congress, eschewing alignment with and opposing comparisons to civilians. In this atmosphere, how could civilians come to identify with military benefits, especially given the reductions in their own government and private sector benefits and services? Though the strategy of separating military from civilian benefits worked for many years, it may now harm more than help soldiers.

For their part, civilians may wish to pay more attention to the fate of seemingly arcane military compensation—and for their own good, too. They ought to take note of the full conversion of military benefits and services to free market models, as the phenomenon will likely reinforce trends toward privatization of civilian social supports. After all, the military is an institution that, despite its changes and challenges, still is held in high regard.[24] Reagan's identification of the military as a central—perhaps the central—institution representing the nation provided the template for subsequent presidents, all of whom have reinforced the symbolic power of the military in American political life. By the early 2000s, one scholar observed that American political leaders seemed to categorize military personnel as "super citizens."[25] If soldiers, sailors, airmen, and marines can have their benefits outsourced and privatized—even while they are at war—what will become of the social programs that remain for civilians? A wide swath of civilian policies protecting economic security, health, and well-being have come under new assault by free market conservatives in the past several years—collective bargaining rights, public pensions, health care, and Social Security, to name a few. If military pensions and health care go the way of vouchers and cash payments, Americans can expect them to be widely adopted in the civilian world.

Instead of universal obligations and social supports, the United States in the late twentieth century created small, separate realms of entitlement and obligation, of worthiness and reward, and the military social welfare system was one of the most powerful. Though it was built on the logic of a distinct, closed circuit to benefit soldiers, it is nevertheless being dismantled together with civilian spheres of social welfare. Even as incomes and employment stagnate, advocates of the free market and against social welfare continue to unravel the patchwork of social and economic support that evolved in the United States over the course of the twentieth century. Divided by decades of divergent histories of social welfare, soldiers and civilians in the twenty-first century may now face a shared fate.

APPENDIX

ABBREVIATIONS

NOTES

ACKNOWLEDGMENTS

INDEX

Appendix

The appendix that follows provides an overview of the major military social welfare and support programs, highlighting briefly their scope and history.

Major Military Social Welfare and Support Programs, by Category

Program (and date of implementation, where relevant)	Scope and history
Housing	
For single soldiers • Barracks	Traditional military benefit
For families • Military Housing/Basic Allowance for Housing • Variable Housing Allowance (1986), Rate Protection (series of changes in 1990s) • CONUS COLA or Overseas COLA (Cost of Living Allowances) • Used to pay for on-post housing (housing allowance deposited directly into either military accounts or private contractor) or housing "on the economy" in the private local real estate market (housing allowance paid to soldier who then pays private entity)	Traditional military benefit for officers and their families, expanded to career enlisted in 1950s, and then to all enlisted with families, both CONUS and overseas, with switch to volunteer force
Health Care	
For soldiers	Traditional military benefit
For families • Space available in army facilities (1956) • CHAMPUS (1966) • Tricare (1995)	Some career enlisted and officer families treated in military facilities on space available basis beginning 1956; CHAMPUS (1966) and then Tricare (1995) covered families systematically

Commissaries and Exchanges • Subsidized groceries (1867) • Subsidized consumer products (1895)	Traditional military benefit
Child and Youth Programs • Child care: Child Development Centers (CDC), Family Child Care (FCC) (in-home day care on bases), Military Child Care in Your Neighborhood (payment and location assistance for private sector child care for active duty personnel without access to a CDC) • School Age Care (SAC): Programs for children aged 6–12 before and after school and on weekends	Subsidized, 1980s–
Travel, Transportation, Moving, and Temporary Lodging Allowances • Moving costs • Travel costs • Per diem • Temporary housing allowances	Traditional benefit covering soldiers and, in the case of "sponsored tours," families. Reserved for career enlisted and officers, extended to junior enlisted soldiers and families in 1979
Family Support Services (1980s–) • Family Advocacy Program • Family Support Groups/Family Readiness Groups • Family counseling/marriage counseling • Deployment Assistance • Spouse Employment Assistance	

(*continued*)

(continued)

Program (and date of implementation, where relevant)	Scope and history
Adult Education Assistance • On-duty education and training for military jobs • Courses in person or by correspondence in off-duty hours • GI Bill postservice educational benefits (1985)	For soldiers, but GI benefits now extended to use by family members
Schooling • Department of Defense Dependent Schools (overseas and Washington, DC) (1946)	Traditional benefit extended to officers and career enlisted whose families were "sponsored," extended to junior enlisted families in 1979
Morale Welfare and Recreation (1940s–) • Sports and recreation • Hotels, motels, camping • Leisure activities	
Subsistence • Basic Allowance for Subsistence	Traditional military benefit for career enlisted and officer and families, extended to junior enlisted families with switch to volunteer force
Financial Literacy/Financial Readiness Assistance • Range of financial related services, education, and counseling	Originated in volunteer Army Community Service programs in 1960s to help especially junior enlisted personnel; regularized and staffed in 1980s and 1990s

Tax Advantages • Numerous, but including Combat Tax Benefits (1918) and tax exempt allowances for housing and subsistence	
Legal Assistance (1943, expanded fully in 1980s)	
Disability	Traditional military benefit, codified in pensions after Civil War
Death and Burial benefits	Traditional military benefit for eligible personnel and veterans
Life Insurance (1940)	
Postservice (Non-Veterans Administration) Programs • Army Career and Alumni Program (on every base) • Partnership for Youth Success (PAYS) (preferred placement option with various employers after discharge) • Troops to Teachers program	

(*continued*)

(continued)

Program (and date of implementation, where relevant)	Scope and history
• Retirement Benefits • Thrift Savings Plan	

Sources: CMH, *Department of the Army Historical Summary*, Fiscal Years 1973–1999 (Washington, DC: CMH); Office of the United States Secretary of Defense, *National Defense Budget Estimates Fiscal Year 2005* (Washington, DC: DoD, 2004); Office of the United States Secretary of Defense, *National Defense Budget Estimates Fiscal Year 2007* (Washington, DC: DoD, 2006); GAO, *Active Duty Benefits Reflect Changing Demographics, but Opportunities Exist to Improve*, GAO-02–935 (Washington, DC: GPO, 2002); "Military Compensation: Army Benefits," GoArmy.com, www.goarmy.com/benefits/total_compensation.jsp.

Abbreviations

ACS. . . . . Army Community Service
AFAP. . . . . Army Family Action Plan
AFGE. . . . . American Federation of Government Employees
AFL-CIO . . . . . American Federation of Labor and Congress of Industrial Organizations
AFQT. . . . . Armed Forces Qualification Test
AFTB . . . . Army Family Team Building
AMC . . . . Army Materiel Command
ARI . . . . Army Research Institute
ASVB. . . . . Army Service Vocational Battery test
AUSA. . . . . Association of the U.S. Army
AVF . . . . All-Volunteer Force
BAH . . . . Basic Allowance for Housing
BENS. . . . . Business Executives for National Security
BRAC . . . . Base Realignment and Closure
CBO . . . . Congressional Budget Office
CECOM. . . . . . Communications-Electronics Command
CFSC. . . . . U.S. Army Community and Family Support Center
CHAMPUS. . . . Civilian Health and Medical Program of the Uniformed Services

CRS. . . . . Congressional Research Service
CSA. . . . . Chief of Staff of the Army
DAHSUM. . . . . Department of the Army Historical Summary
DARPA . . . . . . Defense Advanced Research Projects Agency
DBB . . . . Defense Business Board
DCSPER . . . . . Deputy Chief of Staff for Personnel
DMC . . . . Defense Manpower Commission
DoD. . . . . Department of Defense
DSB. . . . . Defense Science Board
FLO . . . . Family Liaison Officer
FRG. . . . . Family Readiness Group
FSG . . . . Family Support Group
FY . . . . Fiscal Year
GAO . . . . General Accounting Office
GPO. . . . . U.S. Government Printing Office
JET. . . . . Junior Enlisted Travel
LOGCAP . . . . . Logistics Civilian Augmentation Program
MOS. . . . . Military Occupational Specialty
MWR . . . . Morale, Welfare and Recreation
NAF. . . . . Nonappropriated Funds
NPR. . . . . National Performance Review
OACSIM . . . . . Office of the Assistant Chief of Staff for Installation Management
OASD (MRA) later OASD (MRAL) . . . Office of the Assistant Secretary of Defense for Manpower and Reserve Affairs; then Office of the Assistant Secretary of Defense (Manpower, Reserve Affairs, and Logistics)
ODCSPER . . . . Office of the Deputy Chief of Staff for Personnel
OMB . . . . Office of Management and Budget
PCS . . . . Permanent Change of Station
PROVIDE . . . . Project Volunteer in Defense of the Nation
PTSD . . . . posttraumatic stress disorder
PX . . . . Post Exchange

RCI . . . . Residential Communities Initiative
ROTC. . . . . Reserve Officer Training Corps
SAMVA . . . . . . Special Assistant for the Modern Volunteer Army
TAQ. . . . . Total Army Quality
TBI . . . . traumatic brain injury
TDY . . . . Temporary Duty
TQM. . . . . Total Quality Management
USA. . . . . U.S. Army
USAF . . . . U.S. Air Force
USAREC. . . . . . U.S. Army Recruiting Command
USASOC . . . . . U.S. Army Special Operations Command
VCSA . . . . Vice Chief of Staff of the Army
VOLAR . . . . . . Project Volunteer Army
WRAMC . . . . . Walter Reed Army Medical Center

Archival repositories and collections:

MHI . . . . U.S. Army Military History Institute at Carlisle Barracks, PA
- AVAC. . . All-Volunteer Army Collection at MHI
- DRP. . . . Dennis J. Reimer Papers at MHI
- HRP. . . . Harriet E. Rice Papers at MHI
- JWP . . . . John A. Wickham Jr., Papers at MHI
- ODSSPCP . . . Operation Desert Shield/Storm, Provide Comfort Papers at MHI

GMMA . . . . . . George Meany Memorial Archives, Silver Spring, MD
- MUC . . . Military Unions Collection at GMMA

CMH . . . . U.S. Army Center of Military History, Fort McNair, Washington, DC
- MFC. . . . Military Families Collection at CMH

RRPL. . . . . Ronald Reagan Presidential Library, Simi Valley, CA
- MAF. . . . Martin Anderson Files at RRPL

AMCHO . . . . . U.S. Army Materiel Command Historical Office, Redstone Arsenal, AL

JRP . . . . Jimmy D. Ross Papers, collection consulted at MHI, but now housed at AMCHO

Notes

Introduction

1. Patrick J. Kelly, *Creating a National Home: Building the Veterans' Welfare State 1860–1900* (Cambridge, MA: Harvard University Press, 1997); Theda Skocpol, *Protecting Soldiers and Mothers: The Political Origins of Social Policy in United States* (Cambridge, MA: Harvard University Press, 1995); Stephen Ortiz, *Beyond the Bonus March and the GI Bill: How Veteran Politics Shaped the New Deal Era* (New York: New York University Press, 2009); Suzanne Mettler, *Soldiers to Citizens: The G.I. Bill and the Making of the Greatest Generation* (New York: Oxford University Press, 2005); Glenn C. Altschuler and Stuart M. Blumin, *The GI Bill: The New Deal for Veterans* (New York: Oxford University Press, 2009); Kathleen J. Frydl, *The GI Bill* (New York: Cambridge University Press, 2009).
2. On Europe see Deborah Dwork, *War is Good for Babies and Other Young Children: A History of the Infant and Child Welfare Movement in England, 1898–1918* (London: Tavistock, 1987); Derek Fraser, *The Evolution of the British Welfare State*, 3rd ed. (New York: Palgrave Macmillan, 2003); Susan Pedersen, *Family Dependence and the Origins of the Welfare State: Britain and France, 1914–1945* (New York: Cambridge University Press, 1993); Timothy B. Smith, *Creating the Welfare State in France, 1880–1940* (Montreal: McGill-Queens University Press, 2003).
3. Charles Tilly, "Reflections on the History of European State Making," in *The Formation of National States in Western Europe*, ed. Charles Tilly (Princeton, NJ: Princeton University Press, 1975), 42; Charles Tilly, "War

Making and State Making as Organized Crime," in *Bringing the State Back In,* ed. Peter Evans, Dietrich Ruschemeyer, and Theda Skocpol (New York: Cambridge University Press, 1985), 169; Tristram Coffin, *The Armed Society: Militarism in Modern America* (Baltimore: Penguin Books, 1964), especially 75–82.

4. As of 2006, 8,873,071 people volunteered for duty after 1973. The total number of personnel serving would be higher—though that figure is not available—because of holdovers serving from years before the military switched to the volunteer force plus those after 2006. See Office of the Under Secretary of Defense for Personnel and Readiness, "Population Representation in the Military Services, FY 2006," http://prhome.defense.gov/portals/52/Documents/POPREP/poprep2006/.
5. For long-term budget figures see Office of the Undersecretary of Defense (Comptroller), *National Defense Budget Estimates for FY 2007,* (U.S. Department of Defense: Washington DC, March 2006) (It is referred to as the Green Book.). The Tenth Quadrennial Review of Military Compensation in 2008 admitted that even the DoD did not know the costs of its support programs. "The large number of quality of life programs, along with their multiple funding sources, make it difficult to estimate the total cost of quality of life services." See DoD, *Tenth Quadrennial Review of Military Compensation: Report of Deferred and Noncash Compensation,* vol. 2 (Washington, DC: GPO, 2008), 91. Indeed, determining "manpower" or "support" costs is so difficult because they are not drawn solely from the DoD personnel budget. Many of the costs of benefits and social services are in other parts of the defense budget, including Operations and Maintenance, which funds child care and other family and counseling programs; Military Family Housing, which funds family housing; and the general Construction budget, which funds construction of community centers and morale, health, and welfare sites. Though the percentage of the defense budget devoted to manpower and support fell below 50 percent in the 1980s, that was only because under President Ronald Reagan military spending on weaponry and materiel rose so precipitously. The absolute spending on manpower and support programs for soldiers and families rose steadily from the 1970s.
6. Morris Janowitz, "A New Role for the Military Forces," *Current,* June 1972, 45.
7. Tom Ricks, "The Great Society in Camouflage," *Atlantic,* December 1996, 24; Colonel R. Philip Deavel, "The Political Economy of Privatization for the American Military," *Air Force Journal of Logistics* 22, no. 2 (Summer 1998): 7; Brian Gifford, "States, Soldiers, and Social Welfare:

Military Personnel and the Welfare State in the Advanced Industrial Democracies" (PhD diss., Columbia University, 2003), viii.

8. For a recent take on that joke see a half-kidding quote from retired General Wesley Clark in Nicholas Kristoff, "Our Lefty Military," *New York Times*, June 15, 2011, www.nytimes.com/2011/06/16/opinion/16kristof.html.
9. So-called traditional welfare scholarship focused solely on government programs for insurance and assistance. More recent scholarship has unearthed the vast and more complex public-private nature of American governance. See Christopher Howard, *The Hidden Welfare State: Tax Expenditures and Social Policy in the United States* (Princeton, NJ: Princeton University Press, 1997); Christopher Howard, *The Welfare State Nobody Knows: Debunking Myths about U.S. Social Policy* (Princeton, NJ: Princeton University Press, 2007); Elisabeth Clemens, "Lineages of the Rube Goldberg State: Building and Blurring Public Programs, 1900–1940," in *Rethinking Political Institutions: The Art of the State*, ed. Ian Shapiro, Stephen Skowronek, and Daniel Galvin (New York: New York University Press, 2006), 380–443; Jacob Hacker, *The Divided Welfare State: The Battle over Public and Private Social Benefits in the United States* (New York: Cambridge University Press, 2002); Jennifer Klein, *For All These Rights: Business, Labor and the Shaping of America's Public-Private Welfare State* (Princeton, NJ: Princeton University Press, 2003); Brian Balogh, *A Government Out of Sight: The Mystery of National Authority in Nineteenth-Century America* (New York: Cambridge University Press, 2009); Suzanne Mettler, *The Submerged State: How Invisible Government Policies Undermine American Democracy* (Chicago: University of Chicago Press, 2011); Andrew Morris, *The Limits of Voluntarism: Charity and Welfare from the New Deal through the Great Society* (New York: Cambridge University Press, 2009).
10. Skocpol, *Protecting Soldiers and Mothers*.
11. Ortiz, *Beyond the Bonus March;* Jessica L. Adler, "Paying the Price of War: Soldiers, Veterans, and Health Policy, 1917–1924" (PhD diss., Columbia University, 2013).
12. Mettler, *Soldiers to Citizens;* Mark Boulton, *Failing Our Veterans: The GI Bill and the Vietnam Generation* (New York: New York University Press, 2014). Boulton demonstrates how the Vietnam-era GI Bill did not match the World War II–era bill.
13. There has been a lively popular scholarship on this divide since the advent of the volunteer force, represented most recently in Andrew Bacevich, *Breach of Trust: How American Failed Their Soldiers and*

Their Country (New York: Metropolitan Books, 2013). A more academic scholarship has paralleled this. See David R. Segal, *Recruiting for Uncle Sam: Citizenship and Military Manpower Policy* (Lawrence, KS: University Press of Kansas, 1989); Jerald G. Backman, Jon D. Blair, and David R. Segal, *The All-Volunteer Force: A Study of Ideology in the Military* (Ann Arbor, MI: University of Michigan Press, 1977); Charles Moskos, John Allen Williams, and David R. Segal, eds., *The Postmodern Military: Armed Forces after the Cold War* (New York: Oxford University Press, 2000).

14. Gifford, "States, Soldiers, and Social Welfare"; James L. Quinn and Ronald V. Grabler, *Military Unions: The Advantages and Disadvantages of Unionization within the Armed Forces* (Wright-Patterson Air Force Base, OH: Air Force Institute of Technology, 1971), 8–26; Ezra Krendel, "Trade Unionism and the US Armed Forces," in *Military Unionism and the Volunteer Military System*, ed. Peter B. Lane, Ezra S. Krendel, and William Jesse Taylor (Washington, DC: National Defense University, 1977), 15–17; Tobin Dean Seven, "A Military Union in the United States Army? An Attitude Survey" (MPA thesis, San Jose State University, 1978), 54–64; David Cortright, "Unions and Democracy," *Military Review* 57, no. 8 (August 1977): 35–44.
15. If the army is disaggregated from the total defense budget, the impact of spending on soldier and family support is more marked. The manpower budget of the army dwarfed the other portions of its budget up through the early 2000s, when the operations and maintenance budget of the Iraq and Afghanistan wars briefly overtook it between 2003 and 2006. Given that many army benefits and supports resided outside the personnel budget, just like the overall DoD budget, in housing construction and operations and maintenance, the total costs of soldier and family support dominate the army budget.
16. Robert Griffith, *The U.S. Army's Transition to the All-Volunteer Force, 1968–1974* (Washington, DC: CMH, 1997), 18, 31, 53.
17. Beth Bailey, *America's Army: Making the All-Volunteer Force* (Cambridge, MA: Harvard University Press, 2009); Andrew Bacevich, *The New American Militarism: How Americans Are Seduced by War* (New York: Oxford University Press, 2005); Bernard Rostker, *I Want You! The Evolution of the All-Volunteer Force* (Santa Monica, CA: RAND Corporation, 2006); Griffith's *U.S. Army's Transition* stands as the army's first and most detailed history of the its internal transformation to the volunteer force.
18. Bailey, *America's Army*.
19. On the professionalized officer corps see Charles Moskos, "Toward a Postmodern Military: The United States as a Paradigm," in Moskos et al.,

The Postmodern Military, 19; Curtis Gilroy, Roger Little, and J. Eric Fredland, *Professionals on the Front Lines: Two Decades of the All-Volunteer Force* (Washington, DC: Brassey's, 1996).

20. I thank Michael Allen for suggesting this term.
21. As Michael Sherry explained, starting in the 1930s, Americans began to bend their economy, politics, and culture to the imperatives, modes, and metaphors of the military. Michael Sherry, *In the Shadow of War: The United States since the 1930s* (New Haven, CT: Yale University Press, 1995). Additional scholarship on the militarization of American society includes Mary Dudziak, *War Time: An Idea, Its History, Its Consequences* (New York: Oxford University Press, 2012); James T. Sparrow, *Warfare State: World War II Americans and the Age of Big Government* (New York: Oxford University Press, 2013); Laura McEnaney's *Civil Defense Begins at Home: Militarization Meets Everyday Life in the Fifties* (Princeton, NJ: Princeton University Press, 2000); Ann Markusen, Peter Hall, Scott Campbell, and Sabina Deitrick, *The Rise of the Gunbelt: The Military Remapping of Industrial America* (New York: Oxford University Press, 1991);Tom Englehardt, *The End of Victory Culture: Cold War America and the Disillusioning of a Generation*, rev. ed. (Amherst, MA: University of Massachusetts Press, 2007); Catherine Lutz, *Homefront: A Military City and the American Twentieth Century* (Boston: Beacon Press, 2001); Bailey, *America's Army;* Bacevich, *New American Militarism;* Cynthia Enloe, *Does Khaki Become You? The Militarization of Women's Lives* (London: Pandora Press, 1983); Cynthia Enloe, *Maneuvers: The International Politics of Militarizing Women's Lives* (Berkeley, CA: University of California Press, 2000); Meredith Lair, *Armed with Abundance: Consumerism and Soldiering in the Vietnam War* (Chapel Hill, NC: University of North Carolina Press, 2011); Michael Allen, *Until the Last Man Comes Home: POWs, MIAs, and the Unending Vietnam War* (Chapel Hill, NC: University of North Carolina Press, 2009); Amy Rutenberg, "Citizen-Civilians: Masculinity, Citizenship, and American Military Manpower Policy, 1945–1975" (PhD diss., University of Maryland, 2013).
22. Bacevich, *New American Militarism*, 108–110.
23. See poll results reported in Terry Muck, "Return of the Big Stick," *Christianity Today*, September 4, 1987, 18; "Where Our Trust Lies," *Christianity Today*, February 1989, 40. See also, Question: Would you please tell me how much confidence you, yourself have in the military: a great deal, quite a lot, some, or very little? Results: great deal and quite a lot 63%, Method: In Person, Sample Size: 1539. Gallup Organization. Gallup Poll # 1266G, July 1986 [dataset]. USAIPO1986-1266G, Version 2. Gallup Organization [producer]. Storrs, CT:Roper

Center for Public Opinion Research, Roper*Express* [distributor], accessed Mar-13-2015.

24. I thank Kimberly Morgan for first introducing me to the concept of delegated governance. See Kimberly Morgan and Andrea Louise Campbell, *The Delegated Welfare State: Medicare, Markets, and the Governance of Social Policy* (New York: Oxford University Press, 2011).
25. Daniel Rodgers, *Age of Fracture* (Cambridge, MA: Harvard University Press, 2011).
26. Rostker, *I Want You!* See the accompanying CD.
27. Of special note for researchers is the unprocessed collection of files at the CMH regarding military families, collected for a never-written army history of military family programs. Though it has no official name, I have referred to it as the Military Families Collection, CMH.
28. Cynthia Enloe, foreword to *Wives and Warriors: Women in the Military in the United States and Canada,* ed. Laurie Weinstein and Christie White (Westport, CT: Bergin and Garvey, 1997), ix; Enloe, *Does Khaki Become You?,* 213–215; Enloe, *Maneuvers,* 34.

1. Army Benefits in a Free Market Era

1. Beth Bailey argues that the volunteer force was by definition a market-based institution. She also demonstrates the vital and growing importance of advertising as a market tool for the army. See Beth Bailey, *America's Army: Making the All Volunteer Force* (Cambridge, MA: Harvard University Press, 2009).
2. For a brief spell from 1947 to 1948 the draft was suspended.
3. Charles Moskos, *The American Enlisted Man: The Rank and File in Today's Military* (New York: Russell Sage Foundation, 1970), 47.
4. Ibid., 49.
5. David R. Segal, *Recruiting for Uncle Sam: Citizenship and Military Manpower Policy* (Lawrence, KS: University of Kansas Press, 1989), 33.
6. As evidence of the role that avoiding combat played in volunteering for service, the army calculated that of all of its "true volunteers," no more than 2.5 percent volunteered for the infantry. Robert Griffith, *The U.S. Army's Transition to the All-Volunteer Force, 1968–1974* (Washington, DC: CMH, 1997), 53.
7. Ibid., 18, 31.
8. Patricia Bloebaum, "Must the Services Take Care of Everybody?," *The Times Magazine,* May 29, 1978, 7.

9. Robert Stafford et al., *How to End the Draft: The Case for an All-Volunteer Army* (Washington, DC: National Press, 1967), 38. The authors of this book were all members of Congress, some of whom attended the 1966 University of Chicago meeting on the draft. Economist Stephen Herbits, soon-to-be Gates Commission staffer, provided research and writing assistance to the members of Congress.
10. U.S. President's Commission on an All-Volunteer Armed Force, *The Report of the President's Commission on an All-Volunteer Armed Force* (Washington, DC: GPO, 1970), 52, table 5-II.
11. U.S. Senate, Committee on Armed Services, *Hearings on Selective Service and Military Compensation*, 92nd Cong., 1st sess., February 2, 4, 8, 9, 10, 19, and 22, 1971, 43.
12. "Low Pay, High Costs Put Soldiers on Welfare," *Los Angeles Times*, November 13, 1969, A9.
13. "Poverty in Uniform," *New York Times*, June 1, 1971, 38.
14. David Rosenbaum, "Senate Bars Plan Designed to Bring Volunteer Army," *New York Times*, August 26, 1970, 1.
15. Barbara A. Bicksler, Curtis L. Gilroy, and John T. Warner, eds., *The All-Volunteer Force: Thirty Years of Service* (Washington, DC: Brassey's, 2004), 1; "The Draft: On Nixon's Pledge to 'Bury It,'" *New York Times*, February 2, 1969, E4.
16. Editorial, ". . . And on the Draft," *New York Times*, February 1, 1969, 28. Between the end of World War I and the beginning of World War II, conscription was abandoned and the United States operated a small, professional armed forces.
17. David E. Rosenbaum, "Congress Expected to Give Draft Issue Urgent Priority," *New York Times*, January 11, 1971, 6.
18. Burke Marshall, *In Pursuit of Equity: Who Serves When Not All Serve? Report of the National Advisory Commission on Selective Service* (Washington, DC: GPO, 1967).
19. Editorial, ". . . And on the Draft," 28.
20. Dale Van Atta, *With Honor: Melvin Laird in War Pace, and Politics* (Madison, WI: University of Wisconsin Press, 2008), 247; Griffith, *U.S. Army's Transition*, 21.
21. Griffith, *U.S. Army's Transition*, 25, 69.
22. Meg Jacobs, "The Conservative Struggle and the Energy Crisis," in *Rightward Bound: Making America Conservative in the 1970s*, ed. Bruce Shulman and Julian Zelizer (Cambridge, MA: Harvard University Press, 2008), 203.
23. For Friedman's ideas on the relationship of the market to governance see Milton Friedman and Rose D. Friedman, *Capitalism and Freedom*

(Chicago: University of Chicago Press, 1962); Milton Friedman and Rose D. Friedman, *Free to Choose: A Personal Statement* (New York: Harcourt, 1979).

24. For scholarship on the public-private nature of American governance see Christopher Howard, *The Hidden Welfare State: Tax Expenditures and Social Policy in the United States* (Princeton, NJ: Princeton University Press, 1997); Christopher Howard, *The Welfare State Nobody Knows: Debunking Myths about U.S. Social Policy* (Princeton, NJ: Princeton University Press, 2007); Elisabeth Clemens, "Lineages of the Rube Goldberg State: Building and Blurring Public Programs, 1900–1940," in *Rethinking Political Institutions: The Art of the State*, ed. Ian Shapiro, Stephen Skowronek, and Daniel Galvin (New York: New York University Press, 2006), 380–443; Jacob Hacker, *The Divided Welfare State: The Battle over Public and Private Social Benefits in the United States* (New York: Cambridge University Press, 2002); Jennifer Klein, *For All These Rights: Business, Labor and the Shaping of America's Public-Private Welfare State* (Princeton, NJ: Princeton University Press, 2003).

25. With the backing of disaffected businessmen like the founders of the American Liberty League, free market ideologies found material support in the postwar era. The international Mont Perelin Society and the American Foundation for Economic Education became outposts of free market thinking that made their way into universities such as the University of Chicago and think tanks such as the American Enterprise institution in the 1950s. See Kim Phillips-Fein, *Invisible Hands: The Businessmen's Crusade against the New Deal* (New York: W. W. Norton, 2010), 3–53.

26. In some of the new arenas they entered, free market economists fused new subdisciplines. In history, for example, they founded cliometrics and applied neoclassical economic theory to subjects such as American slavery. In law, economists applied microeconomic methods and theories to questions of law, suggesting adjudication based on cost more than rights, and creating a new field of law and economics.

27. John T. Warner and Beth J. Asch, "The Record and Prospects of the All-Volunteer Military in the United States," *Journal of Economic Perspectives* 15, no. 2 (Spring 2001): 190.

28. Oi's work influenced others. See Walter Oi, "The Costs and Implications of an All-Volunteer Force," in *The Draft*, ed. Sol Tax (Chicago: University of Chicago Press, 1967), 221–251; Walter Oi, "The Economic Cost of the Draft," *American Economic Review* 57, no. 2 (1967): 39–62; Anthony Fisher, "The Cost of the Draft and the Cost of Ending the Draft," *American Economic Review* 59, no. 3 (1969): 239–254; W. Lee Hansen

and Burton A. Weisbrod, "Economics of a Military Draft," *Quarterly Journal of Economics* 81, no. 3 (1967): 395–421; Larry A. Sjaastad and Ronald W. Hansen, "The Conscription Tax: An Empirical Analysis," in *Studies Prepared for the President's Commission on an All-Volunteer Armed Force* (Washington, DC: GPO, 1970), vol. 2.

29. Rosenbaum, "Senate Bars Plan," 1.
30. President's Commission, *Report,* 23–25.
31. David R. Henderson, "The Role of Economists in Ending the Draft," *Econ Journal Watch* 2, no. 2 (2005): 363–364, 374.
32. Milton Friedman and Rose D. Friedman, *Two Lucky People: Memoirs* (Chicago: University of Chicago Press, 1998), 378.
33. "An Analysis of the Factors Involved in Moving to an All-Volunteer Armed Force," unpublished manuscript, July 4, 1967, in *I Want You! The Evolution of the All-Volunteer Force,* ed. Bernard Rostker (Santa Monica, CA: RAND Corporation, 2006), CD, S0032. See, for example, pp. 2 and 17 for use of Friedman and Oi.
34. Rostker, *I Want You!*, 34.
35. John McClaughry to Anderson, memo, July 1, 1981, folder Military Manpower Task Force (8 of 17), CFOA 87, MAF, RRPL, 1.
36. The research staff was comprised of economists like Walter Oi and Stuart Altman, acolytes of Friedman. Warner and Asch, "Record and Prospects," 169.
37. Henderson, "Role of Economists," 369.
38. President's Commission, *Report,* 10, 52, 58.
39. Mark O. Hatfield, "A Volunteer Army Is the Answer," *New York Times Magazine,* March 30, 1969, 38; Barry Goldwater, "For an All-Volunteer Army," *New York Times,* February 8, 1971, 33.
40. President's Commission, *Report,* 63.
41. Griffith, *U.S. Army's Transition,* 35.
42. President's Commission, *Report,* 62, 63.
43. Ibid., 63.
44. Ibid.
45. Randall Shoemaker, "Military Pay Underrated," *Army Times,* November 12, 1975, 4.
46. Martin Binkin, *The Military Pay Muddle* (Washington, DC: Brookings Institution, 1975); Donald Rumsfeld, "Report of the Third Quadrennial Review of Military Compensation—Military Compensation: Modernized System, 1976 [Working Draft]," in Rostker, *I Want You!,* CD, S0168. PDF, 20.
47. Robert Altmeyer, "Is the Army a Welfare State? Let's Hex the PX," *National Review* 22, March 24, 1970, 300.

48. Rostker, *I Want You!*, 297–300.
49. Commission on the Organization of the Executive Branch of Government, *Business Enterprises: A Report to Congress* (Washington, DC: GPO, 1955), 3.
50. Stephen Howard Chadwick, *Defense Acquisition: Overview, Issues and Options for Congress* (Washington, DC: Congressional Research Service, 2007), CRS-1.
51. President's Commission, *Report*, 8, 92.
52. Richard V. L. Cooper, *Military Manpower and the All-Volunteer Force: A Report Prepared for Defense Advanced Research Projects Agency* (Santa Monica, CA: RAND Corporation, 1977), 301.
53. Martin Binkin, *Shaping the Defense Civilian Work Force: Economics, Politics and National Security* (Washington, DC: Brookings Institution, 1978), 61–70.
54. Ibid., 66.
55. Cooper, *Military Manpower*, 293.
56. Mike Causey, "Private Contract Worker Push Revives," *Washington Post*, February 7, 1974, H11. Though Nixon tacked early and often between various ends of the electorate, sometimes augmenting the size and scope of government, often cutting it, by 1972, as the economy slowed and his reelection contest loomed, he shifted to the right across a spectrum of issues. In early 1973, encouraged by a growing language of tax revolt and a deepening discord over social spending, when drawing up his annual budget he dug deep into social programs to try to close the federal budget gap. The fiscal year 1974 budget cut welfare and other antipoverty programs, Medicare, housing, and federal manpower and job training programs, among others, while preserving or creating corporate tax subsidies and other tax advantages for businesses and the wealthy. See Hobart Rowen, "1973 Issue: Nixon's Cuts in Social Programs," *Washington Post*, February 4, 1973, K1.
57. "Roy Ash—Biographical Note," Richard M. Nixon Presidential Library and Museum, http://nixon.archives.gov/forresearchers/find/textual/central/smof/ash.php. Litton had grown over the years to acquire over two dozen firms with over fifty plants in nine countries and $900 million in sales. See "Roy L. Ash, American Business Leaders of the Twentieth Century," Harvard Business School, www.hbs.edu/leadership/database/leaders/roy_l_ash.html; Causey, "Private Contract Worker," H11; Mike Causey, "Bolling Contracts for Cleanup Work," *Washington Post*, July 9, 1973, B9.
58. Ash assumed the leadership of OMB upon termination of his role as committee chair. Causey, "Private Contract Worker," H11. Ash's OMB revitalized the effort to put public activities out for private sector bids.

"New studies," Causey reported, "aimed at gathering data that may justify replacement of many of the government . . . workers with private contract employees."

59. First, OMB altered the computations used by federal agencies when comparing the costs of public sector activities to private sector activities in order to favor the private sector. Under Ash, in-house employees had their retirement cost (as part of the A-76 comparison process) increased. Previously, the retirement cost had been calculated at 7 percent of basic pay. Now, OMB more than tripled that cost to 24.7 percent, virtually guaranteeing that government bids to retain or undertake new commercial activities would be higher than the private sector bids. Binkin, *Shaping the Defense,* 23.
60. OMB, "Presidential Management Initiatives," Memorandum to Cabinet Members and Heads of Major Agencies, July 27, 1976, quoted in Binkin, *Shaping the Defense,* 23.
61. Binkin, *Shaping the Defense,* 24.
62. CMH, *DAHSUM: FY 1973* (Washington, DC: GPO, 1977), 144.
63. Ibid., 95–96.
64. CMH, *DAHSUM: FY 1975* (Washington, DC: GPO, 2000), 104.
65. CMH, *DAHSUM: FY 1973,* 112; CMH, *DAHSUM: FY 1978* (Washington, DC: GPO, 1980), 138; CMH, *DAHSUM: FY 1979* (Washington, DC: GPO, 1982), 112–113.
66. CMH, *DAHSUM: FY 1978,* 145–146.
67. CMH, *DAHSUM: FY 1979,* 87–88.
68. CMH, *DAHSUM: FY 1977* (Washington, DC: GPO, 1979), 28.
69. Griffith, *U.S. Army's Transition,* 17–19, 31, 34–37.
70. Dale Van Atta, *With Honor: Melvin Laird in War, Peace, and Politics* (Madison: The University of Wisconsin Press, 2008), 247.
71. David Rosenbaum, "Kennedy and Hatfield Disagree at Hearing on Volunteer Army," *New York Times,* February 5, 1971, 12.
72. Senate Committee, *Hearings on Selective Service,* 50.
73. Griffith, *U.S. Army's Transition,* 37.
74. Colonel Robert L. Phillips, USAREC, June 80–82, "Historical Development of the Army College Fund," series II, box 10, folder 3, Official Papers Reports, AVAC, MHI, 2.
75. Ibid., 1–2. Senate Committee, *Hearings on Selective Service,* 585.
76. Senate Committee, *Hearings on Selective Service,* 585.
77. Harold G. Moore, "A Busy Year of the 'Hard Look' at People Policies," *Army Magazine,* October 1975, 10, 25, 45.
78. Memorandum to Assistant Secretary of the Army for Manpower and Reserve Affairs from William B. Fulton, Director of the Army Staff, January 23, 1976, series II, box 13, folder 11, AVAC, MHI, 2. The slogan

"The Army Takes Care of Its Own" originated during World War II, through the Army Emergency Relief program, a volunteer program that helped army families in emergencies.

79. CMH, *DAHSUM: FY 1978*, 145–146, 59.
80. CMH, *DAHSUM: FY 1979*, 138.
81. CMH, *DAHSUM: FY 1973*, 61. Commanders felt that menial tasks unrelated to military training reduced the quality of the force and resulted in a less professional army.
82. It began pilot projects at three posts, including Fort Carson, Colorado, to give commanders $5 million to hire civilians to perform these previously military duties. Within months, these programs expanded abroad to European posts, and, within a year and a half, throughout the whole army. By 1972, the army had accomplished the full civilianizing of Kitchen Police duty, mostly through contracting, at a cost of $66 million that year. CMH, *DAHSUM: FY 1973*, 144.
83. CMH, *DAHSUM: FY 1975*, 95–96.
84. Phillips, "Historical Development," AVAC, MHI, 1–2.
85. Moore, "Busy Year," 38.
86. Harold Moore, "On Pay and Benefits, a 'Balanced Approach,'" *Army Magazine*, October 1976, 101. Emphasis in original.
87. Griffith, *U.S. Army's Transition*, 30–33.
88. CMH, *DAHSUM: FY 1972* (Washington, DC: GPO, 1972), 93.
89. Griffith, *U.S. Army's Transition*, 39.
90. Ibid., 84–85.
91. Carl S. Wallace, Assistant Secretary of the Army, to Principal Deputy, Assistant Secretary for Defense, memorandum, October 19, 1973, series II, box 7, folder 6, AVAC, MHI, 1–2.
92. In the course of administering a personnel survey to soldiers, leaders at Fort Benning, Georgia, made a discovery: 65.7 percent of the enlisted first-tour responders reported that their wives disliked their being in the army either somewhat or a lot. When these groups were asked, "Do you think your wife's feelings about the Army will have any influence on your decision to reenlist or leave the Army when your present term of service is up?" 61.3 percent of the enlisted first-tour servicemen reported that her feelings would have "A Great Influence." Robert G. Nivens to Lieutenant Colonel Doctor, memorandum, Final Evaluation Report, Modern Volunteer Army Experiment, Fort Benning, Georgia, June 7, 1972, series II, box 8, folder 2, AVAC, MHI, Tab B-155.
93. Ibid., inclusion 18.
94. Ibid., inclusion 26.
95. Staff Sergeant D. L. Manley, letter to the editor, *Army Times*, August 13, 1975, 13.

96. Griffith, *U.S. Army's Transition*, 49.
97. Edward L. King, *The Death of the Army: A Pre-Mortem* (New York: Saturday Review Press, 1972); George Walton, *The Tarnished Shield: A Report on Today's Army* (New York: Dodd, Mead, 1973); William L. Hauser, *America's Army in Crisis: A Study in Civil-Military Relations* (Baltimore, MD: Johns Hopkins University Press, 1973); Haynes Johnson and George C. Wilson, *Army in Anguish* (New York: Pocket Books, 1972).
98. Griffith, *U.S. Army's Transition*, 37.
99. "G.I. Dependents: Aid and Comfort," *Time*, April 14, 1980, 67.
100. Senate Committee, *Hearings on Selective Service*, 46.
101. Representative Bob Wilson (R-CA), quoted in "Jr. EM Travel Pay Pushed," *Army Times*, May 29, 1978, 22.
102. Staff Sergeant (E-5) Larent P. Fronts, USAF, letter to the editor, *The Times Magazine*, August 7, 1978, 35.
103. Joan Hodges, letter to the editor, *The Times Magazine*, August 7, 1978, 42.
104. CMH, *DAHSUM: FY 1972*, 93–94.
105. "Jr. EM Travel Pay Pushed," 22.
106. President's Private Sector Survey on Cost Control (Grace Commission), *A Report to the President* (Washington, DC: GPO, 1984), III-156. See also GAO, *DOD Competitive Sourcing: Results of A-76 Studies over the Past 5 Years* (Washington, DC: GPO, 2000), 8; GAO, *DOD Functions Contracted Out under OMB Circular A-76: Contract Cost Increases and the Effects on Federal Employee* (Washington, DC: GPO, 1985).
107. Citing "an outdated and entrenched bureaucratic mindset" and "risk aversion," the influential defense lobbying organization Business Executives for National Security (BENS) judged the influence of the private sector on the military to have occurred "in name only." See Paul Taibl, *Outsourcing and Privatization of Defense Infrastructure* (Washington, DC: BENS, 1997), 1, 4, 6. Also available at www.dtic.mil/dtic/tr/fulltext/u2/a530702.pdf.
108. Office of the Under Secretary of Defense for Acquisition and Technology, *Report of the Defense Science Board Task Force on Outsourcing and Privatization* (Washington, DC: 1996), 10A.

2. Is Military Service a Job?

1. Walter Mossberg and Richard J. Levine, "Union Plans '76 Drive to Represent Servicemen; Legalities Are Explored, and Pentagon Shudders," *Wall Street Journal*, June 27, 1975, 1.
2. West Germany, the Netherlands, Denmark, Norway, Belgium, and Sweden were among the Western European countries that had recently

unionized their military forces. On NATO countries with unionized armed forces see Ezra Krendel, "Trade Unionism and the U.S. Armed Forces," in *Military Unionism and the Volunteer Military System,* ed. Peter B. Lane, Ezra S. Krendel and William J. Taylor (Washington, DC: National Defense University, 1977), 15–17; Tobin Dean Seven, "A Military Union in the United States Army? An Attitude Survey" (MPA thesis, San Jose State University, 1978); James Quinn and Ronald Grabler, "Executive Summary: Military Unions—The Advantages and Disadvantages of Unionization within the Armed Forces," in *Military Unions,* ed. James A. Bandai, Charles Moskos, and William J. Taylor (ca. 1975–1977), MHI, 8–26.

3. David Cortright, "The Union Wants to Join You," *Nation,* February 21, 1976, 206.
4. John Finney, "The Pentagon Budget: Up High and a Likely Target," *New York Times,* February 9, 1975, 175.
5. William Proxmire quoted in James Treires, "A Poverty-Stricken Pentagon? Nonsense!," *Los Angeles Times,* January 22, 1979, A7.
6. George Marker, "Military to Have Own Labor Group," *Army Times,* November 10, 1977, 4; "Unionizing: An Interview with Clyde M. Webber, National President of the American Federation of Government Employees," *The Times Magazine,* September 24, 1975, 23.
7. See T. Roger Manley, Charles W. McNichols, and G. C. Saul Young, "A Quick-Look Analysis of a Survey Examining the Perceptions of Air Force Personnel towards Military Unionization," Department of Systems Management, School of Engineering, Air Force Institute of Technology, Wright-Patterson Air Force Base, Ohio, June 197, box 38, folder 3, MUC, GMMA, 22, 3, 12; Seven, "Military Union"; James McCollum and Jerald F. Robinson, "A Study of Active Army Attitudes toward Unionization," paper presented at the 39th Military Operations Research Society Symposium, Annapolis, MD, June 1977.
8. Joseph A. Fry, *Debating Vietnam: Fulbright, Stennis, and Their Hearings* (Lanham, MD: Rowan and Littlefield, 2006), 116.
9. Seven, "Military Union," 34–35.
10. Lucia Mount, "Big Government—Big Pensions," *Christian Science Monitor,* May 27, 1976, 14.
11. Social programs endured some of the biggest blows. As the Ford administration struggled to produce a lean federal budget, it targeted programs for lower-income Americans. It decided to "cut back on social programs," reported the *New York Times,* "such as Social Security, food stamps, Medicaid and health programs." For the poor and elderly, budget cuts were dire. Finney, "Pentagon Budget," 175.

12. Mount, "Big Government," 15, 16.
13. "Bio: Les Aspin, 18th Secretary of Defense," U.S. Department of Defense, www.defense.gov/specials/secdef_histories/SecDef_18.aspx.
14. John Finney, "U.S. Challenged on Arms Estimate", *New York Times*, March 8, 1976, 11.
15. "Unlikely Assistance," Editorial, *Army Times*, March 21, 1977, 13.
16. See these sources in Bernard Rostker, ed., *I Want You! The Evolution of the All-Volunteer Force* (Santa Monica, CA: RAND Corporation, 2006): GAO, "Report to Congress: Problems in Meeting Military Manpower, Washington DC, 1973," CD, S0156.PDF; and DMC, "Defense Manpower: The Keystone of National Security, Report to the President and the Congress, April 1976," CD, S0113.PDF, vii. As Secretary of Defense Donald Rumsfeld acknowledged, "pressures to reduce the Defense budget after the war in Southeast Asia . . . have focused on manpower costs more sharply than on any other area of Defense Resources," quoted in Rostker, *I Want You!*, 297.
17. Phil Stevens, "Military Kids Get Health Care at 'Bargain Basement' Rates," *Army Times*, March 15, 1976, 4.
18. "They're At It Again," *Army Times*, August 9, 1976, 2.
19. See Findlay in ibid.; U.S. Senate, Committee on Armed Services, *Unionization of the Armed Forces*, 95th Cong., 1st sess., March 18, July 18, 19, 20, 26, 1977, 98–99.
20. Mount, "Big Government," 14–15.
21. Quoted in Senate Committee, *Unionization*, 286.
22. Harold Moore, "On Pay and Benefits, a 'Balanced Approach,'" *Army Magazine*, October 1976, 101. Other army analysts made the same point. See Colonel William J. Taylor Jr., "Military Unions for the United States: Huge Misstep in the Right Direction," paper presented at the 1977 Annual Conference of the International Studies Association, Chase Park Plaza, St. Louis, March 1–20, 1977, in Bandai et al., *Military Unions*, vol. 2, item D. Taylor was in the Department of Social Sciences at West Point; William J. Taylor, Roger J. Arango, and Robert S. Lockwood, eds., *Military Unions: Trends and Issues* (Beverly Hills, CA: Sage, 1977), 137–149.
23. "The Enlisted Man," *New Yorker*, March 17, 1973, 33.
24. "Modern Living: GI Dormitories," *Time*, March 26, 1973, 98.
25. "In the Volunteer Army—One Way to a Free Education," *U.S. News and World Report*, June 18, 1973, 47.
26. Frank Coffee, "What the Armed Services Offer You *Now*," *Mechanix Illustrated*, December 1973, 88.
27. Iris Washington, "Women in the Armed Forces," *Essence*, April 1979, 25–26.

28. Catherine Calvert, "If You Think Your Country Owes You a Living . . . Here's How to Get It," *Mademoiselle*, March 1976, 183–184.
29. "If All Else Fails . . . Tell It to Your Uncle Sam. He Understands," *Esquire*, July 1977, 51.
30. John Chamberlain, "Shop Stewards in the Army? It's the Nuttiest of Notions," *Richmond Times-Dispatch*, April 23, 1976; "WBTV Editorial: Unionizing the Military," December 1, 1976; and "Soldiers Don't Belong in a Union, *Milwaukee Journal*, March 9, 1977; all in Senate Committee, *Unionization*, 11.
31. "Military Pay: What the Furor Is All About," *U.S. News and World Report*, August 22, 1977, 28–29.
32. Mount, "Big Government," 14; "The All-Volunteer Army—Too Soft a Life?," *U.S. News and World Report*, September 2, 1974, 44–45.
33. "Military Pay," 28–29. Stories about generous military pay and benefits appeared amidst other reports of the lavish lifestyles of the very highest-ranking military officers. "632 generals of two-star rank and above," reported the first paragraph of an article about "big government," "earned more than all but 28 top officials in government." See Mount, "Big Government," 14. Reporters embellished the stories with photos of the elegant, stately mansions of generals' quarters, stories of generals' use of enlisted soldiers as personal or household aides, the use of limousines by Pentagon brass, accounts of admirals' escalating retirement benefits, and pristine, remote "fly-in fishing camps" for top army generals to use with their guests. Together they painted a portrait in which the excesses of senior officers' lives symbolized the overall profligacy of the military and its benefits. "Proxmire Assails Fishing Camps," *New York Times*, October 14, 1974, 23.

    Waste in procurement and operations in maintenance also amplified concern over unchecked military spending. Discoveries ranged from the seemingly small to the shockingly large. Ernie Larson, a supplier to military posts, noted that he "routinely offers a one percent discount for payments received within 20 days." "Never." he added. "does the government bother to make the deadline" and save money. Worse were the cost overruns to a repair project at the National War College that transformed a $65,000 ceiling renovation into a $1.9 million renovation, and worst of all were the "giant cost overruns" revealed for the fleet of C-5As—a huge, heavy cargo transport aircraft—in 1970. See Mount, "Big Government," 14, 15. For many reporters, generals' fancy perquisites and wasteful procurement was of a piece with excessively generous benefits for soldiers, sailors, and airmen. When it came to defense, it was all too much.
34. "An Analysis and Evaluation of the U.S. Army: The Beard Study," prepared by Jerry Reed, appendix, U.S. Senate, Committee on Armed

Services, *Status of the All-Volunteer Armed Force: Hearing before the Subcommittee on Manpower and Personnel*, 95th Cong., 2nd sess., June 20, 1978, 213. Hereafter cited as "Beard Study."

35. Advertisement, *Army Times*, August 27, 1977, 32.
36. *Army Times*, October 11, 1976, 13.
37. *Army Times*, October 1, 1975, 13.
38. Staff Sergeant Joseph Plantamura, letter to the editor, *Army Times*, March 21, 1977, 13.
39. "Jobless Pay Cut," letter to the editor, *Army Times*, November 8, 1976, 14.
40. "Beard Study," 220.
41. Sergeant First Class (Ret.) Steve Reed, letter to the editor, *Army Times*, March 21, 1977, 14. David Taylor, former assistant secretary of defense for reserve and manpower affairs, relayed how in all the hundreds of visits he made to military bases during his tenure, at only one did Les Aspin's name fail to be raised among the soldiers he spoke with. David Taylor, "On the Erosion of Benefits: Why Things Aren't as Bad as They Seem," *Army Times Magazine*, October 31, 1977, 26.
42. Captain Danial [*sic*] L. Shaw, letter to the editor, *Army Times*, August 30, 1976, 18.
43. "Congressional Benefits", Editorial, *Army Times*, March 29, 1976, 13.
44. Cartoon, *Army Times*, November 7, 1977, 19.
45. Major Robert A. Givens, letter to the editor, *Army Times*, September 13, 1976, 14.
46. Clyde Webber, Testimony before the DMC: Organizing the Military Services into a Union, AFGE, August 18, 1975, RG 98–002, series 1, box 38, folder 3, MUC, GMMA, 7–8.
47. David Cortright, "Unions and Democracy," *AEI Defense Review* 1 (1977): 2.
48. Alan Ned Sabrosky, ed., *Blue-Collar Soldiers? The Question of American Military Unionization* (Philadelphia: Foreign Policy Research Institute, 1977), 14.
49. John F. Kennedy, "Executive Order 10988—Employee-Management Cooperation in the Federal Service," January 17, 1962, The American Presidency Project, www.presidency.ucsb.edu/ws/index.php?pid=58926.
50. Flyer, Building Services Employees' International Union, AFL-CIO, ca. 1962, Walter Reuther Library, Wayne State University, www.reuther.wayne.edu/node/577.
51. Joseph A. McCartin, "'A Wagner Act for Public Employees': Labor's Deferred Dream and the Rise of Conservatism, 1970–1976," *Journal of American History* 95, no.1 (2008): 123.
52. Murray B. Nesbitt, *Labor Relations in the Federal Government Service* (Washington, DC: Bureau of National Affairs, 1976), 387, 388, 380, 374;

on the reversal of no-strike positions see also Sterling D. Sparrow and John M. Cappozzola, *The Urban Community and Its Unionized Bureaucracies: Pressure Politics in Local Government Labor Relations* (New York: Dunellen, 1973), 242–244.

53. McCartin, "Wagner Act," 123.
54. Legislation introduced in Congress in the early 1970s proposed to allow public employees' unions the same right as private unions and to have access to the full "benefits of collective bargaining." McCartin, "Wagner Act," 126–128.
55. Nicholas J. Nolan quoted in Strom Thurmond, "Military Unions: No," *AEI Defense Review* 1 (1977), 19. Webber, Testimony, 7–8.
56. Webber, Testimony, 7–8.
57. Lillian Rubin, *Worlds of Pain: Life in the Working Class Family* (New York: Basic Books, 1976).
58. Unemployment rates are from 1976; Department of Labor, Bureau of Labor Statistics, "Local Area Unemployment Statistics: Current Unemployment Rates for States and Historical Highs/Lows," last modified December 19, 2014, www.bls.gov/web/laus/lauhsthl.htm.
59. Marisa Chappell, *War on Welfare: Family, Poverty, and Politics in Modern America* (Philadelphia: University of Pennsylvania Press, 2009), 210–211.
60. Ibid., 196–198.
61. Ibid., 231, 222.
62. "Unionizing: An Interview with Clyde M. Webber," 23.
63. Senate Committee, *Unionization*, 276.
64. Blaylock quoted in Senate Committee, *Unionization*, 287.
65. RA Retired, letter to the editor, *Army Times*, January 19, 1977, 15.
66. Sergeant First Class Henry D. Jennings, letter to the editor, *Army Times*, August 16, 1976, 14.
67. Senate Committee, *Unionization*, 186.
68. On AFGE see Blaylock quoted in Senate Committee, *Unionization*, 297; Harold Logan, "Soldiers Fight Bill to Bar Organizing of Military," *Washington Post*, May 21, 1977, A4.
69. David Segal, "From Political to Industrial Citizenship," in *The Political Education of Soldiers*, ed. Morris Janowitz and Stephen D. Wesbrook (Beverly Hills, CA: Sage, 1983), 294.
70. Manley et al., "Quick-Look Analysis"; Seven, "Military Union," 45. See also McCollum and Robinson, "Study of Active Army"; James McCollum and Jerald F. Robinson, "The Law and Current Status of Unions in the Military Establishment," *Labor Law Journal* 28, no. 7 (July 1977): 421–430; David Segal and R. C. Karamer, "Orientations toward Military

Unions among Combat Troops," *Journal of Collective Negotiations in the Public Sector* 8 (1977): 108–117; David Segal, "Attitudes toward Unions in the Ground Combat Forces," in Taylor et al., *Military Unions*, 137–149.

71. Cortright, "Union Wants," 208; Seven, "Military Union," 45; Lane et al., *Military Unionism*, 9; Krendel, "Trade Unionism," 30.
72. Robert Nolan, Fleet Reserve Association, National Executive Secretary, quoted in Senate Committee, *Unionization*, 185.
73. Ibid. Surveys bore out the analysis. Manley et al., "Quick-Look Analysis," 13; McCollum and Robinson, "Law and Current Status," 421–430.
74. Senate Committee, *Unionization*, 11, 14, 18, 20.
75. *Kansas City Star*, September 1, 1976, box 38, folder 3, MUC, GMMA, 1.
76. Cartoon, *Army Times*, October 4, 1976, 15.
77. *Blade News* [Bowie, MD], January 22, 1976, box 38, folder 3, MUC, GMMA, 4.
78. David Y. Denholm and Theodore C. Humes, "The Case against Military Unionism," in Sabrosky, *Blue Collar Soldiers?*, 75, 77; on Denholm and the Public Service Research Foundation see McCartin, "Wagner Act," 140–141; on Gallup Poll results see Mike Causey, "Public Opposes GU Union," *Washington Post*, July 7, 1977, B2.
79. Both quoted in Ezra S. Krendel and Bernard Samoff, "Trade Unions and the United States Armed Forces: The Issues and Precedents," in *Unionizing the Armed Forces*, ed. Ezra S. Krendel and Bernard Samoff (Philadelphia: University of Pennsylvania Press, 1977), 9.
80. Quoted in George Wilson, "Brown Proposes Rules on Military Unions," *Washington Post*, July 19, 1977, A4.
81. Quoted in Mossberg and Levine, "Union Plans," 1, and also in Cortright, "Union Wants," 206.
82. Guy Halverson, "Cannons Roar on Unionizing U.S. Military," *Christian Science Monitor*, April 2, 1976, 34.
83. William C. Westmorland, "Against Unionizing the Military," *New York Times*, June 2, 1977, 21.
84. Quoted in Senate Committee, *Unionization*, 189. See this same sentiment in Lieutenant Colonel Maurice L. Lien, "Military Associations: A Positive Force for Defense," *Retired Officer*, December 1975, 22, MUC, GMMA. *Retired Officer*, now called *Military Officer*, was the magazine of the Military Officers Association of America. William J. Rogers, "The Commander's Message: Unionism Would Threaten Military Chain of Command," *American Legion Magazine*, January 1977, 4. Military service associations arose largely in the early part of the twentieth century as professional-cum-fraternal organizations that, over time, came

to advocate for their military members before Congress, the DoD, and the various services. The union's bid for representation posed an obvious threat to their existence. As Colonel William Taylor Jr., put it, "To the extent that unions gain control in representing the interests of military personnel, the nongovernmental lobbying organizations lose their membership, dues, and raison d'etre." Taylor et al., *Military Unions,* 9.

85. Stennis quoted in George Wilson, "Caution Urged on Military Union," *Washington Post,* March 19, 1977, A1.
86. Senate Committee, *Unionization,* 7.
87. Montgomery quoted in Andy Plattner, "Poll Rejects Military Unions," *Army Times,* December 27, 1976, 4.
88. See, for example, the advertisement Thurmond made for candidate Gerald Ford in the 1976 presidential election in which he accused candidate Jimmy Carter of not being "for the South" but for "George Meany and the unions," because he promised to sign a repeal of Southern states' right-to-work laws. Strom Thurmond, "Ford vs. Carter," The Living Room Candidate: Presidential Campaign Commercials, 1952–2012, www.livingroomcandidate.org/commercials/1976/strom-thurmond.
89. Senate Committee, *Unionization,* 8; Thurmond, "Military Unions," 25.
90. Senate Committee, *Unionization,* 7; "Senate Votes a Military Union Ban," *New York Times,* September 17, 1977, 48.
91. William Taylor, "Issues in Military Unionization," in Sabrosky, *Blue-Collar Soldiers?,* 21.
92. Mossberg and Levine, "Union Plans," 1.
93. Fred Reed, "Military Union Value Doubted," *Army Times,* December 27, 1976, 2.
94. Blaylock quoted in Senate Committee, *Unionization,* 276.
95. Commission on an All-Volunteer Armed Force, *The Report of the President's Commission on an All-Volunteer Armed Force* (Washington, DC: GPO, 1970), 10, 52, 58.
96. See Moskos's testimony in Senate Committee, *Status of the All-Volunteer Armed Force,* 38. Moskos's "occupationalization" thesis raised alarm bells among those most leery of the transition to a volunteer force.
97. See these sources in Rostker, *I Want You!:* "The Report of the President's Commission on Military Compensation" (Washington, DC, April 1978), 26; Donald Rumsfeld, "Report of the Third Quadrennial Review of Military Compensation—Military Compensation: Modernized System, 1976 [Working Draft]," CD, S0168.PDF, 3–5; and GAO, "Report to Congress," 64–65.
98. Rumsfeld, "Report of the Third Quadrennial Review," in Rostker, *I Want You!,* CD, S0168.PDF, 3–5.

99. "Report of the President's Commission," in Rostker, *I Want You!*, 1.
100. Rumsfeld, "Report of the Third Quadrennial Review," in Rostker, *I Want You!*, CD, S0168.PDF, 12.
101. "Report of the President's Commission," in Rostker, *I Want You!*, 1.
102. "Examples of Pay, Benefits," *Army Times*, April 25, 1977, 1.
103. "Military Pay," 28–29; U.S. Census Bureau, "Current Population Reports," www.census.gov/hhes/www/income/histinc/h05.html; John Finney, "Civil Service Pay Less Than Army's," *New York Times*, November 23, 1975, 25. On government employees' lower pay and benefits see also James C. McCullough, "Washington Assignments: Teach Troops to Cope with Cost of Living," *Army Times*, December 26, 1977, 16. At the same time, the United Services Life Insurance Company, the insurance company founded by army officers and for service personnel, calculated the very high value of "invisible pay" for service personnel. "A second lieutenant receives about $800 per month in such 'invisible pay.'" They calculated what civilians would have to pay from their own pockets for the retirement, health care, life insurance, dependency and indemnity compensation, disability and accident insurance, plus savings from commissary and exchanges. "Study Cites Value of 'Invisible Pay,'" *Army Times*, April 25, 1977, 12.
104. "Examples of Pay, Benefits."
105. "Beard Study," 213–214.
106. Andy Plattner, "48,000 Troops Talk about Pay, Life Styles," *Army Times*, February 28, 1977, 1, 24.
107. Larry Carney, "Rogers Will Try To Halt Erosion of Benefits," *Army Times*, January 17, 1977, 3.
108. Bruce Callender, "Servicemen Viewed as Employees," *Army Times*, October 4, 1976, 33.
109. Gene Famiglietti, "Weyand Issues Call to 'Fight' for Benefits," *Army Times*, November 5, 1975, 7, 6.
110. Rumsfeld, "Report of the Third Quadrennial Review," in Rostker, *I Want You!*, CD, S0168.PDF, 12.
111. Specialist 4 Fatima F. Ebrakini, letter to the editor, *Army Times*, February 21, 1977, 14.
112. Letter from an Officers' Wives Club, *The Times Magazine*, August 13, 1975, 4.
113. "Beard Study," 213.
114. Ibid., 220.
115. Randall Shoemaker, "X-Factor Forgotten: Military Benefits Chart Draws Fire," *Army Times*, December 24, 1975, 15.
116. Ibid.

117. Lieutenant Colonel Dennis J. Morrissey, letter to the editor, *Army Times,* October 11, 1976, 14.
118. Harold G. Moore, "A Busy Year of the 'Hard Look' at People Policies," *Army Magazine,* October 1975, 25.
119. Fred C. Weyand, *Posture of the Army,* Posture Statement presented to the 94th Cong., 2nd sess., February 2, 1976, 25.
120. "Union Threat Not 'Severe,'" *Army Times,* February 14, 1977, 23.
121. Indeed, they often began their stated objections to unions with a preamble about the general good unions had done in U.S. history. See, for example, "AF Chief Says Uncertainty Fuels Drive to Unionize GIs," *Washington Post,* April 5, 1977, A4.
122. In 1973 David Denholm, a conservative and member of the National Right to Work Committee founded the Public Service Research Council, an organization devoted to fighting public sector unionization as a threat not only to the free market and individual "rights to work," but also to democracy itself. The very activism that buoyed public sector unions and represented a boon to AFGE also fueled this backlash, in which Denholm and his allies attacked public sector unions as fundamentally opposed to "the public interest," "the people," and "popular sovereignty." The many strikes by public employees fed into critiques of unions as irresponsible and dangerous. One popular antiunion tract accused the public sector unions of being "arsonists" and "let[ting] our cities burn." Ralph de Toledano, *Let Our Cities Burn* (New Rochelle, NY: Arlington House, 1975), 82, 102, 111, 43.
123. Thurmond, "Military Unions," 19.
124. Senate Committee, *Unionization,* 185.
125. Garn quoted in Senate Committee, *Unionization,* 289.
126. Editorial, *Indianapolis News,* September 25, 1976, quoted in Thurmond, "Military Unions," 27–28. See also McCartin, "Wagner Act."
127. Cartoon, *Army Times,* December 6, 1976, 15.
128. "May Be Leaving," letter to the editor, *Army Times,* March 28, 1977, 14.
129. Quoted in Senate Committee, *Unionization,* 191.
130. Blaylock quoted in Senate Committee, *Unionization,* 276; interview by author with David Cortright, November 25, 2008.
131. "Government Employees Reject Proposal to Organize Military," AFL-CIO News Service, September 8, 1977, box 38, folder 3, MUC, GMMA. David Denholm conducted a survey that included public sector union members, and he, too, noted that 71 percent of them opposed unionizing the military. Thurmond, "Military Unions," 21, and appendix B, 30.
132. "AFGE Rejects Move to Organize Military," *AFL-CIO News,* September 10, 1977, box 38, folder 3, MUC, GMMA.

133. U.S. House, Committee on Armed Services, *Hearings on S. 274, Unionization of Military Personnel, before the Investigations Subcommittee,* 95th Cong., 1st sess., October 12, 13, 19, and 26, 1977.
134. Edward F. Sherman, "Military Unions and the Soldier 'Employee,'" *Washington Post,* April 4, 1978, box 38, folder 3, MUC, GMMA; Andy Plattner, "Bill Banning Military Unions Voted," *Army Times,* August 7, 1978, 4.
135. Lieutenant Commander John M. Kutch Jr., letter to the editor, *Army Times,* September 20, 1976, 14.
136. Joseph Guildor, letter to the editor, *Army Times,* January 10, 1977, 15.
137. Quoted in Howard Fleiegar, "On the Other Hand," *U.S. News and World Report,* October 25, 1976, 100.
138. Weyand, *Posture of the Army,* 25.
139. Quoted in Fred Reed, "Anti-GI Union Laws 'Unnecessary,'" *Army Times,* June 20, 1977, 2.
140. Staff writer, "Defense Budget Gets a 'Boost,'" *Army Times,* March 21, 1977, 4; "Aspin Misses 'His' Meetings," *Army Times,* May 29, 1978, 22; CMH, *DAHSUM: FY 1979* (Washington, DC: GPO, 1982), 93.
141. These were the Defense Appropriation Act of 1981, the Servicemen and Women and Compensation Act of 1980, and the Military Pay and Benefits Act of 1980.
142. CMH, *DAHSUM: FY 1981* (Washington, DC: GPO, 1988), 110–111; CMH, *DAHSUM: FY 1980* (Washington, DC: GPO, 1983), 110; Linda Pappas Hale, Thomas Hale, and Peter Oglobin, *Panel: Military Compensation: A New Look at an Old Challenge* (Washington, DC: Hay Associates, 1981). Also available at www.dtic.mil/get-tr-doc/pdf?AD=ADP001413.
143. Jimmy Carter, "Department of Defense Authorization Act, 1981, Statement on Signing H.R. 6974 into Law," September 8, 1980, The American Presidency Project, www.presidency.ucsb.edu/ws/index.php?pid=45003.

3. The Threat of a Social Welfare Institution

1. E. Thomas Wood and Ken Whitehouse, "Remembering Robin Beard," *Nashville Post,* June 20, 2007, www.nashvillepost.com/news/2007/6/20/remembering_robin_beard; "Former Tennessee GOP Rep. Robin Beard Dies at 67," *Roll Call,* June 20, 2007, www.rollcall.com/issues/52_143/-19027-1.html; Nicholas Laham, *Ronald Reagan and the Politics of Immigration Reform* (Westport, CT: Praeger, 2000), 49–51; Sherry

Hoppe and Bruce Speck, *Maxine Smith's Unwilling Pupils: Lessons Learned in Memphis's Civil Rights Classroom* (Knoxville, TN: University of Tennessee Press, 2007), 191.

2. Beard quoted in "Secretary of the Army: Man on the Hot Seat," *Black Enterprise,* 1980, July 1980, 24.
3. "An Analysis and Evaluation of the U.S. Army: The Beard Study," prepared by Jerry Reed, appendix, U.S. Senate, Committee on Armed Services, *Status of the All-Volunteer Armed Force: Hearing before the Subcommittee on Manpower and Personnel,* 95th Cong., 2nd sess., June 20, 1978, 257, 141. Hereafter cited as "Beard Study."
4. Nunn quoted in Senate Committee, *Status of the All-Volunteer Armed Force,* 5.
5. "Beard Study," 257.
6. Robert Griffith, *The U.S. Army's Transition to the All-Volunteer Force, 1968–1974* (Washington, DC: CMH, 1997), 37.
7. John Whiteclay Chambers II, *To Raise an Army: The Draft Comes to Modern America* (New York: Free Press, 1987), 14–19; James Kirby Martin and Edward Lender, *A Respectable Army: The Military Origins of the Republic, 1763–1789* (New York: Arlington Heights, 2006); Edward C. Papenfuse and Gregory A. Stiverson, "General Smallwood's Recruits: The Peacetime Career of the Revolutionary War Private," *William and Mary Quarterly* 30 (1973): 116–113; Steven Rosswurm, *Army, Country and Class: The Philadelphia Militia and the "Lower Sort" during the American Revolution* (New Brunswick: Rutgers University Press, 1999); David Williams, "Class Conflict, U.S.A," in *Encyclopedia of the American Civil War,* ed. David Heidler and Jeanne Heidler (Santa Barbara: ABC-CLIO, 2000), 446–448; Anni Baker, *American Soldiers Overseas: The Global Military Presence* (Westport, CT: Praeger, 2004), 19. Because soldiers occupied a tenuous social status, military benefits, even for veterans of wars, have had to be meticulously and determinedly constructed as a benefit that they deserved and as a reward for service. In the post-Revolutionary era, veterans' poverty had to be carefully distinguished from the morally suspect need of other poor Americans—paupers, drunks, and other failures. John Resch, *Suffering Soldiers: Revolutionary War Veterans, Moral Sentiment, and Political Culture in the Early Republic* (Amherst, MA: University of Massachusetts Press, 1999), 1–10. The Civil War pensions and homes, which formed the basis not only for the modern Veterans Administration system but also for all public pensions, were the product of enormous rhetorical and political work to portray the Civil War–era soldier as an upright citizen deserving of help. Their advocates struggled to distinguish unemployed, physically damaged veterans from

the other poor or unemployed, creating "soldiers homes" rather than "asylums" in an attempt to sever the associations between soldiers and the lower classes. Patrick J. Kelly, *Creating a National Home: Building the Veterans' Welfare State 1860–1900* (Cambridge, MA: Harvard University Press, 1997); David Gerber, ed., *Disabled Veterans in History* (Ann Arbor, MI: University of Michigan Press, 2000).

8. On the lesser known World War I efforts see Nancy Bristow, *Making Men Moral: Social Engineering during the Great War* (New York: New York University Press, 1996).
9. Edward L. King, *The Death of the Army: A Pre-Mortem* (New York: Saturday Review Press, 1972); George Walton, *The Tarnished Shield: A Report on Today's Army* (New York: Dodd Mead, 1973); William L. Hauser, *America's Army in Crisis: A Study in Civil-Military Relations* (Baltimore, MD: Johns Hopkins University Press, 1973); Haynes Johnson and George C. Wilson, *Army in Anguish* (New York: Pocket Books, 1972).
10. Robert McNamara, "Vital Speeches of the Day," December 1, 1967, 101, quoted in Fred Richard Bahr, "The Expanding Role of the Department of Defense as an Instrument of Social Change" (PhD diss., George Washington University, 1970), 139.
11. OASD (MRA), *Description of Project One Hundred Thousand* (Washington, DC: DoD, 1968), MHI, 7, 5; Charles Cobble, "Social Action Programs in the Department of Defense" (PhD diss., University of North Carolina at Chapel Hill, 1969), 19; Bahr, "Expanding Role," 151.
12. Bahr, "Expanding Role," 151. OASC (MRA), *Description of Project,* 16.
13. "Study Finds No Poor-Man's Army," *Army Times,* January 12, 1976, 15.
14. Adam Yarmolinsky and Gregory D. Foster, *Paradoxes of Power: The Military Establishment in the Eighties* (Bloomington, IN: Indiana University Press, 1983), 75.
15. Moskos and Fallows cited in Editorial, "Morality and Military Service," *Washington Star,* April 6, 1981.
16. Jay Fingan, "DoD: All-Vol Forces Reflect National Image," *Army Times,* March 14, 1977, 25.
17. DMC, *Defense Manpower: The Keystone of National Security, a Report to the President and the Congress* (Washington, DC: GPO, 1976), II-11.
18. OASD (MRAL), *America's Volunteers: A Report on the All-Volunteer Armed Forces* (Washington, DC: DoD, 1978), 44; Jay Finegan, "More EM Recruits Coming from Low-Income Families," *Army Times,* January 23, 1978, 29.
19. Moskos quoted in Senate Committee, *Status of the All-Volunteer Armed Force,* 40; Moskos quoted in Editorial, "Morality." See also Yarmolinsky and Foster, *Paradoxes of Power,* 74.

20. Mady Wechsler Segal, "Women's Roles in the U.S. Armed Forces: An Evaluation of Evidence and Arguments for Policy Decisions," in *Conscripts and Volunteers: Military Requirements, Social Justice, and the All-Volunteer Force,* ed. Robert Fullinwider (Totowa, NJ: Rowman and Allanheld, 1983), 10.
21. DMC, *Defense Manpower,* 159; Senate Committee, *Status of the All-Volunteer Armed Force,* 39; Yarmolinsky and Foster, *Paradoxes of Power,* 72.
22. "High School Grad Recruit Totals Dip," *Army Times,* February 14, 1977, 8.
23. A recruiter recalled the practice in an oral history: "And so, therefore, we were testing people, non-graduates, who had scored less than 65, giving them the GED test throughout the state of Indiana. They did not qualify for a diploma through the state of Indiana but they would issue a letter stating that he had averaged a 3 and therefore met the requirements of the Army. And we were putting them in as high school graduates, which of course met the requirement of the GED." Transcript of Proceedings: Robert K. Griffith with Four Recruiters from Transition Period, Ft. Sheridan, IL, October 20, 1983, series II, box 15, folder 8, Oral Histories, AVAC, MHI, 3–4.
24. Ibid., 36.
25. Moskos quoted in Senate Committee, *Status of the All-Volunteer Armed Force,* 39.
26. David Segal and Mady Wechsler Segal, "America's Military Population," *Population Bulletin* 59, no. 4 (December 2004): 23.
27. DMC, *Defense Manpower,* 162; OASD (MRAL), *America's Volunteers,* 38.
28. DMC, *Defense Manpower,* 162.
29. "Beard Study," 146.
30. George Davis, "Blacks in the Military: Opportunity or Refuge?," *Black Enterprise,* July 1980, 23.
31. Moskos quoted in Senate Committee, *Status of the All-Volunteer Armed Force,* 40.
32. The army allowed men without high school diplomas to join but not women, so by definition all female soldiers had at least a high school degree. Many more women than men also had college experience as well.
33. Linda Stern, "Launch a Career with Basic Training," *Working Women,* February 1980, 48, 60.
34. OASD (MRAL), *America's Volunteers,* 70.
35. Institute for Women's Leadership, "Women's Leadership Fact Sheet: Women in the U.S. Military Services" (New Brunswick, NJ: Rutgers

University, 2010), 2. Also available at http://iwl.rutgers.edu/research_njwc.html.

36. Segal and Segal, "America's Military Population," 30; Segal, "Women's Roles," 201.
37. OASD (MRAL), *America's Volunteers*, 234. See also reports of recruiters taking low-scoring, poorly educated Job Corps recruits in the early-to-mid-1970s, in Robert K. Griffith with Four Recruiters, 4–5.
38. Statement of Senator Sam Nunn, Chairman, DoD Authorization for Appropriations for FY 1981, in *I Want You! The Evolution of the All-Volunteer Force*, ed. Bernard Rostker (Santa Monica, CA: RAND Corporation, 2006), CD, S0567.PDF, 1285–1288.
39. Yarmolinsky and Foster, *Paradoxes of Power*, 72.
40. Bernard Rodgers and Clifford Alexander, *The Posture of the Army and Department of the Army Budget Estimates for FY 1979*, Posture Statement presented to the 96th Cong., 1st sess., January 31, 1979, 5.
41. Robert Yerks, "Our Ability to 'Fight Now' Depends on People," *Army Magazine*, October 1979, 61.
42. Ibid.
43. OASD (MRAL), *America's Volunteers*, 235.
44. Yarmolinsky and Foster, *Paradoxes of Power*, 72, 73.
45. "Beard Study," 230.
46. Ibid., 242.
47. Editorial, "Morality."
48. Yarmolinsky and Foster, *Paradoxes of Power*, 71; Segal, "Women's Roles," 83, 7, 29; Richard Hunter, "An Analysis of the All-Volunteer Armed Forces—Past and Future," in *Conscripts and Volunteers: Military Requirements, Social Justice, and the All-Volunteer Force*, ed. Robert K. Fullinwider (Totowa, IA: Rowman and Allanheld, 1983), 23–45.
49. Beard quoted in Senate Committee, *Status of the All-Volunteer Armed Force*, 92.
50. "The Case for a Volunteer Army," *Time*, January 10, 1969, 26. This argument was often made through innuendo. Media coverage of racial problems in the army routinely referred to African Americans who openly protested discrimination in the army as "militants," regardless of their actual political, philosophical, or institutional affiliations. See, for example, "West Germany: Race and the GI," *Newsweek*, 76, November 9, 1970, 37–38. Conservative Republican columnist for the *Washington Post*, Joseph Alsop, was blunt when he connected Black Power with the possibility of an all-black volunteer force: "Does President Nixon propose to root out and suppress black guerilla movements with combat units 40 percent black?" Joseph Alsop, "Some Subtle Dangers Lurk in Nixon's

Plan to End Draft," *Washington Post and Times Herald,* October 25, 1968, A25.

51. Shirley Chisholm, *Congressional Digest* 50, May 1971, 156.
52. Kennedy featured in David E. Rosenbaum, "Congress Expected to Give Draft Issue Urgent Priority," *New York Times,* January 11, 1971, 6.
53. Ronald V. Dellums, "Focus," Joint Center for Policy Studies, in Rostker, *I Want You!,* CD, S0170.PDF, 4.
54. Interview of Howard H. Calloway, Former Secretary of the Army, by Major Robert Griffith, December 23, 1983, Denver, CO, series II, box 14, folder 9, Oral Histories, AVAC, MHI, 11, 12.
55. Ibid., 9.
56. Senate Committee, *Status of the All-Volunteer Armed Force,* 73.
57. Ibid., 68–69.
58. Morris Janowitz and Charles C. Moskos Jr., "Racial Composition in the All-Volunteer Force," *Armed Forces and Society* 1, no.1 (November 1974): 115–119.
59. Segal, "Women's Roles," 21.
60. Memo to Bo Calloway from Donald Rumsfeld, November 15, 1974, in Rostker, *I Want You!,* CD, G0555.PDF.
61. Interview of Howard H. Calloway, 9.
62. Segal, "Women's Roles," 13; Sar Levitan and Karen Cleary Aldeman, *Warriors at Work: The Volunteer Armed Force* (Beverly Hills, CA: Sage, 1977), 182.
63. On Military Occupational Specialties see Segal, "Women's Roles," 201.
64. Yerks, "Our Ability," 63.
65. "Beard Study," 140.
66. David Segal, "Military Organization and Personnel," in Fullinwider, *Conscripts and Volunteers,* 14.
67. Levitan and Aldeman, *Warriors at Work,* 183.
68. "Army Husband: If Mom's a G.I., Who Babysits?," *Time,* April 16, 1979, 82.
69. "Women in the Armed Forces," *Newsweek,* February 18, 1980, 42.
70. General John A. Wickham, "White Paper, The Army Family" (Washington, DC: Department of the Army, 1983), 4.
71. Segal, "Military Organization," 14. For statistics on single parents in the army see U.S. House, Committee on Armed Services, *Military Child Care: Hearing before Subcommittee on Military Personnel and Compensation,* 101st Cong., 1st sess., April 13, 1989, 58.
72. "Women in the Armed Forces," 42.
73. See Oscar Lewis, *Five Families: Mexican Case Studies in the Culture of Poverty* (New York: Basic Books, 1959); Oscar Lewis, *Children of*

Sanchez: Autobiography of a Mexican Family (New York: Random House, 1961).

74. See, for example, Ange-Marie Hancock, *The Politics of Disgust: The Public Identity of the Welfare Queen* (New York: New York University Press, 2004), 57–63; Ellen Reese, *Backlash against Welfare Mothers Past and Present* (Berkeley, CA: University of California Press, 2005); Jennifer Mittelstadt, *From Welfare to Workfare: The Unintended Consequences of Liberal Reform, 1945–1965* (Chapel Hill, NC: University of North Carolina Press, 2005).
75. Michael Daly in the editorial pages of the *Los Angeles Times*, as quoted in Yarmolinsky and Foster, *Paradoxes of Power*, 87.
76. Interview of Howard H. Calloway, 14.
77. Lieutenant General Robert G. Yerks, "ODCSPER: People Support Is What We Are Here For," *Army Magazine*, October 1978, 67.
78. "Soldier," letter to the editor, *Army Times*, January 17, 1977, 14.
79. Beard quoted in Senate Committee, *Status of the All-Volunteer Armed Force*, 92.
80. Michael Klare, "Can the Army Survive Volar?," *Commonwealth*, January 18, 1974, 387.
81. "Big Switch: Military Finding Favor with New Generation," *US News and World Report*, May 3, 1976, 35.
82. "Beard Study," 240, 223.
83. Ibid.
84. Patricia Bloebaum, "Must the Services Take Care of Everybody?," *The Times Magazine*, May 29, 1978, 7, 8.
85. "Beard Study," 242.
86. See, for example, "Low Pay, High Costs Put Soldiers on Welfare," *Los Angeles Times*, November 13, 1969, A9; "Poverty in Uniform," *New York Times*, June 1, 1971, 38; U.S. Senate, Committee on Armed Services, *Hearings on Selective Service and Military Compensation*, 92nd Congress, 1st sess., February 2, 4, 8, 9, 10, 19, and 22, 1971, 718.
87. "The Federal Food Stamp Program . . . Many Military Families Qualify", ca. 1980, 1; on army help with food stamps see also "Welcome to Fort Carson's Army Community Service center," ca. 1980; and "How to Make Ends Meet, Fact Sheet" (Fort Eustis, VA: USATCFE Public Affairs Office, August 1981), 3. All three in Misc. ACS and Military Family 1971–1985, MFC, CMH.
88. Rodgers and Alexander, *Posture of the Army*, 34b.
89. In the twentieth century, the stigma of reliance on public assistance became inextricably associated with women. New state social welfare programs of the Progressive and New Deal eras bifurcated social support

among men and women. The programs offered to working men consisted of non-means-tested social insurance, while programs for women consisted largely of means-tested public assistance. The word "welfare" over time came to be associated with the latter programs, and in the process became feminized. Barbara Nelson, "The Origins of the Two-Channel Welfare State: Workmen's Compensation and Mothers' Aid," in *Women, the State, and Welfare,* ed. Linda Gordon (Madison, WI: University of Wisconsin Press, 1990). When African American women finally gained access to relief after the New Deal, the program also became racialized. Over the second half of the century, the feminized racialization of public assistance produced a juggernaut of stereotypes around welfare programs. Hancock, *Politics of Disgust,* 57–63; Reese, *Backlash against Welfare Mothers;* Mittelstadt, *From Welfare to Workfare.*

90. On soldier self-identification see Carol Burke, *Camp All-American, Hanoi Jane, and the High-and-Tight: Gender, Folklore and Changing Military Culture* (Boston: Beacon Press, 2004); Catherine Lutz, *Homefront: A Military City and the American Twentieth Century* (Boston: Beacon Press, 2001), 244–245; Francine D'Amico, "Policing the U.S. Military's Race and Gender Lines," in *Wives and Warriors: Women in the Military in the United States and Canada,* ed. Laurie Weinstein and Christie White (Westport, CT: Bergin and Garvey, 1997).
91. "G.I. Joe Can't Make Ends Meet," *Newsweek,* March 31, 1980, 31.
92. Senate Committee, *Status of the All-Volunteer Armed Force,* 73.
93. "Beard Study," 220.
94. "Anonymous," letter to the editor, *Army Times,* June 4, 1977, 14.
95. Ibid.
96. Mrs. Joy Lee Lehman, letter to the editor, *Army Times,* January 17, 1977, 14.
97. Senate Committee, *Status of the All-Volunteer Armed Force,* 5.
98. Ibid., 65.
99. OASD (MRAL), *America's Volunteers,* 240.
100. Senate Committee, *Status of the All-Volunteer Armed Force,* 65.
101. Ibid., 40.
102. Segal, "Military Organization," 7.
103. "Beard Study," 231.
104. Colonel Robert L. Phillips, USAREC, June 80–82, "Historical Development of the Army College Fund," series II, box 10, folder 3, Official Papers Reports, AVAC, MHI, 3.
105. Rostker, *I Want You!,* 510.

106. Segal, "Women's Roles," 7.
107. Phillips, "Historical Development," 3.
108. Stephen Herbits to Anderson, April 13, 1981, folder Military Manpower: All Volunteer Force (1 of 3), CFOA 87, MAF, RRPL, 3.
109. Doug Bandow to Anderson, memo, March 25, 1981, folder Military Manpower Task Force (2 of 17), CFOA 86–87, MAF, RRPL, 1.
110. Milton Friedman to Ronald Reagan, June 2, 1981, folder Military Manpower Task Force (7 of 17), CFOA 87, MAF, RRPL, 1.
111. William Hawkins, "The Draft and the Confusion of American Conservatives," *National Review*, August 7, 1981, in folder Military Manpower Task Force (11 of 17), CFOA 87, MAF, RRPL, 891.
112. See introduction in CMH, *DAHSUM: FY 1981* (Washington, DC: GPO, 1988).

4. Supporting the Military in Reagan's America

1. In the 1980s, President Reagan, his Department of Defense, and the service chiefs institutionalized this story of the fall of the military and then its subsequent rise under Reagan. Army leadership made the Reagan administration's message its own, with standard histories of the military fully incorporating this narrative of threat, disrespect, and decline in the 1970s followed by redemption in the 1980s. Edward C. Meyer, "'A Time of Transition—a Focus on Quality,' Article in *Army Magazine*, 1982–83 Green Book Issue," in *E. C. Meyer, General, United States Army Chief of Staff, June 1979–June 1983* (Washington, DC: Department of the Army, 1983), 317–322. See also introduction in CMH, *DAHSUM: FY 1981* (Washington, DC: GPO, 1988).
2. Ronald Reagan, "Address at Commencement Exercises at the United States Military Academy, May 27, 1981," in *I Want You! The Evolution of the All-Volunteer Force*, ed. Bernard Rostker (Santa Monica, CA: RAND Corporation, 2006), CD, G1166.PDF, 1–2.
3. Ibid.
4. Ibid.
5. As Assistant Secretary of Defense Lawrence Korb explained to Congress, "the old GI Bill was enacted in response to the draft and used as a readjustment benefit for the military. A new educational program will be enacted in response to the All-Volunteer Force and used by the services in the best way possible, as a tool to help their recruiting and retention needs." U.S. House Committee on Armed Services, *New Educational Assistance Program for the Military to Assist Recruiting, Hearing before*

the Subcommittee on Military Personnel and Compensation, 97th Cong., 1st sess., September 10, 1981, 51.

6. One of the most concise accounts of curbs and cuts to social programs is Joel Rogers and Thomas Ferguson, *Right Turn: The Decline of the Democrats and the Future of American Politics* (New York: Farrar, Straus, and Giroux, 1986), 124–129.
7. Reagan, "Address at Commencement," 1–2.
8. Ibid., 4.
9. Suzanne Mettler, *Soldiers to Citizens: The G.I. Bill and the Making of the Greatest Generation* (New York: Oxford University Press, 2005); Margot Canaday, "Building a Straight State: Sexuality and Social Citizenship under the 1944 GI Bill," *Journal of American History* 90, no. 3 (2003): 935–957; Glenn C. Altschuler and Stuart M. Blumin, *The GI Bill: The New Deal for Veterans* (New York: Oxford University Press, 2009).
10. On the Vietnam-era GI Bill and its inadequacies, see Mark Boulton, *Failing Our Veterans: The GI Bill and the Vietnam Generation* (New York: New York University Press, 2014). Boulton demonstrates how the Vietnam-era GI Bill did not match the World War II–era bill.
11. "GI Bill's Uncertain Future," *New York Times,* July 21, 1974, 163; "Trims in GI Bill Obtained by Ford," *New York Times,* August 24, 1974, 9.
12. Robert Taber (Principal Deputy) to Assistant Secretaries of the Military Departments, memo, October 3, 1973, series II, box 7, folder 6, AVAC, MHI.
13. Carl S. Wallace to Principal Deputy, memo, October 19, 1973, series II, box 7, folder 6, AVAC, MHI, 1–2.
14. Interview of Howard H. Calloway, Former Secretary of the Army, by Major Robert Griffith, September 23, 1983, Denver, CO, series II, box 14, folder 9, Oral Histories, AVAC, MHI.
15. Robert K. Griffith with Four Recruiters from Transition Period, Transcript of Proceedings, Ft. Sheridan, IL, October 20, 1983, series II, box 15, folder 8, Oral Histories, AVAC, MHI, 64; Rostker, *I Want You!,* 322.
16. Interview of Howard H. Calloway, 13.
17. Robert K. Griffith with Four Recruiters, 64.
18. Ibid.; Rostker, *I Want You!,* 322.
19. Rostker, *I Want You!,* 323.
20. Morris Janowitz and Charles C. Moskos Jr., "Racial Composition in the All-Volunteer Force," *Armed Forces and Society* 1, no.1 (November 1974), 122, in Rostker, *I Want You!,* CD, S0565.PDF, 321–323.
21. U.S. Senate, Committee on Armed Services, *Status of the All-Volunteer Armed Force: Hearing before the Subcommittee on Manpower and Personnel,* 95th Cong., 2nd sess., June 20, 1978, 43; Charles Moskos,

"The All-Volunteer Force," *Wilson Quarterly* 3, no. 2 (Spring 1979): 133–135, 140.

22. Mady Wechsler Segal, "Women's Roles in the U.S. Armed Forces: An Evaluation of Evidence and Arguments for Policy Decisions," in *Conscripts and Volunteers: Military Requirements, Social Justice, and the All-Volunteer Force,* ed. Robert Fullinwider (Totowa, NJ: Rowman and Allanheld, 1983), 7.
23. Moskos, "All-Volunteer Force," 133–135, 140.
24. Rostker, *I Want You!*, 390. Thurman had spent his previous ten years of service in resources and program management at the Training and Doctrine Command and in the Office of the Chief of Staff of the Army. He became so expert in army personnel transformation through his years at the Recruiting Command that he went on afterward to assume the role of deputy chief of staff for personnel and then that of vice chief of staff of the army, the position most accountable for the day-to-day running of the service. Oral history of General Maxwell Thurman (USA, Ret.) interviewed by Colonel Richard Mackey, Senior Officer Oral History Program, MHI, 1992.
25. Rostker, *I Want You!*, 387, n. 42.
26. Ibid., 510.
27. Ibid., 501, n.18.
28. Ibid., 511.
29. Colonel Charles W. Dyke (Military Assistant to the Secretary of the Army) to Chief of Legislative Liaison Director of the Army Budget, memo, OCA, February 11, 1974, box 7, folder 14, AVAC, MHI, 16.
30. Wallace, memo, October 19, 1973, 1–2. Sar Levitan and Karen Cleary Aldeman, *Warriors at Work: The Volunteer Armed Force* (Beverly Hills, CA: Sage, 1977), 111.
31. Colonel Robert L. Phillips, USAREC, June 80–82, "Historical Development of the Army College Fund," series II, box 10, folder 3, Official Papers Reports, AVAC, MHI, 4–5.
32. Ibid.
33. Adam Yarmolinsky and Gregory D. Foster, *Paradoxes of Power: The Military Establishment in the Eighties* (Bloomington, IN: Indiana University Press, 1983), 81; Segal, "Women's Roles," 10.
34. U.S. House, Committee on the Budget, *Statement of Robert F. Hale and Joel N. Slackman before the National Security and Veterans Task Force,* March 12, 1981, 14, www.cbo.gov/sites/default/ . . . /81doc13 .pdf.
35. Congressman Bill Armstrong (R-CO), Editorial, "Sound Military Requires More Pay and a GI Bill," *Washington Star,* April 14, 1981.

36. Edward C. Meyer and John March, *The Posture of the Army and Department of the Army Budget Estimates for FY 1983*, Posture Statement presented to the 98th Cong., 1st sess., February 15, 1983, 10–11.
37. Gillespie V. Montgomery, *Sonny Montgomery: The Veteran's Champion* (Jackson, MS: University Press of Mississippi, 2003), 22–33. His tank unit was in Meridian when the Freedom Riders came through Mississippi in 1965; see p. 38.
38. "Moskos also recalls that 'Jack Marsh called me into his office sometime in the early 1980s and said he liked my AVF GI Bill proposal. But he could not publicly oppose the OSD party line. He said I should see his good friend Sonny Montgomery and say go ahead. I met with Montgomery and the rest is history. When the Montgomery Bill passed the Congress, Sonny called me up personally at home to relay the news.'" Rostker, *I Want You!*, 512, n.21.
39. Reagan Bush Committee, "A Strategy of Peace for the 80s," news release, television address as delivered by Governor Ronald Reagan, October 19, 1980, 13; and "we must restore the GI Bill" in Ronald Reagan, "STRENGTH: Restoring the Margin of Safety," address delivered at American Legion National Convention, Boston, MA, August 20, 1980; both the above items are in folder Military Manpower: All Volunteer Force (1 of 3), CFOA 87, MAF, RRPL. Reagan's Military Manpower Task Force also lent support to the GI Bill, reporting in 1982 that the "way in which you can improve the quality would be to attract those who are heading off to postsecondary education of some sort." U.S. Senate, Committee on Armed Services, *Pay Increases for Military Personnel, Hearing before the Subcommittee on Manpower and Personnel*, 97th Cong., 1st sess., May 7, 1981, 74.
40. Stephen Herbits to Anderson, April 13, 1981, attachment, folder Military Manpower: All Volunteer Force (1 of 3), CFOA 87, MAF, RRPL, 3.
41. Roger Nils Folsom, "Can Conscription Work?," Cato Institute Policy Analysis, May 15, 1981, folder Military Manpower Task Force (5 of 17), CFOA 87, MAF, RRPL, 3–4.
42. Korb in House Committee, *New Educational Assistance Program*, 52.
43. House Committee, *New Educational Assistance Program*, 5.
44. Folsom, "Can Conscription Work?," 3–4.
45. Doug Bandow to Anderson, memo, March 25, 1981, folder Military Manpower Task Force (2 of 17), CFOA 86–87, MAF, RRPL, 1.
46. Taber, memo, October 3, 1973, AVAC, MHI.
47. Robert Hale, CBO, quoted in Rostker, *I Want You!*, 515.
48. House Committee, *New Educational Assistance Program*, 58, 51. A summary report in the Reagan administration explained: "the loss of GI

Bill benefits caused a decline in enlistment supply, but the net gain of the supply of the GI Bill was reduced in half by the decline in retention due to service people getting out of the service to use the Bill. (Cost per enlistee $200,000). Enlistment bonuses are a less expensive means of increasing enlistment. (Cost per enlistee $19,800)." It made the following recommendations: "tie military pay of enlistees to youth civilian earnings on a year-to-year basis. Adjust recruiting budgets to the unemployment rate and the level of CETA programs. Give small increases in recruiters and bonuses above currently programs levels for the Army and the Marine Corps. Taking these steps should ensure that the services meet their recruiting goals in the 1980s." Doug Bandow to Anderson, memo, "Summary of CNA Briefing," November 5, 1981, folder Military Manpower: All Volunteer Force (3 of 3), CFOA 87, MAF, RRPL, 1.

49. Interview of Howard H. Calloway, 21.
50. Ibid., 18–19.
51. Doug Bandow to Anderson, memo, March 25, 1981, MAF, RRPL, 1.
52. Meyer and March, *Posture of the Army,* 10–11.
53. Interview of Howard H. Calloway, 18–19.
54. "The Posture of the Army and Department of the Army Budget Estimates for Fiscal Year 1983" (February 15, 1983), Joint Statement by General E. C. Meyer, Chief of Staff and John March, Secretary, Department of Army before the Committee on Armed Services, US House of Representatives, 98th Congress, 1st sess., 7.
55. Assistant Secretary of Defense for Force Management Policy, *A Report to the Congress on the Montgomery GI Bill Education Benefits Program* (Washington, DC: Office of the Secretary of Defense, 1988), in Rostker, *I Want You!,* CD, G0761.PDF, 2.
56. Ibid., CD, G0761.PDF, 2, 14.
57. NW Ayer, US-NPS—P20020, *TV Guide,* June 12, 1982, courtesy Beth Bailey.
58. NW Ayer, US NPS P10181, *Scholastic,* 1982; NW Ayer, US NPSPP001016, *Time,* September 1980. Both courtesy Beth Bailey.
59. Meyer and March, *Posture of the Army,* 15–16.
60. Ibid., 10.
61. Ibid., 11.
62. Ibid.
63. CMH, *DAHSUM: FY 1982* (Washington, DC: GPO, 1988), 5.
64. Yarmolinsky and Foster, *Paradoxes of Power,* 72.
65. Senate Committee, *Pay Increases for Military Personnel,* 18.
66. David Stockman, *The Triumph of Politics: Why the Reagan Revolution Failed* (New York: Harper and Row, 1986), 300.

67. Rostker, *I Want You!*, 503.
68. DoD, Caspar W. Weinberger, Secretary of Defense, *Annual Report to Congress, FY 1988* (Washington, DC: GPO, 1987), appendix C, 331, 121.
69. John McCloughry to Lawrence Korb, July 27, 1981, folder Military Manpower Task Force (9 of 17), CFOA 87, MAF, RRPL, 1; Doug Bandow to Anderson, memo, "Subject: Campaign Statements on the G.I. Bill," March 13, 1981, folder Military Manpower: All Volunteer Force (1 of 3), CFOA 87, MAF, RRPL, 1.
70. See folders Military Manpower: All Volunteer Force (1 of 3), CFOA 87, and Military Manpower Task Force (3 of 17), CFOA 86–86, in MAF, RRPL. Quote from Don Moran's memo to David Stockman, Ed Harper, and Glen Schleede, March 6, 1981; see also Ed Harper to Anderson, memo, March 9, 1981, both in folder Military Manpower Task Force (2 of 17), CFOA 86–87, MAF, RRPL.
71. House Committee, *New Educational Assistance Program*, 59.
72. Moskos, "All-Volunteer Force," 133–135, 140.
73. Michael D. Parsons, "Federal Higher Education Policy," in *Higher Education in the United States: An Encyclopedia*, vol. 1, ed., James J. F. Forest and Kevin Kinser (Santa Barbara, CA: ABC-CLIO, 2002), 239–244.
74. Robert M. L. Baker Jr., to Ronald Reagan, November 4, 1982, 049,000–051,999, FA003, WHORM: Federal Aid—Education, RRPL, 1. Baker was president of West Coast University, and the only university president author I found in the files to support the president's proposal to cut student aid. He had met Reagan sixteen years earlier when Reagan, then governor, presented him an award in Los Angeles.
75. Edward Elmendorf, Deputy Assistant Secretary of Education for Student Financial Assistance, to Craig Fuller, memo, January 12, 1982, 044,000–044,199, FA003, WHORM: Federal Aid—Education, RRPL.
76. Edwin Harper to Robin Raborn, White House memo, Subject: Horror Stories on Student Loans and Other Financial Aid Programs, March 26, 1982, 063,000–067,999, FA003, WHORM: Federal Aid—Education, RRPL.
77. Ibid.
78. Marcella Zajac to Ronald Reagan, ca. August 1982, 034,000–039,999, FA003, WHORM: Federal Aid—Education, RRPL, 1.
79. White House Office of Policy Information, Issue Update, Higher Education—Student Assistance, May 28, 1982, 071,000–072,479, FA003, WHORM: Federal Aid—Education, RRPL.
80. Irving Spitzberg Jr., General Secretary, AAUP, to Ronald Reagan, February 22, 1982, 062,200–062,999, FA003, WHORM: Federal Aid—Education, RRPL, 1–2.

81. House Committee, *Statement of Hale and Slackman,* 14.
82. Folsom, "Can Conscription Work?," 3–4.
83. Doug Bandow to Anderson, memo, "summary of CNA Briefing," November 5, 1981, MAF, RRPL. The one federal program that they judged to impact enlistment was the CETA program, a federal job training program for the unemployed created by Richard Nixon in late 1973.
84. Reagan, "Address at Commencement," in Rostker, *I Want You!,* CD, G1166.PDF, 4.
85. John McClaughry to Martin Anderson, memo, April 24, 1981, in Rostker, *I Want You!,* CD, R0001.PDF, 2. Reagan's Military Manpower Task Force simultaneously proposed that "innovative approaches that allow student aid programs to be used to help solve military manpower problems should be explored" (I-7). In other words, students applying for Pell Grants or other federal loans should have their loan linked to military service. "Current Military Manpower Issues," April 23, 1981, Folder Military Manpower Task Force (3 of 17), CFOA 86–87, MAF, RRPL, 1–2.
86. "Hearings before the House Armed Services Committee, Subcommittee on Personnel on the New Education Assistance Program, May 7, 1980," in Meyer, *E. C. Meyer,* 92.
87. House Committee, *New Educational Assistance Program,* 61.
88. Edward Bethune, *Report on Student Aid Programs,* June 1982, 086,665 (1), FA003, WHORM: Federal Aid—Education, RRPL, 30.
89. House Committee, *New Educational Assistance Program,* 66.
90. The Military Selective Service Act was signed in September 1982. Women were not required to register for selective service.
91. Alan Gelber, Office of the Tufts Community Union Senate, to Ronald Reagan, ca. March 19, 1983, 130,000–139,999, FA003, WHORM: Federal Aid—Education, RRPL, 1.
92. Ronald Reagan to Theodore Mataxis, November 30, 1982, 111,000–113,999, FA003, WHORM: Federal Aid—Education, RRPL.
93. Brigadier General Theodore Mataxis (USA, Ret.) to Ronald Reagan, October 7, 1982, enclosed "Resolution," Philadelphia Chapter of the Military Order of the World Wars, 111,000–113,999, FA003, WHORM: Federal Aid—Education, RRPL.
94. Gerald Jaynes and Robin Williams, eds., *A Common Destiny* (Washington, DC: National Academy Press, 1989), 343; Martin Carnoy, "Why Aren't More African Americans Going to College?," *Journal of Blacks in Higher Education* 6 (Winter 1994/1995): 68.
95. See, for example, Ramon Cruz et al. to Ronald Reagan, March 12, 1981, 019000–022499, FA003, WHORM: Federal Aid—Education, RRPL.

96. See Joe Biden Jr., et al. to Ronald Reagan, February 17, 1982, 062200–062999, FA003, WHORM: Federal Aid—Education, RRPL.
97. Darlene Gee and Abraham Nelson, *Profiles of Montgomery G.I. Bill and Army College Fund Soldiers* (Alexandria, VA: U.S. Army Research Institute, 1995), 5–13.
98. See note 55 above.
99. CMH, *DAHSUM: FY 1981,* 1.
100. Meyer and March, *Posture of the Army,* 9.
101. Ibid., 15.
102. Meyer, "A Time of Transition," 322.
103. CMH, *DAHSUM: FY 1982,* 5
104. Yarmolinsky and Foster, *Paradoxes of Power,* 72.
105. CMH, *DAHSUM: FY 1981,* 1.
106. Caspar Weinberger, letter to the editor, *Washington Post,* July 19, 1983, in Rostker, *I Want You!,* CD, G909.PDF.
107. Rostker, *I Want You!,* 509.
108. Question: Would you please tell me how much confidence you, yourself have in the military: a great deal, quite a lot, some, or very little? Results: great deal and quite a lot 63%; Method: In Person, Sample Size: 1539. Gallup Organization. Gallup Poll # 1266G, Jul, 1986 [dataset]. USAIPO1986-1266G, Version 2. Gallup Organization [producer]. Storrs, CT:Roper Center for Public Opinion Research, Roper*Express* [distributor], accessed Mar-13-2015.
109. Gillespie "Sonny" Montgomery to Frank Carlucci, February 20, 1988 in Rostker, *I Want You!.* GO726.PDF, 1–2.
110. Frank Carlucci to Sonny Montgomery, n.d., in Rostker, *I Want You!,* CD, G0726.PDF, 1.

5. Army Wives Demand Support

1. "Want Your Soldier to Re-Enlist?," advertisement, *Army Times,* September 19, 1975, 17.
2. Barbara Marriot, "The Social Networks of Naval Officers' Wives: Their Composition and Function," in *Wives and Warriors: Women in the Military in the United States and Canada,* ed. Laurie Weinstein and Christie White (Westport, CT: Bergin and Garvey, 1997), 27–28; Sar Levitan and Karen Cleary Aldeman, *Warriors at Work: The Volunteer Armed Force* (Beverly Hills: Sage, 1977) 16, 56. As more female soldiers joined the military, the number of male spouses did grow somewhat, but their numbers were tempered by the facts that female soldiers had a lower likelihood of marrying and that female soldiers were much more

likely to marry fellow soldiers, and thus not to have a civilian spouse. David Segal and Mady Wechsler Segal, "America's Military Population," *Population Bulletin* 59, no. 4 (December 2004): 30; and Mady Wechsler Segal and Jesse J. Harris, *What We Know about Army Families* (Alexandria, VA: U.S. Army Research Institute for the Behavioral and Social Sciences, 1993), 8–11.

3. Other military spouses organized around more discrete issues including prisoners of war and the rights of divorced military spouses, for example. The first families to challenge the military's treatment of families in a formal way were the wives of prisoners of war and soldiers missing in action in Vietnam. In 1966, Sybil Stockdale created the National League of Families of American Prisoners and Missing in Southeast Asia, usually called by its shorter name, the National League of Families. Hamilton McCubbin, Barbara B. Dahl, and Edna J. Hunter, "Research on the Military Family: A Review," in *Families in the Military System*, ed. Hamilton McCubbin, Barbara B. Dahl, and Edna J. Hunter (Beverly Hills, CA: Sage, 1976), 317. Others followed the league's lead, translating families' increased influence in the Pentagon to the legislative arena. The Military Wives Association was formed in 1969 to represent the needs of Vietnam War widows. The army wives of the late 1970s and early 1980s moved well beyond the small numbers of wives of POWs/MIAs and Vietnam veterans' wives to comprise the spouses of many new members of the All-Volunteer Force and their spouses, elite officers' wives, and eventually the wives of enlisted personnel.
4. Allyson Sherman Grossman, "The Employment Situation for Military Wives," *Monthly Labor Review* 104, no. 2 (February 1981): 60.
5. On the numbers of dual service couples in the 1980s see U.S. House, Committee on Armed Services, *Military Child Care: Hearing before Subcommittee on Military Personnel and Compensation*, 101st Cong., 1st sess., April 13, 1989, 58.
6. Edna J. Hunter, *Families under the Flag* (New York: Praeger, 1982), 8.
7. Elizabeth M. Finlayson, "A Study of the Wife of the Army Officer: Her Academic and Career Preparations, Her Current Employment and Volunteer Services," in McCubbin et al., *Families in the Military System*, 25.
8. Ibid., 26.
9. Joanne H. Patton (Mrs. George S. Patton), "Professionalization of the ACS Volunteer," speech for the American Association of Social Workers, MFC, CMH, 3–4.
10. For the essential role of women in armies see John Lynn, *Women, Armies and Warfare in Early Modern Europe* (New York: Cambridge University Press, 2008).

11. Mary Ellen Condon-Rail, "From Neglect to Concern, 1776–1973," unpublished paper for the Center of Military History, n.d., MFC, CMH, 3.
12. Sondra Albano, "Military Recognition of Family Concerns: Revolutionary War to 1993," *Armed Forces and Society* 20, no. 2 (Winter 1994): 285.
13. Finlayson, "Study of the Wife," 21.
14. Betty Sowers Alt and Bonne Domrose Stone, *Campfollowing: A History of the Military Wife* (New York: Praeger, 1991), 19–20, 26–27, 31; Edward Coffman, *The Old Army: A Portrait of the American Army in Peacetime, 1784–1898* (New York: Oxford University Press, 1986), 118.
15. Albano, "Military Recognition," 286–288.
16. Ibid., 285.
17. See Judy Barrett Litoff and David C. Smith, eds., *Since You Went Away: World War II Letters from American Women on the Home Front* (Lawrence, KS: University Press of Kansas, 1991), 212.
18. Polly Crow to William Crow, June 12, 1944, in Litoff and Smith, *Since You Went Away*, 147.
19. Condon-Rail, "From Neglect to Concern," 23–25; Albano, "Military Recognition," 8–9.
20. Donna Alvah, *Unofficial Ambassadors: American Military Families Overseas and the Cold War, 1946–1965* (New York: New York University Press, 2007); Martha Gravois, "Military Families in Germany, 1946–1986: Why They Came and Why They Stay," *Parameters* 16, no. 4 (Winter 1986): 57–59.
21. Condon-Rail, "From Neglect to Concern," 33.
22. Ibid.
23. Alvah, *Unofficial Ambassadors*, 11.
24. Condon-Rail, "From Neglect to Concern," 38.
25. Elizabeth Wickenden, *The Military Program and Social Welfare* (New York: National Committee on Social Work in Defense Mobilization, 1955), 23–25.
26. Doris B. Durand, "The Role of the Senior Military Wife—Then and Now," in *The Military Family: A Practice Guide for Human Service Providers*, ed James Martin, Leora N. Rosen, and Linette R. Sparacino (Westport, CT: Praeger, 2000).
27. Finlayson, "Study of the Wife," 20.
28. Ibid., 22.
29. Nancy Shea, *The Army Wife* (New York: Harper and Brothers, 1941), 68, 75.
30. Quoted in Lynne R. Dobrofsky and Constance T. Batterson, "The Military Wife and Feminism," *Signs* 2, no.3 (Spring 1977): 675.
31. Quote from "The Officer's Guide, 1942," in Finlayson, "Study of the Wife," 22.
32. Shea quoted in Durand, "Role," 73.

33. Durand, "Role," 73.
34. Ibid.
35. Quoted in Finlayson, "Study of the Wife," 22.
36. Office of the Surgeon General, Department of the Army, "The Army Community Services: A New Program in Army Social Work," ca. 1965, folder The ACS, A New Program—Background to ADC, CFSC files, MFC, CMH, 3.
37. Patton, "Professionalization," 2.
38. Office of the Surgeon General, "Army Community Services," MFC, CMH, 1, 5; on the history of ACS proposals and importance of MWR also see S. G. Davis, "Welcoming Remarks: Beyond Ribbon Cutting," ca. 1967, folder Colonel S. G. Davis (USAR Ret.), OASD (MRA)—Welcoming Remarks, MFC, CMH, 15–16, 18.
39. Office of the Surgeon General, "Army Community Services," 2.
40. Davis, "Welcoming Remarks," 17.
41. *Army Regulation No. 608–1, Personal Affairs: Army Community Service Program* (Washington, DC: Headquarters, Department of the Army, 1965), MFC, CMH, 1–4.
42. "Army Community Service Volunteer Demographics," 1979, Misc. ACS and Military Family 1971–1985, MFC, CMH, 1; "Army Community Service," ca. 1980–1983, folder ACS—Successes and Preplans, CFSC Files, MFC, CMH, 4.
43. "Army Community Service," ca. 1980–1983, 3.
44. Ibid., 1.
45. Patton, "Professionalization," 1.
46. *Army Regulation No. 608–1,* 4–1, 4–2, 4–3.
47. Patton, "Professionalization," 2.
48. "Army Community Service," ca. 1980–1983, 1–2.
49. Davis, "Welcoming Remarks," 21.
50. Patton, "Professionalization," 3–4.
51. Ibid., 2.
52. "Bio: Joanne Holbrook Patton," National Military Family Association, www.militaryfamily.org/our-programs/military-spouse-scholarships/joanne-holbrook-patton.html.
53. Hunter, *Families under the Flag,* 11.
54. "A Tough Fight in West Germany," *Time,* December 26, 1977, 17.
55. "G.I. Dependents: Aid and Comfort," *Time,* April 14, 1980, 67.
56. "Also Concerned," letter to the editor, *Army Times,* November 22, 1976, 16; "Disgusted," letter to the editor, *Army Times,* November 22, 1976, 16.
57. "Nottingham Peasant," "Readers Respond," *Army Times,* October 16, 1976, 14. ("Nottingham Peasant" was a pseudonymous name referring to an article entitled "Greedy Sheriff.")

58. Hunter, *Families under the Flag*, 12.
59. "How to Make Ends Meet, Fact Sheet" (Fort Eustis, VA: USATCFE Public Affairs Office, August 1981), MFC, CMH, 1.
60. Ibid., 2.
61. Ibid, 1, 4.
62. "An Indebtedness Survey of Personnel Entering the United States Army" (Fort Leonard Wood, MO: ACS, ca. 1979–1980), MFC, CMH, 1–3, 5, 7.
63. Carolyn J. Becraft, "The Woman's Movement: Its Effects on the Wives of Military Officers" (MA thesis, University of Southern California, 1978).
64. Hunter, *Families under the Flag*, 18.
65. Dobrofsky and Batterson, "Military Wife," 676.
66. Ibid., 680.
67. Ibid., 678.
68. Hunter, *Families under the Flag*, 9.
69. Ibid., 18.
70. Dobrofsky and Batterson, "Military Wife," 683.
71. Ibid., 681.
72. Ibid., 683.
73. Patton, "Professionalization," 3–4.
74. Ibid.
75. Hunter, *Families under the Flag*, 10.
76. Ibid.
77. Becraft, "Woman's Movement," 11–13, 34–46.
78. Dobrofsky and Batterson, "Military Wife," 678.
79. Ibid.
80. Ibid., 680.
81. Ibid., 676. Rap groups were small, informal, democratic discussions groups.
82. Hunter, *Families under the Flag*, 9.
83. Lucy A. McLean, "Association for Military Kin Proposed," *Army Times*, October 18, 1976, 15.
84. Ron Buryk, Ed van Vranken, and Elwood Hamlin, eds., *The Army Family: Analysis and Appraisal, Proceedings of a Symposium, October 11–12, 1980* (Washington, DC: Association of the United States Army and the Army Officers' Wives Club of the Greater Washington Area, 1980), v.
85. Carolyn Becraft interview by the author, June 3, 2009, 1.
86. Joe Holley, "Obituary: Bettie Alexander Steiger, 74," *Washington Post*, August 13, 2008, www.washingtonpost.com/wp-dyn/content/article/2008/08/12/AR2008081203172.html.

87. Buryk et al., *Army Family*, iii. In 1976, several years before Becraft's arrival, several members of the group had hatched the plan for an international meeting of army spouses about the status of army wives and families. For three years, the proposal was "tabled" because the group lacked the funds and couldn't find sponsors to hold the conference.
88. Buryk et al., *Army Family;* Treasurer's Report, August 10, 1980, folder Army Family Symposium, 1980, Minutes, Planning, Misc., MFC, CMH, 2.
89. Becraft interview, 1.
90. Buryk et al., *Army Family*, iii.
91. Minutes, Steering Committee Meeting, September 29, 1980, folder Army Family Symposium, 1980, Minutes, Planning, Misc., MFC, CMH, 2.
92. Becraft interview, 2.
93. Buryk et al., *Army Family*, 10.
94. Ibid., vi.
95. Ibid., iv.
96. Ibid., 1–2.
97. Ibid., iii–iv.
98. Ibid.
99. Ibid., 3–18.
100. Ibid., 8.
101. Ibid., 10.
102. Finlayson, "Study of the Wife," 31, 33, 38.
103. Ibid., 33.
104. "Army Community Service," ca. 1980–1983, 1; Marie Baird to Joanne Patton, April 12, 1981, Misc. ACS and Military Family 1982–1990, MFC, CMH, 1.
105. Finlayson, "Study of the Wife," 29.
106. Ibid.
107. Ibid., 60.
108. Ibid., 61.
109. Finlayson, "Study of the Wife," 36.
110. Hunter, *Families under the Flag*, 18.
111. Ibid.
112. Grossman, "Employment Situation," 61–62.
113. Ibid., 63.
114. Finlayson, "Study of the Wife," 28.
115. Grossman, "Employment Situation," 62.
116. Finlayson, "Study of the Wife," 36; on the difficulty of women working on isolated posts see "Indebtedness Survey," 3.
117. Finlayson, "Study of the Wife," 25.

118. Ibid., 40, 30.
119. Hunter, *Families under the Flag*, 23–24.
120. Grossman, "Employment Situation," 60, 62.
121. Ibid., 63.
122. Hunter, *Families under the Flag*, 23.
123. Ibid., 18.
124. Finlayson, "Study of the Wife," 22–23, 38.
125. Hunter, *Families under the Flag*, 18.
126. Ibid., 4.
127. By 1980, the majority of army wives believed that personnel decisions regarding soldiers should be informed by the education and job needs of the spouse. See Hunter, *Families under the Flag*, 18; Dobrofsky and Batterson, "Military Wife," 682.
128. Ibid., 8, 11.
129. *The Army Family: The Next Step, Report of the Second Annual Army Family Symposium, October 10–11, 1981* (Washington, DC: FLO, 1981), 2. The second symposium in 1981 focused on creating a cadre of trained spouses whose role was to interface between the army families on local posts and the command structure both on post and at the level of the Department of the Army. As both delegates and army leaders realized, "bureaucratic programs sketched out here at the Department (of the Army) level (in Washington) are no good unless they are implemented vigorously at the local level and get support of the families and the service member they are designed to assist." General John W. Vessey Jr., VCSA, quoted in *Army Family: The Next Step*, vii. When the army took it over, it became the Army Family Action Plan. See U.S. Army, ODCSPER, *Army Family Action Plan* (Washington, DC: CSA, 1984).
130. *Army Family: The Next Step*, 21. As early as 1980 in fact, right after the first Army Family Symposium, local installations from Fort Carson in Colorado to Fort Bragg in North Carolina—ten installations in all—held "their own family symposia" to deal with family issues at a local level as well.
131. Albano, "Military Recognition," 292.
132. *Army Family: The Next Step*, 19.
133. Ibid., 16. The role of family liaison officer was not well defined at first. Observers at the second symposium raised questions about the lack of clear vision of the ODCSPER for the office, particularly its "structure, role, authorities, goals, and interrelationships/networks"; see p. 15.
134. Oral History, General John Wickham, 1991, box 4, Wickham papers, MHI, 39. Several scholars have noted the importance of Wickham's

white paper, including John Sloan Brown, *Kevlar Legions: The Transformation of the Army, 1989–2005* (Washington, DC: CMH, 2011), 341. However, they generally do not acknowledge the role of spouses in directing Wickham's attention to family support.

135. U.S. Army, ODCSPER, *The Army Family Action Plan III* (Washington, DC: CSA, 1986), 4.
136. Albano, "Military Recognition," 292.
137. ODCSPER, *The Army Family Action Plan III.*
138. Becraft interview, 4. See also "Carolyn Becraft: Association Trailblazer," National Military Family Association,www.militaryfamily.org/get-involved/volunteer/trailblazers/carolyn-becraft.html.
139. John A. Wickham Jr., CSA, *White Paper, The Army Family* (Washington, DC: Department of the Army, 1983), 16.
140. "Study: Army Wives Still Hostage to Volunteerism," *Army Times,* August 16, 1993, 16. See also "Pressure to Perform," letter to the editor, *Army Times,* November 16, 1992, 39.
141. Gail Zellman and Anne Johanson, *Examining the Implementation and Outcomes of the Military Child Care Act of 1989* (Santa Monica, CA: RAND Corporation, 1995), 16, 14, 42.
142. U.S. House, Committee on Armed Services, *Military Child Care: Hearing before Subcommittee on Military Personnel and Compensation,* 101st Cong., 1st sess., April 13, 1989, 5, 41, 58.

6. Securing Christian Family Values

1. John A. Wickham, "Address at the Army Community Services Workshop," Arlington, VA, August 17, 1984, in *Collected Works of the Thirtieth Chief of Staff, United States Army* (Washington, DC: Department of the Army, 1987), 64.
2. Department of the Army, "The Army Family—A Partnership/Die Heeresfamilie—Eine Partnerschaft" (Washington, DC: GPO, 1985).
3. Comptroller of the Army, *The Army Budget: FY 1985* (Washington, DC: Department of the Army, 1984), 90; Comptroller of the Army, *The Army Budget: FY 1986* (Washington, DC: Department of the Army, 1985), 94; Comptroller of the Army, *The Army Budget: FY 1988–89* (Washington, DC: Department of the Army, 1987), 73.
4. William Gardner Bell, "John Adams Wickham, Jr.," in *Commanding Generals and Chiefs of Staff, 1775–2005: Portraits and Biographical Sketches of the United States Army's Senior Officer* (Washington, DC: CMH, 2005), 156.

5. Wickham, "Soldier Values: General Address to All Soldiers," November 1985, in *Collected Works,* 150–151.
6. Wickham, "The Heart and Soul of a Great Army: General Address to All Soldiers," February 1986, in *Collected Works,* 153.
7. In 2002, the Presidential Prayer Team awarded Wickham with their "American Inspirations Award," praising him for a career that "stressed strong values and a biblical integrity" in the army. Presidential Prayer Team, "American Inspirations Award Recipient," June 2002, www.freerepublic.com/focus/f-news/701017/posts.
8. Anne Loveland, *American Evangelicals and the U.S. Military, 1942–1993* (Baton Rouge, LA: Louisiana State University Press, 1996), 267.
9. Ibid., 275. Wickham, "Interview with *Soldiers* Magazine," September 1983, in *Collected Works,* 338. For references to God see Wickham, *Collected Works.*
10. Wickham, "Address at the Annual Service in Honor of the Army, Washington Cathedral," Washington, DC, November 13, 1983, in *Collected Works,* 26.
11. Loveland, *American Evangelicals,* 291.
12. Ibid., 165–210. On Wickham as a recognized leader see reports by the *Los Angeles Times* and the *New York Times* mentioning him along with General John Vescey, chairman of the joint chiefs of staff, and Admiral James Watkinds, chief of naval operations, as an openly evangelical military leader in Loveland, *American Evangelicals,* 208.
13. Evangelical leaders like Billy Graham and Harold John Ockenga visited officers and troops in Vietnam. Declassified operational reports register visits and film showings. See 1st Cavalry Division (Airmobile), "Operational Report: Lessons Learned, November 66–January 67," Department of the Army, 12; 52nd Combat Aviation Battalion, "Operational Report: Lessons Learned, Headquarters, period ending October 31, 1967," Department of the Army, 11.
14. "Religion at West Point," *Christianity Today,* November 6, 1981, 77.
15. Ibid., 76.
16. On parachurches see Loveland, *American Evangelicals.* For percentages of officers who were Protestant see the results of an annual survey of soldiers in 1982 commissioned by the Soldier Support Center at the Pentagon: Don Hirst, "Survey Indicates Service Tends to Run in Family," *Army Times,* February 14, 1983.
17. Ole Holsti, "A Widening Gap between the U.S. Military and Civilian Society? Some Evidence, 1976–1996," *International Security* 23, no. 3 (Winter 1998/1999): 5–42.

18. Anne C. Loveland, *Change and Conflict in the U.S. Army Chaplain Corps since 1945* (Knoxville, TN: University of Tennessee Press, 2014), 175.
19. Beth Spring, "Are Military Chaplains Illegal?" *Christianity Today,* February 18, 1983, 25, 27.
20. Jacqueline Witt, *Bringing God to Men: Military Chaplains and the Vietnam War* (Chapel Hill, NC: University of North Carolina Press, 2014).
21. Andrew Preston, "Tempted by the Fires of War: Vietnam and the Transformation of Evangelical Worldview," in *American Evangelicals in the 1960s,* ed. Alex R. Schafer (Madison, WI: University of Wisconsin Press, 2013), 198.
22. Randy Frame, "Is Pat Robertson Raising Money for Anti-Sandinista Guerillas?" *Christianity Today,* November 8, 1985, 50.
23. Sharon Anderson, "Christians Take Sides on Proposed Defense System," *Christianity Today,* April 4, 1986, 43.
24. Clifford Goldstein, "Who's Afraid of a Judeo-Christian America?" *Ministry Magazine,* July 1986, 2. Faith America Foundation was founded by John Conlan, an evangelical Christian right Republican from Arizona.
25. Preston, "Tempted by the Fires," 198.
26. Terry Muck, "Return of the Big Stick," *Christianity Today,* September 4, 1987, 18; "Where Our Trust Lies," *Christianity Today,* February 17, 1989, 40.
27. Wickham, "The Army Family: Statement before the House Select Committee on Children, Youth, and Families," Washington, DC, November 10, 1983, in *Collected Works,* 25.
28. CMH, *DAHSUM: FY 1984* (Washington, DC: GPO, 1995), 196.
29. Jim Tice, "Family Center OK'd, Club Changes Eyed," *Army Times,* October 29, 1984, 30.
30. CMH, *DAHSUM: FY 1984,* 196; Jim Tice, "Army May Replace Clubs with Hotel Chains," *Army Times,* November 5, 1984, 3.
31. Wickham "Interview with 'The Army,'" in *Collected Works,* 356.
32. Tice, "Family Center OK'd," 29–30.
33. Tice, "Army May Replace Clubs," 3.
34. Wickham, "Opening Statement before the House Committee on Armed Services," Washington, DC, February 7, 1986, in *Collected Works,* 156. Some of the drinking, however, simply moved off base, which exacerbated the problem of drinking and driving.
35. David Bates, "Pornography and the United States Army: Ethical Considerations and Policy Implications" (MA thesis, U.S. Army USASD Fort Benjamin Harrison, IN, with Duke Divinity School, 1991).

36. John A. Wickham Jr., CSA, *White Paper, The Army Family* (Washington, DC: Department of the Army, 1983), 1.
37. U.S. Army, ODCSPER, *Army Family Action Plan* (Washington, DC: CSA, 1984).
38. Wickham, "Address to the Army Officers Wives of Greater Washington Luncheon," Washington, DC, April 18, 1985, in *Collected Works*, 94.
39. Comptroller of the Army, *The Army Budget: FY 1985*, 90; Comptroller of the Army, *The Army Budget: FY 1986*, 94.
40. The largest outlay, for example, was for housing for soldiers and their families. On survey after survey, soldiers and spouses named housing as the single most important army benefit. Spouse surveys were mandated by Congress and the Pentagon beginning in 1985. See Zahava D. Doering and Bette S. Mahoney, *Briefing Notes: A Discussion of Military Dependents' Issues* (Arlington, VA: Defense Manpower Data Center, 1986), MFC, CMH, 3, 23–24. After the austerity of the late 1970s, however, the army had spent precious little on housing. By 1980, the army's budget for new construction of housing was totally eliminated. CMH, *DAHSUM: FY 1980* (Washington, DC: GPO, 1983). Wickham's new Army Family Budget therefore allotted funds for building new housing. After housing, child care programs consumed the largest portion of the budget, as the army spent approximately $121 million between 1985 and 1989. Wickham sunk over $100 million into building new child care programs and providing additional training in early education and facilities management for spouse volunteers. Each year from 1984 through 1989 the army added between one and two dozen new child care programs to posts around the world. Most of these were new construction, though some were renovations of existing army facilities. Comptroller of the Army, *The Army Budget: FY 1988–89*, 73. Many installations also extended hours of care and created new child care services such as drop-in care in addition to full-time, weekly care. U.S. Army, ODCSPER, *The Army Family Action Plan III* (Washington, DC: CSA, 1986), 35. In order to increase the number of child care slots quickly, the army also began encouraging and certifying other forms of child care such as in-home "family child care" both on and off post, spending $13.8 million on these in 1986 and 1987.
41. List from Doering and Mahoney, *Briefing Notes*, 29. The sums allocated varied among the many counseling and support programs. In 1985, $200,000 went to the Chaplain's Family Life Centers, $9.3 million to the army's "Exceptional Family Member Program," helping children with mental and physical special needs, and $13.9 million to "dependent youth activities" which were essentially recreational and afterschool and

weekend programs for army children. Comptroller of the Army, *The Army Budget: FY 1985,* 90. Starting in 1985, the army also funded research on army families, and added that to its Army Family Programs. Comptroller of the Army, *The Army Budget: FY 1986,* 94. Beginning in 1986, the army added funding to family alcohol and drug abuse rehabilitation, a child development service curriculum for army spouses who wished to open child care centers, for a "volunteer coordinator" to help direct family voluntarism, and an outreach program for junior enlisted families to make them aware of all the programs the army now offered. By 1987, the army was also programming funding of $8.8 million for spouse employment assistance and $10.6 million for family budget planning. Comptroller of the Army, *The Army Budget: FY 1988–89,* 73. The budgets rose steadily, from $1.3 billion in 1984 to $1.8 billion in 1986 and $2.2 billion in 1989. Wickham, "Leadership is Key in Coping with Wide Threat Spectrum, Annual Army Green Book Report of the Chief of Staff, 1985–86," October 1985, in *Collected Works,* 126; and Wickham, "Opening Statement before the Senate Armed Services Committee," Washington, DC, February 5, 1987, in *Collected Works,* 212.

42. James Dobson to John Wickham, memo, Focus on Family, Armed Forces Mail Analysis, ca. 1986, folder Task Force on Soldiers and Families, box 51, JWP, MHI, 2.
43. Loveland, *American Evangelicals,* 274–286.
44. Ibid., 291.
45. Dobson to Wickham, memo, ca. 1986, 1.
46. Ibid., 2.
47. David Edens to John Wickham, May 16, 1986, folder Task Force on Soldiers and Families, box 51, JWP, MHI.
48. Minutes of the Chief of Staff's Advisory Task Force on Soldiers and Families, July 18, 1984, folder Task Force on Soldiers and Families, box 51, JWP, MHI, 1.
49. Minutes of the Chief of Staff's Advisory Task Force on Soldiers and Families, May 12, 1986, folder Task Force on Soldiers and Families, box 51, JWP, MHI, 8.
50. Loveland, *American Evangelicals,* 274–286.
51. James Dobson to Ronald A. Mlinarchik, February 19, 1986, folder Task Force on Soldiers and Families, box 51, JWP, MHI.
52. Ibid. This video was in wide use even before Wickham became CSA. See reference in Wickham, "Interview with *Soldiers,*" in *Collected Works,* 341.
53. Loveland, *American Evangelicals,* 287.
54. Ibid., 287–288.

55. Comptroller of the Army, *The Army Budget: FY 1985*, 90. The overall Chaplain's Activities budget rested between $15 million and $19 million in these years, with a small portion, $0.2 million, reserved specifically for coordinating the chaplaincy's growing Family Life Centers.
56. Department of the Army, Chief of Chaplains, "OC of CH Policy or Precedent," November 9, 1990, folder MACOM Staff Chaplain, Family Life Ministry/Family Life Unit Ministry Team, Chief of Chaplains Policy, November 9, 1990, MFC, CMH, cover sheet, 2; Kristin Henderson, *While They're at War: The True Story of American Families on the Homefront* (New York: Houghton Mifflin, 2006), 30.
57. Chief of Chaplains, "OC of CH Policy or Precedent," 8, 11.
58. Thomas R. Smith, Deputy Director, U.S. Army Chaplaincy, memorandum for distribution, November 23, 1991, folder Chaplain, Memo for Chaplain Smith from Chaplain Tatum, Sub: Proposal for Army Family Ministry, December 3, 91, MFC, CMH, 11; see also Henderson, *While They're at War*, 83.
59. Esther Smith, "All American Wives: Women Helping One Another," *The Times Magazine*, February 14, 1983, 45.
60. "The Army Family Network," *News for Army Families*, Winter 1990 (this was the first issue of what became the *Army Families* newsletter), folder FLO, *Army Families* Publication 90–97, MFC, CMH.
61. "Chaplain Family Life Centers Provide Unexpected Benefits," *Army Families*, Spring 1993, folder FLO, *Army Families* Publication 90–97, MFC, CMH, 2.
62. Loveland, *American Evangelicals*, 165–210; "Religion at West Point," 76. Between 1987 and 2009, the numbers of conservative, fundamentalist, and evangelical Christians grew enormously and replaced other Christian sects and denominations, both Catholic and Protestant. Catholic chaplains dropped from 20 percent of the corps to 9 percent, and Protestants increased from 70 percent to 90 percent, with the increase more than covered by the conservative Christian accessions. Loveland, *Change and Conflict*, 175.
63. On the movement for lawsuits see Kim Philip Hansen, *Military Chaplains and Religious Diversity* (New York: Palgrave Macmillan, 2012), chapter 5. On the belief that fundamentalist evangelicals were not able to fully follow their beliefs in the army see the work of former army chaplain John D. Laing, *In Jesus' Name: Evangelicals and the U.S. Army* (Eugene, OR: Wipf and Stock, 2010).
64. Spring, "Are Military Chaplains Illegal?" 25.
65. Loveland, *American Evangelicals*, 287.
66. Harry M. Johnson, letter to the editor, *Army Times*, July 1, 1985, 24.

67. "The Military Wife Deserves a Cheer," *Army Families*, Fall 1991, folder FLO, *Army Families* Publication 90–97, MFC, CMH, 2.
68. Kathryn Beuby Cleary and Thomas J. Cleary, "What Makes a Good Marriage?" *The Times Magazine*, February 7, 1983, 45.
69. "Violence in Families," *The Times Magazine*, March 4, 1985, 4, 10.
70. James Martin and Peggy McClure, "Today's Active Duty Military Family," in *The Military Family: A Practical Guide for Human Service Providers*, ed. J. A. Martin, L. N. Rosen, and L. R. Sparacino (Westport, CT: Praeger, 2000), 9.
71. Mady Wechsler Segal and Jesse J. Harris, *What We Know about Army Families* (Alexandria, VA: U.S. Army Research Institute for the Behavioral and Social Sciences, 1993), 10–11.
72. As of 1993, 57 percent of custodial single parents in the army were women: see Segal and Harris, *What We Know*, 10. Proportionally more women were custodial single parents.
73. EXPOSE, "Military Benefits and the Divorced Military Wife," n.d., folder Misc. ACS and Military Family, 1971–1985, MFC, CMH.
74. See "EXPOSE," September 1981, folder Misc. ACS and Military Family, 1971–1985, MFC, CMH.
75. Christine Langtry, "You Earned That Retirement Check, Too," *Army Times Magazine*, March 3, 1980, 7.
76. *Army Times* covered the ex-spouse movement closely, as it generated interest among both male soldier and female spouse readers. Many male soldiers expressed skepticism in letters to the editors while female spouses expressed support. For letters see Mary Lechman (President EXPOSE chapter), letter to the editor, and Roger C. Laudati, letter to the editor, both in *Army Times*, January 9, 1984, 18; name withheld, "Marital Worth," and Helen Rupp, letter to the editor, both in *Army Times*, February 8, 1984, 20; Doris Mosely, letter to the editor, *Army Times*, August 27, 1984, 21; Alan Williamson, letter to the editor, *Army Times*, August 26, 1985, 20; Gerline Runyon, letter to the editor, *Army Times*, December 16, 1985, 25.
77. See "Nonsupport of Family Member Inquires," *Army Families*, Winter 1996/1997, folder FLO, *Army Families* Publication 90–97, MFC, CMH, 4.
78. Richard Halloran, "Army Acts to Help Families Cope with Pressures of Modern Military," *New York Times*, August 17, 1985, 8.
79. Robert McFadden, "Allegations of Child Abuse Studied at West Point Center," *New York Times*, September 24, 1984, B2; "Army Will Close Child Care Center," *New York Times*, November 16, 1987, A17.
80. Tom Burgess, "Reports of Family Violence, Abuse Increase," *Army Times*, April 8, 1985, 10. Some military psychologists insisted that even

though the reported numbers of spouse and child abuse were higher in the army than in civilian life, abuse among military personnel did not exceed that among civilians. "The rigidity of the system [of family advocacy within the armed forces] insists that it be reported," explained Dr. Richard Ridenour. Glen Collins, "Strengths Found in Military Families," *New York Times*, April 22, 1985, B10.

81. "Violence in Families," 4.
82. Ronald Reagan, "Remarks on Signing the National Family Week Proclamation," November 12, 1982, The American Presidency Project, www.presidency.ucsb.edu/ws/?pid=41986.
83. David and Vera Mace, *Sacred Fire: Christian Marriage through the Ages* (Nashville, TN: Abingdon Press, 1986).
84. Carol Siler, "Army Family Named as One of America's 9 Best," *Army Times*, July 16, 1984, 24.
85. Carol Siler, "Love Binds Army's Great American Family," *Army Times*, July 11, 1983, 50.
86. Siler, "Army Family Named," 24.
87. Andrew Bacevich, *The New American Militarism: How Americans Are Seduced by War* (New York: Oxford University Press, 2005), 141; Loveland, *American Evangelicals*, 298.
88. Wickham, "Address at the Army Community Services Workshop," in *Collected Works*, 64.
89. Bacevich, *New American Militarism*, 141. See also Thomas Ricks, *Making the Corps* (New York: Scribner, 1998); David King and Zachary Karabell, *The Generation of Trust: How the U.S. Military Has Regained the Public's Confidence since Vietnam* (Washington, DC: American Enterprise Institute Press, 2003), 61–69; Loveland, *American Evangelicals;* Ole R. Holsti, "Of Chasms and Convergences: Attitudes and Beliefs of Civilians and Military Elites at the Start of a New Millennium," in *Soldiers and Civilians: The Civil-Military Gap and American National Security*, ed. Peter D. Feaver and Richard R. Kohn (Cambridge, MA: MIT Press, 2001), 27.
90. Loveland, *American Evangelicals*, 289–290.
91. Gary Scott Smith, *Faith and the Presidency: From George Washington to George W. Bush* (New York: Oxford University Press, 2006), 318; D. Michael Lindsay, *Faith and the Halls of Power: How Evangelicals Joined the American Elite* (New York: Oxford University Press, 2007), 18.
92. On Bauer and the White House Working Group on the Family see Glen H. Utter and John Woodrow Storey, *The Religious Right: A Reference Handbook*, 2nd ed. (Santa Barbara, CA: ABC-Clio, 2007), 73; Susan Faludi, *Backlash: The Undeclared War against American Women*

(New York: Random House, 1991), 275. Working Group on the Family, *The Family: Preserving America's Future* (Washington, DC: GPO, 1986).

93. Utter and Storey, *Religious Right*, 73; Working Group on the Family, *Family*, 2.
94. Working Group on the Family, *Family*, 4–5.
95. On cuts to child care see Abbie Gordon Klein, *The Debate over Child Care, 1969–1990: A Socio-Historical Analysis* (Albany, NY: State University of New York Press, 1992), 40. After the hostility of the Reagan administration to child care programs, child care advocates set their sights on simply waiting out his term, as "a new administration might be more favorably disposed to such programs." Anne Marie Cammisa, *Governments as Interest Groups: Intergovernmental Lobbying and the Federal System* (Westport, CT: Praeger, 1995), 46.
96. Executive Order 12606—the Family, September 2, 1987, www.reagan.utexas.edu/archives/speeches/1987/090287b.htm.
97. Steve Rabey, "Ministries Could Cash in on Peace Dividend," *Christianity Today*, February 10, 1992, 61.

7. A Turn to Self-Reliance

1. CMH, *War in the Persian Gulf: Operations Desert Shield and Desert Storm, August 1990–March 1991* (Washington, DC: CMH, 2010), 2.
2. Ibid., 4, 17, 23–24.
3. George H. W. Bush, "Address before a Joint Session of Congress on the End of the Gulf War," March 6, 1991, Miller Center, http://millercenter.org/president/bush/speeches/speech-3430.
4. CMH, *War in the Persian Gulf*, 17; "Family Support, Desert Storm After Action Report, 29 May 1991," single folder, MHI, 1.
5. David Melcanon, "Keep Family Support Flexible, Group Told," *Stars and Stripes*, May 7, 1993, 3.
6. On the long history of reforming public assistance in the lead-up to the 1996 Personal Responsibility and Work Opportunity Act see Joanne Goodwin, *Gender and the Politics of Welfare Reform: Mothers' Pensions in Chicago, 1911–1929* (Chicago: University of Chicago, 1997); Linda Gordon, *Pitied but Not Entitled: Single Mothers and the History of Welfare, 1890–1935* (New York: Free Press, 1994); Jennifer Mittelstadt, *From Welfare to Workfare, The Unintended Consequences of Liberal Reform, 1945–1965* (Chapel Hill, NC: University of North Carolina, 2005); Gwendolyn Mink, *Welfare's End* (Ithaca, NY: Cornell University Press, 1998).

7. George H. W. Bush, "Address to the Nation on the Invasion of Iraq," January 16, 1991, Miller Center, http://millercenter.org/president/speeches/speech-3428.
8. "Family Assistance, Support Back Up Deploying Soldiers," *Army Families* (FLO), Fall 1990, MFC, CMH, 1–2.
9. "How Army Families Can Cope with Deployment," *Army Families* (FLO), Fall 1990, MFC, CMH, 3.
10. Ron Buryk, Ed van Vranken, and Elwood Hamlin, eds., *The Army Family: Analysis and Appraisal, Proceedings of a Symposium, October 11–12, 1980* (Washington, DC: Association of the U.S. Army and the Army Officers' Wives Club of the Greater Washington Area, 1980), 7. Likewise, the first Army Family Action Plan in 1984, the blueprint for army policy created by the worldwide, inclusive process of meetings to generate army policy priorities, asked for "an effective Overseas Orientation Program" and official army "training concerning Army lifestyle and community." U.S. Army, ODCSPER, *Army Family Action Plan* (Washington, DC: CSA, 1984), 5.
11. U.S. Army, ODCSPER, *The Army Family Action Plan III* (Washington, DC: CSA, 1986), 4.
12. Suzanne Wood, Jacquelyn Scarville, and Katharine S. Gravino, "Waiting Wives: Separation and Reunion among Army Wives," *Armed Forces and Society* 21, no. 2 (Winter 1995): 217–236.
13. *Family Support Group Model* (Carlisle Barracks, PA: U.S. Army War College, 1986), MFC, CMH, 4, and unnumbered pages.
14. ODCSPER, *Army Family Action Plan III*, 9; Wood et al., "Waiting Wives," 217–236.
15. ODCSPER, *Army Family Action Plan III*, 4.
16. Larry W. Bryant, "Taking Care of Army Families," *Army Families* (FLO), Summer 1991, MFC, CMH, 1–2.
17. Carl Vuono and Michael Stone, "Volunteer Played a Key Role in Desert Storm Victory," letter to the editor, *Army Families* (FLO), MFC, CMH, Summer 1991, 2.
18. "Family Support, Desert Storm After Action Report," 1.
19. Ibid., 1.
20. Melcanon, "Keep Family Support Flexible," 3.
21. "Family Support, Desert Storm After Action Report," 11.
22. Untitled cartoons, 1SG Edward Quay, in Frank Kinsman and Janice A. Osthus, "Soliders [*sic*] Point of View, Operations Desert Shield/Storm, Morale, Welfare and Recreation in a War Zone," Army Arts and Crafts Program, January 1992, no folder, MFC, CMH. Quay submitted at

least six entries, all concerning the relationship between spouses and the army.

23. Nicki Brody interview, box 1 Spouse Interviews, ODSSPCP, MHI, 25.
24. Kathleen Reischl interview, box 1 Spouse Interviews, ODSSPCP, MHI, 11.
25. Kristin Henderson, *While They're at War: The True Story of American Families on the Homefront* (New York: Houghton Mifflin, 2006), 33; Amelia Adkins interview, box 1 Spouse Interviews, ODSSPCP, MHI, 3.
26. Karen Houppert, *Home Fires Burning: Married to the Military—for Better or Worse* (New York: Ballantine Books, 2005), 154.
27. Kathleen Reischl interview, 10.
28. Ibid., 9.
29. Amelia Adkins interview, 15–16, Nicki Brody interview, 10, Kathleen Reischl interview, 18.
30. Nicki Brody. interview, 10.
31. Kathleen Reischl interview, 7.
32. Ibid., 18.
33. Official restrictions on socializing among spouses whose husbands were of different ranks did not exist. Yet the separation sometimes remained very real. See Henderson, *While They're at War,* 33–34.
34. U.S. Army War College Class of 1992, Spouses and Students, *Who Cares? We Do!: Experiences in Family Support* (Carlisle Barracks, PA: U.S. Army War College, 1992), viii, ix, 87, 88, 89.
35. Karen Jowers, "Services' Responsibility Considered," *Army Times,* September 27, 1993, 24.
36. Robert Reinhold, "Marines are First to Admit Wedlock in Corps Can Be Hell," *New York Times,* August 14, 1993, http://www.nytimes.com/1993/08/14/us/marines-are-first-to-admit-wedlock-in-corps-can-be-hell.html?pagewanted=all&src=pm, accessed 1/18/13.
37. "36 Pregnant Aboard Navy Ship That Served in Gulf," *New York Times,* April 29, 1991, A17.
38. Jon Nordheimer, "Women's Role in Combat: The War Resumes," *New York Times,* May 26, 1991, A1. This article, among others, corrected the statistical picture.
39. Adam Clymer, "In Capitol, Debate on Parents in Gulf," *New York Times,* February 16, 1991, 10; Jack Anderson and Dale Van Atta, editorial, "When Soldiers Have Babies," *Washington Post,* March 8, 1991, E3; Dana Priest, "Pentagon Opposes Exempting Parents, Is Reviewing New Policy on Mothers," *Washington Post,* February 20, 1991, A16; Jane Gross, "Needs of Family and Country Clash in Persian Gulf Mission," *New York Times,* December 9, 1990, A1.

40. Brian Mitchell, *Weak Link: The Feminization of the American Military* (Washington, DC: Regnery Gateway, 1989).
41. Francine D'Amico, "Policing the US Military's Race and Gender Lines," in *Wives and Warriors: Women and the Military in the United States and Canada*, ed. Laurie Weinstein and Christie C. White (Westport, CT: Bergin and Garvey, 1997); Deborah Rogers, "The Force Drawdown and Its Impact on Women in the Military," *Minerva: The Quarterly Report on Women in the Military*, Spring 1992, 1–13.
42. Hamilton I. McCubbin, Barbara B. Dahl, and Edna J. Hunter, "Research on the Military Family: A Review," in *Families in the Military System*, ed. Hamilton I. McCubbin, Barbara B. Dahl, and Edna J. Hunter (Beverly Hills, CA: Sage, 1976), 318. By 1976, researchers cited just over 150 studies, and by 1980 that number had tripled, with 432 "known documents" on military family research. Military Family Resources Center, *Review of Military Family Research and Literature* (Springfield, VA: Military Family Resources Center, 1984), 3. The army's research eventually fell under the sponsorship of the U.S. Army Research Institute for the Behavioral and Social Sciences at Walter Reed Army Medical Center. There, army family research projects increased fivefold. ODCSPER, *Army Family Action Plan III*, 46. The increase in army family research was reflected in a 1993 research compendium by the U.S. Army Research Institute for command and unit leaders. "What We Know about Army Families" was based on only 72 of the many existing studies of army families, but tellingly, 65 of the 72 were produced between 1985 and 1992. Mady Wechsler Segal and Jesse J. Harris, *What We Know about Army Families* (Alexandria, VA: U.S. Army Research Institute for the Behavioral and Social Sciences, 1993), 55.
43. Reuben Hill, *Families under Stress: Adjustment to the Crises of War Separation and Reunion* (New York: Harper, 1949).
44. Talcott Parsons and Robert Bales, *Family, Socialization and Interaction Process* (Glencoe, IL: Free Press, 1955).
45. Hamilton I. McCubbin and Barbara B. Dahl, "Prolonged Family Separation in the Military: A Longitudinal Study," in McCubbin et al., *Families in the Military System*, 117; and McCubbin et al., "Research on the Military Family," 298–314.
46. U.S. Army, Office of the Deputy Chief of Staff for Personnel, "The Army Family Action Plan III," (Washington, DC: U.S. Army Chief of Staff, 1986), 44.
47. Reuben Hill, "Foreword," in *Families in the Military System* (1976), 13.

48. Bell worked with Orthner and Bowen on family adaptation research in 1991. See Dennis Orthner et al., *Development of a Measure of Family Adaptation to the Army* (Research Triangle Park, NC: Technical Report 925, U.S. Army Research Institute, 1991). Bell worked as a senior research psychologist at ARI.
49. D. Bruce Bell et al., "Helping U.S. Army Families Cope with Stresses of Troop Deployment to Bosnia-Herzegovina," paper presented at the 1997 Inter-University Seminar on Armed Forces and Society Biennial International Conference, Baltimore, MD, October 24–26, 1997, 13.
50. Ibid.
51. Ibid., 13–14.
52. Gary L. Bowen and Peter Neenan, "Does Subsidized Childcare Availability Promote Welfare Independence of Mothers on AFDC: An Experimental Analysis," *Research on Social Work Practice*, 3 (1993): 363–384; Gary L. Bowen, Dennis K. Orthner, and Laura I. Zimmerman, "Family Adaptation of Single Parents in the United States Army: An Empirical Analysis of Work Stressors and Adaptive Resources," *Family Relations* 42 (1993): 293–304.
53. Lawrence Mead, *Beyond Entitlement: The Social Obligations of Citizenship* (New York: Free Press, 1986); Charles Murray, *Losing Ground: American Social Policy, 1950–1980* (New York: Basic Books, 1984).
54. "Family Support, Desert Storm After Action Report," 11.
55. Ibid.
56. Ibid., 1.
57. Ibid.
58. Murray, "Basic Training," 12–13. Shauna Whitworth, one of the creators of AFTB, hoped it would "institutionalize another learning process called "inculturation"—that is passing wisdom from one individual down to another." "New Program Will Train Soldiers, Families to Improve Readiness," *Army Families* (FLO), Summer 1993, MFC, CMH, 4; "AFTB Training Brings Families into Army Team," *Army Families* (FLO), Summer 1994, MFC, CMH, 2.
59. "New Program," 4.
60. "AFTB Training," 2.
61. Chris Murray, "Basic Training for Army Families," *Army Times*, November 22, 1993, 12–13.
62. Briefing Slides, folder Community and Family Support Center Briefing Slides, box 15, HRP, MHI.
63. For inquiries to MWR concerning the status of the army's social welfare system on the twentieth anniversary of the volunteer army see folder

Media Queries, 1997, and folder Media Queries, (n.d.), both box 26, and folder Media Queries 1997–1998 (1 of 2), box 27, HRP, MHI. Some media inquiries also included the treatment of soldiers pushed out of the force as a result of the drawdown, and what benefits they might receive.

64. Walters quoted in Harriet Rice to Evan Gaddis (BG) et al., memo, subject: Major Media Query, Knight-Ridder, n.d., folder Media Queries 1997–1998 (1 of 2), box 27, HRP, MHI.
65. See Rice's handwritten notes for Lucas on this memo: Nolan Walters to Harriet Rice, memo, May 7, 1997, Media Queries, 1997, box 26, HRP, MHI, 1.
66. Harriet Rice to Evan Gaddis (BG) et al., subject: Knight-Ridder Interview, n.d., folder Media Queries, 1997, box 26, HRP, MHI.
67. "Murder Board: Knight-Ridder Roundtable Interview: Family Support Programs," folder Media Queries, 1997, box 26, HRP, MHI.
68. Dennis J. Reimer to VCSA et al., memo for distribution, April 17, 1996, folder J. T. Scott, memo, 24 June 1996, Sub: Reshaping Family Programs, MFC, CMH, 1.
69. J. T. Scott, Lieutenant General, memo for distribution, June 24, 1996, folder J. T. Scott, memo, 24 June 1996, Sub: Reshaping Family Programs, MFC, CMH, 1.
70. "Family Readiness Vision," folder USASOC Family Readiness Vision/ Mission—97, Human Resources Directorate, MFC, CMH, 1–2.
71. See two memos: from U.S. Army Chaplaincy Services Support Agency, for distribution, November 23, 1991, 2, and to Matthew A. Zimmerman, Chief of Chaplains, November 14, 1991, 2, both in folder Chaplain, Memorandum re: Proposal for Army family Ministry, 1991, MFC, CMH.
72. Slide presentation "Family Support Programs," folder Family Support Groups, Handouts, C and S, May 4–8, 1998, MFC, CMH 1–3.
73. Ibid.
74. Information paper, Subject: Family Readiness Groups, CFSC-SF-A, February 8, 2000, folder Papers from the Commanders Conference, Carlisle, PA, February 24, 2000, MFC, CMH.
75. Operation READY, *The Army Family Readiness Handbook: Family Deployment Readiness for the Active Army, the Army National Guard, and the Army Reserve* (Department of the Army and Texas A&M, 2002), 172. Also available at http://huachuca-www.army.mil/files/ACS_The_Army_Family_Readiness_Handbook.pdf.
76. Paulette Walker, "'The Army Cares': The Message Is Everywhere, But Is It Getting through to Army People?," *Army Times*, September 19, 1994, 12.

77. Paulette Walker, "Former Leaders Say Army Needs to Prove It Cares," *Army Times*, September 19, 1994, 15.
78. James A. Martin and Dennis K. Orthner, "The 'Company Town' in Transition: Rebuilding Military Communities," in *The Organization Family: Work and Family Linkages in the U.S. Military*, ed. Gary Bowen and Dennis Orthner (New York: Praeger, 1989), 164–165.

8. Outsourcing Soldier and Family Support

1. George H. W. Bush, "Remarks and a Question-and-Answer Session at a Luncheon Hosted by the Commonwealth Club in San Francisco, California," February 7, 1990, Public Papers, George Bush Presidential Library and Museum, http://bush41library.tamu.edu/archives/public-papers/1525.
2. Lawrence J. Korb, Laura Conley, and Alex Rothman, *A Return to Responsibility: What President Obama and Congress Can Learn about Defense Budgets from Past Presidents* (Washington, DC: Center for American Progress, 2011), 23.
3. Although the first Base Realignment and Closure (BRAC) effort started under President Reagan, Bush and Cheney pushed for more consolidations and cuts. Defense Base Closure and Realignment Commission, *2005 Defense Base Closure and Realignment Commission, Final Report* (Washington, DC: GPO, 2005), 311. The 1991 BRAC Commission recommended the closure of thirty-four bases and realignment—meaning reorganization and recombination of function—of forty-eight others; see p. 313.
4. Jesse Ellman, et al., *Defense Contract Trends: U.S. Department of Defense Contract Spending and the Supporting Industrial Base* (Washington, DC: Center for Strategic and International Studies, May 2011), 7–8.
5. Office of the Secretary of Defense, *Department of Defense Contract Awards by Service Category and Federal Supply Classification, Fiscal Years 1996, 1995, 1994, and 1993* (Washington, DC: Directorate for Information, Operations, and Reports, 1997), 5–6.
6. Major General John J. Cuddy, interviewed by Ming T. Wong, Senior Officer Oral History Program 2003, MHI, 156.
7. This was not the first time that the military incorporated corporate management practices. Secretary of Defense Robert McNamara introduced "systems analysis"—a management process incorporated from business schools and corporate boardrooms—through which resources were allocated based on long-term and wide-framed programmatic

planning. Most famously, McNamara reformed the Pentagon budgetary process around systems analysis. The adoption of systems analysis in the Department of Defense fostered its adoption throughout federal bureaucracies in a manner that should raise questions about the relationship between military neoliberal practices I describe here and those adopted by other federal agencies.

8. Brigadier Geneeral Ann Dunwoody quoted in Kari Hawkins, "Meeting Demands of a Changing Army," www.army.mil/article/71502/Meeting_Demands_of_Changing_Army/.
9. Army Materiel Command Historical Office (AMCHO), "A Brief History of AMC, 1962–2012" (Redstone Arsenal, AL: AMC, 2013), 4. Also available at www.amc.army.mil/amc/history/A%20Brief%20History%20of%20AMC%20(May%202013).pdf; CMH, *DAHSUM: FY 1990/1991* (Washington, DC: GPO, 1997), 121.
10. AMCHO, "Brief History," 5.
11. "AMC: Confidence, Quality, Service—A Communications Strategy", folder Transition Team Report (Vol. A–1), January 31, 1992 (3 of 3), box 8, JRP, AMCHO, 2. The author consulted the Jimmy D. Ross Papers at MHI, but the collection has since been transferred to AMCHO.
12. CMH, *DAHSUM: FY 1989* (Washington, DC: GPO, 1998), 187–188.
13. Angel R. Martinez Lorente, Frank Dewhurst, and Barrie G. Dale, "Total Quality Management: Origins and Evolution of the Term," *TQM Magazine* 10, no. 5 (1998): 378–386. The original TQM promulgators in the United States worked in the corporate world and academia: Armand V. Feigenbaum, *Total Quality Control: Engineering and Management* (New York: McGraw Hill, 1961); J. M. Juran, Frank M. Gryna, and Richard S. Bingham, eds., *Quality Control Handbook*, 3rd ed. (New York: McGraw-Hill, 1974); W. Edwards Demming, *Quality, Productivity and Competitive Position* (Cambridge, MA: Massachusetts Institute of Technology, 1982); Phillip Crosby, *Quality Is Free* (New York: McGraw-Hill, 1979).
14. "Supplemental History Report to the Transition Team for General Ross," December 23, 1991, folder Transition Team Report (Vol. A-1), January 31, 1992 (2 of 3), box 8, JRP, AMCHO, 5.
15. AMCHO, "Brief History," 4.
16. Institute for Defense and Business, "The First Annual General William G. T. Tuttle, Jr., USA (Ret.) Award for Business Acumen in Defense and Government," *PR Newswire*, www.prnewswire.com/news-releases/the-first-annual-general-william-gt-tuttle-jr-usa-ret-award-for-business-acumen-in-defense-and-government-115269869.html.

17. CMH, *DAHSUM: FY 1990/1991*, 121–122; Bill Tuttle to Reimer, July 16, 1998, box 12, folder 5 General Management Correspondence July 1998 (1 of 2), DRP, MHI.
18. On Christian colleges and free enterprise see Bethany Moreton, *To Serve God and Wal-Mart: The Making of Christian Free Enterprise* (Cambridge, MA: Harvard University Press, 2009), chapters 9 and 10.
19. Memorandum RE: CSA's letter, January 13, 1992, folder Historical Interviews, Topics (Vol. D-A) February 1, 1992–February 28, 1992 (1 of 4), box 21, JRP, AMCHO, 1–3.
20. *A Devotion to Duty: Memoirs of General Jimmy D. Ross, U.S. Army, Retired,* written with Mary Magee and William Moye (Fort Belvoir: AMCHO, 2007), 269–270.
21. "AMC of the 1990s Team," October 25, 1991, folder Transition Team Report (Vol. A-2) February 28 1992–March 31, 1992, box 8, JRP, AMCHO.
22. Memorandum RE: CSA's letter, January 13, 1992, JRP, AMCHO.
23. CMH, *DAHSUM: FY 1990/1991,* 122.
24. CSA, Information Paper, Subject: Total Quality Management, July 26, 1991, box 47, folder 870–5f, VCSA, October 24, 1992 [note: date on folder is wrong; folder contents are from 1991], Total Army Quality Workshop, DRP, MHI, 1. See also PowerPoint presentation, n.d., folder Transition Team Report (Vol. A-2) February 28, 1992–March 31, 1992, box 8, JRP, AMCHO, 1.
25. CMH, *DAHSUM: FY 1992* (Washington, DC: GPO, 2001), 94; CMH, *DAHSUM: FY 1995* (Washington, DC: GPO, 2004), 90.
26. Dennis Reimer, VCSA Speech Book, Remarks to Total Army Quality Workshop, October 24, 1991, box 47, folder 870–5f, VCSA, October 24, 1992, Total Army Quality Workshop, DRP, MHI, 8–9, 11.
27. Korb et al., *Return to Responsibility,* 27.
28. Mark D. Sherry, *The Army Command Post and Defense Reshaping, 1987–1997* (Washington, DC: CMH, 2008), 85.
29. See Clinton's nomination acceptance speech at the 1992 Democratic Convention in which he pledged to "cut 100,000 bureaucrats." William J. Clinton, "Address Accepting the Presidential Nomination at the Democratic National Convention in New York," July 16, 1992, The American Presidency Project, www.presidency.ucsb.edu/ws/index.php?pid=25958.
30. Indeed, Osborne referred approvingly to the Hoover Commissions in public discussions. William J. Clinton, "Press Briefing on *Reinventing Government* by David Osborne and John Sharp," September 7, 1993, The American Presidency Project, www.presidency.ucsb.edu/ws/index.php?pid=60041.

31. Commission on the Organization of the Executive Branch of Government, *Business Enterprises: A Report to Congress* (Washington, DC: GPO, 1955), xii.
32. President's Private Sector Survey on Cost Control (Grace Commission), *A Report to the President* (Washington, DC: GPO, 1984), III–18.
33. David Osborne and Ted Gaebler, *Reinventing Government: How the Entrepreneurial Spirit Is Transforming the Public Sector* (New York: Penguin 1993), cover, 31, 45.
34. William J. Clinton and Al Gore, "Remarks by the President and the Vice President at *Reinventing Government* Anniversary Event," September 14, 1994, National Performance Review papers, University of North Texas, http://govinfo.library.unt.edu/npr/library/anniversary.html.
35. Clinton, "Press Briefing."
36. Alice M. Rivlin, OMB, "NPR Phase II: Remarks," December 1994, National Performance Review papers, University of North Texas, http://govinfo.library.unt.edu/npr/library/speeches/234a.html.
37. On the privatization of social welfare, see early analyses by Sheila Kammerman and Alfred J. Kahn, eds, *Privatization and the Welfare State*, (Princeton, NJ: Princeton University Press, 1989); John D. Donohue, *The Privatization Decision: Public Ends, Private Means* (New York: Basic Books, 1989); and Stephen Rathgeb Smith and Michael Lipsky, *Nonprofits for Hire: The Welfare State in the Age of Contracting* (Cambridge: Harvard University Press, 1993). More recently, see Michael Reisch, "United States: Social Welfare Policy and Privatization in Post-Industrial Society," in Jason Powell and Jon Hendricks, eds., *The Welfare State in Posindustrial Society: A Global Perspective* (New York: Springer Science+Business Media, 2009), 253–270; Pamela Winston, et al., "Privatization of Welfare Services: A Review of the Literature," Report Submitted to the Office of Policy Planning and Research, Department of Health and Human Services, Mathematica Policy Research, Inc, (May 2002), chapter 2, http://aspe.hhs.gov/hsp/privatization02/, accessed 3/27/15. ACS was purchased by Lockheed Martin in 2001.
38. Joshua Gotbaum, "The Business of Government Hour," radio interview transcript, October 2, 2000, IBM Center for the Business of Government, www.businessofgovernment.org/interview/josh-gotbaum-interview.
39. U.S. Senate, Committee on Armed Services, *Statement of Joshua Gotbaum, Assistant Secretary of Defense (Economic Security), before the Subcommittees on Personnel and Readiness*, 104th Cong., 1st sess., May 15, 1995.
40. See Paul Kaminski to the Chairman, DSB, memo, October 18, 1995, in Office of the Under Secretary of Defense for Acquisition and Tech-

nology, *Report of the Defense Science Board Task Force on Outsourcing and Privatization* (Washington, DC: DoD, 1996), appendix A, 2. After leaving DoD, Gotbaum brought "the totality of the value of privatization and outsourcing" to the Treasury Department, the OMB, and then back to the private sector. He ran the Obama 2008 Transition Team, and he currently directs the government's Pension Benefit Guarantee Corporation.

41. With the assistance of Wall Street investment bankers like Gotbaum, the ailing firms merged rapidly: "dozens of contractors" imploded "into just four firms"—Boeing, Lockheed-Martin, Northrop Grumman, and Raytheon—in an attempt to increase profits by capturing a greater share of the market. Each then reaped profits in the range of $15–$30 billion annually. Ann Markusen, "The Rise of World Weapons," *Foreign Policy*, Spring 1999, 41–42, 44.
42. American Consulting Engineers Council, "ACEC Endorses HR 716, Asks DOD to be Leader in Government Outsourcing," *Last Word* 13, no. 7 (March 17, 1996), Internet Archive (Wayback Machine), https://archive.org/web/.
43. The chief of the DSB, Dr. Craig Fields, former head of the DARPA, had overseen development of much of the technology used for the Internet and was vice chair of United Gaming, a division of Bally, which he advised on technology and security. DoD, "Dr. Craig Fields Named Chairman of the Defense Science Board," press release, December 1, 1994, www.defense.gov/releases/release.aspx?releaseid=295.
44. Stephen Howard Chadwick, *Defense Acquisition: Overview, Issues and Options for Congress* (Washington, DC: CRS, 2007), CRS-1.
45. Phillip A. Oden to Chair, DSB, memo, August 27, 1996, enclosure with Office of the Under Secretary of Defense, *Report of the Defense Science Board*, 2, 50.
46. Business Executives for National Security, "About BENS," www.bens.org/page.aspx?pid=406; see also Ann Markusen, "The Case against Privatizing National Security, 2001," *Governance* 16, no. 4 (October 2003): 26.
47. Paul Taibl, Executive Summary, *Outsourcing and Privatization of Defense Infrastructure* (Washington, DC: BENS, 1997), 5.
48. Peter Slatin, "The Ground Floor: Taking Military Housing Private," *Barron's*, May 5, 1997, 43.
49. U.S. Senate, Congressional Record vol. 143, no. 34, March 17, 1997, S2337–S2339, Congressional Record Online through the GPO, www.gpo.gov/fdsys/pkg/CREC-1997-03-17/html/CREC-1997-03-17-pt1-PgS2337-7.htm. Warren Rudman introduced the first Freedom from Government

Competition Act in 1983, but ten years passed until Republicans again pursued a more vigorous effort. Bills were introduced every year or two in the 1990s, and in 2013 a version was finally passed into law and signed by President Obama. See H.R.163—Freedom from Government Competition Act of 1992, 103rd Cong. (1993–1994); H.R.28—Freedom from Government Competition Act of 1995, 104th Cong. (1995–1996); S.1724—Freedom from Government Competition Act of 1996, 104th Cong. (1995–1996); H.R.716—Freedom from Government Competition Act of 1997, 105th Cong. (1997–1998); S.1167—Freedom from Government Competition Act of 2009, 111th Cong. (2009–2010); H.R.2682—Freedom from Government Competition Act of 2009, 111th Cong. (2009–2010); S.785—Freedom from Government Competition Act, 112th Congress (2011–2012); H.R.1474—Freedom from Government Competition Act of 2011, 112th Congress (2011–2012); S.523—Freedom from Government Competition Act, 113th Congress (2013–2014); H.R.1072—Freedom from Government Competition Act of 2013, 113th Congress (2013–2014). For the efforts of industry groups to support the legislation and the overall efforts of BENS and the DSB see, for example, American Consulting Engineers Council, "ACEC and Industry Leaders Support Government Competition Legislation," *Last Word* 18, no. 8 (March 31, 1997) and "ACEC Endorses HR 716."

50. Office of the Vice President, "Department of Defense, Part 2 of 2, Accompanying Report of the National Performance Review," Washington, DC, September 1993, Section DoD: 4, http://govinfo.library.unt.edu/npr/library/nprrpt/annrpt/agnrpt93/dod2.html.
51. Commission on the Roles and Missions of the Armed Forces, *Directions for Defense* (Washington, DC: GPO, 1993), 3-3. Also available at www.dod.mil/pubs/foi/operation_and_plans/Other/734.pdf.
52. Stephen Hill, *Residential Communities Initiative (RCI): A Privatization Model for the DoD?* (Carlisle Barracks, PA: U.S. Army War College, 2004), 1.
53. The army's contracts for services grew even as the service contracts of the other branches declined. Between 1995 and 2000, total air force spending on service contracts fell and navy service contracts held steady and then fell. But army service contracts grew steadily. See Ellman et al., *Defense Contract Trends,* 19–22.
54. Rebecca Loveland et al., *The Massachusetts Defense Industry: Characteristics and Economic Impact* (Boston: UMass Donohue Institute, 2007), figure 18, 31.
55. CMH, *DAHSUM: FY 1994* (Washington, DC: GPO, 2000), 128.

56. Ibid.
57. Dennis Reimer, VCSA Speech Book: Garrison Commanders' Conference Remarks, December 9, 1991, box 48, folder 870–5f, December 9, 1992 [note: date on folder is wrong; folder contents are from 1991], Garrison Commanders' Conference, DRP, MHI, 16–17.
58. CMH, *DAHSUM: FY 1992*, 150.
59. Dennis Reimer, VCSA Speech Book, box 46, folder 870–5f, VCSA, August 18, 1992, Army Installation Management Course, DRP, MHI, 5.
60. PowerPoint presentation "DSCAIM Process Strategy," November 26, 1991, box 48, folder 870–5f, December 9, 1992, Garrison Commanders' Conference, DRP, MHI.
61. CMH, *DAHSUM: FY 1994*, 125–127; see also box 67, folder 870–5f, CSA, GO Installation Commanders' Course, November 4, 1996, DRP, MHI.
62. Dennis Reimer, Untitled Speech, box 63, folder 870–5F, CSA, Army Communities of Excellence, April 1996, DRP, MHI, 3.
63. See box 65, folder 870–5f, CSA, Installation Commanders, September 23, 1996, and also box 67, folder 870–5f, CSA, GO Installation Commanders' Course, November 4, 1996, DRP, MHI.
64. *Life Magazine*, March 7, 1949, 35, 34; Jan Nugent, "Poverty in Europe," *Air Force Times, Family Supplement,* August 2, 1972; Bill Walker, "Living on the Economy: Non-Command-Sponsored Families: Coping with Europe," *Stars and Stripes,* May 11, 1977, A1; Martha Gravois, "Hot Dogs, Apple Pie, and Wiener Schnitzel: Army Families in Germany, 1946–1986" (MA thesis, Shippensburg University, 1986).
65. DoD had over 31,000 family housing units on bases. Pamela C. Twiss, "The Future of Military Housing," in *Pathways to the Future: A Review of Military Family Research,* ed. Peggy McClure (Scranton, PA: Military Family Institute, Marywood University, 1999), 35. And there were major housing initiatives such as one at Aberdeen Proving Ground, Maryland, begun in 1986. See Jay Stanley, Mady Wechsler Segal, and Charlotte Jeanne Laughton, "Grass Roots Family Action and Military Policy Responses," *Marriage and Family Review* 5, nos. 3–4 (1990): 207.
66. Twiss, "Future of Military Housing," 36.
67. Ibid., 49.
68. CMH, *DAHSUM: FY 1995*, 86.
69. Ibid.; Dennis Reimer, memo for distribution, May 1, 1997, box 9, folder 5 General Management Correspondence May 1997 (1 of 2), DRP, MHI.

70. Senate Committee on Banking and Currency, *Review of Military Housing Programs,* 85th Cong., 1st sess., 1957, S. Rep. 231, 29; William C. Baldwin, *Four Housing Privatization Programs: A History of the Wherry, Capehart, Section 801, and Section 802 Family Housing Programs in the Army* (U.S. Army Corps of Engineers, Office of History, 1996), 13, www.acq.osd.mil/housing/docs/four.htm; Tarin Erickson et al., *Mountain Home Modern: Base Housing in the 1950s* (Plano, TX: Geo-Marine, for U.S. Army Corps of Engineers, 2010), 5.
71. Baldwin, *Four Housing Privatization Programs,* 37, 40; CFSC, *Army Family Action Plan, Corporate Report* (1986), 11. U.S. Army, ODC-SPER, *Army Family Action Plan* (Washington, DC: CSA, 1984).
72. Housing privatization was Title 28 of the National Defense Authorization Act, FY 1996, Public Law 104–106, February 10, 1996.
73. Each branch of the services could choose its own deal structure based on its needs and its resources. Hill, *Residential Communities Initiative,* 2; Daniel Else, *Military Housing Privatization Initiative: Background and Issues* (Washington, DC: CRS, July 2, 2001), CRS-6; CMH, *DAHSUM: FY 1998* (Washington, DC: GPO, 2005), 58.
74. RCI, "Information Paper," July 2010, www.rci.army.mil/program information/infopaper.html.
75. Eric Shinseki, *The Army Family: A White Paper* (Washington, DC: CSA, 2003), 31; Hill, *Residential Communities Initiative,* 8.
76. "Military Homes, Civilian Developers," September 24, 2001, *Los Angeles Times,* http://articles.latimes.com/2001/sep/24/news/mn-49241.
77. RCI, Information Paper.
78. Hill, *Residential Communities Initiative,* 10.
79. Else, *Military Housing Privatization Initiative,* CRS-12, CRS-15.
80. Hill, *Residential Communities Initiative,* 15.
81. Natalie Kosteini, "GMH Divisions Live On under New Owners," *Philadelphia Business Journal,* March 6, 2009, www.bizjournals.com /Philadelphia/stories.2009/03/09/focus5.html; Lend Lease, "Who is Lend Lease? An International Leader in Property and Infrastructure," www .lendlease.com/en/Group/Lend-Lease/Worldwide/About-Us/who-is-lend -lease.aspx.
82. Hill, *Residential Communities Initiative,* 3, 10, 13; see also CMH, *DAHSUM: FY 1999* (Washington, DC: GPO, 2006), 108.
83. It is interesting to consider the fact that the privatized military housing boom coincided with the civilian housing construction boom in the 1990s. CMH, *DAHSUM: FY 2000* (Washington, DC: GPO, 2011), 103–104.

84. Assistant Secretary of the Army for Installations and Environment, "RCI Plan: Where We Are Now," 2010, www.rci.army.mil/programinformation/rcioverview.html.
85. Mahlon Apgar IV, "Special Briefing: Army's Residential Communities Initiative in Fort Hood, Texas," transcript, June 29, 2000, www.defense.gov/Transcripts/Transcript.aspx?TranscriptID=1463.
86. My discussions with several military commanders in the late 2000s suggest that their personnel were not aware that their housing had been privatized. Military blogs, which proliferated in the 2000s, only started registering the privatization in the mid-2000s. See, for example, Love My Tanker, "Privatized Housing," *SpouseBUZZ*, January 10, 2007, http://spousebuzz.com/blog/2007/01/privatized_hous.html.
87. Hill, *Residential Communities Initiative*, 13, 21–23.
88. J. Osthus, CFSC, Information Paper, "Degradation of Soldiers Community Recreation Programs," July 14, 1994, folder MRW Marketing, 1994–1995, box 31, HRP, MHI, 1–2.
89. Susan Way-Smith et al., *Army Morale, Welfare and Recreation Programs in the Future: Maximizing Soldier Benefits in Times of Austerity* (Santa Monica, CA: RAND Corporation, 1993), 59; see memo from *Army Times* to Bill Harkey, Public Affairs, December 1, 1994, 1, and also Paulette Walker, "Study: Give Soldiers Cash to Play Off Post," *Army Times*, December 5, 1994, both items in folder Media Queries FY 97–98, box 27, HRP, MHI.
90. Before CSA John Wickham closed the officers' and enlisted clubs in the 1980s as part of his effort to reduce alcohol consumption, these clubs had also been a source of NAFs for MWR. Wickham's "vice elimination" program thus reduced funding for MWR.
91. CMH, *DAHSUM: FY 1992*, 102–103.
92. Ibid.
93. MWR Board of Directors, CFSC, Plans and Policy Directorate, "MWR Strategic Action Plan," 1994, Alexandria, VA, folder MWR Strategic Plan 1994, box 31, HRP, MHI, 2, 10.
94. Ibid.
95. General RisCassi, Army MWR Board of Directors Meeting, April 22, 1993, folder MWR Board of Directors, 1993, box 30, HRP, MHI, last two pages (no pagination).
96. Untitled PowerPoint slides, folder MRW Marketing, 1994–1995, box 31, HRP, MHI.
97. "Morale, Welfare and Recreation," folder MWR Exhibit for DoD Joint Open House—After Action Report, 1997, box 31, HRP, MHI, 17.

98. Harriet Rice, "The Fallacy of Demand-Driven," draft copy of article for feedback, newsletter, folder MRW Marketing, 1994–1995, box 31, HRP, MHI, 4.
99. William P. Bradner, "MWR Office Unveils New Logo," *Fort Hood Sentinel,* June 8, 1995, folder MWR Logo Launch, 1995, box 31, HRP, MHI.
100. "Morale, Welfare and Recreation," 17; *Army Times Almanac* interview, interviewer: Paulette Walker, December 6, 1994, Read Ahead Qs and As, 1, and *Army Times:* Paulette Walker, Follow Up Qs and As, December 6, 1994, Subject: Quality of Life, 2–3, Folder Media Queries, 1994, box 27, HRP, MHI.
101. Harriet Rice, Orientation Briefing, Lieutenant General John Dubia, November 9, 1998, MWR/Family Program A-76 Strategy Slide, folder unmarked, box 44, HRP, MHI.
102. CMH, *DAHSUM: FY 1992,* 165–166.
103. David R. Warren, *Defense Outsourcing: Challenges Facing DOD as It Attempts to Save Billions in Infrastructure Costs, Testimony before the Subcommittee on Readiness, House Committee on National Security* (Washington, DC: GAO, March 12, 1997), 3.
104. G. E. Willis, "Top Doc Hands Off Troubled System," *Army Times,* September 9, 1996, 4.
105. J. Michael Brower, "Outland: The Vogue of DOD Outsourcing and Privatization," *Acquisition Review Quarterly,* Fall 1997, 384–385.
106. Sherry, *Army Command Post,* 146.
107. Warren M. Anderson, John J. McGuiness, and John S. Spicer, "And the Survey Says . . . The Effectiveness of DOD Outsourcing and Privatization Efforts," *Acquisition Review Quarterly,* Spring 2002, 97–98.
108. Bruce D. Grant, *US Military Expertise for Sale: Private Military Consultants as a Tool of Foreign Policy* (Carlisle Barracks, PA: U.S. Army War College, 1998). On the concern over private military service providers, see one of the first media stories, Leslie Wayne, "America's For-Profit Secret Army," *New York Times,* October 13, 2002, B1. Scholar P. W. Singer brought "corporate warriors" to the attention of policymakers and academics. P. W. Singer, "Have Guns, Will Travel," *New York Times,* July 21, 2003, A13; P. W. Singer, *Corporate Warriors: The Rise of the Privatized Military Industry* (Ithaca, NY: Cornell University Press, 2003). Congress held the first hearings devoted to the phenomenon in 2006. A widespread public discussion ensued about the functioning, cost, and meaning of the military's payment of "mercenaries" on America's battlefields. U.S. House, Committee on Government Reform, *Private Security Firms Standards, Cooperation and*

Coordination on the Battlefield, Hearing before the Subcommittee on National Security, Emerging Threats, and International Relations, 109th Cong., 2nd sess., June 13, 2006.

109. Larry Lock, *Is Military Outsourcing out of Control?* (Carlisle Barracks, PA: U.S. Army War College, 2006), 4.

110. Louis Caldara and Dennis Reimer, *Posture of The United States Army FY 2000,* (February 1999), Posture Statement presented to the 106th Cong., 1st. sess., February 1999, 72.

111. The army relied most on Syracuse University's Maxwell School, where it sent its top colonels for a management course. It also sent its one- and two-star generals to a special program of the Maxwell School and Johns Hopkins University for their DoD Executive Management Development and Training Program. See W. K. Sutey to Reimer, memo, March 31, 1997; and Syracuse University Maxwell School of Citizenship and Public Affairs and Johns Hopkins University Institute for Advanced International Studies, "National Security Leadership Course: Department of Defense Executive Management Development and Training Program," brochure, both in box 71, folder 870–5f, CSA, Office Call, Hon Sean O'Keefe, Maxwell School, Syracuse University, April 2, 1997, DRP, MHI. The army also developed a relationship with MIT's Sloan School of Management, through which it organized a "CEO Conference" for the army. By the late 1990s, these programs were of direct concern to the CSA, who met regularly with the deans of both Syracuse and MIT. See Peter Senge to Reimer, March 31, 1997, and Reimer to Senge, April 14, 1997, both letters in box 9, folder 5 General Management Correspondence, April 1997 (2 of 4), DRP, MHI. Relationships with business schools provided not only formal education and training, but also connections to a growing network of corporate executives who also attended the same or similar programs at the schools.

112. On the Captains of Industry Conference see box 12, folder 5, General Management Correspondence, June 1998 (1 of 2); and PowerPoint presentation, box 33, folder 870–56 CSA, Captains of Industry, March 7, 1997, DRP, MHI. For the Wise Person Seminar see folder 870–56 CSA, Wise Person III Seminar, 14–15 January 1998 (1 of 4), box 38, DRP, MHI.

113. As an indication of its identification with corporate models, the army launched a new public relations campaign that touted its transformation into a corporate institution. A nearly $100 million contract with Sy Colman, a communications firm that later won a contract to improve the global image of the United States during the Iraq War, ballyhooed the army's full embrace of corporate values of "quality management," "outsourcing," and "privatization." Colonel Harold Cooney et al., "Army

Strategic Communications Campaign Plan: Briefing for General Dennis Reimer, Chief of Staff," March 10, 1997, box 8, folder 5 General Management Correspondence, March 1997 (3 of 3), DRP, MHI.

Many of the corporations with which the army became even closer were the longtime defense giants of weapons production—Lockheed Martin, Northrup Grumman, Raytheon, General Dynamics, and Boeing. But these firms, long associated with high-tech weaponry, moved into the rapidly growing military support services market in the 1990s, buying out existing support services firms. Northrup Grumman, for example, moved into the management of military housing, both consulting on policy for the military and managing actual housing developments on posts. BAE Systems, formed in 1999, merged its expertise in weapons with new services it purchased ranging from maintenance to supply chain to training. But new firms focused solely on support services also rose to the top of the list of army contractors, creating close relationships with the army. Humana, TriWest Healthcare, and Health Net shared about $9 billion in health care contracts through the new, privatized Tricare program and the privatization of army hospitals, clinics, and care that emerged in the 1990s. Ellman et al., *Defense Contract Trends,* 27; BAE Systems, "Military and Technical Services," www.baesystems.com /what-we-do-rzz/products—services/military—technical-services.

114. Dennis Reimer, *Posture of the United States Army FY 1998,* Posture Statement presented to the 105th Cong., 1st sess., March 4, 1997, in box 69, folder 870–5f, Testimony SASC: FY 98 Army Budget, March 4, 1997, DRP, MHI, 20–22.
115. MWR, Annual Report, 1997, folder MWR Exhibit for DoD Joint Open House—After Action Report, June 1997, box 31, HRP, MHI, 6–7.
116. Gordon Sullivan and Michael V. Harper, *Hope Is Not a Method: What Business Leaders Can Learn from America's Army* (New York: Times Books, 1996); "Review of *Hope Is Not a Method: What Business Leaders Can Learn from America's Army,*" *Kirkus Reviews,* October 1, 1996, posted online May 20, 2010, www.kirkusreviews.com/book-reviews /gordon-r-sullivan/hope-is-not-a-method/.

Epilogue

1. Eric Schmitt, "Iraq-Bound Troops Confront Rumsfeld over Lack of Armor," *New York Times,* December 8, 2004, www.nytimes.com/2004 /12/08/international/middleeast/08cnd-rumsfeld.html.

2. David Baiocchi, *Measuring Army Deployments to Iraq and Afghanistan* (Santa Monica, CA: RAND Corporation, 2012), 2.
3. Hannah Fischer, *Guide to US Military Casualty Statistics* (Washington, DC: CRS, 2014) 1.
4. Colonel Archie P. Davis III, *Confronting Combat Stress Reactions* (Carlisle Barracks, PA: U.S. Army War College, 2010), 6.
5. Fischer, *Guide*, 4.
6. See Department of the Army, *Health Promotion, Risk Reduction, Suicide Prevention Report* (Washington, DC: Department of the Army, 2010), 11, 14, 16.
7. Soldier TBI, PTSD, and suicide have been widely reported on the national media since 2005, but mental health difficulties, including suicide, among military families have not. See Kristina Kaufmann, "Suicide on the Homefront in Military Families," *CNN Opinion*, March 12, 2014, www.cnn.com/2014/03/12/opinion/kaufmann-military-families-suicides/; Richard Sisk, "The Toll of War: MilWives and Suicide," Military.Com, www.military.com/spouse/military-life/military-resources/the-toll-of-war-milwives-and-suicide.html.
8. See Jason Shepherd, "CSA and Wife Discuss Family Readiness," Army.mil, August 3, 2007, www.army.mil/article/4386/Aug__3__2007___CSA_and_Wife_Discuss_Family_Readiness; and Elizabeth M. Lorge, "Army Family Leaders Sign Covenant with Families," Army.mil, October 17, 2007, www.army.mil/article/5641/army-leaders-sign-covenant-with-families.
9. "Psychological Health/Traumatic Brain Injury," Congressionally Mandated Medical Research Programs of the Department of Defense, http://cdmrp.army.mil/phtbi/; Army Medical Department, "The Army's Post-Traumatic Stress Disorder, Mild Traumatic Brain Injury Chain Teaching program," Army.mil, July 16, 2007, www.army.mil/article/4066/the-armys-post-traumatic-stress-disorder-and-mild-traumatic-brain-injury-ptsdmtbi-chain-teaching-program.
10. Department of the Army, *Health Promotion*, 4.
11. "The Road to Resilience: What Is Resilience?," American Psychological Association, www.apa.org/helpcenter/road-resilience.aspx.
12. See "Ready and Resilient FAQ," Army.mil, www.army.mil/readyandresilient/faq. For a review of the evolution and foci in resiliency research see John Fleming and Robert J. Ledogar, "Resilience, an Evolving Concept: A Review of Literature Relevant to Aboriginal Research," *Pimatisiwin* 6, no. 2 (Summer 2008): 7; Mark D. Seery, E. Alison Holman, and Roxane Cohen Silver, "Whatever Does Not Kill Us:

Cumulative Lifetime Adversity, Vulnerability, and Resilience," *Journal of Personality and Social Psychology* 99, no. 6 (December 2010): 1025; Suniya S. Luthar, Dante Cicchetti, and Bronwyn Becker, "The Construct of Resilience: A Critical Evaluation and Guidelines for Future Work," *Child Development* 71, no. 3 (May–June 2000): 543–562. For resilience research on military families see William Saltzman et al., "Mechanisms of Risk and Resilience in Military Families: Theoretical and Empirical Basis of a Family-Focused Resilience Enhancement Program," *Clinical Child and Family Psychology Review* 14, no. 3 (September 2011): 213–230. For a critique of the army resilience program see Roy Eidelson, "The Army's Flawed Resilience Training Study: A Call for Retraction," *Dangerous Ideas Blog,* June 4, 2012, www.psychologytoday.com/blog/dangerous-ideas/201206/the-army-s-flawed-resilience-training-study-call-retraction; Roy Eidelson and Stephen Soldz, "Does Comprehensive Soldier Fitness Work? CSF Research Fails the Test," Coalition for an Ethical Psychology Working Paper Number 1, May 2012, www.ethicalpsychology.org/Eidelson-&-Soldz-CSF_Research_Fails_the_Test.pdf.

13. U.S. Army, Ready and Resilient Campaign, March 1, 2013.
14. Casey quoted in *Stand-To!* daily newsletter, July 1, 2009, www.army.mil/standto/archive/2009/07/01/.
15. Office of the Chief of Public Affairs (OCPA), PSA video *Army Family Strong,* Defense Video and Imagery Distribution System, www.dvidshub.net/video/58505/army-family-strong#.U_IPpUj9rJE; OCPA, "U.S. Army Announces New 'Army Strong' Advertising Campaign; National Advertising Begins Now," Army.mil, October 16, 2006, www.army.mil/article/363/U_S__Army_Announces_New___039_Army_Strong__039__Advertising_Campaign__National_Advertising_Begins_No/; Ira Teinowitz, "Army Rolls Out 'Strong' New Campaign," *Advertising Age,* October 9, 2006, http://adage.com/article/news/army-rolls-strong-campaign/112420/; Kristina Feliciano, "Lauren Greenfield Directs 'Family Strong' Commercials for the U.S. Army," *Stockland Martel Blog,* April 23, 2009, http://stocklandmartelblog.com/2009/04/23/lauren-greenfield-directs-%e2%80%9cfamily-strong%e2%80%9d-commercials-for-the-us-army/.
16. Not until 2013 did the army alter the video and voiceover to emphasize army support for families rather than self-reliance. See the video embedded in "Army Family Strong," GoArmy.com, www.goarmy.com/soldier-life/army-family-strong.html.
17. Dana Priest and Anne Hull published a series of articles based on four months of reporting. Dana Priest and Anne Hull, "Soldiers Face

Neglects, Frustration at Army's Top Medical Facility," *Washington Post,* February 18, 2007, www.washingtonpost.com/wp-dyn/content/article /2007/02/17/AR2007021701172.html.

18. U.S. House, Committee on Oversight and Government Reform, *Hearing on Walter Reed Army Medical Center before the Subcommittee on National Security and Foreign Affairs,* March 5, 2007 (Washington, DC: GPO, 2007); Valerie Baily Grasso, *Walter Reed Army Medical Center (WRAMC) and Office of Management and Budget (OMB) Circular A-76: Implications for the Future* (Washington, DC: CRS, 2008).
19. Steven Vogel and Renae Merle, "Privatized Walter Reed Workforce Gets Scrutiny," *Washington Post,* March 10, 2007, www.washingtonpost.com /wp-dyn/content/article/2007/03/09/AR2007030902082.html. IAP acquired Johnson Controls, the original contractor bidding for WRAMC, in 2005 and continued Johnson Controls' battle for the contract.
20. Tom Bownman, "Walter Reed Was the Army's Wake Up Call in 2007," *NPR News,* August 31, 2011, www.npr.org/2011/08/31/139641856/in -2007-walter-reed-was-the-armys-wakeup-call.
21. See, for example, Special Notice "Q—U.S. Army Medical Department (AMEDD) Community Based Warrior Transition Unit (CBWTU) Licensed Clinical Social Workers (LCSWs)—Personal Services," Federal Business Opportunities, www.fbo.gov/spg/USA/MEDCOM/DADA10 /W81K0413R0023/listing.html.
22. Baker Spring, "Time to Meet the Challenge of Updating the Military Pensions System," Heritage Foundation, September 29, 2011, www .heritage.org/research/reports/2011/09/military-retirement-system -strengthen-benefits-and-entitlements; Baker Spring, "Saving the American Dream: Improving Health Care and Retirement for Military Service Members," Heritage Foundation, November 17, 2011, www .heritage.org/research/reports/2011/11/saving-the-american-dream -improving-health-care-and-retirement-for-military-service-members.
23. A defined benefit plan is a retirement plan in which a defined amount or percentage is contributed by the employer toward the retirement benefit of the employee. In a win–win for corporate advocates, cuts to what they called the "excessive" and "burdensome" human side of the military would simultaneously fund greater spending on expensive weapons and communications systems.
24. David C. King and Zachary Karabell, *The Generation of Trust: How the U.S. Military Has Regained the Public's Confidence since Vietnam* (Washington, DC: American Enterprise Institute, 2003). A poll by the *Economist* demonstrated continued support since 2003; see "Americans

Give Military Highest Approval Rating among Federal Government Institutions," *YouGov*, week of July 14, 2012, http://today.yougov.com/news/2012/07/19/americans-give-military-highest-approval-rating-am/.

25. Catherine Lutz, *Homefront: A Military City and the American Twentieth Century* (Boston: Beacon Press, 2001), 236.

Acknowledgments

American historians of the United States have few research opportunities to see the world, stuck as we are in our own national archive. So when I stumbled on the history of the U.S. Army's social welfare programs, I was fortunate to recognize a chance to set eyes on new horizons. Since the advent of the volunteer force most Americans, like me, have had scant contact with the military. Trying to understand even a small portion of this world—and then to write about what I learned—represented one of the most challenging and rewarding journeys I've taken as a historian.

My expedition would have failed without the generosity of military personnel, former military personnel, civilian defense employees, and military family members who agreed to help me. These conversations were facilitated by invitations to West Point, Georgetown University's MPA program for military officers, and the Woodrow Wilson Center's conference on military families. Very special thanks to Carolyn Becraft, Sheila Casey, Delores Johnson, Lory Manning, Mary Ellen Pratt, Mady Wechsler Segal, and Linda Smith for allowing me to conduct informational interviews. Conversations with David Cortright, Kristy Kaufmann, David Segal, Colonel Bill Eldridge of the U.S. Air Force, Colonel (Ret.) Kevin Farrell of the U.S. Army, Lieutenant Colonel Townley Redfern Hedrick of the U.S. Army, and Lieutenant Marco Stawnyczyj of the U.S. Marine Corps enriched my understanding of military life and history. Robert Griffith endured a sustained and lengthy email correspondence that decisively shaped the book, and for which I am immensely grateful. Finally, I have benefited from time in the classroom with my undergraduate and graduate students who are veterans of the wars in Iraq or Afghanistan. Their honest and direct discussion of the military also helped me understand the volunteer force.

The army's archivists and scholars helped me gather an archive on the army's benefits and supports in the volunteer era where none seemed to exist. Every staff member at the Military History Institute at Carlisle, Pennsylvania, proved ingenious in helping me imagine where the buried history of army social welfare programs might lie. Special thankyous to Terry Foster, David Keough, Isabel Mansky, and Dr. Richard Sommers. At the Center of Military History (CMH) at Fort McNair, Joel Meyerson offered me a desk and a copy machine, and access to the files collected for a never-written U.S. Army history of family programs. Email discussion with Janet Valentine and in-person conversations with her former colleagues at CMH, Dale Andrade, David Goldman, and James Tobias, proved immensely helpful. Alexa Potter at the Library of Congress's Veterans Oral History Project doggedly searched for relevant oral histories and made the time spent there fun. And Chrissie Tate Reilly, an army staff historian at Fort Monmouth, New Jersey, and U.S. Army Communications-Electronics Command generously passed documents and images my way.

The research staffs at nonmilitary institutions helped me round out and follow through on the stories from the army's archive. Eric Novotny at Penn State tracked down early published materials. Dagne Gizaw, Michelle Kamalich, and Janet Spikes at the Woodrow Wilson International Center for Scholars facilitated my access to the vast Library of Congress catalog. Kelly D. Barton walked me through the documents at the Ronald Reagan Presidential Library. The staff at the George Meany Archives located the American Federation of Labor and Congress of Industrial Organizations military unionization files. And Tom Glynn at Rutgers alerted me to relevant databases of all things military that came across his desk.

I received generous material support for this project from several institutions. The Woodrow Wilson International Center for Scholars offered a wonderful home for the research as I was getting started. Both Penn State and Rutgers University provided both funding and time off at crucial points in the process.

I was lucky to have access to the investigative and organizational skills of research assistants at Penn State, the Woodrow Wilson Center, and Rutgers. I am grateful to Merav Beyar, Julia Bowes, Nicholas DeGroot, Kate Devan, Rachel Finklestein, Matthew Kuchtyak, Sarah Lawrence, Anthony Ross, Emily Williams, and the amazing Jesse Bayker.

Discussions with many scholars helped me hone my ideas. I benefited from invited talks at the Woodrow Wilson International Center for Scholars, University of Maryland, George Washington University, Georgetown University, and Princeton University, where I enjoyed both the Modern American Workshop and the Political History Seminar. At professional conferences over the years, I received valuable feedback from dozens of interlocutors. Among all these discussions I'm especially grateful for the comments of Jeff Brune, Rich Friman, Caley

Horan, Alison Isenberg, Meredith Lair, Laura McEnaney, Kimberly Morgan, Aaron O'Connell, Stephen Ortiz, Gul Berna Ozcan, Rebecca Rix, Sarah Rose, Amy Rutenberg, Robert Self, Bettye Collier Thomas, Kara Vuic, and Julian Zelizer.

My colleagues at Penn State and Rutgers provided advice and encouragement. At Penn State, thank you to David Atwill, Alan Derickson, Lorraine Dowler, Tony Kaye, Sally McMurray, Rachel Moran, Gregg Roeber, Carolyn Sachs, Susan Welch, the late Aaronette White, and Nan Woodruff. At Rutgers, Paul Clemens, Jim Masschaele, Jimmy Swenson, and Mark Wasserman assured financial support for my research. John Chambers expressed early enthusiasm. Dorothy Sue Cobble, Toby Jones, Seth Koven, and especially Lou Masur advised me in the publication process. Marisa Fuentes, Jennifer Jones, and Johanna Schoen made sure I made my deadlines. And conversations with Tuna Artun, Mia Bay, Tiffany Berg, Alison Bernstein, Belinda Davis, Rachel Devlin, Anthony Dibattista, Ann Fabian, Nancy Hewitt, Temma Kaplan, Dawn Ruskai, Candace Wolcott Shepherd, and Cami Townsend inspired me, even though we rarely discussed my research.

In addition to providing moral support, many colleagues made time to read parts of the manuscript, and their comments improved the book immeasurably. Michael Allen and Lila Corwin Berman made decisive suggestions on early versions of the research. Dan Rodgers helped me hone my reflections on my research and provided guidance for shaping the book. Eileen Boris, Geoff Field, Josh Freeman, Karen Hagemann, and Sonya Michel expertly edited published pieces of the research. Mark Erbel, Andy Morris, and Keith Wailoo helped me think through outsourcing and privatization. And Beth Bailey in addition to sharing sources, read three chapters with utmost commitment and care.

Four longtime and loyal friends courageously read the entire manuscript, and their editorial gifts adorn every page of the book. Dave Fitzpatrick double-checked my terminology and provided valuable insights from his career as both an army officer and historian. Alexander Shashko put me through his own version of editorial boot camp, though he's the most patient and encouraging drill instructor anyone could ask for. Claire Potter started reading my writing when I was an undergraduate, and I can think of no better "big picture" editor. And Lori Ginzberg has inked up every piece I've published since I was lucky enough to meet her in 2003. She gave this book special care, and I hope I've done her justice.

At Harvard University Press, Joyce Seltzer pressed me harder than any other reader to fully articulate the meaning of the book. Every one of her editorial comments sharpened the chapters and knitted them together. Brian Distelberg patiently and adeptly led me through the publication process. I am grateful for his sound advice. Edward Wade and Paul Vincent's expert eyes improved the text and smoothed the production process. And the two anonymous readers for Harvard provided the kind of guidance of which most authors can only dream—rich, informed, acute, and encouraging.

Though this book marked an exciting voyage, it was mostly a solitary one—and long at that. So many friends provided distraction and support, but I owe very special thanks to Lisa Levenstein, Maria Mesner, Shalei Pilgrim Simms, Susan Stolar, Felicia Thomas, and Maria Truglio.

I am lucky to have family who never tired of asking how the writing was coming along, and never flinched when I gave the same answer—"It's coming!" Thank you to my parents, Linda and Peter Geiss and Paul Mittelstadt, and to my extended family—Amy Howell, Joel Mittelstadt, Bob and Roberta Matthews, and Rebeca Matthews.

Lucas was born at the same time I hatched the idea for this book. And Adelaide has never known a moment when I wasn't writing it. Like the rest of my family, they cheerfully accepted the long, often boring (for them), and painstaking process. I'm so grateful that they genuinely love history. I'm even more thankful for Aaron, who, though he may not love history, loves me, and spent countless hours helping. As always, he has made the time spent writing—and not writing—this book better than I could hope.

Index

CPSIA information can be obtained
at www.ICGtesting.com
Printed in the USA
BVHW031940190122
625753BV00013B/265/J